The Viking Road to Byzantium

The Viking Road to Byzantium

H. R. ELLIS DAVIDSON

London
GEORGE ALLEN & UNWIN LTD
Ruskin House   Museum Street

First published in 1976

This book is copyright under the Berne Convention. All rights are reserved. Apart from any fair dealing for the purposes of private study, research, criticism or review, as permitted under the Copyright Act, 1956, no part of this publication may be reproduced, stored in a retrieval system, or transmitted, in any form or by any means, electronic, electrical, chemical, mechanical, optical, photocopying, recording or otherwise, without the prior permission of the copyright owner. Enquiries should be addressed to the publishers

© George Allen & Unwin Ltd, 1976

ISBN 0 04 940049 5

Printed in Great Britain
in 11 point Plantin type
by The Aldine Press
Letchworth, Herts

CONTENTS

Introduction   *page* 11

PART ONE: TRADE AND TRIBUTE
1 Across the Baltic   17
2 Finnmark and Biarmaland   32
3 Journeys into Russia   45
4 The Coming of the Rus   57
5 Markets and Fortresses   68
6 The Road to Constantinople   80
7 The Wares They Carried   97

PART TWO: FIGHTING IN THE EAST
1 The Rus as Warriors   109
2 The First Attacks on Constantinople   117
3 The Campaigns of the Rus   126
4 The Great Svyatoslav   137
5 The Varangians in Russia   148
6 The Last Links with Scandinavia   164

PART THREE: NORSEMEN IN BYZANTIUM
1 The Varangian Guard   177
2 Life in Miklagard   193
3 A Norwegian Prince in Byzantium   207
4 In the Service of the Emperor   230
5 The Holy City   247

PART FOUR: IDEAS FROM THE EAST
Introduction   269
1 Marvels and Portents   271
2 The Role of the Shaman   283
3 Odin in the East   300
Conclusion   313

Bibliography   319
Index   331

ILLUSTRATIONS

PLATES
Between pages 176 and 177

1. The Vikings threaten attack
2. Wall paintings in St Sophia, Kiev
    (a) The Emperor at the Games
    (b) The daughters of Yaroslav
3. The Rider and the Woman on Stones from Gotland and Thrace
    (a) Halle Broa, Gotland
    (b) Tomis, Romania
4. The Rider to the Other World
    (a) Top panel of stone from Alskog, Gotland
    (b) The Thracian Rider, Ziatna Panega, Bulgaria

FIGURES

1	Merchant's balance from Birka	page 70
2	The dress of the Rus	111
3	Runes and dragon figures from Constanza	245
4	Platform on Oseberg Tapestry	289
5	Amulets of rider and woman	305
6	Plan of a Russian grave suggesting suttee	310

MAPS AND PLANS

1	Scandinavia and the Baltic region in Viking times	18
2	The Eastern regions	48–9
3	Position of Vitichev and fort	78
4	The Dnieper rapids	83
5	Constantinople and environs	119
6	Plan of the Great Palace in Constantinople	184
7	Plan of Byzantine Constantinople in the Viking Age	194
8	The Byzantine Empire in the early eleventh century	240

ACKNOWLEDGEMENTS

Above all my thanks are due to Lucy Cavendish College, Cambridge, and to the Trustees of the Calouste Gulbenkian Foundation for a Research Fellowship held from 1969 to 1973. This enabled me to make regular visits to Cambridge for research, and led ultimately to my return there, and the encouragement and help received from the College have been a source of strength during the years that this book has been in progress. I am grateful also to the School of Oriental and African Studies in the University of London for the award of the Louis H. Jordan Travelling Fellowship in Comparative Religion in 1969, making it possible to spend some time in Istanbul and to collect material in Romania and Bulgaria. An earlier grant from the Leverhulme Trust acknowledged in a previous book, *Pagan Scandinavia*, must be mentioned again, because it made it possible for me to visit museums in the USSR.

Among many friends and colleagues who have helped me, I should like to mention Charlotte Roueché, who read the section on Byzantium and kindly permitted me to make use of her translations of two important passages from Greek sources; Linda Hatfield, who translated passages from John Scylitzes for me; and Ursula Lyons, who was most generous with help over sources and references relating to the Arab geographers. I am grateful to the Director of the Archaeological Institute at Bucharest, and to Dr Ion Barnea and other members, who were most helpful during my visit there in 1970, and also to members of the staff of the Archaeological Museum at Sofia. I should like to thank Professor Philip Grierson and Professor Harold Bailey for helpful discussions, Dr R. I. Page for replies to queries and Mr Stephen Lees of the Cambridge University Library for help with Greek names. In spite of the help I have received I am very aware of the possibility of errors and inconsistencies in the spelling of Greek, Russian and Arab names of people and places, and can only claim the indulgence of the reader for one, who, like the eastern Vikings, has been wandering in unfamiliar paths.

INTRODUCTION

Much has been written on the activities of the Vikings in the West, and many archaeological finds have increased interest in their campaigns, their short-lived territorial gains, and their gradual abandonment of pagan cults for Christian ways. The controversy as to their role of raiders and destroyers as opposed to that of traders and settlers has long occupied historians, and the old romantic picture of the last representatives of a splendid heroic tradition, together with a more cynical approach to the Vikings as ruthless thugs and uncultured pirates, have both been replaced by a more cautious appraisal of their way of life. The main interest has turned to study of their laws and coinage, their ships, weapons and market towns, and the nature of their trade, and economic reasons have been put forward for their movements and activities. The value of the Icelandic sagas as reliable historical documents has been doubted and denied, as also the fulminations of the church chroniclers against the raiders, and sources are now slowly being revised in accordance with a different historical approach. If we may feel sometimes that we possess more accurate knowledge of the building of Viking ships than the doings of their kings, it is none the less worth remembering that we have a veritable treasure-house of literary material, produced not so very long after the reverberations of the Viking Age had died away, and much of it eminently readable. Some of this material has been misinterpreted in the past, but this is no sensible reason for rejecting it wholesale. In this literature there is a good deal concerning the Viking road to the East, across the Baltic instead of the North Sea and the Atlantic, reminding us that there were plenty of eastern Vikings as well as western ones.

We have tended to neglect this side of Viking history because of a natural interest in events round our own coasts and in the tantalising records of the American voyages. The vigorous Scandinavian thrust, however, was as strong in the eastern direction as in the western one, and the little island of Gotland in the Baltic might be viewed as a kind of Clapham Junction of the Viking Age, a centre from which routes led out in many directions.

We have to make a determined effort to seek out literary traditions for these regions, for although both Norwegians and Danes and some Icelanders took part in the eastern journeys, the impetus came largely from Sweden, and here no saga literature has been preserved to compete with that of Iceland. To make up for this there is much information from outside sources, and Icelandic literature gives us many clues, although they may prove difficult to unravel.

At first the attraction lay in the fertile countries of the southern and eastern Baltic and the cold regions abounding in fur-bearing animals. The prospect of gathering tribute from Finno-Ugric, Balt and Slav peoples led the more warlike kings of Sweden and Denmark into repeated expeditions over sea, and encouraged traders and raiders to penetrate further into the barren lands of the northern Finns and Lapps. Gradually the ambitious traders were led eastwards in search of markets like Bulghar on the Middle Volga. Precarious settlements and fortified trading posts were established, and the great Russian rivers offered a road to those skilled in the use of small ships, although it was a path open only to the toughest merchants and adventurers. Gradually fresh routes and possibilities were explored, and as Scandinavian leaders established themselves in small centres from which to operate in the country round, the way was open for conquest and plunder in the more powerful states. Thus the Vikings made contact with the Bulgars on the Volga and their kinsmen on the Danube, with the Jewish Khazars and the Muslim peoples of the Caliphate, and they finally reached the most powerful and wealthy region of south-eastern Europe, the Byzantine Empire.

The story of the encounters of the Eastern Vikings is not unlike that of their doings in western Europe; they traded, plundered, raided, made alliances and fought as mercenaries, attempted to take over towns and fortified centres and make settlements, but achieved no lasting conquests. Their gains melted away when they were opposed by expert cavalry and established armies, and although they fought fine campaigns from their ships, using the rivers and inland seas of eastern Europe, they were finally outclassed by the organised forces and scientific methods of fighting at which the Byzantines excelled. The exploits of the Vikings, however, won them a place in the Byzantine world, and they gained the respect of the emperors for their endurance, loyalty and splendid fighting qualities. The long line of Scandinavians, mostly anonymous, who served the Byzantine rulers in the army and fleet and finally in a section of the Imperial Guard in Constantinople makes a stirring story and has left its mark on the saga literature of far-off Iceland.

It was as a pagan people that the Scandinavians began to penetrate eastern Europe, but even after Christianity reached Kiev in the tenth century and was in general accepted by those serving the most Christian Emperor of the Byzantines, there was still reason to travel eastwards. Besides the attractions of Constantinople as a market and of adventure and good pay in the campaigns overseas, there was the lure of the Holy Land and the great churches of the Byzantine capital, filled with holy relics which were the wonder of the Christian world. The eastern road was followed by Christian kings of Norway and Denmark, and contacts kept up with Kiev and Novgorod until Tatar invasions put an end to the old pattern and blocked the way east.

The purpose of this study is to indicate the rich and varied contacts open to the Scandinavians who used the eastern road, and the importance of the links made with the peoples of eastern Europe, the Muslim Caliphate and the Byzantine Empire. The influence of these may be seen not merely in the hoards of silver found on Scandinavian soil, but also in the art and mythology of the North and the tales of the marvellous in the literature of medieval Iceland. Scandinavian mythology, as found in the poetry of Iceland, the imagery of the sculptured stones in Gotland and Sweden, and the funeral symbolism of the pagan period, seems to have possessed considerable vigour in the last period of heathenism. In particular the picture given both by literature and art of the cult of Odin and his heroes contrasts in some ways with what we know of earlier Germanic religion. The strength and complexity of mythological lore in the late Viking Age may be partly due to the encouragement which pagan concepts received in the eastern region, where bands of Scandinavian adventurers lived a barbaric life in the old heroic style, and encountered even more barbaric customs among the wilder peoples with whom they came into contact. At the same time they were becoming acquainted with the elaborate and sophisticated civilisation of Constantinople, and taking part in military enterprises on a scale beyond anything which they had known in the North. The effect of such varied experiences is one of the many questions prompted by a study of the eastern Vikings, and the last section of this book is concerned with the world of ideas and the adventures of the mind. After surveying the evidence of the movement into eastern Europe, an attempt will be made to estimate possible influences on the thought and literature of the late Viking Age and the period which followed it.

PART ONE

Trade and Tribute

CHAPTER 1

Across the Baltic

Some indication of the potential wealth to be gained by trade with eastern Europe in the Viking Age is given by the archaeological records of the little island of Gotland, its vast number of medieval churches with elaborate carved stones from the pre-Christian period built into the walls or hidden under the floors, and its many hoards of coins and broken silver, ornaments and metal vessels. The Gotlanders paid for their prosperity by constant attacks from pirates and raiders, and treasures were continually hidden in the earth in times of stress and danger. About half the vast number of silver coins from abroad discovered in Scandinavia have been found in Gotland, and a large proportion of these came from the Islamic East.

In the Viking Age the Baltic was a great centre for both traders and pirates, and youths of good family frequently took a share in both activities when they needed extra wealth and had a summer to spare. The exploits of Scandinavians as raiders were rivalled by the Kurlanders and Ests from across the sea, and it is said that in the eleventh century men used to pray in Danish churches that God would save them from the Kurlanders.[1] Scandinavian activity in the Baltic must have begun well before the Viking Age. Kivikosti mentions two finds which can be dated to the sixth century, one from the island of Tytärsaari in the Gulf of Finland and the other from the island of Riekkala in Lake Ladoga.[2] In both cases there are Swedish grave-goods with isolated burials, suggesting raiding enterprises in these regions. The importance of the fur trade probably acted as a stimulus to such expeditions and may furnish an explanation of the surprising number of Anglo-

[1] Gimbutas (1963), 155.
[2] Kivikosti, 89-90.

MAP 1

Saxon brooches which have been found in the eastern Baltic area.[1]

Although written accounts from the early Viking Age of what went on round the Baltic shores are few and unreliable, there are hints of a stormy past to be found in medieval literature, and memories of expeditions across the sea from Denmark and Sweden. Saxo Grammaticus in his Latin history of the Danes tells how one

[1] Vierck, 380 ff.

of his early heroes, Hadingus, made a bond with the god Odin, whom he encountered in the guise of a rover called Liserus, and together they made war on Lokerus, the 'tyrant of the Kurlanders', but were defeated. Odin then carried off Hadingus to his own realm and gave him good counsel.[1] This story is left unfinished, but Saxo mentions another campaign between Hadingus and Handvanus, 'King of the Hellespont', who was entrenched behind strong fortifications at Duno. This must be one of the many strongholds of the Baltic provinces in or near the Duna or western Dvina, while the Hellespont represents the river route southwards to the Dnieper and Black Sea; the geographers of Saxo's time accepted a general theory of a water route from the Black Sea to the Baltic, some knowledge of the great Russian rivers being grafted on to the lore of Latin scholars who placed Scythia and the Black Sea far to the north of their actual position.[2] Hadingus won Duno by the old trick of fire carried by birds, a widespread traditional tale (p. 215 below), and then allowed the King to ransom himself with gold. He is one of the semi-mythical heroes who cannot be dated, but Saxo places him almost at the beginning of his history, making him the son of Gram and giving him a Finn princess for mother.

Another king in Kurland, Dorno, is said to have been attacked by Hadingus' son Frodo, and to have applied a scorched earth policy against him.[3] Frodo in turn conquered by a ruse and held the Kurlanders' capital on the lower Dvina, where extensive earthworks have been excavated.[4] Saxo tells us that Frodo aspired to *imperium Orientalis*, the empire of the East, and numbers Polotsk in Russia among his conquests. These legends survived in Danish tradition, and others were current among the Swedes.

In the *Ynglinga Saga* of Snorri Sturluson, compiled in the thirteenth century from poems and traditions, some of the early kings of the Swedes are said to have made expeditions across the Baltic. King Sveigdir, second in descent from the god Freyr and possibly himself a mythical figure,[5] went to Sweden the Great (Russia) and

[1] Saxo I, 23, 28 ff.
[2] Leake, 56 ff.; Wright, 312 ff.
[3] Saxo II, 39, 46 ff.
[4] Gimbutas (1963), 169.
[5] *Ynglinga Saga*, 12; Sveigdir is one of the names of the god Odin (H. Falk, *Odinsheite* (Kristiania 1924), 27).

to the land of the Turks to seek for Odin and the home of the gods; he was away five years and met many kinsmen there. On a second expedition to Estland he followed a dwarf inside a great rock in his desire to find Odin and was never seen again. A good many years and reigns later, a certain King Yngvar went harrying into the Baltic and was defeated and killed in the same place, Stein, and buried at Adalsysla, opposite the island of Ösel.[1] Attempts have been made to identify his grave with a long mound at Saastamaa, called Porimägi (Treasure Mound), not far from the sea, but this identification seems to have been prompted by antiquarian speculation rather than genuine tradition.[2] The poet Thjodolf of Hvin, from whom Snorri drew much information, stated in *Ynglingatal* that Yngvar was buried near the Baltic Sea after he had been killed by the Ests. The term *sysla* was used for an administrative district for taxation or tribute, and Schuck believed that *Adalsysla* was the region round the Frisches Haff.[3] Clearly this region of the Baltic was a favourite one for raiders, and Yngvar's successor, Anund, called the 'foe of the Ests' in *Ynglingatal*, went over to Estland to avenge his father and is said to have brought much booty home to Sweden. Later in Olaf Tryggvason's reign Eirik Jarl went raiding in the same area, and Olaf the Holy was busy there also in his youth.[4]

The greatest of the Swedish leaders who raided in the eastern region in the seventh century was Ivar the Far-Reacher, King of Skåne, who slew Anund's son Ingjald and took his kingdom. Snorri says of him that he won all Denmark, part of Saxony, a fifth part of England (presumably Northumbria) and 'the whole of the eastern realm'.[5] While this is hardly a reliable historic record, it shows that there were memories of large-scale conquests across the Baltic in his reign, even though no one pretended that they were lasting. According to *Hervarar Saga*,[6] Ivar took Kurland, Estland and all the eastern kingdom up to Gardariki, while in the *Sǫgubrot af Fornkonungum*[7] he is said to have been killed on an expedition

[1] Ibid. 32.
[2] Nerman (1929), 13.
[3] Ibid. 12.
[4] *Heimskringla, Óláfs Saga Tryggvasonar*, 90; *Óláfs Saga ins helga*, 8.
[5] *Ynglinga Saga*, 41.
[6] *Hervarar Saga*, 11.
[7] *Sǫgubrot af Fornkonungum*, 3.

Across the Baltic

against a king in Gardariki, who had married his daughter against her father's will; both sagas use Thjodolf as a source. Ivar's achievements were continued by his daughter's son, Harald Wartooth, who ruled both Denmark and part of Sweden, and it is clear that Swedes and Danes alike were eager to establish authority and collect tribute along the southern Baltic shores. Ivar's death, according to Nerman, took place about 675,[1] so that there was much activity in the eastern Baltic at an early date. One runic stone, about 800 in date, in Östergötland in Sweden records the death of a certain Øyvind, who 'fell in the East' with a companion,[2] and this serves to confirm raids or trading expeditions or a mixture of both by this time in the far Baltic.

In the early years of the ninth century a Danish king, Godfred, who died in 810, was extorting tribute from various Slav tribes who had moved westwards and settled on the Baltic coast, as well as from the Frisians.[3] The Obodrichi and the Pomeranians (known as Wends) were part of the Slav advance, which resulted in the closing of the old trading routes between Scandinavia and southern Europe in the seventh century,[4] and so led to new activities in the Baltic area. The Franks had been making alliances with these peoples for their own advantage, and Godfred, feeling his trade threatened, attacked the Obodrichi and destroyed their trading centre at Rerik, moving Danish merchants to a new market under his own control at Sleastorp, which is usually assumed to be Hedeby.[5] This important centre was certainly founded about this time and much of the eastern trade passed through it (p. 68 below).

We have one valuable source of information for the ninth century in the Latin biography of Bishop Anskar of Hamburg, who lived from 801 to 865; this was written by his successor Rimbert about 870. Some of Rimbert's information came from eye-witnesses, and he makes it evident that attacks by raiders were part of the normal pattern of life in the Baltic lands. On one occasion in 829 Anskar was taking a small library of nearly forty books to be used on a mission to the heathen Swedes, but pirates attacked the ships and took the books, together with gifts from the German

[1] Nerman (1929), 14.
[2] Ruprecht, 139; Leistøl (1970), 121.
[3] Adam of Bremen I, 14, 20.
[4] Lewis, 136; Lot, I, 303 ff.
[5] *Annales Regni Francorum* (edited Pertz and Kurze, Hanover, 1895), 126.

Emperor to the King of the Swedes.[1] These were hard times for scholars and churchmen, for in a later chapter we read that the bishop himself barely survived Rorik's raid on Hamburg, when the church was burnt down and many books, including the Bible, destroyed.[2]

Rimbert also gives an account of a successful Swedish campaign in Kurland soon after 850, a time when Swedish power in the area appears to have been declining.[3] The Kurlanders had rebelled against the Swedes and refused to pay further tribute, and the Danes took advantage of this by sending a fleet there in order to gain control over the region. Their forces were defeated, however, by the warlike Kurlanders and they were forced to pay a large sum in ransom money and to surrender a valuable store of weapons. The Swedish King Olaf of Uppsala then sent over an army, captured Seeburg (probably on the site of modern Grobin) and advanced against the stronghold of Apulia, where a large force awaited him inside the fortifications. After eight days' fighting he had made little progress, and he and his men then drew lots to ascertain the will of the gods, but received no indication of any help until they called upon the god of the Christians. This may well be apocryphal, but at all events the sudden offer from the Kurlanders to come to terms was sufficiently surprising to be claimed as a miracle. It was agreed that the gold and weapons taken from the Danes should be handed back, and tribute to the Swedes resumed.

We know something of Apulia in Lithuania, which was excavated before the Second World War.[4] It was later known as Apuole, and the spelling *Appule* is found in a letter of 1253, so that it was not a Latinised name but evidently had the ending in *e* characteristic of the Kurland language. The fort still rises fifteen metres above ground level, and there are remains of an extensive 'town' or settlement outside it, as well as a cemetery of flat graves nearby, so that Rimbert's estimate of 15,000 men assembled there may not be an excessive exaggeration. The grave-goods indicate settlement in the eighth and ninth centuries, and similarities to finds from Sweden suggest that the Swedes held Apulia for some

[1] Rimbert, 10.
[2] Ibid. 16.
[3] Ibid. 30.
[4] Nerman (1958), 196 ff.; Gimbutas (1963), 154. The modern name is Litauens.

time between 650 and 800, during which period the settlement expanded and became prosperous. Archaeological evidence fits in with Rimbert's date of 855 for the retaking of the fort by the Swedes. About 150 arrow-heads, many bent and broken, were found in the hill plateau and in the wall of the fort at about the same level, suggesting a fierce battle or series of attacks, and it is conceivable that these were shot in the campaign described by Rimbert. The fortress of Seeburg was destroyed by King Olaf during the attack, and must presumably have been inside the area of old Kurland and not far from the sea; Nerman believes that it was the original settlement at Grobin. Here there are three separate cemeteries, and the grave-goods suggest that Gotlanders remained to trade after the force of Swedes was driven out, until they too left after the destruction of the town.

In the mid-tenth century Danish expansion in the south Baltic continued under Gorm and his son Harald. Harald founded the stronghold known as Jumne, Julin or Jomsborg, presumably to be identified with the modern Wollin at the mouth of the Oder.[1] Jomsborg is famous in saga literature as the legendary centre of tremendous Viking champions, said to have been formed by Harald Bluetooth either when he was driven out of his kingdom and took refuge among the Wends or when he was at the height of his power.[2] If the identification is correct, however, there is no trace of the stronghold and the large stone harbour described in the saga, and Jomsborg seems to have been a fortified centre like others in the Baltic area, occupied by a Scandinavian garrison (p. 72 below). The saga descriptions may possibly have been influenced by military camps of the Trelleborg type established later in Denmark.[3]

There was also Norwegian activity in the eastern Baltic. At the end of the ninth century the twin sons of Harald Fairhair, Halfdan the Black and Halfdan the White, were said to have been making an attack on Estland when Halfdan the White was killed.[4] The Norwegians found the Baltic a profitable area for raiding, and the

[1] Blake, introduction vii–ix; cf. Kunkel and Wilde.
[2] Weibull argued that traditions about Jomsberg were completely fictitious (*Nordisk Historia* I, 1948, 349 ff.), but this extreme view has been rejected by most scholars and he himself revised it later.
[3] Foote and Wilson, 267 ff.
[4] *Heimskringla, Haralds Saga ins hárfagra*, 32.

Danes endeavoured to gain control over the Slav peoples of the Baltic coast, but the main interest of the Swedes lay further to the east in the area of Kurland and Estland. An allusion to Swedish power in this region is found in the account by Snorri Sturluson of the Thing or Assembly held at Uppsala in 1016.[1] Thorgny, the chief Lawman, an impressive old man from Tiundarland, was trying to dissuade King Olaf from grandiose plans of war against Norway. The king's daughter Ingigerd, who had hoped to marry Olaf II of Norway (p. 164 below), had already reminded her father that he would do better to turn his attention eastwards as his predecessors had done,[2] and Thorgny took up the same theme:

'Of a different mind now are the kings of Sweden from those of former days. My grandfather Thorgny could remember Eirik Emundarson as king in Uppsala, and said of him that as long as he remained active he took an army every summer across the sea and subdued Finland and Karelia, Estland and Kurland, and far into the eastern regions. You can still see the earthworks there and other fortifications which he built.'

The list of Swedish kings given in the later part of this speech is not complete. Nerman estimated that Eirik Emundarson lived in the ninth century and died an old man in 882, so that the period of his conquests would be in the fifties or sixties.[3] According to Snorri he was the grandfather of Eirik the Victorious, who ruled about a century later. However, the general picture, that of a time of expansion in Kurland and Estland in the mid-ninth century, is borne out by other sources. Fortifications across the Baltic are mentioned by Saxo,[4] and in the account of the eastern Baltic recorded by Alfred the Great, Wulfstan states that there were many 'towns' among the Ests, the Finno-Ugric people next to the Kurlanders, each with its own ruler.[5] In the Baltic states many hill forts like that at Apulia survive and hundreds await excavation. Impiltis in Kurland has been excavated, Dagmale and Tervete in Semigallia, and Nemencine in Lithuania, as well as a number of

[1] Ibid. *Óláfs Saga ins helga*, 72.
[2] Ibid. 80.
[3] Nerman (1929), 51.
[4] Saxo II, 40, 47 ('A town of undoubted strength' etc.).
[5] King Alfred's Orosius, *Early English Text Society*, 79 (1883), 17–21.

others.[1] These so-called towns were settlements which grew up round the hill strongholds, some of considerable size. The surviving earthworks are impressive and by the tenth century had been equipped with ramparts, wooden fences, towers of wood or stone and log-houses. Impiltis had a rampart as great as ten metres high, protected by water or marsh on three sides and on the fourth by a deep ditch crossed by a bridge, leading to a portcullis and a gate flanked by towers. There were deep wells inside the fortifications which made it possible to withstand a long siege, and some of the forts enclosed huge areas within the ramparts, so that supplies of food could be stored and animals kept there. The strengthening of the forts seems to have begun between the sixth and eighth centuries, probably as a defence against increasing Scandinavian attack. No doubt many Swedish expeditions were merely to collect tribute or quell opposition and did not involve permanent settlement. Nerman, however, believes that Seeburg was built or at least enlarged by the Swedes as a fortress on the Alanda river, where a small earthwork already existed in the Roman period, and claims that the earliest finds of a Swedish type, an arrowhead and some fragments of pottery, indicate a settlement there by the second half of the seventh century.[2] At this time the coastal region of Kurland was sparsely inhabited, and the Swedes could have established themselves there in the time of Ivar the Far-Reacher. The river could have taken its name from the Swedish *āland, 'river land' and the name later adopted by the Kurlanders. Nerman's arguments are based on the two cemeteries to the north and east of Grobin,[3] where the dead were nearly all male, laid in mounds with their weapons in Swedish fashion, and possibly members of a warrior garrison from central Sweden. The third large cemetery south of the river was of a different type, for it contained flat cremation graves characteristic of Gotland, and held many women's ornaments of Gotland type. It seems likely that the Gotlanders formed a trading centre there under Swedish protection and brought their women with them; this would account for the growth of the little colony into a prosperous town.

In the ninth and tenth centuries, the time of the notorious Viking

[1] Gimbutas (1963), 168 ff.
[2] Nerman (1958), 180 ff.
[3] Ibid. 3 ff.

raids on the monasteries and towns of Anglo-Saxon England, Ireland, France and Germany, trading in the Baltic could hardly have been a peaceable occupation. Merchants had to travel in company, carry arms and be prepared to fight for their goods and lives, with the dismal prospect of being themselves sold as slaves in some Baltic market if luck turned against them. Nevertheless trade flourished, as the evidence from Scandinavian cemeteries and trading centres on either side of the Baltic indicates. Nerman's picture of a trading colony forming in the wake of a military garrison at Grobin gives some idea of how this developed, while tribute taken from subject peoples or weaker neighbours like the Kurlanders would be in the form of goods such as skins or perhaps grain and honey, all adding to the prosperity of the Swedes. Trade at this period was not the same as that in modern times, based on money economy and the profit motive, for much of it was in the form of barter and many luxury objects found in the graves may have been taken as plunder or received a gifts.[1] But even if this is borne in mind, it is clear from the evidence of the trading centres (p. 68 below) that there was much wealth to be gained from increasing contacts with the lands across the Baltic.

How early the Scandinavians penetrated beyond the eastern Baltic into Russia is a subject on which there had been much controversy. Vernadsky claims that they reached the mouth of the western Dvina and settled there before 700,[2] but archaeological evidence hardly supports this, although no doubt there were isolated raids (p. 17 above). Nerman puts together three sources which indicate a movement towards Russia in the 850s:[3] first, Rimbert's account of the recapture of Apulia; secondly, the date 852 given in the Russian *Primary Chronicle* for the arrival of the Varangians, together with mention of taxes imposed on Slavs and Finns in 859; and thirdly, Snorri's account of the achievements of Eirik Emundarson at about the same date. There is evidence, however, that as early as 838 certain Swedes had found a way down the Dnieper to Constantinople (p. 57 below), so that it seems likely that there was penetration into Russia by small bands in the early part of the ninth century. The method by which advances

---

[1] Grierson (1959), 123 ff.
[2] Vernadsky (1943), 266 and in later publications.
[3] Nerman (1929), 46 ff.

were made into Baltic territory was evidently by setting up fortified centres with permanent garrisons, from which tribute could be collected from the surrounding land; these could be strengthened by reinforcements from home, and traders could settle in the vicinity as soon as it seemed safe to do so. Nerman found traces of Scandinavian occupation at Saulakuas in West Latvia, at Jaci, ten kilometres north-west of Grobin, and in a few other sites, but the traces are slight and insufficient to prove permanent settlement.[1] Finds have also been made round Elbing, which was probably the Truso mentioned by Wulfstan in the late ninth century.[2] There is little here which can confidently be identified as ninth-century Scandinavian work, and Rimbert's description of a general withdrawal of the Swedes and re-establishment of the Kurlanders about this time would account for this. Merchants may have continued in Truso until about 900, but in general the Swedes evidently transferred their interest further east to southern Finland and western Russia. Nerman's dating of sword-hilts and tortoise brooches from the Baltic countries supports this view;[3] many swords of a non-Baltic type were found on the island of Ösel, a favourite area for Scandinavian raiders. Some ornaments seem to originate from Gotland, and after the main Swedish influence waned ships from Gotland still visited Ösel and the Latvian rivers, and certain harbours continued to be used by them. Weapons were indeed still carried to the Baltic countries in the thirteenth century, since there were protests from the Popes against trading with the heathen and supplying weapons to those fighting Christian soldiers.

Snorri Sturluson was clearly interested in the south-eastern Baltic, and in *Egils Saga*, which may possibly have been his work,[4] there is a lively account of an expedition to Kurland by the hero, Egil, who accompanied his elder brother Thorolf on a voyage abroad.[5] The tale is probably fiction, but it gives a glimpse of Kurland through the eyes of a thirteenth-century saga writer, showing how trade and plundering went on side by side. Thorolf fitted out a large longship and spent some time raiding in the

[1] Ibid. (1958), 183 ff.
[2] Gimbutas (1963), 153.
[3] Nerman (1929), 69 ff.
[4] Jones (1960), 20 ff.
[5] *Egils Saga*, 46.

Baltic before moving on to Kurland for 'a fortnight's peace and trading'. After this short truce, they set out to raid along the coast, and reached the mouth of a great river with woods on either side. They went ashore in parties of twelve and raided a settlement where the Kurlanders fled before them. Young Egil's party went on further through the forest and came to a region of fields and isolated farms. The nearest one was deserted, so they took what they could find and prepared to return. Then a company of Kurlanders appeared and drove them into a corner against the high fence which surrounded the farm, threw spears at them and at last, after several had been wounded, took them prisoner. They were left bound in an outhouse to wait till morning, when more fun, it was suggested, could be had torturing them; but after a struggle Egil freed himself and untied his companions. They broke through a partition wall in the log building, and found three Danes in a pit under the floor, a man called Aki and his sons. These had been captured in a battle the previous summer; Aki had been treated well and put in charge of the farm, but the sons were treated as thralls and they had been recaptured while trying to escape. Aki led the Icelanders through a granary and up to a loft over another building where servants were making up beds for the night. There was a good store of weapons there, so they killed the servants, and Aki then opened a trap-door into a store-room below, where the farmer kept his wealth. They carried off as much as they could, Egil taking a small meadcask which later proved to be full of silver.

On the way back, Egil insisted on returning to the farm, saying that it was cowardly to rob the farmer without letting him know. He did so alone, found the Kurlanders feasting in the hall and serving-lads carrying in trenchers from the cookhouse, where cauldrons hung over a great log fire. Egil seized a log, which had been set alight at one end 'as was the custom there', and thrust the burning end into the thatch. The men inside knew nothing until the roof was alight, and when they ran to the door Egil was waiting there to cut them down as they emerged. Finally the roof fell in, and Egil set off to rejoin the ship.

This is a fine adventure story, showing the strength, reckless courage and vindictiveness which were to distinguish Egil through his life, but the background details are realistic, and seem to be based on some knowledge of conditions in Kurland. The farm consisted of thatched log-houses divided by partitions, including a granary, hall, cookhouse and sleeping-quarters over a storeroom all surrounded by a high fence. There is no mention of women or children, and the farm seems to have been run as an armed camp, with a supply of weapons in the sleeping-loft. Reliable captives were used as overseers, and men from various farms banded together to meet raiders, share an evening meal in the hall, and sleep in the loft at night.

There is little doubt that raiders continued to infest the Baltic coasts till the end of the Viking Age and after. Among the memorial stones which record deaths of men who died abroad or came home to Sweden after journeys in the East, Ruprecht gives thirteen which refer to the eastern Baltic, most of them belonging to the eleventh century. At Frugården in Västergötland there is a stone erected for Olaf, a young man killed in Estland in the early part of the century.[1] Another, Bjorn from Uppland, fell in Virland, in south-east Estonia, along with a kinsman or neighbour, in the second quarter of the eleventh century.[2] Nerman refers to a certain *Aistfari*, a traveller to Estland, mentioned on a stone at Släbro, Södermanland.[3] Ruprecht has another possible *Aistfari* (*isifara*) who dies among the Greeks, named on an inscription at Droppsta in Uppland.[4] Three brothers, apparently older men, perished in the river Windau in north-west Kurland or near it, and their sisters raised the stone for them in the churchyard at Sjonheim in Gotland.[5] Semigallia is mentioned on a stone raised for Svein by his widow in Mervalla, Södermanland.[6] Like many of these inscriptions, this includes two lines of alliterative verse:

'Often he sailed to Semigallia,
with a fine ship, round Domesness.'

This suggests a merchant ship, used for trading with the Baltic countries and beyond, and Domesness was the northern point of Kurland, on the route to the Dvina. There is also a copper bowl, made to hold a merchant's scales, which has on it a runic inscrip-

[1] Ruprecht, 38 (132).
[2] Ibid. 137 (152).
[3] Nerman (1929), 57.
[4] Ruprecht, 159 (156).
[5] Ibid. 192 (164).
[6] Ibid. 82 (142).

tion stating that it was brought home from Semigallia by a certain Djarf; it includes two lines of verse in skaldic style, describing how an eagle tore the death-pale robbers,[1] possibly a quotation from a poem describing adventures abroad. At Åda in Södermanland there is a stone commemorating Bergvid, raised by his brother after Bergvid was drowned in Livonia, the area east of the Gulf of Riga north of the river Dvina.[2]

We have no idea what Bergvid was doing in these regions, but in the same area there is evidence for some kind of fighting force, perhaps for collecting tribute, under a certain Frøygeir. This was established at Tavestia in Finland, where Frøygeir shared command with Brusi; the latter had succeeded his brother Egil, according to the inscription on a stone at Söderby, Gastrikland.[3] Another of Frøygeir's followers was Asgeir, for whom his father erected a stone at Veckholm, Uppland, and who is said to have fallen in Livonia in Frøygeir's company.[4] It is not certain where Frøygeir himself ended his life, except that it was somewhere in the Baltic; two other men mentioned on the stone at Leginge, Uppland, recording his death were probably brothers and died in the land of the Greeks.[5] Yet another man, Gisli, whose name occurs on a stone at Tibble, Uppland, is said to have fallen abroad in Frøygeir's company.[6] Frøygeir himself is said to have died *in silu*, which might stand either for Salo in the Gulf of Finland or for the island of Ösel. If it is the same man mentioned on all four stones, which seems reasonable, then his company travelled over a considerable area of the eastern Baltic. They could have been a band of armed merchants, explorers or collectors of tribute, or a combination of all three, or even a mercenary band assisting some ruler in Finland and then going on elsewhere. On the whole references to Finland are rare, and when it occurs the reference is to the south-west section of modern Finland only; an eleventh-century stone at Söderby-Karl in Uppland was raised by parents for their son Otrygg, who was killed there.[7]

[1] Ibid. 173 (159).
[2] Ibid. 97 (144).
[3] Ibid. 187 (162).
[4] Ibid. 146 (154). (The name is incomplete here.)
[5] Ibid. 130 (151).
[6] Ibid. 144 (154).
[7] Ibid. 143 (153).

Such stones were important records of death and inheritance, and those which can be deciphered indicate much activity in the East Baltic. They show that a number of men proceeded beyond Kurland and Estland and were killed, possibly on the way to Russia. A number of stones state that the dead man perished 'in the East', without giving further details, and we shall see later that others provide evidence for men dying in Russia or in the land of the Greeks.

CHAPTER 2

Finnmark and Biarmaland

While the Danes and Swedes took a great interest in the southern and eastern Baltic, the Norwegians were led to explore the country further north, and they too were drawn eastwards, through Finnmark, to the mysterious Biarmaland. The exact position of Biarmaland is not easy to determine, in spite of the many references to journeys there. The traveller whom King Alfred of Wessex called Ohthere, but whose Scandinavian name would be Ottar, gave the King a detailed account of a voyage to the White Sea in the late ninth century, and this was inserted into the Old English version of the history of Orosius.[1] It has remained of outstanding importance for our knowledge of the territories to the east of Norway in Viking times.

In his sober and cautious account, Ottar described how he sailed up the coast of Halogaland from his home in northern Norway, where he lived in the most northerly settlement along the western coast. He set out to follow the coast northwards, past a region where the only inhabitants were nomadic Lapps (*Finnas*), living by hunting and fishing. At last he reached the White Sea and the mouth of a great river, which appears to be the Verzuga, flowing into Kandalaks Bay. Beyond this lay the first cultivated land which he had seen since leaving home.[2] He did not dare to proceed further into the region beyond the river, since it belonged to the Biarmians, who spoke a language resembling that of the Lapps. Although he did not enter their territory, he was able to communicate with them, and they told him much about their own lands and

[1] See note 5, p. 24 above.
[2] The verb *bu(g)an* can mean 'to inhabit' or 'to cultivate'. Ottar is referring to a settlement in contrast to the temporary dwellings of the Lapps, but from his statement that the land is well *gebud* it would seem that the meaning here is cultivated and that the Biarmians practised agriculture.

those of their neighbours; unfortunately this information is not recorded, since Ottar was not sure how reliable it was.

His journey would seem to have been prompted not so much by the desire to explore as from eagerness to find new routes for trading and new sources of wealth. He told the King that excellent ivory could be obtained in the northern seas, and that walrus skins made good mooring ropes; his own considerable wealth, he said, had come partly from walrus hunting and partly from the herds of reindeer which he owned, but his greatest profits were from the tribute which he obtained from the Lapps. They paid him in reindeer hides, birds' feathers (which gave down for pillows and warm clothes), walrus ivory, whalebone, ropes made from seal and walrus hides, and animal furs. A rich Lapp might pay as much as fifteen marten skins, five reindeer hides, one bearskin, two measures of feathers, a tunic of bear or otter fur, and two ropes of seal and walrus hide, each sixty ells long.

This gives some idea of the potential wealth of the northern territories, where nomadic peoples lived without cultivating the land. The Norwegians of Halogaland claimed a kind of lordship over the Lapps, which did not go unchallenged. Ottar told Alfred that the Cwens lived north of the Swedes and east of the Halogalanders, and that they frequently made raids against his people, crossing the lakes in their light boats and carrying these overland, from one waterway to another. Ross has shown that it would be possible for Cwens to cross Lake Alta and Lake Leina, carrying their boats over the watershed and arriving by way of the Bardu and Malselva rivers in the area round the Malangen Fiord where Ottar lived.[1] Light boats of skins sewn together, roughly equivalent to a modern rubber dinghy, were used in north Scandinavia up to recent times and could easily be carried on a man's shoulders.

A further picture of tribute-gathering from the Lapps comes from *Egils Saga*.[2] King Harald Fairhair of Vestfold was said to allot the tribute-collecting in the north to one of his landed men, Brynolf, who like Ottar lived in Halogaland. After Brynolf's death it was given to Egil's uncle, Thorolf Kveldulfson, who had been in the King's bodyguard and was now given an estate in the north in return for loyal service. We are told how Thorolf sup-

[1] Ross (1954), 337–45.
[2] S*Egils aga*, 9 ff.

ported his household: he obtained large catches of herring and cod, killed seal and took birds' eggs, so that he was able to dispense lavish hospitality. In winter he set off with about a hundred men to collect the Lapp tribute; first he declared a truce, so that a market for skins could be held, and then he journeyed through Finnmark, which, as the saga-teller is careful to explain, extended over much of Norway east of Halogaland, over the central mountains to the land of the Finns and Cwens and the Karelian peninsula. Next year the Cwens asked for his help against the Karelians who were raiding in the Mark, offering him a share of booty equal to that of their king, namely one third of the total with sole right to all beaver, sable and marten skins. With Thorolf's help the Karelians were driven out, and he acquired much wealth in skins. Meanwhile, however, his enemies had been slandering him to the King, accusing him of keeping much of the tribute for himself, until finally Harald gave the collecting of it to the sons of Hildired, who hated Thorolf. They went to Finnmark with a small party only; consequently the amount of skins which they took was much smaller than before and of poorer quality. Next winter Thorolf again went to help the Cwens, and came back with sufficient skins to load a merchant ship with 'grey wares' (grey squirrel skins) and 'white wares' (wadmal cloth and sheepskins), together with hides and dry fish for England. The ship returned with a cargo of wheat, honey, wine and cloth, but King Harald had in the meantime been persuaded that Thorolf was robbing him of his Lapp tribute, and he seized the cargo; then he led an attack on Thorolf, who went down fighting after the burning of his hall.

Much of this may be assumed to be fiction, but the detailed account of the collecting of skins and the contacts with Lapps and Cwens is of great interest. It has been suggested that the writer of the saga was using a twelfth-century source for his description of the geography of Finnmark in chapter 12.

Evidently Biarmaland lay beyond the lands of the Cwens and the Lapps; according to Ross it probably extended over two main regions, one near the White Sea at the head of Kandalaks Bay beyond the Varzuga river, the region visited by Ottar, and another, known as Further or Eastern Biarmaland, around the northern Dvina, which runs into the White Sea near Archangel. Possibly Biarmaland extended right round the shores of the White

Sea, so that these two regions were joined. Ross gives his arguments in detail in a study published in 1940, based on a close scrutiny of all references to Biarmaland in Anglo-Saxon, Old Norse and Latin sources. In Scandinavian tradition Biarmaland represented the edge of the known world, and beyond it men believed there lay fabulous lands and strange peoples. It figures in many tales as a place of wild adventure, with sacred places surrounded by high palisades, burial mounds filled with silver, and images of the god the Biarmians worshipped, *Jómali*, with a bowl of treasure in his lap. *Jumala* is the Finno-Ugrian word for 'god', and it is this, in conjunction with other evidence, which leads Ross to identify the Biarmians with Baltic Finns, probably the people known as Karelians, speaking a Finno-Ugrian language.[1] It is implied in Norse sources that their speech was a foreign tongue to the Scandinavians, and in one account it is compared to the chattering of birds (p. 39 below), and an interpreter is needed to translate it. There were resemblances between Baltic-Fennic and Lapp at the period when Ottar visited the region, so he may well have been able to communicate with the Biarmians if he or one of his party understood the Lapp language, and it would be reasonable for him to remark on the resemblance between the two tongues. Another significant point is that the Finno-Ugrians, unlike the Lapps, were cultivating land at an early date. The Karelian Finns are known to have practised agriculture, although, as is evident from the account in *Egils Saga*, they were considered a war-like people and a threat to their neighbours.

Many attempts have been made to identify Biarmaland with Permia, round the upper Kama river in north Russia, because of the similarity of OWN *Bjarmar* and O. Russ. *Per(e)m*. A legend of rich graves and a high standard of wealth and culture in this region was current in the eighteenth century, and accepted by many Russian scholars. Kuznetzov, whose views on Biarmia have been conveniently summarized by E. Koutaissoff,[2] argues against this identification, and it is also opposed by Ross, on the grounds that the northern Permians or Komi do not appear to have lived near the White Sea, and that their language was widely different from Lapp. Kuznetzov points out that silver and gold objects

[1] Ross (1940), 48 ff.
[2] Koutaissoff, 20 ff.

found in the Permian region were unlikely to have been made there, but must be due to trade or plunder. However, the fact that so much had been found in this area must have helped to build up the tradition of the power and wealth of the Biarmians and of the possibilities of treasure to be found in northern Russia.

The difficulties encountered in attempts to identify this elusive people might be overcome if *biarm* is taken as a descriptive word rather than as the name of an ethnic group. It has been suggested that it was applied to a type of Finn hunter who undertook long expeditions through forest regions; such men could be found over a wide area ranging from Finnmark to the White Sea, and as far south as Lakes Onega and Ladoga. This is the interpretation favoured by Kivikosti and Tallgren.[1] The tradition of the wealth of these people could be based partly on the treasure found in Permia, which included silver vessels of Asian origin and decorated idols, and partly on finds among the Tshuds near Ladoga, where there was a relatively high culture between 850 and 1100, indicated by over two thousand burial mounds holding weapons, ornaments and occasional huge hoards of silver coins. Around the northern Dvina river, the region usually specified in Norse sources which deal with visits to Biarmaland, there have also been finds of treasure from graves or hoards, some of Balt origin and some Permian from the eleventh century, although the majority of the population there appears to have been Karelian. This whole area, with its mixture of tribes, mostly of Finno-Ugrian stock, certainly derived much benefit from the increase of trade between Scandinavia and the regions around the Volga in the Viking Age. Strandberg[2] suggests that the Karelian peninsula occupied a position in relation to Finland which can be compared with that of Gotland in relation to Sweden, and that the tribes there gained much prosperity from being on a direct trade route.

The most realistic account of an expedition to Biarmaland after that of Ottar is the journey of Thorir Hund and the brothers Karli and Gunnstein, which took place in 1026.[3] Thorir lived at Bjarkey in Halogaland [4] and was the chief man of King Olaf the Holy in

---

[1] Kivikosti, 148; Tallgren, 118.
[2] Strandberg, 168.
[3] *Heimskringla, Óláfs Saga ins helga*, 133.
[4] Ibid. 106.

Finnmark and Biarmaland

that region, presumably responsible for collecting the Lapp tribute for his king; he was a man of ruthless cunning, reputed to be skilled in the magic of the Lapps, as we are told in the poem *Erfidrápa*.[1] Karli was trading on King Olaf's behalf and his brother Gunnstein on his own account. Thorir asked to join their party of twenty-five and surprised them by arriving with a longship and eighty men. They first visited a trading station and bought a quantity of grey squirrel, beaver and sable skins; this was on the river Dvina, and they afterwards began raiding along the coast. Thorir proposed plundering a burial place, since rich Biarmians were buried in the woods with much gold and silver in their mounds. They went through flat tundra until they reached the forest where they marked trees to guide them on the way back, till they reached a clearing where there was a mound surrounded by a fence with a locked gate. Thorir and Karli hooked their axes over the top and climbed over to let the rest in; they took much treasure mixed with earth out of the mound. The image of the god of the Biarmians, called Jomali, stood beside the mound, with a rich neck-ring and a silver bowl full of coins on his lap, which Thorir forbade them to touch. As they were leaving, however, he seized the bowl and emptied the coins into his tunic. Karli, not to be outdone, struck at the neck-ring and knocked off the Jomali's head. The noise was heard by a party of Biarmians on their way to keep watch at the burial place, and they blew horns to fetch help. However, the plunderers escaped, for Thorir managed to conceal them from their pursuers by strewing something 'like ashes' behind them, a practice elsewhere attributed to the Lapps.[2] Later on the sharing out of the treasure caused touble, and Thorir treacherously killed Karli and nearly succeeded in killing his brother Gunnstein as well.

Similar stories of plundering a sacred place, some perhaps inspired by this account, are found in the *Fornaldar Sǫgur*. In *Bósa Saga*, in addition to some fantastic elements like a vulture's egg and an enchanted bull, Bosi and Herraud took a crown and collar from a Jomali and a silver bowl filled with gold from his knee.[3] In *Sturlaugs Saga* the account is more confused: a temple

---

[1] *Skjaldedigtning* B1, 242 ff.; Strömbäck, 201.
[2] e.g. Saxo V, 165, 203; *Heimskringla, Haralds Saga ins hárfagra*, 32, where Gunnhild learns the trick from the Lapps.
[3] *Bósa Saga ok Herrauðs*, 8.

in Biarmaland was dedicated to the deities Thor, Odin, Frigg and Freyja, and contained an image of Thor with a silver table, a playing-board of gold and a great auroch's horn.[1] In *Hálfs Saga*, the hero broke into a mound by the Dvina and obtained much wealth.[2] In *Ǫrvar-Odds Saga*, which has much material to do with the eastern Baltic, there is a long account which is worth examining, since it is in a different class from the others.

The Norwegian hero Odd was known as Arrow-Odd or the Far-Travelled, and he won great fame for his exploits in Biarmaland. He and his father, Grim Hairy-cheeks, and his grandfather, Ketil Salmon, were landowners in Halogaland, in close contact with the Lapps and showing interest in the northern territories lying east of Norway. Ketil settled in or near the island of Narvey, and his son Grim was born to his non-Scandinavian wife during an expedition to Finnmark. All three generations had contacts, both friendly and hostile, with Lapps, Biarmians and other tribes of the north-east, who are sometimes represented as very strange beings and called trolls or giants. Nevertheless, a reading of the three sagas in the *Fornaldar Sǫgur* collection makes it evident that these folk have their roots firmly established in the Baltic regions and do not come out of the common stock of western romance.

In his youth Odd's destiny was foretold by a Lapp woman, called a *vǫlva* or seeress, who visited the home of his foster-father Ingjald in Norway. The account of the ceremony corresponds with those of divination ceremonies held by shamans among nomadic peoples of northern Europe and Asia (p. 285 below). The seeress was called Heid, and held to possess the power to foretell the seasons and the destinies of individuals. She brought with her to the farm fifteen youths and fifteen maidens, who were used as a kind of choir for the singing of spells; she practised her special arts while the household slept, and next day a feast was held when she answered specific questions of importance to the community. Then those present went up in turn to question her about their futures, but Odd refused to take any part and lay on a bench under his cloak. When the seeress addressed him directly he told her not to babble about his affairs, as he put no belief in her words. However, she went on to tell him about his

[1] *Storlaugs Saga Starfsama*, **18**.
[2] *Hálfssaga ok Hálfsrekka*, **5**.

long and famous career and to prophesy his death (p. 129 below). Strömbäck came to the conclusion [1] that this account of the divination ceremony is among the earliest of this type in the sagas.

Odd struck the seeress and she left the house in anger; this led to a break with his foster-father and his departure abroad. The first journey which brought him fame was to Biarmaland,[2] where he robbed a sacred mound beside the river Dvina. When he first arrived there he visited a hall where a funeral feast was being held and stood at the door watching. He could not understand the language of the Biarmians, which is likened to the chattering of birds, but he saw someone he took to be a Scandinavian acting as cup-bearer, and when the man came to refill his cup from a great silver vessel by the door, Odd and his companions seized him and carried him off. The man was reluctant to speak, but finally told them he had been there for three years and found the life hard; he also told them that there was a mound near the river containing much silver, since offerings were made there every time a man died or a child was born among them. Odd's men made two expeditions to the mound; the first party took away much silver mixed with earth, but when Odd was leaving with the second party, he saw their former captive approaching with a large force of natives. Odd asked why he had betrayed them, and he replied that the Biarmians were ready to hold a market and exchange their silver weapons for the iron ones of the Norwegians. This sounds like a typical heroic challenge to battle,[3] and the fight began, Odd warning his men to throw anyone who was killed into the river, since the Biarmians might work magic if they obtained dead bodies. Odd's party won and took away the treasure from the mound, together with a pile of 'silver' weapons (presumably spears and swords ornamented with silver) obtained from the defeated.

The Biarmians are not said to have used magic, in spite of Odd's fears, but the Lapps certainly did so, for when they were sailing past a Lapp settlement which they had plundered of furs on their way out, a storm was raised against them. Odd told them to throw

[1] Strömbäck, 96 ff.
[2] Ǫrvar-Odds Saga, 4.
[3] cf. the OE poem on the Battle of Maldon (45 ff.): 'They will give you spears for tribute. . . . Such wargear as will do you no good in battle,' Byrhtnoth's reply to the Vikings who demanded tribute.

all the skins they had taken into the sea, whereupon these were immediately swept towards the shore, and he insisted that if they had not done this their ship would have been lost. As it was, they were driven on to an island, and the people from the mainland, who were apparently not Lapps, but are described as huge, ugly and black-haired, tried to dislodge them. Odd, however, set up a bearskin on a pole with hot cinders in the bear's mouth, and this kept the natives away. At last they got a favourable wind and sailed back to Halogaland, and Odd won such fame from this expedition, according to the saga, that there has never been any journey from Norway to equal it.

Here we have what on the whole is a rational account, differing considerably from those of travellers who meet with fantastic adventures and visit enchanted temples. Nora Chadwick [1] has even raised the question of whether this famous journey could possibly have been the same as that recorded of Ottar of Halogaland in King Alfred's *Orosius* (p. 32 above), the famous voyage to the White Sea in the late ninth century. Later on we shall also be faced with the question of the relationship between Odd and Oleg the Wise of Kiev (p. 128 below). There are three parts to Odd's story: the voyage to Biarmaland round northern Norway, the pillaging of a sacred mound, and the battle near the river Dvina. All three are familiar motifs, repeated in a number of prose sources, and it is scarcely possible to decide who was the original hero of each episode. The funeral feast and the details of the battle, however, belong to *Ǫrvar-Odds Saga* alone, and one can only say that these have a more convincing ring than other accounts of Biarmian journeys in the *Fornaldar Sǫgur*, and that it is possible that the family history of the hero and his repeated associations with regions to the east of Halogaland are based on genuine early traditions from this region.

Accounts of fighting with the Biarmians occur in a number of other sources. Saxo refers to tribute in skins taken from both Lapps (or Finns?) and Biarmians in the fifth book of his History.[2] He tells how Arngrim of Sweden went to fight the Finns, whose way of life is described in some detail: they were skilled in throwing spears and used large arrows; they lived a nomadic life as

[1] Chadwick (1946), 170 ff.
[2] Saxo V, 165, 203 ff.

hunters and travelled on skis or snowshoes, and their skill in spells and magic arts made pursuit difficult. Finally, however, they surrendered to Arngrim, and the tribute imposed on them was a load of reindeer skins every three years from each group of ten men. Arngrim also defeated Egtherus, King of the Biarmians, in single combat, and imposed a tax of one skin from every man in his tribe. He won great fame and was congratulated by the rulers of the Danes and Swedes for adding 'the edge of the world' to the Danish realm. The warlike quality of the Biarmians is confirmed by Saxo's story of Ragnar in his ninth book;[1] he had succeeded against many foes, but on meeting the Biarmians found himself 'dragged by an armed and uncouth race into the utmost peril'. On a second attempt to defeat them, he was helped by Kurlanders and Samians (the East Prussians south of Kurland), who showed proper respect for his authority, but he only succeeded because he managed to trap the Biarmians in an ambush. Finally he killed both the King of the Biarmians and the King of the Finns, and set up a memorial of his victory by carving an inscription on a rock. Ragnar is represented as marrying a Biarmian princess in *Ragnars Saga*.[2]

In *Hálfdanar Saga Eysteinssonar* Biarmaland is placed within easy reach of Alaborg and Aldeigjuborg, and not far from Novgorod. The rulers of Aldeigjuborg by Lake Ladoga, Alaborg on Lake Onega, Karelia and Biarmaland all take part in campaigns, and at one point three routes to Biarmaland are noted.[3] The first is by sea, taking five weeks, and is dangerous on account of pirates and Vikings. The other two are by land; one a very difficult route over mountains and wild country, with no specified time given, and the other a more direct way, through three areas of forest where there is nothing to eat but berries and sap from the trees, and then across a great river to Biarmaland, taking three weeks in all. In the *Tale of Eymund* (p. 159 below), the Biarmians act as allies to the brother of the King of Novgorod when he attacks the town; they are brave fighters but so greedy for plunder that Eymund takes advantage of this and like Ragnar lures them into an ambush. The sagas have preserved a number of traditions about the Biarmian royal family,

[1] Ibid. IX, 308, 372 ff.
[2] Chadwick (1946), 156.
[3] *Hálfdanar Saga Eysteinssonar*, 16.

and these belong to the more bizarre aspect of Biarmian traditions. Odd came several times into contact with an outstanding Biarmian champion called Ogmund or Kvillamus,[1] who is described as wearing black felt with his face covered, so that only eyes and mouth could be seen. This might merely represent the winter costume of men of the far north, but Ogmund was possessed of marked supernatural powers, and might be seen as a shaman (p. 299 below).

In *Egils Saga* Thorolf Skallagrimsson, the elder brother of the hero, is said to have taken part in an expedition made by the young Prince Eirik Bloodaxe to Biarmaland in 925.[2] Later on his death is described in a battle in England, in a strange passage which is so like and yet unlike other accounts of the famous battle of Brunanburh when King Athelstan defeated a number of Viking chiefs and northern rulers that it has aroused much discussion. The battle took place by the river *Vina*, and this has led Campbell to suggest that the saga-teller has confused two different battles, and that Thorolf's death really took place in Biarmaland, the river Vina indicating as usual the northern Dvina.[3] The poem composed by Egil on his brother's death states that he fell 'on an island in the north', and this could refer to the Biarmian campaign, but unfortunately no poem on Eirik Bloodaxe's expedition survives. We know that the writer of the saga took great interest in events east of Norway (p. 27 above), gaining his information partly from family traditions about his Icelandic hero and surviving poems by Egil, and partly from other accounts of expditions into the north.

A later Norwegian raid in the same area is referred to by the poet Glum Geirason; this was made by King Harald Greycloak in 965:[4]

'The conqueror of kings, bold in speech, reddened the fiery sword in the east, north of the town where I saw the Biarmians in flight. The maker of treaties won good renown on this expedition; the young Prince did battle on the Dvina banks.'

In a less realistic tale messengers are sent by Harald Fairhair to the

[1] *Qrvar-Odds Saga*, 13; 19; 23.
[2] *Egils Saga*, 37; *Heimskringla, Haralds Saga ins hárfagra*, 32.
[3] A. Campbell, *The Battle of Brunanburh* (London 1938), 74–5.
[4] *Heimskringla, Haralds Saga Gráfeldar*, 14, verse 100.

region round Gandvik, the name usually given to the White Sea.[1] They take a ring, two flitches of bacon and a barrel of butter to the King's 'fostermother', Heid. She is described as a huge and ugly figure in a skin kirtle, a kind of giantess showing marked resemblance to the supernatural protectors of Siberian shamans.[2] She helps Hauk, one of the messengers, by warning him of an attack by a rival group of Swedes; she heals his wounds after a fight, and finally leads him back to the trading station 'where the merchants were'. This implies a background of rivalry between explorers and traders from different areas in the far north, while the practical gifts of bacon and butter, much appreciated by Heid, suggest genuine contacts between Scandinavians and the northern peoples which have left a mark on tales of magic and witchcraft in Icelandic literature. The tradition of marriages between Norwegian men and Lapp or Finn women points in the same direction.

Indeed a fairly consistent picture emerges of a temporary Scandinavian overlordship over certain northern areas east of Norway, where Norwegians, Danes and Swedes by show of force took tribute in skins from the Lapps and from various Balt and Finno-Ugrian people over a wide area. Traditions about Biarmaland are for the most part associated with the region round the Dvina river beyond the White Sea, but also with that north of Novgorod and Ladoga. Considerable interest is shown in tales of raids in this area, in the winning of treasure from mounds and sacred places, and in battles with the natives, who show themselves adversaries worthy of respect, as well as in the strange religious customs of these regions and the peculiar traditions associated with their rulers. These tales are of a very different kind from those told of the Lapps, who are no great fighters and seldom resort to force, while they lead a nomadic life without cultivating the earth and dwell in tents. It is questionable whether the term *Finnr* necessarily denotes a Lapp, for in many cases it could refer to people of Finno-Ugric tribes further east, who competed with the Scandinavians for the Lapp tribute in skins, or even to the Balt peoples. The work done by Ross, Tallgren and Kuznetzov shows the wide variety of tribes living in modern Finland and northern Russia in the ninth and tenth centuries, most of them of Finno-Ugric stock,

[1] *Flateyjarbók*, I, 467, 579 ff.
[2] Davidson (1973/2), 27 ff.

and the term Biarmian was probably used loosely to cover a number of these. The relationship of the Scandinavians with these peoples varied from outright hostility to temporary alliances and meetings for trade and mutual benefit. Their way of life and their religious practices seem to have made a powerful impression on the storytellers, and the importance of this has not always been recognised by scholars in their arguments over the precise identity of the Biarmians and their territories. For over two hundred years, while the increase in eastern trade and the influx of eastern silver brought them prosperity along with their Swedish neighbours, these tribes were in close contact with the traders and adventurers of the Viking Age, and stories about them, rejected by Ottar because of their doubtful reliability, undoubtedly made their way back to Scandinavia by other channels and even reached as far as Iceland.

CHAPTER 3

Journeys into Russia

Development of trade in the Baltic and possibilities of collecting furs and plunder led naturally to further exploration. The first direction in which the Scandinavians moved was eastwards across northern Russia, the area inhabited by Finno-Ugric tribes. The route up the western Dvina from Kurland led to the head waters of the river Volga, while another road further north was by way of the Gulf of Finland and the river Neva to Lake Ladoga. At Staraja Ladoga, south of the lake, there is evidence for Scandinavian settlement, although as yet no systematic study of the many burial mounds between Lake Ladoga and Lake Onega has been carried out, nor has the cemetery for the settlement been found. Thus it is not possible to distinguish with confidence between the Finnish, Slav and Scandinavian settlements which may have existed here. Clearly Staraja Ladoga, known as Aldeigjuborg to the Norsemen, was a place of considerable importance.[1] It was probably a Scandinavian trading centre long before Novgorod, where the Swedish Rurik mentioned in the *Primary Chronicle* is said to have settled (p. 63 below).

The centre seems to have been a small fortified town rather than a fortress, and the houses were replaced as they fell into decay, and were used as family dwellings. Ploughs and farm implements show that agriculture was practised, and the inhabitants kept domestic animals and went fishing. Like the Baltic towns, Aldeigjuborg had an earth rampart and was protected by a river and a ravine; it stood about seven miles up the river Volkhov and not on the lake itself, which would make it easier to defend, and this position may be compared to that of Grobin and other Baltic sites.[2] Swedish

[1] Raudonikas (1930, 1951); Gimbutas (1971), 156. The 1958 excavations have not been fully published, but there is a useful survey by Davidan.
[2] Nerman (1955), 197–8.

occupation here appears to have begun early in the ninth century, the time of gradual expansion of trade and Swedish moves eastward, and the site probably existed already as a Finno-Ugric one, which may have been taken over by the Swedes or shared on a friendly basis. Above the earliest layers the foundations of large, square log-houses were found, provided with an annexe for stores or cattle, and these may have been occupied by the Scandinavian traders; some were used as workshops and one was a smithy. These houses stood far apart, and above them were one-roomed dwellings of characteristic Slav type, which were much closer together and set in rows to form streets, with a paving of planks providing a thoroughfare. One significant piece of evidence for the presence of Scandinavians is a piece of wood with a long runic inscription, which is a verse in elaborate skaldic style, referring to mythological beings. The various interpretations unfortunately differ considerably,[1] but the existence of such an inscription, which must presumably have been made in the settlement, indicates the presence of a group of men interested in court poetry, and the runes are believed to be of ninth century date. It was at one time suggested that the wood formed part of a bow, but there seems little doubt that it is a *runakefl*, a piece of wood used for runes of the type found at Bryggen in Bergen; Aslak Liestøl has published a number of these which bear inscriptions in metrical form.[2] The discovery has been taken to corroborate the theory of a Scandinavian state established at this date,[3] but one runic inscription alone is not a proof of permanent settlement, and Aldeigjuborg may have been a garrison settlement established by the Swedes on the pattern of Grobin, with a trading and farming population of local people under their protection.

Although we have no proof that the Scandinavians founded the town, objects of Scandinavian type have been found at the lowest level. There were glass beads of the type found at Hedeby and in Gotland, and mentioned by Ibn Fadlan as much valued by the Rus (p. 66 below), and also remains of a particular kind of shoe, with the heel extended in a triangle, which differs from

[1] G. Høst, *Norsk Tidsskrift f. Sprogvidenskap*, 19 (1960) 418 ff.
[2] Liestøl (1963).
[3] Stender-Petersen, *Historische Zeitschrift*, 191 (1960), 1 ff. For objections, see *Kuml* (1960), 135–7.

that found in Slav sites from the eleventh century onwards, but which has also appeared in the lowest level of Novgorod excavations and at Pskov and Beloozero.[1] There were also combs which could have been made by Scandinavian craftsman. Another find of considerable interest, not yet published, is the figure of a tall wooden man in war-gear found in a small timber structure in the excavations of 1958;[2] this building had a hearth of upright blocks, which contained burnt bones of animals, birds and fish. It resembles the descriptions of wooden posts carved with human heads to whom the Rus made sacrifices and prayed for good luck in their trading, according to Ibn Fadlan's account (p. 65 below).

We hear much of Aldeigjuborg in Norse literature. It was remembered as a great exploit of Eirik, Jarl Hakon's son, that he made an expedition against the town and burnt it after the death of his father and the taking over of family estates in Halogaland by Olaf Tryggvason in 995. This is mentioned in the poem *Banddrápa* by Eyjolf Dadaskald, quoted in *Heimskringla*:[3]

> You Prince destroyed Aldeigju;
> we have learned the truth of this.
> Men had grim fighting there;
> you came east into Gardar.

The settlement formed a convenient half-way halt between Novgorod and the Baltic. It was there that messengers arrived to invite Magnus to become King of Norway in 1034, while both Magnus and later Harald Sigurdson stopped there to get their ships ready for the voyage across the Baltic.[4] Beyond Aldeigjuborg there was a possible route along the Svir to Alaborg on Lake Onega, and then south down the Vytegra, with a portage to the Kovska, and so along the Shelsna to the Volga.

The men who travelled by such routes would be influenced in their choice by the relative dangers of cataracts on the rivers and the amount of portage necessary, when boats had to be dragged overland or in extreme cases emptied of their cargo and carried on

---

[1] Davidan, 87.

[2] Ibid. 83; Gimbutas (1971), plate 67.

[3] *Heimskringla, Óláfs Saga Tryggvasonar*, 90, verse, 151; *Skjaldedigtning* B1, 201.

[4] *Heimskringla, Óláfs Saga ins helga*, 251; *Magnúss Saga ins góða*, 1; *Haralds Saga Sigurðarsonar*, 17.

MAP 2

BIARMIANS
Izhma R.
Pinega R.
Onega R.
N. Dvina R.
L. Onega
Alaborg Nytegrea
P
White L.
P
Beloozero
Sheksna R.
Kama R.
P E R M I A
Yaroslavl
P
Rostov
P
Volga R.
Volga R.
Suzdal
Kliazma R.
Oka R.
Viatka R.
Kama R.
Sura R.
Bulghar
Moskva R.
BURTAS
VIATICHI
Khopel R.
Yalk R.
Seim R.
Don R.
Belgorod
Volga R.
Donets R.
Samara R.
Rapids
S
K H A Z A R
Sarkel
Don R.
K H A G A N A T E
Atil
SEA OF
AZOV
Kuban R.
Kuma R.
Tmutorokan
CASPIAN
Terek R.
SEA
SEA
GEORGIA
Kura R.
ARMENIA
Bardha'a
Trebizond
ARMENIA
E M P I R E

men's shoulders. It is difficult for us now to estimate the relative importance of such obstacles, but the main portages continued to be used throughout Russian history, as Kerner has shown in his detailed study of river routes, and the position of Russian towns at key-points on the river system. Once at Beloozero ('White Lake'), the travellers were over the great watershed and within easy reach of the mighty river Volga, the main highway east and south. Scandinavian objects have been found in this area, said in the *Primary Chronicle* to be the place where one of the Scandinavian leaders settled. The old town was abandoned at the time of the Black Death and replaced by the modern Belozersk some distance away.[1] To the north-east of Moscow isolated finds of Scandinavian swords and oval brooches have been made, and also in the Volga basin, but no indication of extensive settlements of recognisable Scandinavian character have been discovered, and in view of the excessive claims made by some Swedish archaeologists, it must be realised that isolated finds might be accounted for by trade or plunder.[2] A number of towns are mentioned in the sagas, all on the routes east or around the head waters of the Volga and its tributaries: Palteskja (Polotsk), Móramar (Murom), Sursdal (Suzdal), Rapstofar (Rostov), Smoleskja (Smolensk) and Syrnes (?Chernigov),[3] and there is archaeological evidence for early settlement at some of these (p. 76 below).

Once the Volga was reached, the Scandinavians left the area of Finno-Ugric tribes and entered that of the Volga Bulgars, who were established between the middle Volga and the river Kama, while between the lower Volga and the Caspian Sea they came into contact with the Khazars. The Bulgars were a northern group of Turko-Hunnish stock, who settled in the region of the Don in the seventh century and were later to a large extent absorbed by Khazars and Avars. By the Viking Age two main groups of Bulgars had survived, the Balkan group in the area round the Danube and the group on the middle Volga. The latter had been partially converted to the Muslim faith, and in the early tenth century were attempting to build up a strong Kalganate of their own and to ward off attacks from their powerful Khazar neigh-

[1] Mongait, 296.
[2] Sawyer, 62 ff.
[3] Cross (1953), 43; 228 (note 67).

bours. The Khazars were an outstandingly capable and cultured people, a branch of the Turkish race, whose rulers had accepted Judaism about 730; many of their subjects remained Muslim or Christian, and these were treated with a rare and admirable tolerance. By the ninth century they formed a powerful state with a standing army between the Volga and the Caucasus.

The Scandinavians who penetrated into this part of Russia had to make a choice between remaining a subservient people, paying tribute to the Bulgars as the Lapps and Finns did to them, or setting up organised opposition; as might be expected from the history of the Vikings, they preferred the latter course and banded together under the leadership of various jarls. Their policy was presumably the same as that in the Baltic countries, the occupation of fortified centres with small settlements attached, from which they could collect tribute from neighbouring peoples. We have seen from *Egils Saga* how this could be done (p. 33 above) and how considerable organisation and show of force were necessary in order to get ample supplies of furs and other commodities such as honey and wax before some more efficient rival stepped in to extort supplies from the unfortunate natives. The term for such levying of tribute in Russian sources was *polyudie*; the collecting was generally done in autumn and winter, and payment in the early tenth century might be in furs, honey or wax, handed over to the prince of Kiev or his accredited representative or subsidiary ruler; the latter would keep one third of the 'tax' and hand the rest over to his superior. Olga seems to have tried to improve the system about 946, by establishing posts to which the contributions could be brought.[1]

The exact nature and size of the Scandinavian bands in Russia in the ninth century has unfortunately remained a subject for bitter controversy ever since the 'Normanist' and 'Anti-Normanist' schools of opinion formed in the last century. Written records are sufficiently contradictory to provide endless material for argument; archaeological evidence might help if systematically collected and made available to western scholars, but may in itself be as misleading as early records. It has been pointed out that if we relied on the evidence of archaeology for our knowledge of the Vikings in England, we should gain a very inadequate picture of

[1] Jenkins (1962), 59–60.

their settlement there.[1] In any case, the shifting fortunes of the early adventurers would no doubt make it difficult to trace their progress along the eastern road, even if more exact evidence were available. At least we can feel certain that the Scandinavians had a number of trading posts in Russia in the ninth century, and that they found contacts, adventures and profits there which made the obstacles worth surmounting and which led them to accept the considerable dangers and hardships involved.

The main lure which attracted men down the Volga was their desire to obtain silver from the Islamic world. There were good prospects for traders at the great market of Bulghar on the middle Volga, the capital of the northern Bulgar kingdom, where for the first time they were able to meet Eastern merchants for their mutual profit. The Volga branch was known as the Silver Bulgars in the *Primary Chronicle*, presumably because of their control over this desirable form of wealth. The Scandinavians had no silver mines of their own and, once the influx of gold and silver from the Roman Empire came to an end and the trade-routes were blocked by barbarian peoples moving west, they could only obtain precious metals by trade or plunder, and for this the eastern world offered great possibilities.[2] Mining for silver had gone on in Tashkent from the late eighth century, and towards the end of the ninth the rich mine of Benjahir was discovered in Afghanistan and became the main source of silver, the production of which reached fantastic proportions in the Caliphate in the course of the Viking Age.[3]

There were also considerable possibilities for tribute from the native tribes as the Scandinavians penetrated into new areas, although they now had to contend with powerful rivals. Already expert at obtaining skins from neighbours nearer home and at forming efficient raiding parties to get what they wanted, they were able to carry valuable wares to Bulghar to exchange for silver, and also to take advantage of the demand for slaves in the eastern world. In the ninth and tenth centuries vast hoards of Kufic coins reached Sweden and Gotland, together with silver ornaments which could have been made in the Volga region or in the Caliphate.

[1] Wilson (1970), 107 ff.
[2] Lewis 136 ff.
[3] Bolin (1953), 12 ff.

These often survive as hacksilver, ornaments and coins broken in pieces in order to be weighed for trading purposes. Hoards of silver mark the route from Bulghar back to Sweden, and the important researches of Sture Bolin [1] show that in the late ninth century the composition of hoards found in Russia is practically identical with those from Scandinavia, indicating that the coin stocks in both areas was the same. Evidently money was coming in a continuous stream westwards, rather than moving from Islamic territories into Russia and then from Russia to Sweden in two separate stages.

Many Arabic and Kufic coins reached Sweden and Gotland only to be hidden away by their possessors in periods of unrest and never recovered until modern times. If we take into account the vast amounts which must have come to light during the intervening centuries, not to mention the wealth put to practical use by its owners, then the total number of coins and silver treasures coming into Scandinavia during the Viking Age reaches staggering proportions. Eastern coins are valuable evidence for dating, since they commonly bear a date of issue, and this, together with the distribution of the hoards, has added greatly to our knowledge of contacts and conditions during the period. Sawyer takes as a typical ninth-century hoard one from Fittja in Uppland found in 1873.[2] This consisted of 136 coins, ranging from the early seventh to the mid-ninth centuries; one was pre-Muslim; another minted soon after the Arab conquest; nine came from between Damascus and Isfahan and were minted for the Umayyad Caliphs, twenty-four from Mohammidijah south of the Caspian, thirty-five from Baghdad, one from Cordova in Spain, and the rest were issued by the rebel ruling houses of the Tahirids from such centres as Bokhara, Merv, Samarkand and Tashkent. These last could have reached Bulghar by the caravan route from Khiva, south of the Aral Sea, and the few silver Pehlevi from Persia which have been found in Scandinavia could have come the same way. Some of the Kufic silver could have travelled by way of the Khaganate of the Khazars, but in the first half of the ninth century the route from

---

[1] Bolin's main work, *Studier over Mynt och Myntfynd i Ostra och Norra Europe* has not yet been published but a helpful survey has been provided by Sawyer, 103 ff.
[2] Sawyer, 92 ff.; Linder, 109 ff.

Bulghar seems to have been the important one for Scandinavian traders. There are few western coins in the hoards, and even fewer from Byzantium in this early period.[1] Nearly all the hoards which can be clearly dated are found in eastern Scandinavia and especially in Gotland, and it is clear that few Kufic coins reached Denmark and Norway until the tenth century.

Some gold also found its way along this northern trade route. In the Hon hoard at Oslo there are nine gold dinars which presumably came by way of the Volga, and although Gotland has only three gold coins from this period, there are more than 130 gold objects from the east among the finds there. The comparative rarity of gold coins may be due to the fact that these tended to be converted at once into ornaments, gold leaf or gold thread. It was not customary to place either gold or silver in graves, perhaps because raiders were so active in the Baltic area and there was much risk of grave-robbing, as the Biarmian traditions indicate.

While the Volga route was clearly of major importance in the ninth century, that southwards down the Dnieper gradually superseded it. About 965–70 the stream of Kufic silver coins from Bulghar dried up, and the market of Birka ceased to flourish (p. 70 below). There were some political reasons for the closure of the northern route, since in the second half of the tenth century the rulers of Kiev were at war both with the Bulgars and the Khazars, and were seeking new directions for conquest and profit. Another reason for the abandonment of the northern route may be seen in the silver crisis in Islam in the late tenth century.[2] The silver mines began to fail, so that the influx of Kufic coins dried up after that period and the latest date on coins found in Russia is 1015. Alternative sources for silver for Scandinavians were Germany and England, and by the tenth century Byzantine coins also appear, although never in the same quantities as the Kufic ones of the earlier period. Evidently there were strong reasons for turning to the Dnieper route, which led southwards to Constantinople and the rich lands round the Black Sea.

Interest in this was apparently shown by Scandinavians in the

[1] A survey of hoards in Russia (*Archaeology of the USSR, a corpus of archaeological sources* G4/4 and E4/4) was published in 1961 and 1962. See M. W. Thompson, 'Byzantine coins in Russia', *Mediaeval Archaeology* 10 (1966), 145–146.

[2] Sawyer differs from Bolin here.

Kiev region early in the ninth century (p. 58 below). However, it was no easy route to develop, since instead of Finno-Ugrian peoples of the North there were different and for the most part hostile tribes who spoke unfamiliar languages. The Krivichi around Smolensk, the Dregovichi and the Drevljane to the west of the Dnieper, and the Radimichi to the east, were Slav peoples. Further down on the lower Dnieper were the Poljani, later driven out by the Magyars; they in their turn were replaced by the Pechinegs, a particularly warlike and turbulent people with whom the holders of Kiev had long and chequered relations, and who played an important part in the foreign policies of Byzantium.[1] None of these tribes were likely to welcome the Scandinavian interlopers, while to the east of the Slav area was the state of the Khazars, with well-organised armed forces who had already been collecting tribute from the Slavs and were anxious to get firm control of the tribes round the Dnieper. Beyond, again, stretched the shadow of the great and powerful Byzantine empire. Beside the dangers from hostile peoples, the great cataracts of the lower river formed a serious obstacle.

However, the desire for trade and the need for silver spurred on the Scandinavians in their search for new routes. Archaeological work near Smolensk suggests that by the tenth century there was a settlement at Gnezdovo, a little way down the Dnieper. Here there were over three thousand burial mounds, the earliest of which are now dated by Soviet archaeologists to the tenth century.[2] They admit that this cemetery held Scandinavian graves and finds of characteristically Scandinavian type, although they differ from Swedish archaeologists as to the amount of Scandinavian material there. There are swords, for instance, with hilts of types found in Norway and Sweden, which are fairly reliable indication of the presence of Viking forces, even if individual weapons, like one with an inscription in Old Slavonic on the blade, later fell into Slav hands. This settlement on the river confirms a new interest in the Dnieper route in the tenth century, and may have been deliberately chosen as a centre from which progress down the river could be made. It is not necessary to assume that vast Scandinavian

---

[1] For a summary of what is known of the Pechinegs, see Macartney, 342 ff.

[2] Avdusin, 52 ff., and further discussion in the *Norwegian Archaeological Review*, 6 (1973).

forces were involved here or elsewhere, and they may have been in close touch with the previous inhabitants, either as overlords or allies, which would explain the mixed nature of the gravegoods. Smolensk, which was evidently in existence before the establishment of the Gnezdovo site, was the main centre of the Krivichi, who occupied the region of the Upper Dnieper, the Volga and the western Dvina. The prospects of possible wealth from regions further south was bound to lead the Scandinavians at some stage to attempt the route down the Dnieper in search of markets, plunder and possibilities of conquest, and once Kiev became one of their centres there was a chance to achieve this.

CHAPTER 4

The Coming of the Rus

It is in the ninth century that we first hear of the Rus, who were well known to Arab geographers, and whom the Byzantine Greeks called *Rhos*. The identity of these people is a subject on which so many books and articles have appeared that it is difficult to view the evidence clearly through the fog of controversy surrounding it. For most western scholars, the name *Rus* is taken primarily to denote the Scandinavian settlers in Russia, particularly those established at Kiev in the ninth century. In this they follow the lead of Thomsen, who in a famous series of lectures given at Oxford in 1876 [1] set out to prove 'that the tribe which in the ninth century founded the Russian state, and to whom the name Russ was originally applied, really were "Northmen" or Scandinavians of Swedish origin', and to show the inadequacy of the arguments which had recently been put forward to claim that the Rus were really Slavs.

Thomsen and all those who have followed him emphasised the importance of an entry in the *Annales Bertiniani* [2] for the year 839, according to which Greek ambassadors from the Byzantine Emperor arrived at Ingelheim. This entry occurs in the section written by Prudentius, Bishop of Troyes, a reliable chronicler, and it stated that the Greeks came to seek support from Louis the Pious, bringing with them certain men who said that 'they [that is, their nation] were called Rhos'. These men had been on an embassy to Constantinople, but were unable to get back to their own land by the way they had come because hostile tribes blocked the way. The Emperor Theophilus begged Louis to permit them to return home through his dominions, and Louis was sufficiently

[1] Thomsen, 20.
[2] *Annales Bertiniani*, edited Waitz (Hanover 1883), 19–20.

interested to question the men carefully, suspecting that they might be spies. He learned that they belonged to the nation of the Swedes (*comperit eos gentis esse Sueonum*) and declared that he would keep them for a while and allow them to leave once he was sure that they had no hostile intentions. It is to be presumed that he sent them home, since there is no record of their return to Constantinople, and in fact there was a convenient route from Ingelheim to Kiev.

These Annals are a reliable source, although at this date the appearance of the Rus in Kiev is surprising. Nerman estimated that the penetration of the Scandinavians into Russia did not begin until about half way through the ninth century (p. 26 above). Riasanovsky,[1] anxious to explain away the passage in the Annals, argues that these Swedes must have been ambassadors sent by Slav rulers in Kiev to negotiate with the Byzantine emperor, and that the word Rus was used of their Slav overlords. Since archaeological evidence indicates, however, that the small independent settlements in Kiev did not grow into a town until the tenth century, this is not very convincing, and the theory was in fact refuted long ago by Thomsen. The leader of the Swedes is referred to as *Chacanus* (Khagan) in the Annals, and we know that this title was later used for the princes of Kiev in the tenth century;[2] it seems reasonable to assume that the Rus learned the word from the Khazars and applied it to their own leader.[3] An early group of adventurers had evidently established themselves in the stronghold and were already exploring the possibilities of the Dnieper route to Constantinople. The same situation occurs regarding Viking attacks in Spain and North Africa, in that these are shown by reliable evidence to have begun earlier than is generally assumed, evidently in the form of isolated raids by small numbers of men preceding the main expeditions.[4]

Identification of the Rus with the Swedes is supported by the

---

[1] Riasanovsky (1962), 5 ff.; (1969), 28.

[2] e.g. in the Hudud al-'Alam of 982, and by Ibn Rusteh (p. 64 below); also by the Byzantine Metropolitan Illarion in a sermon alluding to Vladimir and Yaroslav (Riasanovsky (1962), 5). A Finnish historian, Pekkana, suggested that *chacanus* could be an error for the Scandinavian name Hakon (*Varangian Problems*, 141).

[3] Vlasto, 390. cf. 243 ff.

[4] Melvinger, 127 ff.

clear statement of Liutprand of Cremona in the tenth century,[1] when he describes the Rus as a northern people, named perhaps after the colour of their skin (he took the name to mean 'red') but called *Nordmanni* by the Germans among whom he lived. Liutprand died in 975 and is a well-informed and reliable witness, for though he himself was not present when the Rus attacked Constantinople, his stepfather was, and Liutprand himself visited the capital not long afterwards. A third telling piece of evidence comes from an Arab writer, Al-Ya'qubi, who died at the close of the ninth century. He was acquainted with both the eastern and western areas of the Mediterranean, and he identifies the Vikings who attacked Seville in 843–4 with 'the pagans (*al-magus*) who are called Rus'.[2]

The favourite explanation for the name Rus, although by no means the only one, is that it is derived from the Finnish name for Sweden, *Rotsi, later *Ruotsi* (cf. Estonian *Rotsi*), and that this comes from Old Swedish *Rōþer*.[3] This is thought to have had some association with rowing or ships, so that *rōþs-karlar* meant 'rowers' or 'seamen'; alternatively the word stood for 'route where men row' and *rōþs-karlar* would be the men who lived or passed along the rowing route. Another explanation is to link the word with Roslagen on the east coast of Sweden, the area from which many Swedes left for Russia, and to assume that the name was used by the Finns for men who came from this region. Liutprand thought that the Greek form *Rhos* came from the Greek adjective for 'red', probably indicating the red, weather-beaten faces of the Norsemen, while there are other more ingenious but not very convincing theories. The Greek form might be due to contamination from similar words in Greek or Hebrew, understandable if the name reached Byzantium by way of the Khazars.[4]

Those determined to find a non-Scandinavian origin for the name can easily find parallels from south-eastern Europe: there is

---

[1] Liutprand, *Antapodosis*, V, 15, 185.

[2] Birkeland, 13. For the term *al-magus*, originally 'fireworshippers' and later applied to Scandinavians and Normans, see Levi-Provençal in the *Encyclopaedia of Islam* (almadjus). cf. Melvinger, 43 ff.

[3] Ekblom, 47 ff. Brate claimed to read *Roþrslandi* on the Piraeus inscription (p. 220 below).

[4] V. Minorsky, *Encyclopaedia of Islam* (Rus); cf. Jenkins (1962), 20 ff.

a river *Ros*, a tributary of the Dnieper, a tribe in the Bible called *Rosh*, and the people whom Jordanes calls *Rosomanni*. The name in fact is no unusual one.[1] Vernadsky's theory of a merger between the Swedes and an obscure tribe of the Alans called the Rukhs-As, whose name they adopted,[2] is not generally accepted. The term Rus also came to be used in a geographical sense, which is not easy to define with exactitude. It seems originally to have meant the land under the rule of the Prince of Kiev, and then the area round the middle Dnieper.[3]

Vernadsky argued for the establishment of a Scandinavian military base between the Black Sea and the Caspian, with its centre at Tmutorakan, at an early date; he thought that this was afterwards cut off from the north by the expansion of the Khazars and the blocking of the route up the lower Volga. He wished to identify this area with Sweden the Great, of which Snorri writes in the opening chapter of *Ynglinga Saga*:

'Now north of the Black Sea lies Sweden the Great, or the Cold. Sweden the Great some men believe to be no less in area than Serkland the Great, while others equate it with Bláland the Great. The northern part of Sweden the Great remains uninhabited on account of frost and cold, just as Bláland in the south is desert on account of the burning sun. In Sweden there are many kinds of peoples and many languages; there are giants, dwarfs, black men and many strange tribes. There are also beasts and dragons of enormous size.'

The name Sweden the Great was probably modelled on such names as Bulgaria the Great, the kingdom on the Don in the seventh century. It appears to have been applied loosely to the eastern regions, and may have come into use because of a resemblance between the name for Sweden, *Svíþjóð*, and Scythia. It was used for the vast tract beyond the Baltic in which traders and adventurers moved in the Viking Age. Serkland used to be explained as Saracen-land, or even the land round Sarkel on the Don, but a better explanation has been given by Arne, who took it

[1] Ibid. 129 ff.
[2] Vernadsky (1943), 274; cf. *The Origins of Russia* (1959), 175 ff.
[3] Jenkins (1962), 22–3.

to mean Silkland, the region of the Muslim peoples from which silk (*sericum*) could be obtained;[1] in the thirteenth century it was also used for North Africa. Bláland here is Africa, although the 'black men' may be the Black Cumans or some other nomadic tribe.[2]

In such a passage we are dealing with a literary tradition, derived from classical lore concerning the weird people and fabulous monsters said by ancient writers to flourish in the land of Scythia. This was vaguely placed somewhere east of Sweden, not far from the Baltic, and medieval scholars like Snorri Sturluson and the early map-makers accepted this assumption. Adam of Bremen states that the Baltic 'extends a long distance through the region of Scythia as far as Greece', by which he means the Byzantine Empire, and even gives the sea the alternative name of Scythian Lake.[3] Saxo refers to the Hellespont when he clearly has the area just beyond the Gulf of Finland in mind, and to a 'vast accumulation of motley barbarism' east of Sweden across the Baltic,[4] equating this area with Scythia and its marvels and monsters as represented in the writings of Greek and Latin geographers. It is necessary to draw a sharp distinction between the geography of scholars and churchmen, taken from books, and that of merchants, soldiers and pilgrims, based on travel and exploration. In the Icelandic sources much of the complexity, though also the fascination, arises from the blend of these two kinds of geography.

There is no convincing evidence for the existence of a kingdom of Tmutorokan before the expansion of the Khazars. Vernadsky relies on isolated references, such as a complaint from a Persian general in the mid-seventh century that he was caught in south Russia between the Khazars and the Rus, but Dunlop takes this to be a late addition, and there is nothing to confirm it from elsewhere.[5]

There is, however, general agreement that in the ninth century

---

[1] Ruprecht, 55. The interpretation 'Saracenland' is given by Braun (1924), 150.
[2] Altheim and Stiehl, *Die Araber in der alten Welt* (Berlin 1965), II, 530.
[3] Adam of Bremen II, 18, 64; IV, 10, 193; we may compare his remark in IV, 15, 196: 'Those who have a knowledge of geography also assert that some men have passed by an overland route from Sweden to Greece.'
[4] Saxo, preface, 8, 13.
[5] Dunlop, 48.

the important Rus state on the Dnieper around Kiev was formed. The evidence comes from various sources, particularly the Russian *Primary Chronicle*, the *Povest Vremennykh Let* (Chronicle of Past Years). This is no longer assumed to be the work of Nestor, a monk in Kiev in the late eleventh century, but is thought to be a mixture of early annals, Khazar sources and oral tradition, composed partly in Nestor's time and partly in the twelfth century. The *Primary Chronicle* preserves memories of a centre at Kiev before the coming of the Scandinavians, and describes the establishment of the first Scandinavian kingdom there. It appears that Kiev was an early Slav sanctuary, whose inhabitants paid tribute first to the Drevljane, then to the Khazars and finally to the Varangians. This last term was used by Greeks and Arabs as well as Russians for the Scandinavians, and was probably derived from the Old Norse *vár*, 'pledge', used of a group of men binding themselves into a company and swearing to observe certain obligations and to support one another loyally, as well as sharing the profits.[1] It was a word familiar at the time when merchant adventurers pledged themselves to travel into the eastern regions, making a trading agreement among themselves and undertaking to fight in one another's defence. It was also used for men from abroad who agreed to enter the service of an overlord for a specified period, and was applied to the Scandinavians who came to fight for the rulers of Kiev and Novgorod in the eleventh century. The *Primary Chronicle* uses the phrase 'Varangians from beyond the sea' for Scandinavians coming from their own country. However, it is probably wrong to assume that the term must always refer to a particular ethnic group; the Vikings were ready to ally themselves with Finns or Slavs if it suited them, and so the same problem confronts us as when considering the identity of the Biarmians or the Rus. The name Varangians was no doubt applied to associations of people or bands of allies acting along with the Scandinavians.[2] Of those holding power in Kiev we are told:[3] 'These particular Varangians were known as Rus, just as some are called Swedes and other Norsemen, Angles and Goths (? Gotlanders), for they were thus named.'

[1] Blöndal (1954), 10 ff.
[2] Boba, 15 ff.
[3] *Primary Chronicle*, 860–2, 59.

The attraction of Kiev as a centre for Scandinavian traders is easy to understand. The *Primary Chronicle* states that the tribes round the Dnieper paid tribute to its ruler in furs, and that when the Khazars controlled this area they had demanded one squirrel and one beaver skin from every household. The Varangians took over the collection of tribute; after a while the tribes around Kiev are said to have driven them out, but later to have invited them to return because without them they found they were in a constant state of warfare among themselves. The next three centres established, according to the *Primary Chronicle*, were Novgorod, Beloozero and Izborsk, but according to the Hypatian redaction Ladoga replaces Novgorod, which was founded later. The three towns are said to have been taken over by three brothers, a familiar pattern for a story of the origin of a state. The choice of Ladoga accords with archaeological evidence and probability, and the name Novgorod (New Town) implies the existence of an earlier settlement. It seems likely that the first travellers to Bulghar bypassed the site of Novgorod and took the direct route from Ladoga to the Volga. Some time during the ninth century, however, Novgorod became the main centre for the Rus in Gardar, and was known as Holmgard ('island town') with Aldeigjuborg as a convenient halt between this and the Baltic (p. 47 above). There was a link between the two settlements provided by the Volkhov river, while the river Lovat offered a route to the Volga, and a portage brought travellers to the head of the Dnieper near Smolensk. The third town mentioned, Beloozero, was an important point on the road to Bulghar.

A description of the Rus has been left by the Arab geographer Ibn Rusteh, who compiled his work in the early tenth century from an earlier account by Jarhani, now lost, and possibly other sources also.[1] This means that what we possess is a secondary source, to be treated with caution, but one of early date. He describes a centre which might be Novgorod, since it is thought of as in island, and might be a hill-fort in the area of swampy ground beside Lake Volkhov:

'Concerning the Rus, they live on an island (? peninsula) which

[1] Birkeland, 14 ff. French translation by G. Wiet, *Les Atomes précieux* (Cairo 1955), 163 ff.

lies in a lake. The island on which they live is three days journey in extent, and covered with wood and thick scrub. It is very unhealthy, and so marshy that the ground quivers when one treads on it. They have a leader called Khagan-Rus. They fight with the Slavs (*Saqaliba*) and use ships to attack them; they take them captive and carry them to the Khazars and there sell them as slaves. ... They have no villages, no estates or fields. Their only occupation is trading in sable and squirrel and other kinds of skins, which they sell to those who will buy from them. They take coins as payment and fasten them into their belts. They are clean in their clothing, and the men adorn themselves with gold arm-rings. They treat their slaves well and wear showy clothes, since they engage in trade with much thoroughness (?).[1] They have many 'towns'. They are generous with their possessions, treat guests honorably and act handsomely towards strangers who take refuge with them, and all those who accept their hospitality. They will not allow any of their own people to molest these or do them harm.'

This description could hardly refer to the Scandinavian peninsula or the hypothetical kingdom round Tmutorokan, as has been suggested, but it agrees with what we know of the early settlement at Novgorod, near a lake in a very marshy area where plank roads had to be laid down and constantly renewed in the medieval town (p. 76 below). The absence of agriculture or villages such as were characteristic of the Slavs, the whole-hearted enthusiasm for trading, the taking of slaves and the number of fortified centres, which are also called 'towns' in the Norse sources, all fit in with what we know concerning the kind of life led by the Swedish traders. Although it is unlikely that the compiler of this passage, Ibn Rusteh, himself visited the region, he has left us a most convincing account of the fighting qualities of the Rus and their religious practices, which is confirmed by other evidence which we possess.

His account also agrees with that given by Ibn Fadlan, who took part in an embassy from the Caliph of Baghdad to the King of the Volga Bulgars in 921–2. The King had asked for assistance in building a fortress to defend the Bulgars from Khazar attacks, and

[1] Uncertain. De Wiet's interpretation is that they clothe their slaves well in order to sell them.

was prepared to receive instruction in the Islamic faith. Ibn Fadlan was an authority on canon law, and he acted as secretary to the expedition, but when the religious instructor refused to go beyond Gurganiya, he took over his duties as well. He was praised by the King, who gave him the name of the Truthful, or so he claims, and this reputation has been confirmed by those who have studied his work.[1]

Ibn Fadlan was a born traveller, fascinated by the strange customs and traditions of the various peoples whom he encountered on the difficult journey from Baghdad, across the land between the Aral and Caspian Seas and then up the Volga to the Bulgarian capital. He wrote a long account of this journey, extracts of which were preserved in Yaqut's *Geographical Dictionary* and in 1933 a manuscript of the complete work was discovered in a library in Baghdad by Zeki Validi Togan. This may go back to the eleventh century, and it has been edited and translated into various languages, so that it is now easily accessible.[2] About one-fifth of the vivid and detailed account is concerned with the people of the Rus, whom he encountered at Bulghar.

They were engaged, he tells us, in selling their merchandise to traders who came to the international market there, and they brought with them many sables which they used in place of gold coins when they wished to buy. He tells how they prayed to their gods, figures of wood stuck into the ground near the place where they moored their ships, a description which calls to mind the carved figure discovered at Staraja Ladoga (p. 47 above). The Rus begged their deities, in return for offerings of food and drink, to send a merchant with many silver coins who would buy what they had to sell and not question what they told him. As well as furs, they brought slave-girls to sell. They arrived in boats along the Volga, and were permitted to build large wooden houses, each of which held from ten to twenty persons. Each trader had his own quarters in one of the buildings and sat on a couch there with his slaves around him. Each of the leaders had his own special slave to

[1] Smyser, 93–4.
[2] English translation, H. M. Smyser; also R. P. Blake and R. N. Frye, *Byzantine-Metabyzantine* I(2) 1949, 7–37; French translation, M. Canard, *Annales de l'institut d'études orientales* 16 (1958), 41–146. German translation with commentary, Zeki Validi Togan, *Abhandlungen für die Kunde des Morgenlandes*, 24, 3, (1939).

serve him, and also his concubine, and it must be these who are described as the 'wives' of the Rus, and who were treated generously, wearing splendid ornaments, neck-rings of gold and silver, strings of green glass beads, which were greatly prized, and large 'boxes' on their breasts which were probably the large tortoise brooches fashionable at this time. The traders could hardly have brought their wives on the difficult journey down the Volga, but like Hoskuld the Icelander in *Laxdæla Saga* (p. 102 below) they were accustomed to take concubines when away from home, and these had recognised rights. The King of the Bulgars could claim one slave out of every ten brought to Bulghar for himself.

Whereas Ibn Rusteh described the Rus as kind to their slaves and clean in their dress, Ibn Fadlan accuses them of filthy habits and of living like wild asses; this, however, seems to have been largely due to the fact that they did not, like Muslims, use running water to wash or wash between meals. He describes how a large bowl was carried round the hall each day, so that each man could wash his face and hair, which implies at least certain standards of cleanliness. Smyser even draws a parallel between life in the halls of the Rus and that in the king's hall at Heorot in the Anglo-Saxon *Beowulf*.[1]

Some parts of the account appear to be based on hearsay or misunderstanding, like the description of the King of the Rus behaving like an oriental despot; moreover, it seems hardly likely that the traders had intercourse with their slaves in public, since this would certainly decrease their value as merchandise. When, however, Ibn Fadlan claims to describe what he himself saw and heard, as in the case of the cremation ceremony of a chief, putting questions to an interpreter and giving the answers he received, it is generally felt that he has given a reliable account of what he has observed at first-hand. His description provides important evidence for the identification of the Rus as Scandinavian traders, since the details of the ship-funeral are in close accord with archaeological evidence from ship-graves of the Viking Age in Scandinavia.[2] The spirit of their religious beliefs, their attitude to their gods, the symbolism of the door of the dead in the funeral ceremony leading to the realm of their dead ancestors, and their fierce joy when the ship

[1] Smyser, 102 ff.
[2] Davidson (1967), 113 ff.

was consumed by the cremation fire, are all in keeping with other evidence from Old Norse literature. He refers also to an inscription on a post set up to commemorate the dead, and another Arab writer, An-Nade, claims to have seen symbols engraved in wood by the Rus; Liestøl takes both passages as referring to the carving of runes.[1] Most of the Arab sources are fragmentary and difficult to interpret, but in the lengthy account of Ibn Fadlan we have evidence of outstanding value, adding greatly to our knowledge of the kind of life lived by Scandinavian traders in northern Russia in the early tenth century.

[1] Liestøl (1970), 125.

CHAPTER 5

Markets and Fortresses

It seems that by the early ninth century Scandinavian traders were moving eastwards along the great Russian rivers. Their progress made possible the growth of market centres in the eastern Baltic, and the stimulus of markets further east, such as Bulghar, and contact with other travellers there must have encouraged adventurous men to attempt new journeys in search of profit. Meanwhile trade with the British Isles and the Rhineland was also helping to expand the trading centres in Scandinavia.

An important market on the south Baltic coast was Hedeby in south-eastern Denmark, probably founded by Godfred in 808 (p. 21 above). This was admirably suited for trade both with the North Sea and the Baltic, since it was joined by earthworks with Hollingstedt, a small port on the west coast only eleven miles away. Hedeby has been thoroughly excavated by archaeologists from Kiel and Schleswig, and much is now known about its lay-out and trading history.[1]

After its foundation in the ninth century, it grew rapidly until it was destroyed in the eleventh, probably by Harald Sigurdson of Norway in 1050. At the time of its greatest prosperity it was protected by a rampart, which was increased in size as the settlement grew, and by a stockade and ditches. Three road tunnels for use by pedestrians and wagons pierced the stockade, and there were two main streets and many dwelling houses. A brook ran through the town, and the river Schlei provided good anchorage for ships. The large area inside the ramparts may have included open market-places, with room for merchants to set up their tents and stalls; there was also a section where the craftsmen lived, producing

[1] Detailed information about the site is given by Jankuhn (1963) and Schietzel (1969).

pottery, woven materials, jewellery of metal and amber, glass beads, objects of horn and bone, and iron weapons made from lake ore from Sweden. It may also have been here that the first Danish coins were minted. Such work kept the town prosperous all the year round, although the main trading season was the summer. The chief attraction of Hedeby was the collection of luxury goods from both western and eastern Europe to be found there; these included furs and slaves from the eastern Baltic and beyond, and there were also regular supplies of pottery, glassware and weapons from the west and soapstone vessels from Norway. After the destruction of Hedeby its place as a trading centre was taken by Schleswig.

The Swedish town of Birka on the island of Björko in Lake Mälar came into being as a direct result of trade with the eastern regions, replacing the earlier Helgö where access for ships was limited.[1] Birka had a splendid position on an inland lake, between the two great estates of Uppland and Södermanland, and was under the protection of their rulers. A fort stood on a small hill to the south-west, and in the tenth century the town seems to have been enclosed by a wall with timber towers. Rimbert refers to the Thing or Assembly of the town,[2] where under a *praefectus regis* fair treatment for merchants and traders from abroad was provided. The southern outlet through Södertälge was probably still open at this period,[3] so that ships could sail direct to Gotland and the Gulf of Finland, while there was an inland waterway to northern Sweden by lakes and rivers which could have been used as an ice road by traders bringing furs in winter. The sheltered lake waters offered excellent harbourage with bays of varying depth for the ships anchoring there, while in addition an artificial harbour was constructed in the most prosperous period of Birka's history. Excavations of the extensive cemeteries there, dating from about 800 onwards, have added much to our knowledge of the trade which kept the town thriving. There were glass and pottery from the Rhineland, but many more goods from the East. Traces of silk were found in forty-five graves, and one type with a gold pattern is believed to come from China.[4] While there were coins of western

[1] Arbman (1939 and 1940); *The Viking* (London 1966), 44 ff.
[2] Rimbert, 19, 65; 27, 93.
[3] Sawyer, 183–4.
[4] Geijer, 58 ff.

Europe in thirteen graves, there were ninety-two whole or fragmentary coins from the Islamic East and a number of ornaments of eastern origin, like the amethyst ring with an Arabic inscription believed to come from beyond the Caspian. There are three examples of the delicate balances used by merchants to weigh out silver, and many graves contained small metal weights. Skates, ice-picks, and crampons on the shoes of the dead suggest that the town was inhabited in winter as well as summer, and indeed this would be the best time for fur trading. Crafts like metal-working, making

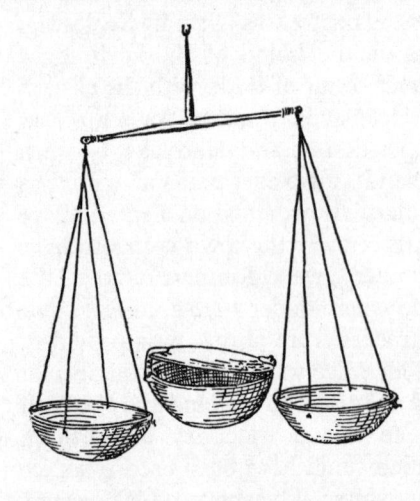

Fig. 1. A merchant's balance with its metal case, of the type used in the Viking Age (after E. Wilson, J. Simpson, *Everyday Life in the Viking Age*, Batsford 1967).

of beads and horn articles and the minting of coins may have gone on here also, although the evidence is less clear than at Hedeby. The importance of workshops has been pointed out by Birgit Arrhenius;[1] in one of these copies of an oriental pendant were being manufactured, a secondary effect of the flow of goods from the eastern regions. The exact date of the foundation of Birka is not known, but it was probably between 780 and 830.[2] Its end seems to have come about during the second half of the tenth century, due to the closing of the Volga route on which the trade of the town largely depended. The inhabitants probably moved to Sigtuna, which was founded in the period 960–75; according to Adam of

[1] Arrhenius (1968 and 1970).
[2] Sawyer, 184.

Bremen, there was nothing to be seen at Birka by the late eleventh century.

Further west in Norway was the trading centre called by the Anglo-Saxons Sciringesceal, visited by the Norwegian Ottar on his voyage south (p. 32 above), and identified with Kaupang ('market'), a site along a narrow strip of land on the west side of Oslo Fiord. It is no longer open to ships from the sea, but was accessible in the Viking Age, although the way in must have been difficult without a pilot. This site and the extensive cemeteries nearby have been systematically excavated by Charlotte Blindheim.[1] Kaupang was a harbour which seems to have been in use for a time as a summer market, with a small settlement of six houses, where metal-work, weaving, the making of soapstone dishes and probably the working of amber was carried on. There is evidence for goods from the eastern Baltic, the British Isles and the Rhineland; dried fish and down from the eider duck may have been additional home products which left no traces behind, and boat-building would have been an additional source of profit. The finds show links with those from Hedeby, and in the accounts of voyages recorded for King Alfred (p. 24 above), Kaupang and Hedeby are mentioned along with the eastern Baltic market of Truso. Kaupang flourished for some time in the ninth until the early tenth century, when the lowering of water in the channel may have led to its abandonment. The original attraction was probably the harbour and the existence of a sacred place which brought travellers there, since three large cemeteries continued to be used after the settlement had been abandoned, and a large number of ship-burials was crowded on to one headland. Possibly men from western and central Norway found it convenient to assemble there before sailing on expeditions further east, in order to gain protection against pirates.[2] There are other sites called Kaupang in Norway, and a number of small trading centres of this kind, which never developed into towns, are now known in Scandinavia from the Viking Age.

The eastern Baltic centre at Truso is said in Wulfstan's account for King Alfred to have been near the mouth of the Vistula, which

[1] Blindheim (1960, 1969). Additional articles on trade at Kaupang in *Viking* 33 (1969); cf. *Kiel Papers*, 41–50.
[2] Sawyer, 190–1.

separated the land of the Wends from that of the Ests, on the shore of a lake where the river Ilfing (the Elbing) entered Estmere, the modern Frisches Haff. Truso was probably on the site of the present-day Elbing, where near the railway station a cemetery of the Viking Age was found with objects of Gotland type in the graves.[1] The sagacious Alfred of Wessex evidently realised the importance of the route from western Norway to the eastern Baltic when he put the accounts of Ottar and Wulfstan together in his translation of Orosius.

There must have been many other trading centres in the Baltic. In the eleventh century Adam of Bremen declared that he had heard 'great and scarcely credible things' in praise of Jomsborg, which he claimed was the largest of all cities in Europe, a mainly pagan town to which people of all nations came.[2] Legends about the Jomsborg garrison and its exploits may already have been current, but his description suggests a prosperous trading centre, and excavations bear this out. Much valuable information about early wooden buildings of various types has been gained from the work carried on there from 1934 onwards,[3] and some of the ninth-century houses are of Scandinavian stave construction.

An account of what is probably Hedeby, although Jomsborg has been suggested, is left by al-Turtushi, a Spanish Jew from Cordova, whose work survives only in translations.[4] He was in northern Europe soon after the middle of the tenth century and was not over-impressed by the town he visited, which seemed to him a poor place. There were wells of sweet water there, he noted,[5] and the inhabitants lived largely on fish. Women had considerable freedom and the right to divorce their husbands, and babies were thrown into the sea if their parents could not feed them. Christians had their own church in the town, but most of the people were heathen, holding festivals in which they ate and drank in honour of their god, sacrificing animals and hanging up the carcases on

[1] Nerman (1953), 189 ff.
[2] Adam of Bremen II, 19, 66.
[3] See Kunkel and Wilde.
[4] Birkeland, 101, 159, but see Sauvaget, 135. The traveller's full name was Ibrahim b.Ya'qub al-Turtushi.
[5] Haegstad, 84, suggests that this is a euphemism for the women of the town, but in view of the general interest shown by the geographers in sweet as opposed to brackish water, this seems an unnecessary complexity.

poles outside their houses. He thought they worshipped Sirius. Both men and women used eye make-up to preserve their looks.[1] He found their singing harsh and unpleasant, worse than the growling of dogs.

This account could well apply to Hedeby. There were wells there which supplied piped water, and Adam of Bremen refers to a Christian church visited by Rimbert in the ninth century. Sacrificial feasts, freedom of women, destruction of unwanted children at birth and the eating of fish are what we would expect of Scandinavians of the Viking Age, while the singing of northerners would no doubt be unattractive to a man from the south. The reference to Sirius is tantalising, but may be based simply on the conventional assumption that pagans must worship idols and stars.

Further east there must have been an important trading centre on Gotland, perhaps at Vläslagen (formerly Västergarnsviken), where a large semi-circular earthwork has been found, and traces of a trading settlement may have been covered by sand; there is an excellent natural harbour here, but since it was open to the sea it would have been hard to defend against raiders. Gotland's key position on the route east makes the existence of important market centres certain, but possibly the small ships of the Viking Age could be beached at various points round the island.[2] If trade were mainly with the pagan peoples of the south Baltic coast, this might explain the silence of Christian writers on the subject.

Once we reach Russia, the subject of towns becomes highly controversial. In the thirteenth century the Icelanders called the region *Garðariki*, meaning the kingdom of fortified settlements or 'towns', and it was earlier referred to as *Garðar* in runic inscriptions.[3] It seems probable that small settlements were already in existence when the Scandinavians began their penetration eastwards. Recent research has shown a general growth of urban settlement between the seventh and ninth centuries in the Baltic countries, Russia and the state of Great Moravia which came into existence in the early ninth century, as well as in Scandinavia

---

[1] Haegstad interprets this as 'they wore amber which does not deteriorate with age'.
[2] Floderus, 65 ff.; Lundstrom, 99 ff.; *The Viking* (London 1966), 51 ff.
[3] Kleiber, 71.

itself.[1] The Bulgars and Khazars had towns of some size, although they were ruled, like the Moravians, by a monarchy of basic nomadic type. The market at Bulghar drew Swedish merchants along the Volga route because they could meet with eastern merchants there and get a good price for slaves and furs, and we know from Ibn Fadlan that they had their own quarters on one bank of the river, where they were permitted to build their own halls. Similar settlements for traders must have grown up beside other towns in Russia.

When Kiev was excavated, Karger traced three early settlements there which combined in the tenth century to make a single town, and which was further enlarged by Yaroslav.[2] It is said in the *Primary Chronicle* that when Olga visited the Drevljane in 945 (p. 135 below): '... the waters flowed below the heights of Kiev and the inhabitants did not live in the valley but upon the heights'. At that time the only settlement was probably on the hill, and there is archaeological evidence for fortifications on one of the three heights on which the city stands;[3] here the Scandinavians could have turned the small settlement into a strong fortified centre. The lower area of the town where craftsmen lived, the *Podol*, close to the river, developed by the tenth century, so that we have a striking parallel to Nerman's outline of the growth of Grobin (p. 25 above).

The foundation of Kiev is dated in the *Primary Chronicle* at about 860. It must have been established earlier than this, and Vasiliev suggests a date about 840,[4] while others would put it still earlier. The story in the *Chronicle* is that two 'boyars', who in Scandinavian terms would be jarls as distinct from kings, and who were connected with Rurik, the founder of Novgorod, sailed down the Dnieper and came upon a little settlement on a hill. They were told that it had been built by three brothers, and that the people living there were Poljani and paid tribute to the Khazars. These two leaders were called Askold and Dir (ON *Hǫskuldr* and *Dyri*); they took over the hill, gathered their followers together and took command of the Poljani. Besides its advantages as a centre for

[1] Gimbutas (1971), 146 ff.; *The Great Moravian Exhibition* (Czecho-Slovak Academy of Sciences, Prague, 1964).
[2] Tikhomirov, *The Towns of Ancient Rus* (Moscow 1959), 16 ff.
[3] Hensel, 45.
[4] Vasiliev (1946), 9 ff.

collecting tribute, the stronghold was on the route leading westwards to Poland, and so formed a link with the Moravian Empire which grew up in the ninth century. While Novgorod appears to have been gradually absorbed into Swedish territory, Kiev seems to have been taken over by Norwegians and ruled by hereditary jarls, perhaps from Halogaland. Joint rulership of this kind is not uncommon in early Norse tradition, and there is no need to assume that the names must represent a single ruler. Askold and Dyr are credited with the attack on Constantinople which took place in 860 (p. 123 below). From the record of the Rus arriving in Constantinople as early as 838, probably to negotiate a trade agreement (p. 57 above), it appears that interest in the Dnieper route must have begun early. However, hostile tribes blocked the way between Kiev and the Byzantine capital, so that the representatives of the Rus were unable to return, and it was only when Kiev had been firmly established as a centre with overlordship over the surrounding tribes that it was possible to organise regular expeditions down the river every year with merchandise, as is clear from the treaties recorded in the *Primary Chronicle* (p. 89 below). These indicate that convoys of merchants moved down the river under the authority of the Prince of Kiev, and came from a number of Rus centres to join the trading voyage.

In the course of the ninth century Novgorod also became a major centre of Scandinavians in Russia. Extensive excavations there have revealed much of the lay-out of the medieval town,[1] but few Scandinavian remains have been found, possibly because their settlement was on the east bank of the river which has not yet been excavated; a runic alphabet carved on a bone has, however, been discovered. A hill-fort about three kilometres upstream is known as Rurik's fort, and traces of Scandinavian settlement might perhaps be expected here, since this area was occupied as early as the ninth century. It is not far from the remains of an ancient sanctuary, Peryn, presumably called after the god Perun, at the point where the river Volkhov enters Lake Ilmen. This has been excavated, and found to consist of a circular area surrounded by a ditch, with eight lobes, so that it resembled an eight-petalled flower. In the centre had stood a large wooden post, possibly a

[1] For an account of the excavations, see Artsikhovsky, summarised in English by Thompson. Cf. Mongait, 296 ff.

stand for an idol or part of an idol itself. In Novgorod occupation appears to go back to the tenth century, and the city may have grown out of a trading centre set up in the vicinity of the ancient sanctuary and near the hill-fort in the marshy land near the river. The town had a winding main street where planks were laid down over the mud, and this remained the chief highway until the seventeenth century. Many workshops of the twelfth and thirteenth centuries were found, and a large number of 'letters' written in Old Slavonic on birchbark. There was an excellent drainage system to deal with the high water level, and large wooden pipes were made in two halves and joined by birch bark, while there were also wells and barrel sumps. Due to the water in the soil, much of the original wooden material has been preserved.

Thus the two main towns, Kiev and Novgorod, appear to have begun their development as Scandinavian outposts, challenging Khazar influence over neighbouring tribes. There must have been other less important fortified centres from which the Rus could continue trading and collecting of furs. There are traditions of an early Slav settlement at Smolensk, where three ancient dwelling-sites existed by the eighth century, one on the hill where the cathedral stood later, and here the main development into an urban centre took place from the close of the ninth century onwards.[1] The *Primary Chronicle* describes Smolensk as a populous town avoided by Askold and Dir in 863, but in 882 Oleg, who by then had control of Kiev, is said to have forced the inhabitants to recognise him as their overlord. Thus it seems like Kiev to have begun as a small fortified place on a hill, while the main population settled on lower ground; the settlement represented by the large cemetery at Gnezdovo must have been established later than Smolensk itself (p. 55 above). Polotsk also seems to have begun as a hill fort; Vitebsk was occupied by the ninth century, and Suzdal has some finds of tenth century date, including a comb with a ship on it which could be Scandinavian work. Chernigov and Pskov may also go back to the ninth century, and possibly also Ozborsk and Rostov, while at Sizov there was a strong military element in the first occupation, with women occasionally interred in the graves of warriors.

The *Chronicle* tells us that Oleg in 882 began to build fortified

[1] Tikhomirov, *The Towns of Ancient Rus* (Moscow 1959), 26 ff.; Avdusin, 53 ff.

places, and archaeological evidence for one of these from a later period was found by Rybakov in 1961 at Vitichev on the Dnieper, about forty kilometres below Kiev. Remains of a tower were found, which had been used as a base for a beacon, and there were traces of two fortified centres there, the earlier dating from the late tenth or early eleventh century. Vitichev was at a strategic point for defence against the Khazars and other peoples attacking from the east, and the beacon appears to be Varangian work and has no parallels elsewhere in Russia. There would be a good view from the tower, and the church at Kiev could be seen from it; it seems to have been constructed for purposes of signalling, as in Scandinavia and the Orkneys. The suggestion has been made that Vitichev was the place mentioned by Constantine in the account of the voyage down the Dnieper (p. 82 below) and also the *Vitaholm* on the runic inscription at Alstad in Norway.[1]

In an illuminating study on the origin of towns in the medieval period, Hensel suggested that there were two essential features, the fortified hill round which the town grew, and the existence of a fertile hinterland to provide food for the population. A position on an important trade route which could also be easily defended was an additional factor to encourage growth. His study helps to explain the contribution of the Scandinavians to the growth of towns in Russia. They evidently took over villages, or more often hill-forts, which might have small settlements already attached to them, and strengthened the defences, so that they could be used as centres for collecting tribute from the region round. If such centres were well placed, they grew rapidly, and a *podol* for craftsmen established itself as part of the town. The Scandinavians, with their natural instinct for trading and their ability to collect tribute, would be just the invaders to encourage such growth, and they were always ready to join themselves to Finns or Slavs who would acknowledge them as overlords or work with them as allies. They are unlikely to have concerned themselves much with the organisation of the larger centres, so long as they benefited from them and the townsmen caused no trouble, and later on we know that such urban communities became strong enough to hold their own with the Varangians and to dictate policies for themselves.

It is essential to take into account the evidence from the Baltic

[1] Kleiber, 66 ff.

MAP 3

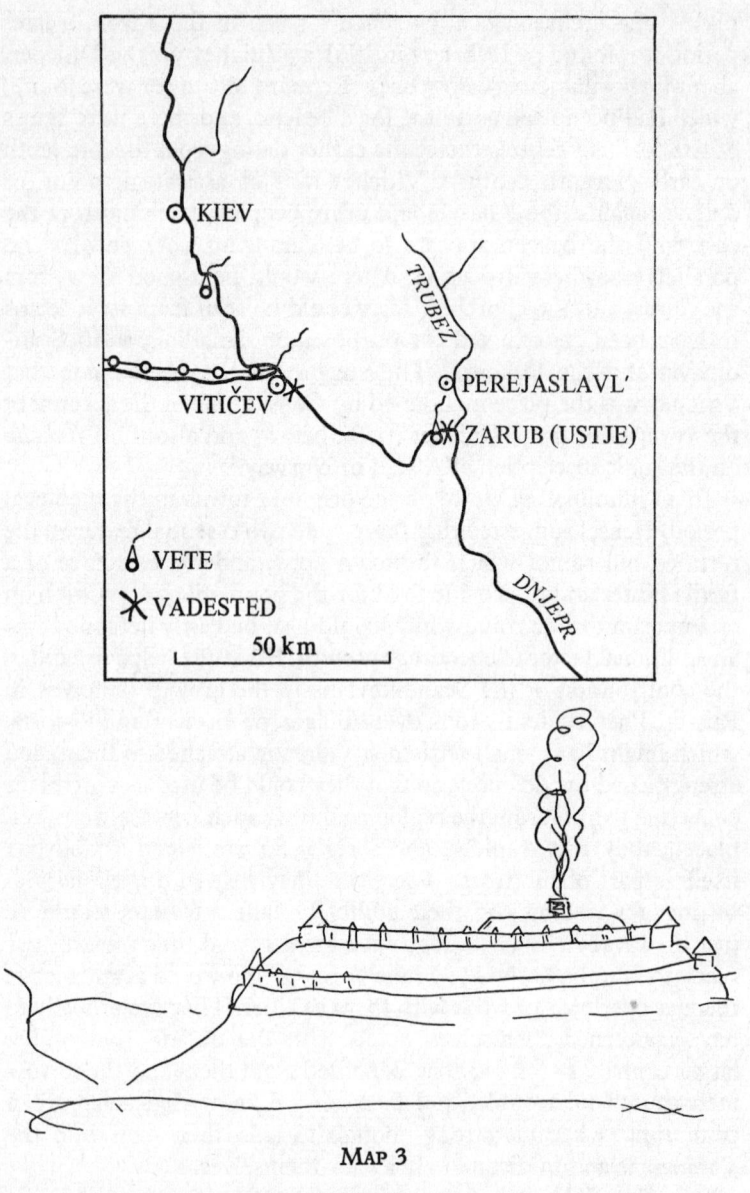

Position of Vitichev on the Dnieper and reconstruction of fort with
beacon (from B. Kleiber, *Viking* 29 (1965)).

market centres to understand what happened in Russia. Many scholars have assumed that the invaders must have stayed in neat ethnic groups, easily recognisable by contemporaries, and that they would have insisted on building houses of their own native type and continuing to use their own style of weapons and ornaments. This goes against the dictates of common sense. The Vikings were practical colonists and explorers, they would travel light and adapt to existing conditions, while intermarriage with women of different races or the taking of concubines among their captives must have complicated household arrangements and possessions to an even greater degree. Many bitter arguments might have been avoided if the participants paused to consider the conditions of everyday life likely to prevail among Scandinavians in Russia, and ceased to regard them men as determined to perpetuate their old way of life in the new land to which they had come. While the first arrivals might leave clear evidence in graves or on dwelling sites, this would not be so with the second or third generations. Indeed the outstanding quality of the Scandinavians who travelled east seems to have been flexibility and adaptation to the changing and difficult circumstances of their hard and dangerous life.

CHAPTER 6

The Road to Constantinople

As the Rus had taken furs and slaves to Bulghar, so they carried the same wares to Constantinople in the tenth century, down the Dnieper waterway. We have an account of their journey in the book by the Emperor Constantine Porphyrogenitus (912–59), written for the edification of his son, *De Administrando Imperio*.[1] This contains a long description of the difficulties faced by the Rus in bringing their boats down the Dnieper, a subject in which the Emperor clearly took great interest. This section of the book is believed to have been compiled about 944, based on an account by someone who had made the journey, perhaps a Byzantine envoy who had been to Kiev and returned with the merchant convoy. It appears to have been someone familiar with Constantinople, from references to the Hippodrome and the royal polo ground, and according to Jenkins the style suggests that the account was taken down from an oral description. The informant appears to be familiar with both Scandinavian and Slav languages, from the names given to the rapids, although these may have been supplied by a Varangian with local knowledge. The fact that the names of the rapids are given in both languages is of considerable importance, not only because they provide one of the most valuable pieces of evidence for the identity of the Rus, but also because we have here the only surviving example of the language they used at this period, while the Slavonic names are among the earliest surviving examples of the language of the Eastern Slavs.

[1] Edited and translated by G. Moravcsik and R. J. H. Jenkins (Budapest 1949), 57 ff. A commentary by Jenkins is published in a separate volume (London 1962), and a revised translation by Jenkins, Dumbarton Oaks, Washington, 1967.

The account tells of the assembling of the merchants who were to make the voyage down the Dnieper. Early in November every year those in Kiev left to collect tribute, mainly in furs but perhaps also in slaves, from tribes in the surrounding regions. Meanwhile some of the Slavs who paid tribute to Kiev built boats for the voyage and were paid for these; it seems that a new fleet was supplied every year and the old vessels broken up. These boats are called *monoxyla* and the term indicates a vessel hollowed out of a single tree-trunk, a kind of dug-out canoe. These are known to have been used by the Slavs from the seventh century onwards, and Priscus mentions such boats in an account of his visit to Attila's court in 448; they have also been found at Novgorod.[1] Presumably on war expeditions the Rus used larger vessels of Scandinavian type, but the boats on the Dnieper were for trading purposes, presumably best suited to the conditions of the voyage, the crossing of the rapids and the journey across the Black Sea to Constantinople. The expeditions were clearly arranged by treaty with the Emperor,[2] and it is probable that vessels which might be used for more warlike purposes would be discouraged by the Byzantines as far as possible.

It has been queried whether such primitive craft would be capable of transporting large parties of merchants with their cargoes of goods and slaves, but this could be made possible by raising the sides by means of planks, as on clinker-built ships. Some of the vessels found at Novgorod were fitted with frames to hold the planking in this way. On two occasions in the account of the voyage it is stated that 'tackle' was added to the boats, and this might mean the building up of the sides as well as the addition of masts and sails. Boats used by the Cossacks in the seventeenth century appear to have been constructed on the same principle; they were built without a keel, but on 'bottoms made of the wood of the willow', and were about 45 feet long; when raised with planks, pinned or nailed over one another, they were as much as 12 feet high and 60 feet in length, according to a description by a French traveller, Guillaume Levasseur de Beauplan.[3] The journey

[1] Gimbutas (1971), 99; Avdusin, 106.
[2] Sorlin, 456 ff.
[3] G. L. de Beauplan, *A description of Ukraine*, translated A. and J. Churchill, *A Collection of Voyages and Travels* (London 1704), I, 591.

must have been a gruelling one, which accounts for the fact that new boats were provided each year; the treaty of 907 (p. 90 below) states that the returning merchants received from the emperor provisions, ropes, sails and so on for the voyage according to their needs. The return voyage with such cargoes as silk, wine, and luxury goods would mean that the boats were less heavily loaded, and perhaps could be reduced in number. However, since they had to be taken upstream even greater difficulties would presumably be incurred while passing the rapids. While the Slavs provided the boats the Rus themselves were responsible for oars and fittings and planks for the sides.

The boats were brought down the river from the forest regions where they were made, perhaps in the Valdai hills; they were fitted out at Kiev and then taken down the river to Vitichev, about forty-five kilometres from Kiev, to await the rest of the convoy which came from other towns. This was a fortified place (p. 77 above) and was probably chosen to enable boats from Pereyaslavl on the lower Trubezh to join them. They would have to leave in June to enable them to make the voyage to Constantinople and back before the river froze. It has been estimated that the whole voyage might take as long as five or six weeks, reckoning ten days to the rapids, a day or two to pass them, a day on St Gregory's Island, four days to the Dnieper mouth, and then past the mouth of the Dniester to the Danube, where the boats could be made ready for the open sea. Finally they set off for their voyage to the capital from Mesembria,[1] which might have taken as many as twenty days for what must have been slow, clumsy craft. It was probably for this reason that they preferred to follow the coast round to the mouth of the Danube by Constanza, Varna and Mesembria. The emphasis in the treaty on equipment for the return voyage may mean that they sailed back to the Dnieper mouth direct.

At Vitichev boats joined the convoy from various points further north, and moved down the river until the rapids were reached, at a point just beyond the modern town of Dnepropetrovsk (see Map 4). There were seven of these, forming a serious obstacle to travellers, and it was only possible to pass them during a few weeks in the year while the water was high; in the nineteenth century the best time was early in May, but the Rus seem to have left later than

[1] Sorlin, 348 (note).

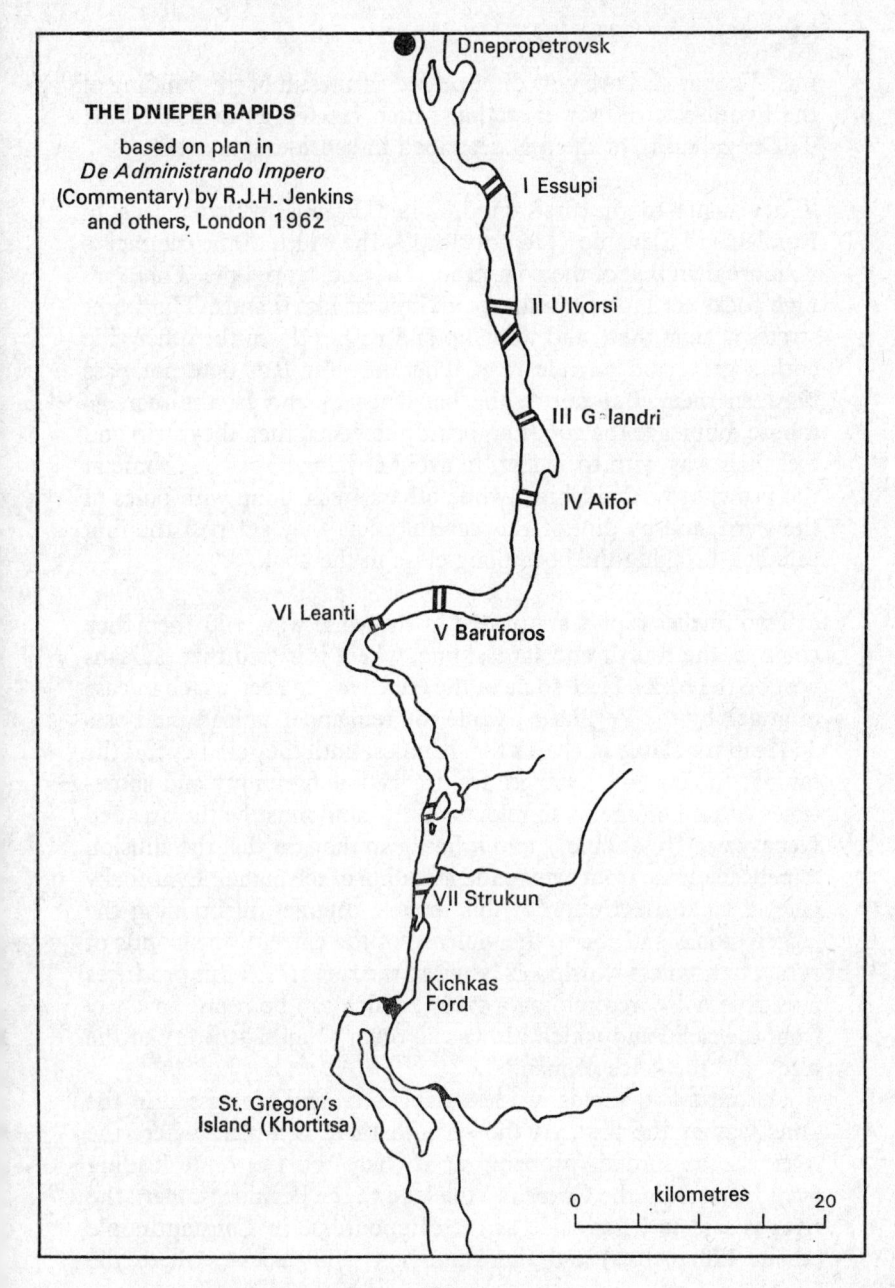

MAP 4

this. The rapids have now disappeared as a result of the building of the hydro-electric power station which created an artificial lake. The negotiating of them is described in considerable detail:

'They come to the first rapid, called Essupi, which means in Russian and Slavonic "Do not sleep"; the width of the cataract is no more than that of the polo-ground in Constantinople. There are high rocks set in the middle, standing out like islands. The water strikes against these and wells up and rushes down the other side with a great and terrible roar. Therefore the Rus dare not pass between them, but put to the bank nearby and let the men go ashore, but leave the goods on board the boats, then they strip and feel their way with their feet, to avoid striking a rock ... some at the prow, some amidships, while others push along with poles at the stern, and by dint of this careful effort they get past the first cataract, bringing the boat along close to the bank.'

Two further rapids are passed in the same way, and then they come to the fourth and largest one, where it is said that pelicans nest on the rocks. Here some of the crew have to keep watch in case of attack by the Pechinegs, while the remainder unload the boats and lead the slaves in chains for six miles, until they are beyond the rapids; the boats are sometimes dragged along empty and sometimes carried on men's shoulders. This rapid must be the dreaded Nenasytets ('insatiable'), and it has been thought that the allusion to pelicans arose from a misunderstanding of the name.[1] Evarnitsky gives a vivid description of this terrible cataract, mentioning the jagged stones and rocks, the violence of the current, the clouds of spray, bottomless whirlpools between the rocks: 'All this produces a terrible noise, resembling a groan, which can be heard far away from the rapid and which drowns all other sounds—the cry of the birds and the voice of man.'

The next two rapids are less dangerous and are passed in the same way as the first. At the seventh there is a place where the river can be forded (probably at Kichkas) on the route leading from Cherson in the Crimea to the land of the Pechinegs. Here the river is said to be as wide as the Hippodrome in Constantinople (about 120 metres) and there are high cliffs above, where the

[1] Thomsen, 58.

Pechinegs and their allies often lie in wait to attack travellers. It was at Kichkas that five swords of Scandinavian type were discovered in the river bed in 1928, during the construction of the Dnieper dam; they were of tenth century date and were thought to have been lost all at the same time.[1] This could conceivably have been at the time of the attack on Svyatoslav, which led to his death in 972, but from the account it seems probable that many battles took place at this crossing.

When the last rapid had been safely passed, the travellers reached St Gregory's Island, whose Russian name is Khortitsa, lying like a huge ship in the middle of the river, with high cliffs on three sides. It is called Varangian Island in a source of 1223.[2] Here there was a huge oak-tree, and the Rus made sacrifices of cocks, drawing lots to decide which of the birds should die, and also offerings of food, setting a ring of arrows in (or round?) the oak. A great oak of colossal size and great age on this island is described by a traveller in 1876, soon after it had fallen,[3] and said to have been the traditional meeting-place for Zaporog Cossacks. From this point the party was free from danger from the Pechinegs, since the river widened and the banks were low on either side, unsuitable for an ambush by archers. There might still, however, be some danger if the boats were driven ashore at the river mouth. At the island of St Aitherios or Berezan in the Dnieper estuary a Swedish runestone was discovered in 1905, the inscription stating that it was erected by Grani in memory of his comrade Karl, who evidently perished on the journey at some time in the eleventh century.[4] The boats seem to have followed the Dniester to the Danube estuary, where they could be fitted with sails, masts and rudders for the final section of the journey across the Black Sea to the capital, where, as Constantine's account puts it, 'at last their voyage, fraught with travail and terror, difficulty and danger' was at an end.

This account gives a most convincing picture of the hardships entailed by trading in Russia in the tenth and eleventh centuries, the tremendous physical labour of getting the boats past the rapids,

[1] Ravdonikas (1933), 598 ff.
[2] *Voskresenskaya Leroptis* (Polnoe Sobranie, Russkikh Letopisey VII), 130.
[3] Jenkins (1962), 55.
[4] Cleve, 250 ff.

and the difficulties facing those who wished to bring slaves, furs and other wares safely to the capital, with constant threat of enemy attacks on the way. The names of the rapids, carefully recorded in both Slav and Rus languages, have been much discussed by scholars, and there seems no doubt that the Rus names are Scandinavian in origin, although in a number of cases there is considerable disagreement as to their exact form. They have probably been taken down from an account given orally, leaving plenty of margin for error. They are Old Swedish in form, and the Slav names are East Slavonic; some scholars detect traces of Bulgarian influence in these, although Falk,[1] using the earliest MS, claims to discern Ukrainian influence. He suggested that the Rus first named the rapids and that the Slavonic names are translations. The local people must presumably have had their own names for them before the coming of the Rus, but it may be that the names given by Constantine were the particular ones used by the men from Kiev who regularly made the voyage. They are the kind of descriptive names which attach themselves to the great rapids in the rivers of North America, and they help to conjure up a picture of the river road.

The list given in the Greek account runs as follows:[2] First, *Essupi*, possibly from *asupi*, 'always sucking in', or *ei sofi*, 'do not sleep' (the interpretation given in the text), or alternatively *ves uppi*, 'be wakeful'. Only one name is given for this rapid, perhaps because the two forms were sufficiently alike to be mistaken for the same word. Second, *Ulvorsi*, from *holmfors*, 'island rapid'. Third, *Gelandri*, from *gjallandi*, 'yelling' or 'loudly ringing', which would be in agreement with the later Russian name *Zvonets* from *zvon*, 'ringing sound'. Fourth, *Aifor*, either from *eiforr*, 'ever-fierce', or *edfors*, 'portage rapid'. Fifth, *Baruforos*, either from *barufors*, 'wave rapid', or *varufors*, 'cliff rapid'. Sixth, *Leanti*, either from *hlæjandi*, 'laughing', or *leandi*, 'seething'. Seventh, *Strukun*, from *strukum*, 'rapid current', or *strukn*, 'stream', 'small fall'. The fourth of these names, *Aifor*, is named in a runic inscription on a stone at Pilgards in Gotland, which refers to five brothers making a journey south with a man called Vifil as leader; the stone is raised

---

[1] K. O. Falk, 226 ff., but many have disagreed with this. For full references see Jenkins (1962), 41.
[2] Ibid. 42.

The Road to Constantinople

in memory of a man called Rafn, who died in Aifor, apparently on the return journey.[1]

The account of the rapids in the Greek treatise may be compared with a description from one of the legendary sagas, *Yngvars Saga Viðforla* (p. 167 below). This saga deals with a journey made by a party of Swedes under the leadership of a Swedish prince called Ingvar down a great Russian river, and includes a struggle to pass a number of cataracts. The first which they reached was at a point where the river ran through a deep ravine, and they were able to pull boats along by ropes. At the second rapid, however, this was not possible:[2]

'They came to a great cataract. There was such a tumult from it that they were forced to go ashore ... the cliffs were so high that they could not draw the ship along by ropes. They brought their boats in between the rocks, where the river curved with the current. There was a gap visible between the rocks, and there they went ashore; it was flat and wet. Ingvar told them to get busy making digging tools, and this they did. They began digging, and measured out a deep broad ditch so that the river could flow through it. But it took a month before they were able to take their boats through this.'

At the end of the saga there is a note about the traditions which the saga-writer claims to have used, which contains the interesting comment:[3]

'Some say that Ingvar and his comrades went on for two weeks, and were unable to see anything unless they lit a candle, because the cliffs met above the river and it was like rowing for two weeks inside a cave. Wise men, however, think this cannot be true unless the river flowed through so narrow a ravine that the rocks met overhead, or else that the woods were so dense that the trees met above as the cliffs neared one another.'

The plot of the saga is muddled and cannot be wholly rational-

[1] Pipping, 175 ff.
[2] *Yngvars Saga* (edited E. Olsen, Copenhagen 1912), 19.
[3] Ibid. 48.

ised, but it appears to preserve genuine traditions of a famous expedition to Russia in an attempt to open up the lost trade-routes down the Volga to the Caspian Sea. The account of passing the rapids certainly recalls conditions on the Dnieper, and might be based on stories of that river. The importance of a knowledge of languages on the journey, much stressed in the saga, would apply here also. Ingvar is said to have spent three months in Russia before he began his journey, and he learned to speak several tongues. When he encountered the wise Queen Silkisif, he kept silent for a while to discover how many tongues she knew, and found to his approval that she spoke Latin, Greek, German and Scandinavian, as well as 'many others known on the eastern road'.[1] Another ruler, the King of Heliopolis, could speak many languages, but his native tongue was Greek.[2] After Ingvar's death his son decided to follow his father's example and spent a winter at a school, 'where he learned to speak many tongues known to be used on the eastern road'.[3] The complex of languages and cultures south of Novgorod was indeed such as to make it essential that a party of merchants voyaging south should have good interpreters with them. This is clear also from Ibn Fadlan's account of his long journey from Baghdad up the Volga to Bulghar, and again from an episode in the Old Russian life of St Antonus;[4] this saint in the early twelfth century was said to have met a Greek merchant in Novgorod who spoke Latin, Greek and Russian; he found that the man was a Hellenised Greek from the Crimea who had learned Russian through commercial contacts with the northern zones.

At the end of the voyage, the traders arrived at the magnificent capital of the Byzantine Empire, Constantinople. To them it was the Great Town (*Miklagarðr*), and the impact of its sophistication and luxury must have been enormous. It also offered an irresistible temptation to raiders, and in the late ninth and early tenth cencentury a number of attacks were made by Rus ships, of which we learn a good deal from Byzantine sources (p. 118 ff. below). The Byzantines countered this threat by their two favourite methods, diplomacy on the one hand, and on the other the policy of playing

[1] Ibid. 15.
[2] Ibid. 17.
[3] Ibid. 32.
[4] Vasiliev (1932/1), 327.

off one enemy against another. About 874 Basil I was sending gifts to that 'most unconquerable and impious people the Rus'.[1] In his treatise Constantine is careful to point out that the Rus could not reach the Imperial City either for trade or warfare unless they were on good terms with the Pechinegs, so that if the emperor kept the Pechinegs on his side, neither Rus nor Turks could attack, nor 'extract from the Romans large and inflated sums of money and goods as the price of peace'.[2] In spite of their raids on the city, the Rus were permitted to trade there, and the importance of this trade to the empire is indicated by the carefully drawn up 'treaties' or agreements preserved in the *Primary Chronicle*, under the dates 907 and 911.

The *Chronicle* records an attack in 907 (p. 123 below), and after this negotiations are said to have been made, and the emperor led the Rus envoys round the city, showing them the treasures for which Byzantine was famous and sending them back home with gifts of silk, gold, fruit and wine. It is generally agreed that these two documents are genuine ones, even if they are not, as the *Chronicle* claims, treaties made on two separate occasions, after hostilities had taken place; it is possible that the first is a preliminary draft and the second the agreement in final form,[3] but after a detailed and careful examination of the text and of the work done on it by Russian scholars, Irene Sorlin has come to the conclusion that the 911 treaty is not merely a ratification of the earlier one, although both are genuine and hang together.[4] She points out that while the 907 agreement summarises the rights of the Rus, that of 911 outlines the civil law which applies to the Rus who come to trade in Constantinople. Both have presumably been translated into Russian from a Greek original.

The importance of the agreements lies in the picture which they offer us of relations between the Rus and the Byzantines in the early tenth century, and of the way of life lived by traders and merchants who visited the city. A number of names are added to the treaties, and some of these are clearly Scandinavian; they show that the Scandinavian element was still predominant at the court

[1] Ibid. (1951), 168.
[2] Jenkins (1967), 219.
[3] Vasiliev (1951), 219.
[4] Sorlin, 345; 351; 472 ff.

of Kiev and those of other Russian centres which subscribe to the agreement.[1] In the 907 document, the names are Karl, Farlof, Velmud, Rulav and Stemid: the Norse forms of these could be Karl or Karli, Farulfr, Vermundr, Hroðleifr and Steinviðr. These names reappear in the second treaty, and fresh ones are added: Ingeld, Gudy, Ruald, Karn, Frelaf, Ruar, Aktevu, Truan, Lidul and Fost. These have been interpreted as Ingjaldr, Góði or Guði, Hróaldr, Karni, Friðleifr, Angantyr (suggested by Thomsen but less convincing than the rest),[2] Þróndr or Þrándr, Leiðulfr and Fastr or Fasti. The names recognisably Scandinavian appear to be Swedish in origin, but some on the list may be Finnish. Nora Chadwick noted that some of these names occur in the saga of Ǫrvar-Odd and other legendary sagas of Iceland.[3]

While the names pose some problems, the points made in the agreement are strictly practical and far removed from adventure or fantasy. The 907 agreement, which may be a précis of a longer document, is concerned mainly with trade:

'The Rus who come hither shall receive as much grain as they require. Whoever come as merchants shall receive supplies for six months, including bread, wine, meat, fish and fruit. Baths shall be prepared for them in any volume they require. When the Rus return homeward, they shall require from your Emperor food, anchors, cordage and sails and whatever else is needed for the journey.'

It is stipulated that no Rus who arrives without merchandise shall receive provisions, and none of them shall commit acts of violence in the town or the countryside during their stay. They must dwell in the St Mamas quarter of the city. This was the section on the Bosporus, not far from the sultan's palace of later times, so that the merchants had their own place of residence outside the walls of the city (as at Bulghar) and a harbourage for their ships.[4] On arrival, their names were to be recorded by government officials, and they received a monthly allowance, given first to those from

[1] Ibid. 474.
[2] Thomsen gives a list of equivalents, although not all these have been accepted by later scholars. See Sorlin, 329 ff.
[3] Chadwick (1946), 27.
[4] Pargoire, 261 ff.

Kiev and then to those from other Russian cities, including Chernigov and Pereyaslavl. They might only enter the city through one gate, and could bring in no weapons with them, and they had always to be accompanied by an official. While on business in the city, they were not liable to taxes.

The 911 agreement has a number of separate clauses. It includes undertakings against the plundering of cargoes of Greek ships by the Rus, who are to furnish aid to any Greek vessel in difficulties:

'If a ship is detained by high winds upon a foreign shore, and one of us Rus is nearby, the ship with its cargo shall be revictualled and sent on to Christian territory. We will pilot it through every dangerous passage until it arrives at a place of safety. But if any such ship thus detained by storm or by some terrestrial obstacle cannot possibly reach its destination, we Rus will extend aid to the crew of this ship and conduct them with their merchandise in all security, in case such an event takes place near Greek territory. But if such an accident befalls near the Rus shore, the ship's cargo shall be disposed of, and we Rus will remove whatever can be disposed of for the account of their owners. Then when we proceed to Greece with merchandise or upon an embassy to your emperor, we shall render up honorably the price of the sold cargo of the ship. But if anyone on that ship is killed or maltreated by us Rus, or if any object is stolen, then those who have committed such acts shall be subject to the previously provided penalty.'

It seems unlikely that Greek vessels would be wrecked on Rus territory, but there might be contacts along the Black Sea coasts or at the Dnieper mouth, and in any case such clauses about shipwreck were normal Byzantine procedure when making agreements with other powers.[1]

Other clauses refer to the ransom or return of slaves. A Rus prisoner from any region sold on Byzantine territory, or any Christian prisoner sold on Rus territory, could be ransomed for twenty bezants and sent home. If a Rus slave escaped or was stolen or sold, he must be returned to his Rus master if the claim to possession was substantiated. Other clauses refer to criminal acts such as murder or robbery with violence committed by Rus on Greek

[1] Sorlin, 357.

territory; it appears that they were allowed to settle such matters if they concerned themselves only, but if Greeks were involved, then they had to submit to such penalties as were imposed in Byzantium. One clause of some interest refers to Rus who desired to enter military service under the Emperor; if this were their serious desire, then they were permitted to stay in the city, no matter what their number was or at what date they had arrived; this indicates that already Scandinavians were taking service in the forces. There is reference also to the settlement of the estate of any Rus who should die when 'professionally engaged' in Greece, and a distinction is made between those engaged in trade and those who were casual travellers; there is also mention of men who incurred debts while residing in Constantinople, and both sides agreed to send such men back home. This must apply to Rus who had resided in the capital for some time, possibly those serving in the army.

It is important to realise that these terms were exceedingly generous ones. The normal time permitted for residence in the capital was three months, and only specially privileged Syrians and the Rus were allowed to stay as long as six. Lopez accounts for this by the value set on the goods which they brought to the city;[1] possibly also they made less demands than the troublesome Bulgars, who were despised by the Greeks. Beside this extra residential period, the Rus received total customs exemption, a kind of collective passport, and quarters conveniently near the centre of Constantinople. However, these special privileges were not mentioned in the *Book of the Prefect*, and it is possible that they were never enforced. It would seem that normally the traders returned in the autumn after a short stay.

As time went on, there were more Rus raids, and in 945, after an attack by Igor had been defeated with the aid of Greek fire (p. 130 below) a second agreement is quoted in the *Chronicle*, which gives more information about the conditions of trade. Again there are doubts as to the dates and the number of the attacks, but the agreement appears to be a genuine one and conforms in every way to Byzantine diplomatic usage. Sorlin thinks that two versions of this agreement were prepared by the Byzantine chancellery, one to be signed by the emperor and the other for the Rus; the ambassadors

[1] Lopez, 34 ff.

gave their signatures to this, but it would also need ratification by the ruler of Kiev. This time the Byzantine undertakings as well as those of the Rus are given, and the terms are rather less favourable to the Rus, who were at a disadvantage after their attack on the city had failed. Agents and merchants had previously been supplied with silver seals as credentials, but now they had to produce a certificate which gave the number of ships despatched: 'by this means we shall be assured that they come with peaceful intent.' The use of documents instead of seals implies the growth of diplomacy at Kiev, and the use of writing by this time by the Rus.[1] Men who arrived without such certificates could be arrested and killed if they refused to surrender.

The purchase of silk plays an important part in this document. It might be purchased to the value of fifty bezants, and a receipt for it had to be stamped by an imperial official. This meant less favourable terms than in the earlier agreement, but on the other hand the Rus were allowed five times as much in *pallia* (large pieces of silk) than were the provincial Greeks at this time. These terms appear to have been enforced. The loss of a slave on Greek territory could also be compensated by the payment of two pieces of silk per slave, provided one of the Rus could swear to the loss. If the Rus brought back Greek captives from outside Byzantine territory, they should receive a ransom of ten bezants for each young man or girl, eight for middle-aged persons, and five for old folk or children. They were not to enslave any member of the crew of a Greek ship which went aground, or remove anything from it – a simplification of the clause in the earlier treaty. The Rus were forbidden to winter at the mouth of the Dnieper but were to return home each autumn, and they were forbidden to interfere with the Chersonian fishermen in this area. This implies that pillaging expeditions had been made from Berezan. In case of a killing, it appears that the Rus were unable to force their own wergeld laws on the Greeks, but were subject to the penalties of Byzantine law. It is interesting that this agreement includes reference to Christian Rus and to their sanctuary at Kiev.

It becomes clear from these agreements that the two most desired objects of trade with Constantinople were Greek money and silk. Byzantine silk was famous throughout the world, since

[1] Sorlin, 457.

the state kept its finest silk, that used for the imperial robes and ecclesiastical vestments, as a non-commercial production. Such robes were symbols of imperial authority, possessing almost magical significance; they might never be purchased, but were occasionally sent as diplomatic gifts to other states. There were private guilds, however, which manufactured silk of second quality, and this was worn by citizens of the capital; it could be bought and taken out of the city under strict regulations only, and in limited quantities. Palace officials received gifts of such silk as part of their salaries. Foreigners who were permitted to remain three months in the capital were now allowed to buy articles of clothing in silk of a single piece, or silk cloaks above a certain value. We may note the unhappy experience of Liutprand, who, when leaving Constantinople for the last time after some unpleasant interviews with the Emperor Nicephorus and what he considered markedly discourteous treatment, was finally deprived by customs officials of what he had assumed to be his rightful ration of *pallia* to take home to the German Emperor.[1] The prestige attached to the possession of Byzantine silk was enormous, and added greatly to the image of the city as a centre of treasure such as the richest men in the West could not purchase. There was also a law forbidding the export of gold, which might be brought in by traders but not taken out again, so that there had to be a series of exchanges before the merchant was permitted to leave with his profit. The fact that compensation in silk for escaped slaves was now offered to the Rus, whereas in the earlier agreement it was in gold, indicates that they preferred silk; since slaves formed so valuable a part of their wares, the loss of one was clearly a serious matter and recognised as such by the Byzantine government. The value of trade with the Rus is made obvious by the fact that such trouble was taken to draw up a fair trading agreement, with considerable advantages for the Rus, in spite of attacks which they had made against the city.

As to whether Scandinavian traders proceeded still further east, it is difficult to find a clear answer. Even if we do not accept Vernadsky's theories about an early trading centre in Tmutorakan (and Sorlin's examination of the treaties furnishes us with addi-

[1] Liutprand, *Relatio de Legatione Constantinopolitana* (translated Wright), 53–4, 267 ff.

tional arguments against this),[1] we know that there was a ruler here related to the royal house of Kiev by the eleventh century. There were certainly raids on the Caspian (p. 126 below) which may well have been based on hopes of setting up centres there for collecting tribute and establishing markets as had been done in western Russia. In a ninth-century account, the earliest reference to them in Arabic sources,[2] Ibn Khurdadbeh (c. 825–912) refers to the Greek Emperor charging a tithe on the goods of the Rus when they reached the Black Sea, and to the king of the Khazars imposing one when they sailed down the Don. He calls the Rus a 'kind of *Saqaliba*', a term sometimes used of the Slavs, but which here may simply mean that they were Europeans. There are too many difficulties involved in this account for us to accept unreservedly his picture of the Rus proceeding down the Volga and selling sword-blades, furs and Khazar spears on the shores of the Caspian.[3] Then they take to their ships, he continues, and afterwards carry their wares by camel to Baghdad, while European slaves act as interpreters for them there. It has been suggested that here the Arab writer was confusing the Rus with Jewish merchants, who are known to have travelled widely and to have organised a great part of the slave trade with the East. On the other hand, he knew Baghdad well, and his reference to interpreters implies that there was only a small group of such merchants. It is not unreasonable to suppose that a few of the Rus proceeded down the Volga beyond Bulghar, trading with the Khazars on the way as long as their ruler permitted, and so reached the Caspian, paving the way for the attack launched in this area in the tenth century (p. 133 below). We have evidence from Scandinavia of objects from the Far East, such as Chinese silk, a figure of the Buddha, Persian glass, purses from India and so on, but these could well have been obtained either by raids during the Caspian campaign or in markets like Bulghar or Constantinople from eastern merchants.

In the course of the eleventh century the Pechinegs, always a hazard to trade, occupied part of the Dnieper route along with some Slav allies, and the Crimean peninsula gained in importance

[1] Sorlin, 318; 463.
[2] Birkeland, 10 ff. The name sometimes appears as Ibn Horradadbeh and in other forms.
[3] Dunlop, 226.

as an intermediary trading centre between the Byzantine Empire and Russia.[1] The Chersonians bought furs, hides and wax from the Pechinegs,[2] who may have obtained these from the Rus, and Byzantine merchants from Constantinople and Asia Minor brought their goods to the Crimea and exchanged them for other merchants' wares. There was a land route from the Crimea to Kiev, probably crossing the Dnieper at Krarion, but this must have depended on the movements of nomadic peoples in this area. A great source of Chersonian wealth was in salt fish, and the fishing region at the mouth of the Dnieper was specially safeguarded in the 911 treaty with the Rus, and was of great economic importance. Salt was procured from the north-west corner of the Sea of Azov. After the twelfth century Soldaia replaced Cherson as a trading centre, and it is interesting to find William of Rubeck, as late as the thirteenth century,[3] mentioning Turkish merchants who traffic in Russia bringing in ermine and grey squirrel skins, while those going into Russia took cotton clothes, silks and spices, and ships came to the mouth of the Dnieper to buy dried fish. He was advised not to hire a cart for his baggage, but to buy a covered cart of the kind used by the Russians for their skins. With the Tatar invasion of the thirteenth century, however, the old trading patterns came to an end and new ones had to be gradually established.

[1] Vasiliev (1932/1), 326 ff.
[2] Jenkins (1967), 186.
[3] *Journal of Friar William of Rubeck* (*Contemporaries of Marco Polo*, edited M. Komroff, London 1929), I, 76; 78.

CHAPTER 7

The Wares They Carried

The account of the Rus given by Ibn Fadlan confirms the general picture derived from Scandinavian literature, which is that the main wares carried by the traders were furs and slaves. We have seen how the fur trade depended largely on contacts with the Lapps and Balts and Finno-Ugric peoples round the Baltic, northern Scandinavia and Russia, and how tribute in skins was imposed on the Slav peoples further south. Good skins fetched high prices both in Europe and the East, a point made by Adam of Bremen when he wrote of the East Prussians: [1]

'They have an abundance of strange furs, the odour of which has inoculated our world with the deadly poison of pride. But these furs they regard indeed as dung, to our shame, I believe, for right or wrong we hanker after a martenskin robe as much as for supreme happiness. Therefore they offer their very precious marten furs for the woollen garments called *faldones*.'

Furs were indeed much sought after as luxury goods, and were obtained by hunting, trapping, plunder, barter and forced tribute, since money did not enter into these transactions. A picture of how the trade was carried on in the far north is given by an Arab, Abu al-Fida', in the early fourteenth century. He wrote of people in the far north who traded without seeing their trading partners: [2]

'Still further north there are people who enter into trade without seeing the travellers with whom they are bargaining. A man who

---

[1] Adam of Bremen IV, 18, 199 (J. T. Tschan's translation).
[2] *Geography of Abu al-Fida'*, translated M. Reinaud (Paris 1848) under the heading 'Northern Regions of the World', 284.

has visited these regions states that the inhabitants dwell on the edge of the northern sea, and adds that when caravans come to these lands they begin by announcing their arrival. Then they make their way to the place agreed on for buying and selling. Here each merchant lays his wares down with a price ticket and goes back to his lodging. The natives come out and lay beside these wares their weaselskins, fox, lynx(?) and other skins and then go away. The traders come back, and those satisfied with the goods offered in exchange take them. He who is not satisfied leaves the goods behind, and the trade continues in this way until both sides are in agreement.'

Such is the 'silent trade', for which there is plenty of evidence between different races at different levels of civilisation.[1] As Ibn Battuta, a traveller of the fourteenth century, probably drawing here on the work of other geographers,[2] remarked, the traders in the far north did not know whether those who bought their wares were men or genies, since they saw nobody. When there was direct contact, what went on might be on the lines of the trading described in one of the Greenland Sagas, when Karlsefni's men encountered natives (either American Indians or Eskimo) in Vinland.[3] The natives arrived in their skin boats, and the Greenlanders raised their shields as a sign of truce and began to trade. They refused to sell weapons, but offered red cloth in exchange for unblemished furs and grey skins. The natives accepted a span's length of cloth in exchange for a skin, tying the cloth round their heads:

'So the trading went on for a while, and then the supply of cloth which Karlsefni's people had began to run short, so they cut it into small pieces no broader than a finger, and the Skraelings gave just as much in return as before, or even more.'

In the tenth century Ibn Fadlan emphasises the importance of

[1] P. J. H. Grierson, *The Silent Trade* (Edinburgh 1903).
[2] *The Travels of Ibn Battuta*, translated H. A. R. Gibb (Hakluyt Society (2), 117, Cambridge 1962), II, 492, 'Account of the Land of Darkness', cf. S. Janicsek, 'Ibn Battuta's Journey to Bulghar', *Journal Royal Asiatic Society* (1929), 792–800.
[3] *Eiríks Saga Rauða*, 11.

the sable skins which the Rus used instead of coins to buy goods in Bulghar (p. 65 above). Other writers mention the market there for furs. Al-Muqaddasi, writing about 985, gives a long list of those obtainable there: sable, Siberian squirrel, ermine, marten, weasel, beaver and coloured hare.[1] Al-Mas'udi, who was writing before 947, noted that of all skins the black fox from the region round Bulghar was most valued, and such a skin cost at least 100 dinars; the kings of the barbarians and the Arabs were eager to obtain caps and coats made from them.[2] Later in the tenth century Ibn Hauqal gives the same information, claiming also that black fox skins retain heat better than any other kind, so that they are excellent for old men and invalids.[3] Ibn Rusteh refers to the Rus trading in sable, squirrel and other skins as their main occupation (p. 64 above) and notes that other peoples along the Volga brought sable, ermine and grey squirrel skins to Bulghar.[4]

Clearly many traders were anxious to exploit the possibilities of the immensely rich fur-producing lands of northern Russia, but the Scandinavians, with their long contacts with Lapps and Finns and their capacity for enduring cold and hardship, must have been at a considerable advantage here. In *Landnámabók* there is a reference to an Icelander who was a fur-trader and who had been at Novgorod:[5] '... he was a great traveller and merchant who went many times on the eastern road, and had better skins to sell than most other traders, and because of this he was called Biorn the-Skins'. Biorn came from Norway and was the son of a distinguished man called Skeggi; when he had had enough of trading he came out to settle in Iceland. There is also a runic inscription from Stenkumla, Gotland, referring to a man who lives in the south 'with skins'.[6]

The other main type of merchandise carried by the Scandinavians consisted of slaves. Ibn-Fadlan's account of their activities

[1] Al-Muqaddasi, *Descriptio Imperii Moslemici*, edited M. J. de Goeje (Leiden 1877), 324–5. I am indebted to Dr Ursula Lyons for this reference and for help with the passage.
[2] Al Mas'udi, *Meadows of Gold*, etc., translated A. Sprenger (London 1941), 17, 412; Birkeland, 30 ff.
[3] Ibn Hauqal, *Le Livre de l'avertissement*, translated B. Carra de Vauz (Paris 1896), 93–4.
[4] Ibid. 15.
[5] *Landnámabók*, S. 174; H. 140, 212–13; passage quoted from M, note 2, 212.
[6] Liestøl (1970), 130.

in Bulghar indicates that their slave-trading there was on a fairly small scale, carried on privately without attempts to sell large batches of slaves in the public market. It would hardly have been possible to bring large numbers in small boats along the river routes, and the traders appear to have aimed at quality rather than quantity in their wares. The same is true of the voyage down the Dnieper, where we are told that at one point the slaves had to walk six miles in chains when the traders were passing the rapids (p. 84 above). It has been suggested that the reference in the *Primary Chronicle* to Vladimir's 800 concubines at Kiev indicates not a harem in the oriental style but his wealth in slaves which could be sent to Byzantium for trade,[1] although in either case the number seems likely to have been exaggerated.

There is no doubt that prices in the tenth century were high for the right kind of young slave of either sex who could be trained in music and the other arts and sold in Islam. Mez states that in 912 a 'pretty girl' might fetch 150 dinars (about 1,500 marks), but that a talented slave might be sold for as much as 13,000 dinars, while the price for white slaves was far higher than for coloured ones.[2] Slav boys and girls were particularly prized, and many were taken from Bulghar to Samarkand to be sold in the markets there. It was, however, degrading for a good slave to be sold publicly; they usually changed hands privately or through a dealer, and this was the type of trade which seems to have been practised by the Scandinavians. Mez's well-documented account shows that the fate of the slaves sold at Bulghar was not necessarily a cruel one; there were strong moral obligations on slave-owners to treat their slaves well, and many reached great heights in the courts of Muslim kings and nobles. The uncertainty and humiliation for those of free and aristocratic upbringing, however, must have been very hard to bear, and it was this type of slave which was particularly sought after by the traders.

There is no doubt that slavery was fully established in the Viking world, and indeed it had continued among the Germanic peoples of northern Europe from the time of the fall of the Roman Empire.[3]

[1] Vasiliev (1932), 325–6.
[2] A. Mez, *The Renaissance of Islam* (1937), 157 ff.
[3] A. M. Wergeland, *Slavery in Germanic Society during the Middle Ages* (Chicago 1916), preface xi.

Welsh and Irish youths were regularly bought and sold in markets along the Bristol Channel and in Dublin, and taken to farms on the northern islands, to Iceland and Norway.[1] Captives taken in raids on the Baltic countries, including Slav territories there, were also sold into slavery. Adam of Bremen accuses the Danish King of permitting Viking raiders to plunder and enslave not only barbarians on the Baltic coasts, but their own countrymen as well:[2] 'As soon as one of them catches another he mercilessly sells him into slavery either to one of his fellows or to a barbarian.' He adds that they immediately sell women who have been raped. The markets for slaves existed in tempting numbers, ranging from central Europe and the Mediterranean ports to new territories explored by the traders in the eastern region. Rimbert gives a glimpse of the harsh realities of the trade.[3] He tells how Anskar in the ninth century would buy Danish and Slav boys on sale in Hamburg 'to redeem them from captivity' and put them into monasteries to be trained in the service of God. He quotes a case of a widow's son taken as a slave to Sweden, whom the bishop released and brought home, and he was angry with some of the Christians on the south Baltic coast because they refused to help escaped slaves and sold them to other Christians; he insisted that they must be left free. Adam of Bremen tells us that Rimbert, Anskar's successor, followed the same policy, not hesitating even to sell church vessels if the money could redeem captives. At Hedeby, where he had a church, he once saw a crowd of slaves dragged along by a chain, and when one of them claimed that she was a Christian nun, reciting a psalm to prove it, he bought her by giving up his own horse.[4] The redeeming of a woman captive by the payment of a horse, this time to Arab raiders in southern France, is mentioned again in a poem by a cleric written in 826. A certain Datus or Dado blamed himself bitterly for not having ransomed his mother for the price of his horse since she was afterwards killed by the raiders, and he founded the monastery of Conques in reparation.[5]

Christian slaves from the west were used as thralls on Scandi-

[1] Bromberg, 133 ff.; Charles, 34 ff.
[2] Adam of Bremen IV, 6, 190.
[3] Rimbert, 15; 35; 38.
[4] Adam of Bremen I, 39 and 41; the full story is in the *Vita Rimberti*.
[5] Melvinger, 120.

navian farms to do the hard work; they seem on the whole to have been fairly well treated and to have been given a reasonable chance to earn their freedom.[1] Such at least was claimed to have been the policy of Erling Skjalgsson, a great landowner in Rogaland under Olaf the Holy, renowned for his shrewdness and generosity. He was said to have kept many slaves in addition to his free-born servants, and the slaves worked for him until they earned their freedom by an agreed amount of labour. Snorri in *Heimskringla* states that they worked for him during the day and had their own piece of land to cultivate in the evenings, and that a thrifty man might earn freedom in three years or even less.[2] Erling bought others to replace them when they were free, and the earliest account in the oldest Saga of King Olaf, dated about 1180, mentions that some of his former slaves made much money and possessed much land. According to tradition Aud the Deep-minded gave land in Iceland to several slaves whom she brought with her from Scotland, saying of one of them:[3] 'I have given freedom to the man called Erp, the son of Jarl Meldun, for it is no desire of mine that a man of such high birth should bear the name of thrall.' Mael-Duin is a Celtic name, and Erp could have been captured in the Scottish wars, as is stated in *Landnámabók*; here it is said that Aud bought Erp's mother Myrgiol, an Irish princess, from Jarl Sigurd for a high price.

Slaves whom the Vikings collected on their way home or took in raids in the Baltic might be disposed of in home markets. In *Laxdæla Saga*[4] the visit of the Icelander Hoskuld to a market near Goteburg is described, held on an occasion when chiefs from different districts came together for a meeting. Among the tents of the merchants there was one apart from the rest, in which sat a man dressed in fine woven cloth with a Russian hat of fur. He was Gilli the Russian, known as a very prosperous merchant. Hoskuld asked if he had a bondwoman for sale, and the merchant drew back a curtain and revealed twelve women sitting in the back of the tent. One was shabbily dressed but very handsome, and Hoskuld agreed to pay the high price of three marks of silver for her, although the

---

[1] For conditions of slaves in Scandinavia, see Foote and Wilson, 65 ff.
[2] *Óláfs Saga ins helga*, 23.
[3] *Laxdæla Saga*, 6; cf. *Landnámabók* I, S. 96, 138, and Heller, 35.
[4] *Laxdæla Saga*, 12.

price of the others was only one mark. Gilli told him that the woman was dumb. Much later Hoskuld discovered that she could speak and that she was the daughter of an Irish King; she bore Hoskuld a son, the famous Olaf the Peacock. This is a romantic episode, probably introduced to give Olaf an impressive family background, and indeed it follows the familiar folktale pattern of the disguised princess motif; in his study of this tale, Heller concludes that the main features have been suggested by the tradition about Erp, noted above, and by incidents in Odd's life of Olaf Tryggvason, said to have been sold as a slave when a child.[1] However, realistic details are given about the transaction, and it is interesting to note that the price of one mark, reckoned in refined silver, was equivalent to that of four milch cows.[2] Hoskuld paid out the money from his purse, and it was weighed in Gilli's scales. The price asked for the young Olaf is given by Odd as nine marks, on account of his great wisdom and beauty.

Odd's story of Olaf and his mother is included by Snorri in *Heimskringla*, and he appears to have added some references to Estland. The story is unlikely to be based on historic fact, although the reference to Queen Allogia (Olga) perhaps indicates that he took his information from a Russian source.[3] He tells how Olaf and his mother Astrid were on their way to Russia after his father's death when the ship was attacked by pirates from Estland and mother and child separated and sold as slaves, while Olaf's fosterfather, an elderly man who would be of little value, was killed. The child Olaf was bought by a farmer and well treated, but later again put up for sale at a market in Novgorod when he was seven years old, and there he was recognised by a kinsman and brought up as befitted his birth. Years later his mother was also recognised in a slave market in Estland by a rich Norwegian called Lodin, who was out trading. He bought the queen, now pale, thin and ill-clad, on condition that she agreed to marry him. She consented with the goodwill of her kinsmen and bore him several children.

Less romantic is a verse from one of Harald Hardradi's poets,

---

[1] Heller, 34 ff. Cf. Braun (1924), 176–7.
[2] *Íslenzk Fornrit* V (Reykjavik 1968), 23–4.
[3] *Heimskringla, Óláfs Saga Tryggvasonar*, 6; cf. Jones (1967–8); Braun (1924), 177.

Valgard, referring to the prince's capture of women in the eleventh century: [1]

> 'Those Danes who still lived, fled, but fair women were taken. The maidens were locked in fetters. Many women went past you to the ships; bright chains bit greedily on their flesh.'

This was in a raid on Zealand and Funen by a mixed Scandinavian force under royal leaders. We have another glimpse of ruthless slave-taking in the famous *Sermo Lupi* of Wulfstan, Archbishop of York at the beginning of the eleventh century, when he laments that many times the thrall now binds the man who was once his lord and sells him as a slave, and that [2] 'two or three seamen drive bands of Christian men from sea to sea throughout the whole of this nation, chained together, to the open shame of us all'. Wulfstan was a man with considerable knowledge of the slave trade, since he saw its effects in Bristol, where he stayed for some months preaching so eloquently against it that nearly all the Christians in the region renounced any further part in it.[3] In general, however, slavery was condoned by the Church, even though individual churchmen like Anskar and Wulfstan preached against it, as long as Christians were not sold in pagan markets and allowed to fall into Muslim hands. Christians as well as pagan Vikings were prepared to sell heathens like the Wends in Bulghar and Constantinople.

Besides furs and slaves, there must have been luxury goods worth taking to eastern markets. Al-Muquaddasi gives a long list of goods which could be bought at Bulghar in the tenth century. This includes the following items, as well as furs and slaves: sheep, cattle, goatskins and leather; hawks; honey, wax, nuts, coriander seeds, grapes and dried figs; maple wood (for bowls); corn, amber, brocade, lengths of cloth, thread, caps; fish-glue and fish-teeth (which might mean walrus ivory); arrows, swords and mailcoats. Some of these could have been obtained from the lands of the Bulgars or their near neighbours, but the Rus might have brought wax and honey, fish products and ivory, silk (once contacts with

---

[1] *Skjaldedigtning* B1, 362, 9.
[2] *Sermo Lupi ad Anglos*, edited D. Whitelock (3rd edition 1963), 60.
[3] Lamb, 180–1.

Byzantium had been made), amber, swords and armour. Honey and wax had considerable value in the tenth century. The Rus may have procured it from either the Balts or the Slavs, for the latter collected it from nests of wild bees in the forests; a wooden cup filled with honey and wax was found in one of the fortified villages of the Dnieper region, Vishneva Gora.[1] The Khazars are said to have obtained honey from either the Bulgars or the Rus,[2] and wax had a ready market in Byzantium, since there was a great demand for wax candles in palaces and churches. The importance of wax in the economy is shown by evidence from the Ivanskoye Sto in Novgorod, the earliest of the merchant guilds there, whose charter goes back to the twelfth century.[3] Members of this guild had the right to weigh wax, to collect dues from both local and foreign merchants coming to trade, and also to supervise weights and measures, a right shared with the bishop. Their stores of wax were kept in the cellar of the guild church, St John the Baptist, which was important enough to possess cathedral status. When Igor sent the Greek envoys back from Kiev, according to the *Primary Chronicle*, they took with them gifts of furs, slaves and wax,[4] and these were evidently the three most important types of merchandise taken by the Rus to Constantinople. Some swords also may have been carried to Bulghar, since the type used by the Scandinavians was much sought after by the Muslim peoples. These and other weapons would not be difficult to transport in small boats, while a market like Bulghar offered good opportunities for bartering plunder of any kind obtained on the way and getting a good price for luxury articles.

Memories of travellers returning from Byzantium recorded in the Icelandic Sagas give some idea of the impact on those who stayed at home. In *Laxdæla Saga* Bolli Bollason returned from a stay of some years in Constantinople, where he had served in the Emperor's Guard, and he and his eleven companions rode back from their ship:[5]

'They were all wearing clothes of scarlet cloth, and they sat on

[1] Gimbutas (1971), 92.
[2] Dunlop, 93; 225.
[3] Tikhomirov, *The Towns of Ancient Rus* (Moscow 1959), 119 ff.
[4] *Primary Chronicle*, 945, 54, 77.
[5] *Laxdæla Saga*, 77.

gilded saddles; all were men of distinction, but Bolli outdid the rest. He wore clothes of silk, given him by the king of Miklagard; he had on a scarlet cloak over his clothes, and he was girded with Legbiter, its hilt ornamented with gold and with gold thread round the grip. On his head he had a gilded helmet and a scarlet shield at his side, with a knight on it outlined in gold. He carried a lance in his hand as is the custom in foreign lands. Wherever they took lodging the women could do nothing but stare at Bolli and his finery and that of his companions.'

This picture is not to be attributed solely to the influence of romances on Icelandic literature; gold and silver, scarlet cloth and silk and splendid weapons were symbols of the wealth of Byzantium, and there was good reason for this. Lances were part of the Greek soldier's equipment, while lengths of the coveted Byzantine silk were presented to those holding positions in the palace (p. 200 below). Much treasure and not a little glamour travelled from east to west during the Viking Age, leaving its mark on the literature as well as on the graves and treasure-hoards. Bolli, however, was no merchant, and in the later Viking Age it was by their prowess as fighting men and suitability as mercenaries that many Scandinavians laid hands on the wealth of eastern Europe. This will be the subject of the following section.

PART TWO

Fighting in the East

CHAPTER 1

The Rus as Warriors

We have seen how from the outset the story of trade in the eastern regions was inseparable from fighting. The expeditions across the Baltic were primarily military ones, and the trade posts set up across the sea were equipped with armed garrisons. The rich series of traditions which attached themselves to the Jomsvikings shows that the Baltic region was a fruitful source of heroic legend and a birthplace of tales of reckless fighting, and resistance to the end such as once formed a part of the cult of the battle-god Odin. Visits to Biarmaland, Estland and Kurland, to the realm of the Bulgars, the Khazars and the Slavs, were never wholly peaceful enterprises, and vague and confused memories of campaigns and heroic adventures permeate such of the sagas as are concerned with the eastern road. Once armed settlements were established in Gardar the Vikings were not slow to engage in conflict, not only with lesser peoples but with the might of Byzantium itself. There were also battles between rival Scandinavian groups for power and influence.

The picture of the Rus given by Arab writers is a composite one of trader-warriors, with strong heroic undertones. Ibn Rusteh's description of them was compiled in the early tenth century, and taken in part from even earlier sources (p. 63 above). After his account of the trading methods of the Rus there is a graphic account of them as fighting men. They were loyal to one another, he tells us, and if one were attacked the rest would come to his aid. If two of them had a dispute and the leader could not decide between them, he would tell them to settle the case with their swords, 'and victory will belong to the sword which is keenest'. They were brave and heroic, and when attacked would not desist until they had gained a complete victory, taking the women captive and selling the men into slavery. They preferred attacking by water rather than by land. He tells us something of their appearance, of their baggy trousers tight below at the knee and their excellent swords. A Rus warrior would carry his sword everywhere with him, since there was little security and much treachery everywhere, and when he went outside to relieve himself he would take as many as three men with him to keep guard. This last vivid detail emphasises the danger of life in the eastern regions, and constant threats of attack and ambush in the armed settlements. If a son were born to one of the Rus, he would take a sword from the scabbard and throw it down before the child, with the words: 'I shall leave you no possessions; you will only have what you yourself can win by the sword.'

Miskawaih, who died in 1030, gives in his history [1] a consistent picture of the Rus as men with 'vast frames and great courage' who refused to acknowledge defeat but fought on until either the enemy or themselves were slain. They carried many weapons: swords, spears, shields and daggers, and also tools such as axe and hammer. The *Hudud al-'Alam*, a Persian work of the late tenth century, probably based on the same early sources as Ibn Rusteh, gives a slightly less favourable picture of a warrior people who were ill-tempered, quarrelsome and arrogant in their bearing. Their dress is mentioned again as consisting of baggy trousers and woollen hats with a piece falling over their necks.[2] Marvazi, writing in the eleventh century,[3] again emphasises the fighting qualities of the Rus, remarking that one of them was equal to a number of men of any other nation, and that if they had horses and were riders 'they would be a great scourge to mankind'. This was a shrewd observation, as will be seen from accounts of campaigns in which the Rus took part in southern Russia. In addition we have Ibn Fadlan's description of the followers of the King of the Rus:[4] '... the bravest of his companions and those on whom he can rely. These are the men who die with him and let themselves be killed for him.'

---

[1] Miskawaih, *Eclipse of the Abbasid Caliphate*, translated Amedloz and Margoliouth (Oxford 1921), V, 67.

[2] *Hudud al-'Alam* (Regions of the World), translated V. Minorsky (Oxford 1937), 159.

[3] *Sharaf al-Zaman Tahir Marvazi* (edited and translated V. Minorsky (London 1942), 36.

[4] Smyser, section 93, 101.

On the memorial stones of Gotland, the baggy trousers of oriental type and caps described by these writers can be recognised. The fame of the swords of the Rus is well attested by other descriptions from the Arab world, particularly those given by al-Kindi in the ninth century and al-Biruni in the eleventh.[1] The most striking part of the descriptions, however, is the emphasis laid by contemporaries on the loyalty, reckless daring and scorn for death shown by the Rus, their faithfulness to their leader and their readiness to come to the aid of their comrades. Such descriptions might come straight from the heroic literature of the Germanic peoples, and the world pictured by the Arabs is that of the prince

Fig. 2. The dress of the Rus. Two figures in baggy trousers shown on a memorial stone of the Viking Age from När Smiss, Gotland (after E. Wilson, op. cit.).

and his *comitatus*, the bodyguard of armed warriors supporting their leader and existing on booty won from the enemy. The use of ships rather than land fighting is characteristic of the Vikings, and the rivers, lakes and inland seas of the eastern region made it possible for them to use the same techniques as in western Europe. Their fine weapons were much coveted by the eastern peoples, and after the invasion of Bardha'a in 943 (p. 133 below), when they left many of their number dead by pestilence and had to quit the region, the Muslims are said to have opened their graves to take out the swords which they buried with their dead, and these, wrote Miskawaih in the early eleventh century, 'are in great demand to this day for their sharpness and excellence'.[2]

The fury of the Rus in battle and their characteristic blend of clemency and ruthlessness, reasonableness and greed, is illustrated by the detailed account of the attack on Bardha'a given by the same writer. At first, when they arrived, the Rus were met by a

[1] Zeki Validi (1936); Davidson (1962), 115 ff.
[2] Miskawaih, V, 73.

local force, who did not know, we are told, that these fighting men would prove very different from Greeks and Armenians. The Rus quickly seized the town and then told the inhabitants that they had no objection to them continuing to practise their own faith, providing that they acknowledged the Rus as overlords and gave them loyal support. 'They behaved well', comments another writer, Ibn Athir.[1] But the common people threw stones at them and made continual attacks, until the Rus gave them three days (Ibn Athir says ten) to evacuate the town. When the majority ignored this, the Rus began to slaughter them, shut up the women and children of the richer inhabitants inside a fortress and demanded that the men should pay ransom. Many were ready to do this, but disputes began as to the amount to be paid, and finally the Rus lost patience and slew them all, keeping the women and boys as slaves. We are told how one merchant ransomed his life for an agreed sum, and when one of the Rus accompanied him to his shop and found that there was a hoard of wealth hidden there, he took it all, but offered the now penniless man a piece of stamped clay which would serve him as a safe-conduct.

Thus we have glimpses of the Rus as efficient plunderers and raiders, winning wealth with their swords, famous for their sudden attacks and for their skill and daring in battle. We also see them giving up their lives in the grand heroic manner when the odds turned against them. Miskawaih had heard marvellous tales of their prowess when outnumbered by their enemies. One story repeated to him by several witnesses told how five of the Rus on one occasion were defending themselves in an orchard against attack by a large force of Muslims. Among them was a handsome boy, the son of one of the Rus leaders by a concubine. The Muslims tried to take them captive, but none of them would surrender, and they were all killed after they had slain many times their own number. The last survivor was the youth, whom they were particularly anxious to take alive, but he climbed a tree and slashed at himself with his sword until he fell dead to the ground.

The Rus descended like locusts on the fertile fields, orchards and gardens of southern Russia. In 968 there was a major attack on the Khazars, and the capital, Atil, was captured by the Rus. Ibn

[1] Ibn Athir, translated C. Huart, 'Les Mosâfirides de l'Adherbaïdjân', *A Volume of Oriental Studies presented to E. G. Browne* (Cambridge 1922), 236.

Hauqal heard from a man who visited the place soon afterwards that where there had previously been forty thousand vineyards now scarcely a leaf was left on the bough and not a grape or raisin remained in that place after the Rus descended on it.[1] It was indeed by excessive feasting upon the fruit of Bardha'a that they are said by Miskawaih to have brought about their own ruin, for they ate such quantities, and according to Moses of Khorene so many olives and cucumbers [2] that they suffered severely from some form of dysentery. The epidemic grew so serious that large numbers died, and the survivors were forced to withdraw from the town by night, with what plunder and captives they could carry away with them.

Another vivid picture of the Rus as fighting men has been left by the Greek Leo the Deacon, in the eighth and ninth books of his *History*.[3] Leo himself was present during Svyatoslav's campaign against the Byzantine army in Bulgaria in 970, as secretary to the Emperor, who led his own forces. He could scarcely have been aware of the traditions of the cult of Odin, yet the picture which he has left us of tough, fearless and dedicated warriors, prizing glory above all else, refusing to recognise the possibility of defeat, and if needful prepared to die by their own hands, is in close accordance with the heroic traditions of the North as we see them reflected in the literature. Typical also of what we know of the cult of Odin is the wild madness with which Svyatoslav's followers fought, shocking the sophisticated Greeks; they roared, he noted, like wild beasts, howling in a strange, disagreeable fashion. They fought with an animal ferocity and blind frenzy, while their leader, Svyatoslav, is described as attacking the Greeks like a madman. When one of his followers felt that the position was hopeless, he would plunge his sword into his own body, like the youth at Bardha'a, preferring to die by his own hand rather than be killed or captured by a man whom he despised. Leo accounts for this by a belief that if slain in battle these warriors were doomed to serve their slayer in the next world, but it seems more likely that it was capture and slavery or mutilation by the Byzantines which was dreaded, and that a heroic death by one's own sword ensured a

[1] Dunlop, 242.
[2] Miskawaih V, 71 (note 2).
[3] Leo Diaconus (*Corpus Scriptorum Historiae Byzantinae*, Bonn 1828).

glorious entry into the realm of the god of battle. Certainly it seems that few prisoners were taken in the last battles between the Emperor John and Svyatoslav, described in much detail in Leo's account, although there is mention of numbers being captured in the earlier campaigns when the Bulgarians were fighting alongside the Rus. When he urged his men to continue the fight against heavy odds, Svyatoslav exhorted them to remember the valour of their forefathers and their high reputation as warriors, which had enabled them to capture whole cities with little bloodshed. It was not their custom, he reminded them, to return as fugitives, but they must either live as victors or die gloriously after proving their courage to the full. Cedrenus, getting his information from John Scylitzes,[1] gives a similar picture: if they lost, Svyatoslav told them, they should choose a glorious and happy death rather than a life of ignominy and shame, for if they saved themselves by running away, life would be unbearable for them, and they would be a laughing stock to the neighbouring tribes who had previously held them in great respect. So his followers agreed to fight on in a last desperate effort to defeat the powerful Byzantine army, and Leo tells us that the decision was a joyful one.

The care for those who fell in battle after the heavy losses on the Bardha'a campaign is confirmed by Leo's observations. After a costly battle outside the walls of Dristra, the Rus came out by night in the light of the full moon, sought out their dead on the battle-field and lit great funeral pyres of logs beside the walls, on which they burned the bodies of their fallen. Leo mentions sacrifices of captives, both men and women, and of animals and birds thrown into the Danube. This took place after the death of one of their leaders with the Scandinavian name of Ingvar, and the elaborate funeral ceremony may have been held in his honour. Another custom which shocked the Byzantines, accustomed to their own more sophisticated forms of barbarity, was the raising of the head of an enemy commander on to a spear on one of the towers of Dristra. This particular man and his horse had been so splendidly adorned that when he was killed the Rus at first imagined that they had slain the Emperor himself and rejoiced accordingly. Cedrenus also mentions that after one of the fiercest battles the Greeks discovered the bodies of Rus women on the field, dressed in men's

[1] Cedrenus, *Compendium Historium* (ibid. Bonn 1839) II, 407.

clothes, which is like an echo of the tradition in the Norse sagas that certain women wore armour and went out to fight (p. 311 below).

Leo also tells us something of the equipment and method of fighting used by the Rus on the Bulgarian campaign. They carried long shields, the height of a man, and many wore mailcoats. Before battle they drew up their forces in a close line and advanced in formation with levelled spears. Svyatoslav, their leader, was mounted, but his men were for the most part on foot, fighting with swords, bows, spears and javelins. Leo makes it clear that it was their inability to use horses and their disadvantage against experienced cavalry which prevented them from overcoming the Greeks. Thus their leader, Ingvar, fighting magnificently, was brought down by Anemas, an Arab who held a high position in the Emperor's guard. His technique was to gallop with drawn sword straight at his opponent, then to rein in his horse and to strike at the neck of his enemy. Svyatoslav avoided a similar attack by sliding off his horse and escaped with a wound, but a man on foot was virtually helpless against this cutting stroke from above. On one occasion the Rus tried a sortie on horseback, but failed because they were unable to control their steeds, and they were soon routed by the skilled Byzantine cavalry. Another serious weakness was their lack of equipment. The Greeks used incendiaries, probably pots of petroleum thrown by a catapult, against the tower in which the Rus took refuge inside the walls of Dristra. Attempts to take the building by storm had failed, and as many as 150 Greeks are said to have been killed at the narrow doorway by the defenders, but when they set the building on fire the Rus were forced to come out into the open. Svyatoslav's men tried without success to destroy a Greek war-machine which had been firing stones over the wall of the town and caused them severe losses. Finally the skilful placing of ships loaded with Greek fire on either side of the Danube made escape impossible for the ships of the Rus, and they were unable to slip away by night as they had done at Bardha'a when pressed too hard. Although Greek fire was never used on this campaign, its importance as a deterrent is unmistakable.

The final picture of Svyatoslav, the heroic leader, realising the hopelessness of his position and saddened by his great losses, coming to a swift decision to make the best terms possible with the Emperor, is also characteristic of Rus tactics. The Emperor, who clearly respected the Prince as a formidable enemy, agreed to meet him, and rode down to the Danube in impressive array, attended by a band of horsemen splendidly caparisoned. The Rus prince on the other hand, in a white robe only distinguishable from those of his companions, as Leo somewhat sarcastically points out, by its cleanness, came up the river by boat, rowing on a bench along with his men. Leo was clearly contemptuous of such a leader, but it is refreshing to find the old tradition of the Germanic heroic age, that of the king who marched, worked and suffered along with his loyal followers and was honoured accordingly, still continuing in the tenth century among the Rus led by the great warrior-prince of Kiev.

CHAPTER 2

The First Attacks on Constantinople

Many of the campaigns of the Rus, supported by various tribes who joined them as allies, are recorded in the *Primary Chronicle* and in the works of Greek and Arab historians. Fighting in Russia seems at first to have been sporadic; the Scandinavians traded and plundered and took tribute where they could, quarrelling with their rivals and supporting one another in small bands against hostile peoples, as in the lands further north. With the formation of the kingdoms of Kiev and Novgorod, however, organised fighting began on a larger scale. The Rus took over the organisation built up by the Khazars for collecting tribute from the tribes round the Dnieper, and had to be prepared to fight to keep it, while for the first time they won access to the region of rich townships and cultivated lands round the Black Sea. The Greek cities of the region and above all the magnificent Byzantine capital offered possibilities for plunder and extortion even greater than the Vikings had found in the West, and they were not slow to take advantage of the new world opening before them.

Evidence for raids on the Byzantine capital before 860 has been rejected by Vasiliev in his detailed study of the events of that year,[1] which reveals the complex and difficult nature of the sources from which a history of the Eastern Vikings must be reconstructed. The Rus must have been in contact with Constantinople as early as 838, when a party of Swedes visiting the capital were unable to return because their way was blocked by what are described as a 'barbarous and ferocious people' (p. 57

[1] Vasiliev (1946); cf. Mango (1958), 74, note 2.

above). The tribes blocking the way back to Kiev could have been the Magyars, whose advance at that time was being encouraged by the Khazars as a means of keeping the troublesome Pechinegs occupied. Only trading of a specific nature can have gone on between Kiev and the capital between 839 and 860.

The events of the year 860 are hard to determine with certainty, since there was an attack by the Normans about this time on Constantinople, probably in 861 at the end of a successful Mediterranean campaign, and they too are said to have pillaged the islands and shores round the capital after entering the Sea of Marmora. The Byzantines at this time were suffering considerably from rapacious neighbours and plunderers, and their defences were not strong enough to keep invaders out of the Hellespont. In 860 the fleet was engaged with the Arabs further east, and the Emperor was on his way to conduct the campaign against them. It was a tempting moment for the Rus to make their first serious attack. and we are fortunate in having a good deal of information from contemporary Greek sources about its effects on the city.

The most valuable source of information consists of two sermons preached by the Patriarch Photius in the cathedral of Hagia Sophia; one of these was delivered in June while the attack was in progress, and the second soon after the Rus ships had withdrawn.[1] Since, as Mango points out, these are public pronouncements, they are the most authoritative of the sources available. The sermons are in the elaborate rhetorical style typical of Byzantine homilies, but make clear the fury of the attack, the terror of the Greeks, and the loss of life and property in the country round. The ships arrived so quickly that the citizens were taken completely by surprise; there were not even rumours of their approach and the blow came 'like a thunderbolt from heaven'. The description of the attackers is significant: they are called a fierce and savage tribe, a barbarian people, 'obscure, insignificant, and not even known until the incursion against us', and 'an obscure nation, a nation of no account ... insignificant but now become famous'. They are also described as 'an uncaptained army', 'equipped in servile fashion'. Their land is said to be sundered from the land of the

[1] Photius, Homilies III and IV; for translation and commentary, Mango (1958), 74 ff.

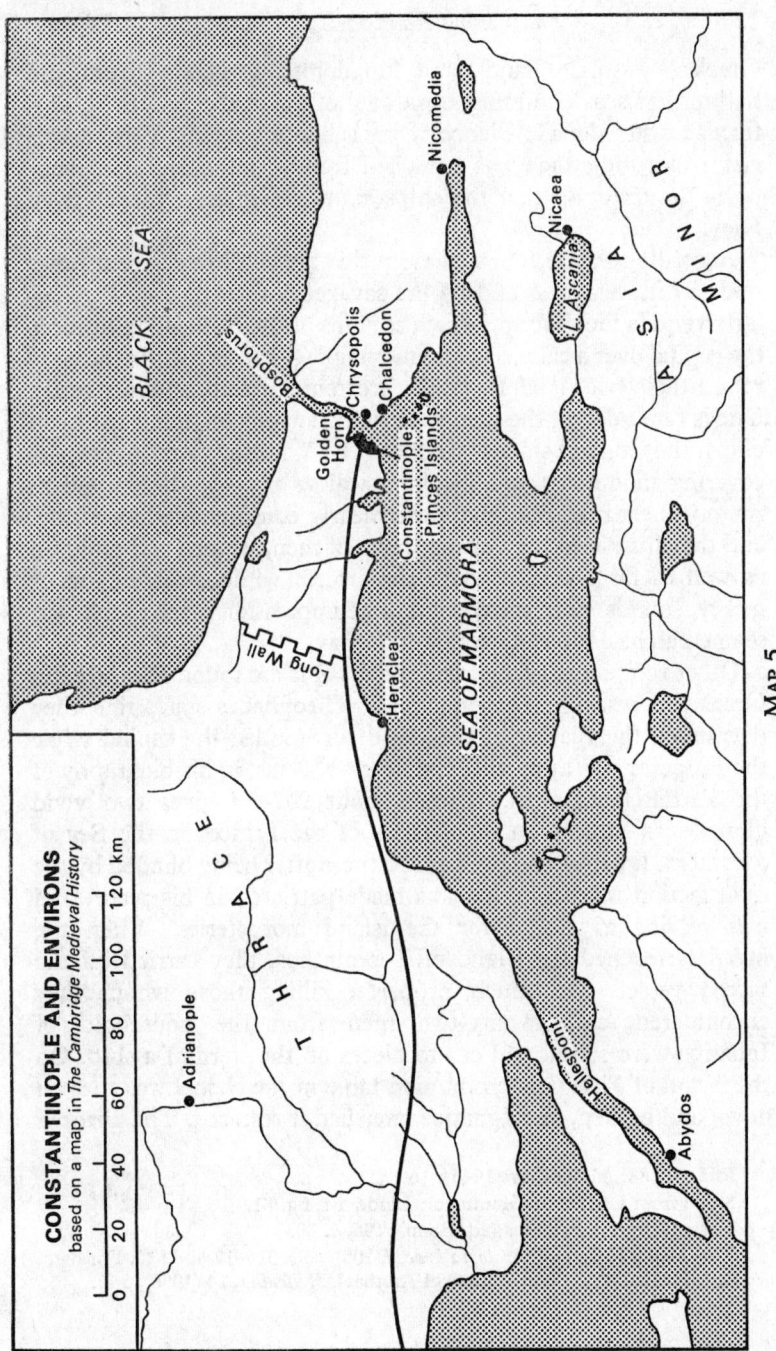

CONSTANTINOPLE AND ENVIRONS
based on a map in *The Cambridge Medieval History*

MAP 5

Greeks by 'many lands and kingdoms, navigable rivers and harbourless seas', and they came 'out of the farthest north'.[1] This furnishes additional evidence, if any is needed, against Vernadsky's claim that the attack was launched from Tmutorakan, and supports the tradition that the ships came down the Dnieper from Kiev.

According to the fourth homily this attack differed from other raids by its swiftness and by the savagery of the enemy. Particularly vivid is the description of the ships of the Rus sailing towards the capital over a calm sea, and moving past the city while the crew raised their swords aloft, 'as if threatening death by the sword'. One is reminded of the men with raised swords manning a ship on one of the Gotland stones (see Plate 1).[2] While accounts of corpses covering mountains and blocking valleys may be discounted as rhetorical exaggeration, there was clearly considerable loss of life, and the allusion to the cutting down of men, women and children as well as farm animals with the sword, without distinction or mercy, sounds more convincing. The impression given is that the seamen attacked in a state of wild frenzy.

Other references to the attack of the Rus are found elsewhere in Greek sources. The Continuator of Theophanes states that they devastated the Black Sea coast and surrounded the capital while the Emperor was away with the fleet.[3] Nicetas, in his biography of the Patriarch Ignatius, written about 907–9,[4] gives two vivid glimpses of attacks on the Islands of the Princes in the Sea of Marmora. Ignatius had been exiled there after being blinded by the rival faction when Photius was made patriarch in his place, and was serving as Abbot for the island monasteries. When the invaders reached the island of Tereninthos, they carried off the sacred vessels and much property, killing those whom they encountered, and twenty-two men from the household of Ignatius were seized and cut to pieces on the stern of a ship. On the island of Plati the communion table in the chapel was thrown down and broken, and Ignatius later had it restored. The *Brussels*

---

[1] Ibid. 82, 88; cf. Vasiliev (1946), 169 ff.
[2] Stone from Lärbro St. Hammars: Lindqvist, fig. 81.
[3] Theophanes Continuatus (ed. Bonn), 196, c. 33.
[4] *Vita Ignatii* (Migne, *Patrologia graeca*, 105), cols. 516–17 and 532. For date, see R. J. H. Jenkins, 'Eight Letters of Arethas', *Hellenika*, 14 (1956), 346.

The First Attacks on Constantinople

Chronicle, probably composed in the eleventh century,[1] gives the exact date of the attack as 18 June 860 and states that the Rus arrived in 200 ships (the number is multiplied by ten in the *Primary Chronicle*).

It seems clear from the Homilies that the enemy could have entered the city and that nothing could have been done to oppose them. Photius believed that they intended to capture it; he refers to them taking up arms against the empire and being 'puffed up with the hope of taking the queenly city as a nest of birds', and refers to the helplessness of the citizens, who wept and lamented and recited litanies all night in an appeal to the Blessed Virgin to save them. It is possible that the Acathistos Hymn to the Virgin and two poems to the Blessed Virgin of Blachernae referring to miraculous help given in time of need were composed by Photius, but more likely that they come from an earlier period and that Photius borrowed from the Hymn in his sermon.[2] The poems could have been inspired by the attacks of the Avars in 626, and reference to the barbarians bending their stubborn necks when they saw Her at the head of the army, and of the destruction of the enemy by water and not by the sword would be appropriate to the earlier occasion. However, it is likely that such hymns were used by the citizens in 860 in their appeals to the Virgin, just as passages from Photius' homilies in their turn were used during the Turkish attack of 1422; the Byzantines were continually looking back to their past history and formed composite legends of miraculous deliverance from their enemies which grew as the years went by.

Photius refers to a procession round the city walls, bearing the Virgin's robe, in the fourth homily; he says that he himself carried it, supported by the whole city, and that it was at this point that the enemy ships unexpectedly withdrew. In a group of chronicles derived from that of Symeon Logothete the story varies, and it is implied that the attack lasted for some time, and that the news reached the Emperor so that he started for home. He and the Patriarch took the Virgin's robe round the city and the Emperor dipped it in the sea, whereupon a storm blew up and the Rus ships

---

[1] An important source discovered by Cumont (*Anecdota Bruxellensia* I, 33, Université de Gand, *Recueil des travaux publiés par la Faculté de Philosophie et Lettres*, fasc. 9, 1894). For this and other sources, see Mango (1958), 75 ff.

[2] Vasiliev (1946), 97 ff.; Mango (1958), 81–2.

were scattered, thus saving the city. However, if this were true it seems incredible that no mention was made of the Emperor's presence or of the miraculous storm by Photius, whose second sermon was probably preached early in July. Attempts have been made to explain the discrepancy.[1] Possibly the attack was meant only as a plundering expedition, and the Rus left for home after gaining ample booty, their departure hastened by a superstitious fear of the procession or the more practical dread of the return of the fleet. They may have run into a storm after leaving the capital, so that the news did not reach the city in time for Photius to allude to it in his sermon. In any case, the theory that the attack lasted for some months, as Vasiliev argued, seems unconvincing; it is contradicted by the fourth homily and also by the fact that by December legates were arriving at Constantinople for a council. There are grounds for believing that the departure of the Rus took place on 25 June,[2] which would mean that the raid was crowded into a week of concentrated violence and terror. It is possible that the Emperor returned with a small force after the ships had retreated, and that he took part in a service of thanksgiving which was confused in the Chronicle of Symeon with the earlier occasion. The only reference to a defeat of the Rus is in the *Brussels Chronicle*, but it seems certain that they suffered heavy losses at some point, since in the *Primary Chronicle* they are represented as returning ignominiously to Kiev and no claims are made for a victory: 'there was in Kiev great weeping', comments the *Nikonovski Chronicle*.[3] The plunder which they collected during their progress round the coast may have been lost in the damage which their ships suffered in the storm.

There are records of negotiations taking place with the Greeks. In the *Vita Basilii* of Constantine Porphyrogenitus he refers to these being arranged by Basil I, and also mentions a bishop being sent to instruct members of the Rus embassy who had expressed a desire to become Christians.[4] A request for baptism is referred to by Photius in an Encyclical, while it is also mentioned in the *Primary Chronicle*, and this appears to have been made between

---

[1] Ibid. 78 ff; Vasiliev (1946), 226 ff.
[2] Gregoire and Orgels (1954), 141 ff.
[3] Vasiliev (1946), 226.
[4] *Vita Basilii* (ed. Bonn), 342, chapter 97.

864 and 867.[1] Perhaps the sight of the procession round the walls and the Blessed Virgin's protection of her people did after all have some effect on the invaders. In spite of the unhappy end to the expedition, it seems that they gained something by it, since a friendly treaty was evidently concluded, and in a later agreement of 911 (p. 91 above) reference is made to a state of amity between the Greeks and the Rus which continued for many years. It may have been at this point that the Rus began to serve as mercenaries in the Byzantine service, since by 910 there seem to have been as many as 700 of them in the Byzantine naval attack on the Arabs. If the Rus were impressed by the riches and the strong defences of Byzantium and the powers of her supernatural protectress, the Byzantines in turn were now aware of the potentialities of these threatening people from the North, and as usual were prepared with diplomatic measures to avoid further attacks.

The first raid on Constantinople is attributed to the leaders Askold and Dir in the *Primary Chronicle*, the Scandinavians who took over the stronghold of Kiev (p. 74 above). They in their turn were killed by the Rus leader in Novgorod, a kinsman of Rurik called Oleg (ON *Helgi*), who had fostered Rurik's young son Igor (ON *Ingvarr*). Igor married Olga, said to be a Swedish princess, whose Scandinavian name was Helga, and who may possibly have been Oleg's daughter. After Oleg killed Askold and Dir, he established himself as leader of the Scandinavians in Kiev, and the *Primary Chronicle* states that his followers, Varangians, Slavs and others, were known collectively as Rus. Oleg was a successful leader, imposing tribute on neighbouring tribes and building stockaded centres in which he placed garrisons. Not only the Drevljane but also the Severi and the Radimichi now acknowledged him as their overlord and paid no more tribute to the Khazars.

All too little is known about this Scandinavian trio, Helgi, Ingvar and Helga, but there are certain resemblances between Helgi and the Norwegian hero Qrvar-Odd, to which we shall return (p. 128 below). Oleg's main achievement, according to the *Chronicle*, was a successful attack on Constantinople in 907, but there is considerable doubt as to whether this ever took place. Like his predecessors, he is said to have had a force of 200 ships and a number of horses, to be used on foraging expeditions according to Viking custom.

[1] Vlasto, 244.

The Golden Horn was closed by a chain, but he disembarked, killed many Greeks and damaged their buildings, and then put wheels on his ships and let the wind take them over the land between the Bosporus and the Horn. The Greeks came to terms, offered him poisoned food which he shrewdly refused, and then promised to pay him tribute; they swore on the Cross while Oleg and his men swore by their gods Perun and Voles. Oleg demanded silk sails for his ships and linen ones for his Slav allies, and hung his shield over the city gate in sign of victory. Gifts of gold, wine and fruit were given them when they left for Kiev, and before departing the Rus were shown something of the splendours of the city and told about the Christian faith.

For this event we have no corroboration from Greek sources, and the reliability of the tradition has been seriously doubted and even the existence of Oleg called into question. Such extreme scepticism, however, is hardly justified, as Sorlin and Ostrogorsky have shown.[1] Part of the account may be copied from other tales of attacks on the capital, but nothing in the story is in itself improbable. The taking of ships over the land was managed by the Turks in 1453, and the Rus were experienced in the use of rollers and the art of portage. The poison and the silk may be popular motifs introduced into the account (pp. 133, 262 below), but the raising of a shield was a recognised sign for a truce.[2] The Arab writer Al-Mas'udi refers to a certain Alawang who fought the Greeks, which could represent the Scandinavian name Helgi.[3] Jenkins has suggested that an obscure passage in the Greek *Chronicles of the Pseudo-Symeon*, referring to the Rus putting their trust in oracles, could refer to this campaign.[4] The list of placenames given could indicate the voyage to Constantinople, and Oleg's name *veshchi*, 'the wise', is a word relating to foreknowledge and skill in divination rather than shrewdness and intelligence. However, if the tradition of Oleg's attack is based on historical fact, it may have been merely one of a number of small expeditions made by the

---

[1] For the case against Oleg, see Gregoire (1937), 80 ff. But see also Ostrogorsky (1939) 47 ff.; 296 ff.; (1969) 259; Obolensky (1971/1), 185 ff.; Sorlin, 336 ff. and additional references there given.

[2] cf. *Eiríks Saga Rauða* 11, where Karlsefni's party raise their shields as a sign that they will trade with the Skraelings.

[3] Vasiliev (1951), 178.

[4] Jenkins (1949/2), 403 ff.

Rus, magnified by the *Primary Chronicle* into a major victory and supported by motifs from other tales of conquest. There is some evidence for such raids taking place.[1] Leo VI in *Tactica*, written about 905, advises that the ships of the Greek navy should be equipped differently according to the type of attack they were called on to face. The Saracens, he noted, used a larger and slower type of vessel, while the Northern Scythians, by which he must mean the Rus, used ships which were smaller and much faster, since they were unable to bring their larger vessels down the river to the Black Sea.[2] Sorlin suggests that the account of Oleg's victory may have been inserted in the *Chronicle* at this point to account for the treaty of 907, which she believes is complementary to that of 911 and not a separate treaty made after a previous campaign. In the existence of the treaties we are on firmer ground, and it is clear that only respect for the fighting power of the Rus and an eagerness to benefit by their trade would have persuaded the Byzantines to draw up the favourable terms offered them in these documents (p. 92 above).

The evidence for the earliest attacks on Constantinople, although in many respects vague and unsatisfactory, show us nevertheless that by the beginning of the tenth century contact with the Byzantine capital had been established, on the usual Viking basis of military threats by sea linked with offers of profitable trade. Although little seems to have been achieved by the first attack and the evidence for the second is insubstantial, the inference of the practical details of the trading agreements is undeniable. The account of Oleg's victory, however dubious its details, may give a reasonably reliable picture of successful plundering and extortion of payment from the Greeks, as well as the new respect felt by them for the Rus and their northern allies. The next attack on Constantinople in 941 must have strengthened this impression.

---

[1] Vasiliev (1951), 172 ff.
[2] Sorlin, 339.

CHAPTER 3

The Campaigns of the Rus

While progress was being made towards Constantinople by Oleg or by other leaders now forgotten, there were attempts also to push further east, towards the lands of the Caliphate. There is little information about this in the *Primary Chronicle*, but raids on the Caspian area are described in detail in Arab writings of the tenth, eleventh and thirteenth centuries, and there is general agreement between the accounts, although it is difficult to establish how many raids took place or to date them with certainty. The earliest attempt came between 864 and 884, in the reign of Hasan ibn Zaid, and the raid is referred to by Ibn Isfandiyar, a native of Merv, writing in the early thirteenth century.[1] He states that the Rus attacked Abasgun, near the modern Gümüsh-täpo in the southeastern corner of the Caspian, and records another raid in 910, when sixteen ships appeared on the Caspian and made a successful attack in which a number of Muslims were killed. This last statement is uncorroborated, but a slightly later attack in 912–13 is described in detail by a contemporary, al-Mas'udi, who was writing in 943 and is known to have visited the Caspian area.[2]

Al-Mas'udi describes how the Rus occupied one shore of the Sea of Azov and used it as a base for their ships without meeting any opposition. About 912–13 a large fleet of about five hundred ships, each holding a hundred men, came to Sarkel at the mouth of the Don where the river enters the Black Sea. They sought permission of the Khazar king to cross his territory and so reach the Volga, which would give them entrance to the Caspian (here called the Khazar Sea), and offered in return to give him half the plunder

[1] Ibn Isfandiyar, translated E. G. Browne (London 1905), 199.
[2] Al-Mas'udi, *Les Prairies d'Or*, translated C. Barbier de Meynard and P. de Courteille (Paris 1863) I, 458, 18 ff.

The Campaigns of the Rus

which they won on the expedition. This generous offer shows how dependent they were on a Khazar alliance, since Sarkel was strongly fortified and there was no other route by which they could get from the Black Sea to the Caspian. They sailed some way up the Don and then crossed to the Volga, which brought them into the Caspian Sea, where, as Mas'udi emphasises, no vessels had hitherto been seen except fishing boats and merchant ships. The Rus overran a wide area round the coast, sending out raiding bands on horseback to attack towns and villages inland. They reached Jill, Daylam, Tabaristan and Abaskun on the Jurjan coast, and even penetrated into the oil country round Baku in Azerbaijan, as far as Ardabil, three days' march from the sea. They defeated local forces which were sent out against them, killed many of the inhabitants, carried off women and children as slaves, burned and plundered and wrought great destruction. Then they anchored in the islands in the south-west part of the sea, not far from the oil region, and the King of Shirwan, 'Ali ibn-al-Haytham, led a force of soldiers in merchant vessels and small boats against them. These were easily routed by the Rus, well experienced in sea-fighting, and thousands of Muslims were killed or drowned. After this the Rus sailed round the coast unchecked for many months, and all that the people of the region could do was to keep a constant watch for the enemy and make what preparations they could against attack. The picture which al-Mas'udi gives could be paralleled from the British Isles in the same period, when Viking attacks were at their height and unprotected monasteries and villages suffered grievously.

Finally, with much booty and many slaves, the Rus returned to the Volga estuary and sent a share of what they had obtained to the Khazar king as promised. The Khazars themselves had no fleet, al-Mas'udi points out; otherwise they themselves could have done much harm in the Caspian area. However, by this time the news of the Rus expedition had reached the Muslim people in the Khazar state, and in great indignation at the harm done to those of their own race and faith they insisted on attacking the Rus fleet as it returned home. The king could not restrain them and could only send a message to the Rus leader warning him of the approaching army. About 150,000 men are said to have marched down the Volga, well armed and equipped with horses, supported by

Christians from the town of Atil. The Rus saw the army approaching and left their ships to fight, and the battle continued for three days. In the end the Rus were overcome by superior numbers, and so many were slain or drowned that al-Mas'udi reckons about 30,000 perished, which would be about two-thirds of the original force. Some ships got away to the eastern bank of the river, but most of their crews were killed either by the Burtas or the Muslim Bulgars further up the Volga, so that a further 5,000 may have been lost. Al-Mas'udi says that this attack on the Caspian area was not repeated, although the Rus had not abandoned their plans for getting control of this region, as will be seen.

It seems probable that the expedition had been intended as the perliminary to a deliberate plan of invasion and conquest on the Kiev pattern. The advantages of the scheme are obvious, for the region was rich and fertile, with no well-organised defences, and included the source of the invaluable petroleum oil on which the Byzantines depended, 'as important as iron and more precious than gold or silver', which provided them with a weapon against attacks from the sea.[1] The difficulties are also obvious, for the Caspian could only be reached by water by the goodwill of the Khazars, whose stronghold at the mouth of the Don was strongly guarded. We have no information in the Russian Chronicle about the effect of this defeat on the Volga, which must have been a crushing blow, but somewhere about this period we have the strange story of the death of Oleg, which is one of the main problems in the early history of the Scandinavians in Russia. It occurs after the account of his Constantinople victory.

Oleg had been told by 'wonder-working magicians' that his much-prized horse would be the cause of his death; accordingly he made a vow never to ride it or look on it again, although he gave orders that it should be fed and tended. Five years later he returned to Kiev and learned that the horse was dead, whereupon he laughed and declared:[2] 'Soothsayers tell untruths and their words are naught but falsehood. This horse is dead but I am still alive.' He then rode out to view the skeleton, stamped on the skull while still mocking at the prophecy, and as a result was bitten by a

[1] Forbes (1959), 79.
[2] *Primary Chronicle* 912, 69. For problems of Oleg's dates, see Chadwick (1946), 49 ff.

snake which crawled from it and died soon afterwards. He was buried on a hill, where it is said that his tomb could still be seen.

This story is remarkably close to that told of Odd the Far-travelled, the man from Halogaland who was renowned for his journeys in Biarmaland and the eastern region (p. 38 above). His death also was foretold, although this time it was by a Lapp seeress who visited the house of his foster-father in northern Norway while Odd was still a youth.[1] She prophesied that a horse on the farm would be the cause of his death, and Odd immediately killed the animal and buried it. At the end of a long and successful career he went back to the deserted farm in Norway where his foster-father had lived and caught sight of a horse's skull, 'very polished and ancient, large and grey on the outside'. He wondered if this could be the skull of the horse Faxi, and as he stuck his spear into it, an adder crawled out and bit his ankle. His leg swelled with the poison, and after he had composed a poem on his exploits and given directions about his funeral he died. They placed him in a stone coffin of great size, and afterwards cremated him, according to his commands, and the saga mentions that the coffin could still be seen.

In the story of a fulfilled prophecy we have what is basically a folktale, the motif being that of the inevitability of fate in spite of the clever man's attempts to evade it; it is a motif with literary associations and classical precedents concerning the oracle of Delphi and similar prophecies. Stender-Petersen [2] gives four versions of the tale in which the horse is the central factor; besides the two stories of Oleg and Odd, there is an English variant of the death of a knight foretold by an old woman, which might have been derived from Scandinavia, and a Serbian-Turkish version which he believed came from Byzantium and originated in traditions about the death of the Emperor Michael III in 867. This ruler was obsessed with horses and neglected state business for them, and he was finally assassinated by his groom Basileus, who had won his favour by taming a splendid horse which the emperor had been unable to ride. The groom's treachery had been foretold by several ominous prophecies, ignored by the emperor. There is no serpent, however, in this version, and it seems unlikely that it formed the

[1] *Ǫrvar-Odds Saga*, 2.
[2] Stender-Petersen (1953), 184–8.

basis of the story of the death of Oleg. From his nickname 'the wise' Oleg seems to have had a reputation for foreknowledge (p. 124 above), so that some misunderstood prophecy about his fate may have formed the basis of the story in the *Chronicle*.

The name of the leader who perished in the fighting on the Volga in 913 is not given in the Arab sources, but it is said that he was slain, along with a large part of his army. This may conceivably have been how Oleg really met his death. Nomad chiefs were often referred to as serpents in the Russian byliny,[1] and if Oleg's death took place in battle a figurative expression of this kind in a poem could have been taken literally by the chroniclers and resulted in the strange story of the serpent. It seems unlikely that such an incident could have originated in Norway, although without fresh evidence it is not possible to prove this. The description of the skull of the horse in the Icelandic saga is impressive, and sounds as if it came from a poem, and it may have been in the form of narrative poetry that the story of the leader's death reached the North. The tradition that Oleg was laid in a stone coffin before being cremated also suggests a Russian rather than Norwegian source, the story being perhaps linked with some local antiquity. It is at least noteworthy that there is a basic resemblance between the careers of Oleg and Qrvar-Odd: both won fame by eastern journeys, both were leaders of fighting forces in the East, and both died in fulfilment of a prophecy.

The next name to emerge in the *Primary Chronicle* is that of Igor (ON *Ingvarr*), who is said to have been the foster-son of Oleg. It is to him that the next attack on Constantinople in 941 is attributed, and this is corroborated by a detailed account by Liutprand, later Bishop of Cremona, who was in Constantinople in 949 on a diplomatic mission, and whose stepfather had been there at the time of the raid itself and witnessed the beheading of the survivors after the sea-battle.[2] Liutprand tells us that the attackers were the people known in his country as the Nordmanni (p. 59 above) and that Igor their king collected over a thousand ships and sailed against the city at a time when the imperial fleet was away fighting the Saracens. Igor and his men moved round the shores of the Black Sea, devastating the coastal regions as they

[1] Chadwick (1946), 146.
[2] Liutprand, *Antapodosis* V, 15, 185.

The Campaigns of the Rus

went, while the Emperor Romanus spent sleepless nights in his anxiety for the capital. Then he learned that there were some old galleys in the shipyards, and called in carpenters to repair them and to equip them with flame-throwers, so that Greek fire could be projected on all sides against the enemy vessels:

'When the galleys had been equipped according to his instructions, he collected his most skilful sailors and bade them give King Igor battle. So they set out; and when King Igor saw them on the open sea he ordered his men to capture them alive and not kill them. But the merciful and compassionate Lord willed not only to protect his worshippers who pray to him and beg his aid, but also to give them the honour of victory. Therefore he lulled the winds and calmed the waves; for otherwise the Greeks would have had difficulty in hurling their fire. As they lay, surrounded by the enemy, the Greeks began to fling their fire all around; and the Rus, seeing the flames, threw themselves in haste from their ships, preferring to be drowned in the water rather than burned alive in the fire. Some sank to the bottom under the weight of their cuirasses and helmets which they were never to see again; some caught fire as they swam among the billows; not a man that day escaped save those who managed to reach the shore. For the Rus ships by reason of their small size can move in very shallow water where the Greek galleys because of their greater draught cannot pass.'

Clearly the Rus losses were heavy. Leo the Deacon, referring to this defeat in an account of a message sent by the Emperor John to Svyatoslav later on (p. 143 below), stated that out of the huge fleet only ten ships escaped to the other side. We now know a considerable amount about Greek fire, based on a petroleum compound and discharged through a metal tube (p. 276 below); much of its effect depended on the fact that the tube could be turned in different directions, and when the sea was calm, as on this occasion, great damage could be done to wooden ships and to the crew. The flaming petroleum burned on the water as well as on clothing, as is evident from Liutprand's account. Some of those who reached the shore were evidently captured, for Liutprand's stepfather saw them being beheaded in Constantinople. A few ships reached the other coast, because of their ability to enter shallow water where the Greek ships could not follow them, and with these survivors Igor returned home. The Russian *Primary Chronicle* corroborates the Greek account, giving additional details of raids along the Black Sea coast as far as Heraclea and Paphlagonia and all over Nicomedia. The Rus are accused of killing their prisoners with great cruelty, using them as targets for arrows and driving iron nails through their heads; this information seems to come from George Harmartolos and appears also in John Scylitzes, though he does not make it clear when all this took place.[1] At one point, according to the *Primary Chronicle*, an army from the eastern provinces marched against the raiders, but after an indecisive encounter the Rus embarked by night and sailed out of reach. Then follows an account of the meeting with the Greek fire-ships commanded by Theophanes,[2] and there is another vivid description of the Rus in panic throwing themselves into the sea to escape the flames:

'When they came once more to their native land, where each one recounted to his kinsfolk the course of events and described the fire launched from the ships, they related that the Greeks had in their possession the lightning from heaven, and had set them on fire by pouring it forth, so that the Rus could not conquer them.'

The *Primary Chronicle* goes on to say that in 944 Igor returned with an army of Slavs and Pechinegs and another fleet. The Emperor was warned of his approach by the Chersonians of the Crimea and agreed to pay the Rus tribute, as he had done to Oleg, sending gifts of silk *pallia* and gold to Igor's Pechineg allies. Igor's men were in favour of accepting the offer, so he returned home, leaving the Pechinegs to ravage Bulgaria. After this comes the long and detailed treaty already discussed (p. 92 above), and from the favourable terms given it seems yet again that the impression made by the Rus attack must have been considerable, in spite of the defeat and loss of their ships.

[1] Muralt, *Georgii Monarchi Chronicon*, 841.
[2] Gregoire and Orgels (1954) claim that there were two separate sea-battles, one on 11 June to defend the city and another in September when the Rus turned their attention to the Black Sea coasts. It is difficult, however, to reconcile this with Liutprand's circumstantial account.

Almost immediately after this expedition comes the attack on Bardha'a in the Caspian area. Possibly Igor wished to make use of the army he had collected now that it was no longer needed against Constantinople. This expedition, like the previous one in the same area, is ignored in the *Primary Chronicle*, but described in great detail by Miskawaih and referred to in a number of other Arab writers.[1] We are not told this time how the Rus reached the Caspian, but once there they travelled by way of the Kura river, which rises in the mountains of Azerbaijan and Armenia. They proceeded up the river, and were met by the governor of Bardha'a at the head of a force of some 600 men with many local volunteers, making an army, according to Ibn al-Athir, of about 5,000 in all.[2] The Rus put them to flight without difficulty, 'within an hour'. All able to leave the town then did so, and it was occupied by the Rus. Thereupon followed the events already described (p. 111 above), the offer of a truce, the refusal of the townspeople to come to terms, and the killing or enslavement of a good many of them. Moses of Kalankatuk, writing in the late tenth century,[3] states that 'the women of the city, knowing the method, made the Rus drink a cup of death, who, understanding the deceit, without pity cut down the women and children'. This seems likely to refer to the occupation of the town, and might indeed have been linked with the outbreak of the epidemic which proved such a calamity to the Rus, if this were due, or thought to be due, to tampering with supplies of food and water by the women. Whatever its cause the epidemic spread swiftly, and many of the Rus died. Meanwhile opposition was built up by Marzuban ibn Muhammad, the ruler of Azerbaijan. He made several attempts to retake the city, but was always forced to withdraw. Finally he arranged an ambush and staged a false attack, withdrawing quickly so that the Rus would pursue his men as they fled. The Rus came out after them, with their leader mounted on a donkey; this has puzzled some commentators, but it was usual in Viking campaigns for a mounted leader to direct his men, and there were no horses available, since we are told all transport had been taken by those who fled from the town. At first Marzuban's plan seemed a failure, because once his

[1] Miskawaih V, 67 ff.
[2] Ibn al-Athir, translated Huart, 236 ff.
[3] Chadwick (1946), 55.

men had begun to run away, they were unable to stop; it was not until he himself with his personal staff turned resolutely to face the enemy, expecting instant death, that the rest were shamed into a halt. They shouted to the men waiting in ambush, and these came out and cut off the pursuing Rus from the town, so that the Muslims surrounded them. It is said that the Rus commander and 700 of his men were killed, while the rest retreated to a fortress inside the town and there were besieged by Marzuban.

Meanwhile the epidemic grew worse, and after the Rus had buried many of their dead, they slipped away by night, taking with them what booty they could carry and the most valuable captives; they made for the river Kura and rowed away. God had saved the Muslims from them, concluded Miskawaih. His graphic account is confirmed by other writers. Ibn al-Athir tells a similar story, stressing the fact that the Rus behaved well in Bardha'a until provocation from the inhabitants made it impossible to come to terms with them. He adds that Marzuban's forces dared not pursue the Rus after they left the town, because they had such respect for the fighting power of their opponents.

It was probably as a result of this campaign that relations between Rus and Khazars worsened. The Hebrew document known as the 'Reply of Joseph', which may conceivably be a genuine tenth-century source, implies that the Khazar king denied the Rus entry to the route up the Don and down the Volga to the Caspian: [1] 'I . . . do not allow the Russians who come in ships to come by sea to go against the Arabs, nor any enemy by land to come. . . . If I allowed them for one hour, they would destroy all the country of the Arabs as far as Baghdad.' The occupation of Bardha'a, which may have continued for some months, must have made an enormous impression on the Muslim world. There are references by Ibn al-Faqih to villages occupied by them around the town,[2] and in the *Hudud al-'Alam*, the tenth-century work by a Persian geographer well acquainted with this region, it is said that the Rus camped in the village of 'Mubaraki outside Bardha'a before they made their attack in 943.[3] Marvazi, another Persian writer living in the eleventh century, states that the Rus held

---

[1] Dunlop, 144 ff.; 42.
[2] Ibid. 240 (note 19).
[3] *Hudud al-'Alam*, 144.

The Campaigns of the Rus

Bardha'a for a time.[1] It seems probable that there were more raids and skirmishes with the local inhabitants than are described in the existing accounts, and that they were long remembered in the area. We do not know which Rus leader was responsible for the campaign; the man killed at Bardha'a is unlikely to have been Igor, since his death is recorded in 945 much nearer home.

The *Primary Chronicle* states that Igor's retinue urged him to go out and collect more booty, and although he had already taken tribute from the Drevljane he went out against them a second time with a small raiding party. They not surprisingly protested, and then attacked and killed him, and his tomb is said to be seen near Iskorosten. Leo the Deacon heard another account of his death, since he states that he died at the hands of Germans, who fastened him to two trees and then released them so that he was torn apart.[2] The idea that he was killed by a neighbouring people agrees with the stories of vengeance taken by his widow Olga. The *Chronicle* records that after the Drevljane had killed Igor they sent a deputation to her proposing that she marry their prince in order to unite the kingdoms, and Olga lured them into a stone chamber inside a burial mound and there had them buried alive, seated in rich robes inside their ship. A second embassy was sent, and those who took part in it were burned to death inside a heated bathhouse. After this Olga went to the city of the Drevljane, ostensibly to mourn at Igor's grave, and asked them to brew a great funeral feast for him. She then ordered her bodyguard to massacre them as they lay drunk after the banquet, sent in an army under her young son Svyatoslav before they could take vengeance, and defeated them. She besieged Iskorosten and is said to have captured the city by the ancient ruse of setting fire to it by means of birds with matches tied to their wings, a feat which figures in many tales of war strategies in the classical and medieval world (p. 215 below).

These ruthless acts ascribed to Olga before her conversion to Christianity were thought by Nora Chadwick to originate in Scandinavian oral tradition,[3] and indeed both the character of the strong-minded queen and the kind of action which she took

---
[1] Marwazi, translated Minorsky (London 1942), IX, 5, 36.
[2] Leo Diaconus VII.
[3] Chadwick (1946), 29 ff.

against her enemies can be paralleled from Old Norse literature. The ship inside the barrow seems to be based on some misunderstood tradition of ship burial with elaborate funeral rites, such as we know from Ibn Fadlan was practised by the Rus in the tenth century (p. 66 above) while the use of a bathhouse to commit murder is found in an Icelandic setting.[1] Igor's wife, however, is remembered in Russian sources for her conversion to Christianity. In spite of her husband's attack on the city, she visited Constantinople in 957 and was received with much ceremony by the Emperor Constantine, as we know from Greek sources (p. 248 below). She was the first of the royal house of Kiev to become a Christian, but her son Svyatoslav did not follow her example. 'My bodyguard will laugh at me,' he told her, according to the *Primary Chronicle*, and he continued to keep up the traditions of a pagan past and the old policy of raiding and warfare with the support of unconverted northerners. It seems to have been the Slav element at the court of Kiev which welcomed conversion, while the Scandinavian leaders and their followers resisted the new faith.[2] When Svyatoslav was old enough to take over power in Kiev, the Frankish bishop whom his mother had brought there was forced to leave, and the Christians must have been a small minority only. Meanwhile Svyatoslav continued the policy of his Scandinavian predecessors, and followed a vigorous scheme of expansion and conquest in the east and south.

---

[1] *Eyrbyggja Saga* 28; cf. *Þiðreks Saga*, edited Bertelsen, II, 309.
[2] Vlasto, 249–50.

CHAPTER 4

The Great Svyatoslav

Igor's son Svyatoslav was the last of the great heroic leaders in a pagan tradition. By the time he became Prince of Kiev, the kingdom must have become mainly Slav in organisation and policy, and he certainly led Slav troops. But he was of direct Scandinavian descent, and Scandinavians were fighting in considerable numbers at his side, so that we are entitled to regard his campaign as part of the history of the eastern Vikings.

The praise of his achievements in the *Primary Chronicle* sounds as though it had been quoted from panegyric poetry, and we know enough about his campaigns from outside sources to realise his great ambitions and the considerable success which he won before his death in an ambush on the Dnieper. As so often in the history of the Vikings, the conquests of the Rus under Svyatoslav, though spectacular, were not lasting. He set out on a career of conquest on a grand scale, and his armies advanced against the Khazars, the Volga Bulgars, the Danube Bulgars, and finally against the forces of the Byzantine empire. This was the first occasion in which the armies of the Rus met the Byzantine forces in direct conflict, and they came very near to victory.

The reason for Svyatoslav's attack on the Khazars has been discussed in much detail by Vasiliev. Unfortunately much of his argument depends on three fragments known as the *Report of a Greek Toparch*, which were claimed to come from two folios of a manuscript discovered by Karl Hase in the Bibliothèque Nationale, published in 1819.[1] These folios have never been found, and an exhaustive search for them and investigation of Hase's correspondence and his own copy by Ihor Ševčenko makes it now highly probable that the fragments were a forgery by Hase himself.

[1] Vasiliev (1936), 118 ff.

The fragments were presumed to come from three sections of an account written by a ruler in the Crimea, telling how the neighbouring regions were overrun by cruel barbarians, although these were a people previously renowned for mildness and justice. He fortified his city against them, and consulted certain men who had settled there, who were not Greeks; they advised him to seek help from a ruler north of the Danube, whose manners and customs were similar to theirs, and who had a large army. Part of the narrative is missing, but it appears that the ruler promised his help, and the Crimean Toparch returned with his embassy in winter, crossing the Dnieper as soon as the ice would bear, and suffering much from snowstorms and from hostile tribes. The position of the sun in Saturn is mentioned, which made a date in the winter of 962–3 a possibility, although, as Ševčenko shows, other dates are possible, and it seems impossible that such calculations could have been made at the time as is claimed in the account.[1] Vasiliev believed that the cruel barbarians were the Khazars, and the men who gave advice were Rus who had settled in the Crimea, who advised that help should be sought from Svyatoslav in Kiev. He felt that this gave a plausible reason for the campaign against the Khazars by Svyatoslav in the early 60s, and implied that the Prince gained influence for a time over the Crimea, which was of great strategic importance. These arguments can no longer be accepted as valid, although there is good evidence for the attack against the Khazars.

The *Primary Chronicle* records the capture of the Khazar town Biela Viezha ('White Tower' or 'White Tent'), and a victory over the Yas and Kazogs. This town may be Sarkel, the fortress guarding the mouth of the Don, but is more likely to be the capital, Khazaren-Atil (Atil of the Khazars) on the Volga. If so, it was a momentous achievement. A motive for an attack in this quarter might be found in the catastrophe that overtook the army of the Rus twenty years earlier, for it was from Atil, a city with a Christian church and a metropolitan bishop [2] that a force of Christians had come to the support of the Muslim army which won a great victory over the Rus as they returned from the Caspian (p. 128 above). There are other references to the destruction of

[1] Ševčenko, 130.
[2] Dunlop, 92 (note).

Atil about this time. Ibn Hauqal was told in 965 by a man who had visited the town after the attack that its gardens and orchards were devastated and that the Muslims and other people had deserted it.[1] He claimed that the Rus descended on everything, and not only the Khazars but the Burtas on the east bank of the Volga and the Volga Bulgars further north were left with nothing but ruins where their towns had been and were later assisted by the Shirwan ruler, who sent them an army. Miskawaih also refers to the overrunning of the Khazar capital in 965, although he attributes this to the Turks, and to the Khazars appealing to the Muslims for help.[2] It may be noted that the Burtas and the Bulgars had both given help to the Khazars in the attack on the Rus army, and it seems highly probable that Svyatoslav's main motive was a desire for vengeance, while at the same time he would be re-establishing the reputation of the Rus among the eastern peoples. The dispersed Khazars seem to have returned to their city in course of time, but a strange silence comes down on their activities after this, and Dunlop[3] takes 965 as the date marking the end of the independent state on the Volga. At the time of al-Biruni in the early eleventh century Atil was still in ruins, and Sagsen, which was flourishing in the twelfth century, replaced it as a trading centre. There are occasional references to the Khazars, and some scholars believe that they established a small state in the Crimea, but their power and influence were gone.

After this campaign in the south-east, Svyatoslav turned southwards against the Bulgars of the Danube. He was urged on by the wily Emperor Nicephorus, who hoped to play off one troublesome neighbour against another, and no doubt was anxious to get the Rus away from the Crimea. This was an important area for Byzantium, because of its strategic importance, placed as it was between the Empire and the northern peoples and easily reached across the Black Sea, and also a source of information about the movements of the Rus and Pechinegs and other tribes.[4] The Emperor accordingly sent an embassy to Kiev with an offer of 1,500 lb. in gold, 'a sum of money enormous even in those days of

[1] Ibid. 242.
[2] Ibid. 244.
[3] Ibid. 247.
[4] Obolensky (1966), 475, 510–11.

immoderate bribery of nations', as Runciman remarks,[1] to persuade Svyatoslav to invade Bulgaria. The warlike Symeon of Bulgaria had died, so that the region did not seem to offer a major threat to the Empire, but it was desirous to keep it in a state of weakness, as well as to keep the Rus prince from embarking on more dangerous campaigns. However, the ambassador sent to Kiev was Calocyras, a Chersonian from the Crimea and a cunning character; he made a separate agreement with Svyatoslav by which the Rus should be allowed to hold Bulgaria if they supported his claim to the imperial throne. According to John Scylitzes, Svyatoslav made some preliminary raids in the area and decided that a permanent conquest would be well worth while.[2] It appears that he accepted the tempting offer and took the Emperor's gold.

In 967[3] he set off down the Dnieper with his fleet and sailed round the Black Sea coast to the estuary of the Danube. He seems to have taken the Bulgarians by surprise; they were now ruled by Symeon's son Peter, who was unlike his father and a gentle, pious individual. An army of about 30,000 was hastily collected, but after being defeated by Svyatoslav's forces it retired to Dristra, after which there seems to have been no more resistance. Svyatoslav took a number of towns, according to the *Chronicle* as many as eighty, but this number was probably suggested by the list of eighty forts established by Justinian on the Danube as given by Procopius. He then settled down in Pereyaslavets to rule over the north-eastern part of the territory. The exact site of this important stronghold is uncertain, but an attractive suggestion is that it was inside the Byzantine fortress of Dinogetia in Romania, at the point in Dobrudja where the Danube bends round eastwards on its course to the Black Sea.[4] There was a Slav settlement inside the fort, established about the tenth century and inhabited until the twelfth, large enough to hold over 160 houses, and clearly a centre for trade. A close link with Kiev is indicated by a find of spindle whorls of pink slate, such as is only obtainable in the Kiev region, while articles from the area of the Volga Bulgars were also found, and could have come by way of Kiev. Svyatoslav is said to have

[1] Runciman, 200.
[2] Cedrenus II, 660.
[3] For arguments in favour of this date, see Stokes, 44 ff.
[4] Ibid. 474.

received more money from the Emperor, possibly further instalments of the original sum promised, and in general he appears to have been accepted by the Bulgarians, who found occupation by the Rus preferable to the rule of the hated Greeks.

Unfortunately, news reached him from Kiev of his mother Olga's illness and of attacks by the Pechinegs on the town. Svyatoslav was forced to return home, leaving the fleet in Bulgaria while he and his bodyguard went back by land, a journey of about six weeks. The Pechinegs had attacked in force, possibly with the connivance of the Emperor, and Olga was now an ageing woman, while Svyatoslav's sons were still young. She was unable to cross the Dnieper and get in touch with forces on the opposite bank, and soon supplies ran out and there was talk of surrender. Then comes the exciting episode of a young Rus who slipped out of the town and mingled with the nomads, holding a bridle in his hand and telling them in the Pechineg language that he was searching for his horse. He suddenly jumped into the Dnieper and began to swim across, and although the Pechinegs sent arrows after him he survived until a boat from the other bank picked him up. He told the Slav general, Pryetich, of the state of things in Kiev; next morning horns were blown and Pryetich and his men appeared on the river bank. The Pechinegs assumed that Prince Svyatoslav was returning, and retreated, so that Olga and her grandsons were able to cross the river to safety. Then the Pechineg prince came alone to meet Pryetich, who told him that the Prince was on his way home with a huge army; the two made a treaty of friendship and the Slav leader exchanged his breastplate, sword and shield for the spear, sabre and arrows of the nomad. The Pechinegs gave up the siege, and when Svyatoslav finally arrived, he collected an army and drove them back to the steppe. The implication here is that the Slav general, although a loyal ally, was independent of Svyatoslav and could make his own agreement with the enemy.

Svyatoslav remained in Kiev until his mother's death in 969 and her funeral according to Christian rites. He had made it clear that he intended to move to Pereyaslavets, where [1] 'all riches are concentrated: gold, silks, wine and various fruits from Greece, silver and horses from Hungary and Bohemia, and from the Rus furs,

[1] *Primary Chronicle*, 969, 86.

wax, honey and slaves'. He set up his three young sons as viceroys in Kiev, Dereva and Novgorod, and then returned overland to Bulgaria with additional troops from the Rus, the Magyars and the Pechinegs. By now, however, valuable time had been lost and the situation had worsened. The Byzantines had learned of the treachery of Calocyras and the failure of their original plan, and Nicephorus made a fresh alliance with the Bulgarians. We hear of this from the diplomat Liutprand, who arrived in Constantinople in 968 to find to his fury that 'unwashed barbarians' from Bulgaria were being given precedence over all other foreign envoys.[1] Marriages were arranged for two small Bulgarian princesses with two young princes of the imperial family, and the little girls were sent off to Constantinople in a primitive war-chariot with scythes fitted to the wheels. Their fate, however, is unknown, for in December 968 one of the treacherous palace murders for which Byzantium was notorious took place, and Nicephorus was killed in his bedchamber by his wife's lover, John Tzimisces. John soon rid himself of the Empress and proved a far more vigorous ruler than his predecessor, but at first he was not sufficiently secure to take adequate measures against Svyatoslav. However, in January 969 Tsar Peter of Bulgaria died, and was succeeded by his son Boris, who had been brought up in Constantinople and was likely to favour the Byzantine side.

Thus it was that when Svyatoslav returned to Bulgaria he found Boris had retaken Pereyaslavets and driven out the garrison left there under the command of Svyatoslav's *voevoda* Volk, a Slav general. We can gather from what survives of a lost chronicle [2] that the Bulgarians attacked soon after Svyatoslav's departure, and Volk found that his supplies were running out. He collected all the boats he could find, slaughtered his horses and salted the meat, and then set the town on fire. The Bulgarians crowded to the fire, and meanwhile Volk and his men slipped away with supplies of food and sailed up the Danube, taking care that no boats remained behind. They reached Dristra, and there joined the new forces brought back by the Prince.

Svyatoslav prepared to retake Pereyaslavets, but was repulsed with heavy losses. He rallied his men with brave words, and they

[1] Liutprand, *De Legatione Constantinopolitana*, 19, 246.
[2] Stokes, 481, note 80.

The Great Svyatoslav

made a second attempt and recaptured it by evening. The Emperor John Tzimisces then sent him a message offering to continue with the payments as promised if Svyatoslav would move out of Bulgaria. He got back what must rank among the most insolent messages ever sent to Byzantium: Svyatoslav suggested that the Emperor had better cross over to Asia, since the only offer he would accept was that of all the Emperor's possessions in Europe. John replied by reminding him of the disaster which overtook his father Igor on the Bosporus after he had broken his agreements and attacked Constantinople, and he then threatened Svyatoslav with the whole might of the Byzantine army. No need for the Emperor to seek him out, Svyatoslav replied; they would meet outside the gates of Constantinople. He concluded with words which have a proud, heroic ring: the Emperor must realise that the Rus were not mere labourers, living by the work of their hands, but warriors who could use weapons; they were not women to be scared by threats or infants frightened of bogeys.

Since diplomacy had failed, John prepared for war. He summoned his picked body of troops, the Immortals, and sent Bardas and Petros ahead to begin the campaign. Leo gives us a detailed account of this in Books VII, VIII and IX of his history, and since he was present on the campaign as the Emperor's secretary, he should be a good witness. There is further information in the account by John Scylitzes, recorded by Cedrenus. Bardas began by sending spies dressed like the Rus to discover the position of the enemy, and then marched against them with a small force. We are told that Svyatoslav's army was in three sections, Pechinegs, Turks and Rus, together with some Bulgars who gave him support. The Rus here must be understood to mean Scandinavians and their Slav allies. Bardas realised he was outnumbered and remained within the walls of a fortress, in spite of their taunts to him to come out and fight. After a while the Rus and their allies grew careless and no longer maintained their camp, but feasted, danced and made music, wandering about as they chose. Bardas sent out a small force to invite pursuit, arranging other troops in ambush, so that when the Pechinegs pursued the fugitives they were surrounded and cut down almost to the last man. Then there was fierce fighting between the two armies, until Bardas himself brought down one of their chief warriors, a man of great size with splendid weapons who had attacked him with his sword; Bardas, however, had the better weapon and brought him down with a cutting stroke, slicing him almost in two. After this the Rus broke and fled, although this does not seem to have been the decisive victory which Leo claims, and the *Primary Chronicle* claims it as a victory for the Rus.[1] Soon afterwards Bardas left the Danube to begin a revolt on his own account in Cappadocia, so the Emperor himself prepared to lead the spring offensive in 971.

He got ready a fleet of galleys able to project Greek fire and inspected them before they left the city, then he set out with his army. By a fatal oversight Svyatoslav left no guard on the mountain passes, so that the Greeks reached Pereyaslavets while he himself was still in Dristra. Perhaps he was taken by surprise by the Emperor's arrival in Holy Week, or lulled into false security by fresh overtures from the Greeks for a truce, but in any case the mistake was to prove a costly one. The garrison in Pereyaslavets defended themselves with spears, arrows and stones, while the Greeks used catapults to bombard the walls. At last a young soldier led a successful assault up a ladder against the ramparts, beheading a warrior who barred his way, and so the Greeks gained entry. The Rus now withdrew to the tower where the Bulgarian treasures were stored, and defended the narrow door so successfully that before long a vast number of Greeks lay dead before it. At last the Emperor resorted to flame-throwers against the building, which must have been partly built of wood, and the flames forced the Rus out into the open. There was fierce fighting for a while, and then Svinketil (evidently a Scandinavian leader) broke through the Greeks with a small following and got away to Dristra.

After repairing Pereyaslavets and sending prisoners to call on Svyatoslav to surrender, the Emperor marched on Dristra (which the Greeks called Dorystolon), occupying a number of small places on the way. Svyatoslav was furious when the Bulgarians began going over to the Greek cause, and had three hundred leading men beheaded and others imprisoned. He collected as large a force as possible and sent out a band of guerillas against the Emperor's army; they killed a number of Greek soldiers until the Emperor sent search parties into the woods beside the road, cap-

[1] *Primary Chronicle*, 971, 88.

tured the assailants and had them cut to pieces on the spot. At Dristra the Rus were drawn up in battle formation outside the walls, and for a long time there was desperate fighting; not until the Emperor sent the cavalry in did the line break and the Rus retreat inside the fortress. The Emperor then built a camp on a hill nearby, from which stones could be fired into the town. The Rus made one expedition against this on horseback, but proved no match for the experienced Greek riders. Then the fire-ships arrived in the Danube, greatly increasing Greek morale, and were posted along both banks of the river, so that escape for the besieged by ship was impossible.

Next day Svyatoslav's men came out to fight again, but the battle ended with the death of Svinketil, one of the three leaders, and again the Rus withdrew, while the Emperor encouraged his men with gifts and supplies of wine. The wine nearly proved their downfall, for the man in charge of the war-machine in the camp was so sleepy after his midday meal that, when the Rus attacked in an attempt to burn it, he was thrown from his horse and immediately cut to pieces. The Rus imagined from his rich armour and the fine trappings of his horse that they had slain the Emperor and rejoiced greatly. The following day they were out again, but one of the chief men in the Emperor's guard, a skilful Arab horseman called Anemas, cut down another Scandinavian leader Ingvar (Ikmor) with his sword; once more the Rus retreated. That night they collected their dead and cremated them beside the walls, making human and animal sacrifices to the departed. In the morning after the funeral, Svyatoslav held a council; some of his men urged him to come to terms with the Greeks and leave for home, since the fire-ships made flight impossible and they could no longer go out to forage in the country round, as they had done before the ships arrived. Leo and Scylitzes give a summary of Svyatoslav's rousing speech to his followers, reminding them of the brave deeds of their ancestors, their own reputation as warriors, and the pursuit of glory, even though this should mean death (p. 114 above). A similar account in different words is reported in the *Primary Chronicle*: [1]

"'Now we have no place whither we may flee. Whether we will or

[1] Ibid.

no, we must give battle. Let us not disgrace Rus, but rather sacrifice our lives, lest we be dishonoured. For if we flee, we shall be disgraced. We must not take to flight, but we will resist boldly, and I will march before you. If my head falls, then look to yourselves." Then his warriors replied, "Wherever your head falls, there we too will lay down our own."'

The account given by Leo is a far grimmer one, however, than that in the *Chronicle*, which describes Svyatoslav driving back the Greeks and marching towards Constantinople until the Emperor, finding it impossible to tempt him with gifts, came to terms and Svyatoslav agreed because it would take too long to collect reinforcements. According to Leo the final battle, on 24 July 971, was a very fierce one, and the Greeks came near defeat. Ametas attempted to repeat his former success and made for Svyatoslav with drawn sword, as the Rus leader was fighting like a man possessed in the midst of the battle. He cut at him, but Svyatoslav too was on horseback and was protected by a good coat of mail; he slipped off his horse and escaped with a wound, while Ametas was cut to pieces by Svyatoslav's bodyguard. The Emperor called upon his own guard as the Rus advanced, and drums and trumpets were sounded to urge the retreating Greeks on to a fresh effort. At that moment a storm broke in clouds of rising dust and blinding rain, and it was afterwards said that an unknown rider on a white horse suddenly rode forward and led the advance. Afterwards the Emperor sought for this man to reward him, but he was never found, and men said that it was no other than the Holy Martyr Theodore, despatched by the Holy Virgin to save the people of her city in the hour of deepest need. At all events, the Rus gave way, and Svyatoslav, faint from loss of blood from his wound, only just managed to escape in the gathering darkness; according to Leo, 'he raged all night in anger and pain'.

Svyatoslav realised now that his only course was to make terms with the Greeks, and he sent a message offering to surrender the town and to free his prisoners, if the Greeks would allow his ships to leave without using their fire and would furnish them with provisions for the home journey. They could then be on terms of friendship as in the past and continue to trade with one another. The Emperor seized the opportunity, treated the messengers generously and agreed to allow two bushels of corn for each man, while he consented to Svyatoslav's request for a meeting. The Rus leader rowed up the Danube with his men, and Leo gives his famous description of his appearance. He calls him a fine figure of a man, of medium height, with powerful neck and broad chest; he had bright eyes, bushy eyebrows, a blunt nose and smooth cheeks, with a broad moustache on his upper lip. His head was bald, except for a lock of hair on either side, a token of his noble birth (and presumably in the Slav tradition), and in one ear he wore a silver ring decorated with two pearls and a carbuncle. This careful description may be set beside that in the *Primary Chronicle*, where he is pictured as a tough warrior, 'stepping light as a leopard', accustomed to travel with his men without luxuries or comforts, roasting strips of dried meat over the coals and sleeping in the open with his saddle for a pillow. This may be an echo from heroic poems in his praise; we may add it to the picture of Svyatoslav left by the hostile Greek historian and the evidence for his achievements in the field, and are given the impression of an outstanding warrior leader, fit to stand beside any in the literature of the heroic age and the Viking North.

Svyatoslav's campaign against the Greeks was his last expedition. After he had fulfilled his side of the agreement he set off by ship with his followers to return to Kiev. But when they reached the Dnieper, the Pechinegs were waiting in ambush, probably at their favourite place near the cataracts on the river, and in the fighting the prince and many of his men were killed and only a small force returned to Kiev. We are told that the Pechinegs, exulting in their victory over so famous a leader, had his skull made into a drinking cup set in gold, a custom for which there is evidence among the various Altai peoples.[1] To preserve the skull of an enemy in this way was an outstanding honour, and this brief reference in the *Primary Chronicle* indicates something of the awe and terror with which Svyatoslav must have been regarded by the tribes around Kiev.

---

[1] J. Roux, *La Mort chez les peuples altaïques* (Paris 1963), 82 ff.

CHAPTER 5

The Varangians in Russia

After the death of Svyatoslav, a change takes place in the accounts of fighting given in the *Primary Chronicle*. Instead of a heroic leader setting out on a career of conquest, a leader of Scandinavian descent followed by his own bodyguard, building up large armies with the aid of Slav and Pechineg allies, we now find the Scandinavians employed as mercenaries by the rulers of Kiev, Novgorod and other towns in Russia. These Scandinavian forces are known as Varangians (p. 62 above). It becomes clear also that the townspeople were in a position to impose considerable limitations on the doings of their rulers; they could provide wealth to pay troops or object to their employment, raise their own local armies when they felt it necessary, and either urge the princes on to war or refuse to support their campaigns. During the reigns of Vladimir and Yaroslav, Icelandic sources show that there was considerable interest in affairs in Russia.

By the time Vladimir became ruler of Kiev, Slav influence there had greatly increased. Vladimir's mother belonged to the Drevljane, and she had been at Olga's court in charge of her household. This would be an honourable position, but it explains the scornful reply of the Scandinavian girl Ragnheid, whose father Rognvald is said to have come from Sweden and taken possession of Polotsk.[1] She refused to marry Vladimir, declaring that she was not going to pull off the boots of a slave's son. Vladimir's uncle on his mother's side, Dobrynya, acted as adviser to the Prince when he succeeded his father, and ruled Novgorod when Vladimir was in Kiev. Indeed it seems that Vladimir could never have won Kiev without the help of a Slav general Blud, who is called the *voevoda* of Vladimir's brother Yaropolk. Nora Chadwick has suggested that

[1] *Primary Chronicle*, 978–80, 91.

the men who bore this title and clearly played an important part in the government of Kiev were members of the native hereditary aristocracy, on whom the princes of Scandinavian descent depended for their authority and for the necessary support to maintain it.[1] Vladimir is said to have had Varangians in his service and to have been very slow in paying them. On one occasion they captured a city and demanded that they should receive part of the tribute from it, but Vladimir promised to pay them when the marten skins were collected in a month's time, and then did not keep his promise. Consequently large numbers of Scandinavians left him for service with the Emperor, though Vladimir persuaded those whose services he valued most to stay with him, giving them control over certain cities.[2]

The Rus princes evidently relied on the Scandinavian forces, since there was plenty of fighting to be done, although of a different kind from that under Svyatoslav. The rulers of the different towns opposed each other and competed for the all-important tribute from the neighbouring tribes. When Sveinald returned with the army from the Bulgarian campaign, he encouraged Svyatoslav's eldest son, Yaropolk, to fight his brother Oleg. Oleg had killed Sveinald's son and his own body was later found among the slain in the moat of a small town to which he fled. Then Vladimir, helped by Blud, opposed Yaropolk, slew him by treachery in 978 and thus became ruler of Kiev.

To the early part of his reign belongs the story of the Scandinavian princess Ragnheid, whose father Rognvald held Polotsk, told in some detail in a later part of the *Chronicle*.[3] When she insulted Vladimir and refused to marry him, declaring that she wanted his elder brother Yaropolk for her husband, Vladimir's uncle Dobrynya was enraged at the girl's reply, since he was the brother of Vladimir's mother whom she had called a slave. Together with Vladimir he attacked Polotsk, took the ruler and his wife prisoner and urged Vladimir to rape the girl in the presence of her parents. Vladimir is said to have killed her father and, accord-

[1] Chadwick (1946), 113 ff. cf. 36 ff.
[2] *Primary Chronicle*, 980, 93. Cross suggests that the departure for Constantinople belongs to the events of 988 (p. 179 below), but the tradition of Vladimir's meanness and his anxiety to get rid of a number of his mercenary troops may be reliable.
[3] *Codex Laurentianus* for the year 1128; Stender-Petersen (1934), 216 ff.

ing to one account, her brothers also, and then to have made her his wife, calling her Gorislava. Their son was called Izaslav. As time went on, Vladimir took other women and neglected Ragnheid, and one night she attempted to stab him as he lay sleeping. He woke in time to seize her arm, and she told him that she hated him for killing her father and taking the kingdom, and for neglecting her and her son. Vladimir commanded her to put on the royal robe she had worn at her wedding and to lie down on the bed, for he was going to return with a weapon and kill her. While he was gone, she gave an unsheathed sword to her little son and told him that he was to ask his father whether he thought that his mother was there alone. At the child's question, Vladimir dropped his weapon; he went to consult his advisers, who told him that he must spare the Queen for her son's sake, and that he must provide them with a place to live. Vladimir built the town of Izaslavl and gave it to his wife and son.

A less dramatic version of Ragnheid's fate is found in another part of the *Chronicle*,[1] where he is said to have put her away when he married the Byzantine princess Anna, and offered to marry her to one of his nobles, but she indignantly refused. She was baptised and entered a convent under the name of Anastasia. Stender-Petersen thought that the vengeance story belonged to a series of tales of attempted vengeance by brides on their wedding-night, and compares it with other tales of forced marriages, some of which are not very convincing parallels with the story in the *Chronicle*.[2] There are, however, obvious links with one story, that of Olaf Tryggvason's marriage to Gudrun, the daughter of Jarnskeggi, who resisted Christianity and who was killed when Olaf destroyed the temple of Thor.[3] Jarnskeggi had led the landowners in opposition against Olaf, and when the district had been made Christian and terms were arranged between the King and the former rebels, it was agreed that Olaf should marry Gudrun:

'And when the bridal night came, the two, King Olaf and Gudrun, shared the same bed. But the first night that they lay together, when the King slept, Gudrun seized a knife, intending to stab him.

[1] *Codex Laurentianus (Polnoe Sobranie Russkikh Letopisey)* II, 258.
[2] Stender-Petersen (1934), 210 ff.
[3] *Heimskringla, Óláfs Saga Tryggvasonar*, 71.

The King, however, was aware of it and he took the knife from her, and got up from the bed and went to his men and told them what had happened.'

Gudrun and her followers then left, and she and Olaf did not come together again. This story of attempted revenge by a woman married against her will may have been taken back to Norway and later included among the doings of Olaf Tryggvason by Snorri. Very little is made of the story here, but in the account of Ragnheid we have a tale in the Scandinavian heroic manner, with a proud and tragic heroine. How much historical truth lies behind it we do not know, but it recalls the atmosphere of the old heroic world and the acts of revenge committed by Brynhild and Gudrun in the stories of the Volsungs. It is not the only story associated with Vladimir which found its way to the North.

In the early part of his reign Vladimir is said to have made attacks on several neighbouring tribes. The Lyakhs in Polish territory west of Kiev are mentioned, the Vjatici round the upper Oka, south of Moscow, some of whom moved into eastern Prussia as the result of his campaign, and the Radimichi settled in the forest area east of the Dnieper. No details about these attacks are given. He is also said to have made an attack by ship on the Volga Bulgars, presumably along the old Volga route, with the support of the Torks, a nomadic people from the Upper Don who were enemies of the Pechinegs.[1] This campaign was successful, and he concluded a treaty with the Bulgars, establishing peace 'till stone floats and straw sinks'. The *Chronicle* refers to a tradition that the Bulgars offered Vladimir instruction in the Islamic faith, and according to Marvazi a Muslim teacher visited Kiev.[2] However the splendours of the Byzantine ritual and the political advantages of the alliance led Vladimir to accept Christianity according to the eastern rite (p. 203 below).

Vladimir's conversion, to which much space is devoted in the *Primary Chronicle*, inevitably meant closer links with the Empire. Basil II promised his sister Anna in marriage, an outstanding honour, but the arrangements were slow to go forward and Anna was said to be anything but enthusiastic. This was probably why in

[1] Probably the same as the Oghouz; cf. Sinor, 287.
[2] Vlasto, 395 (note 81).

989 Vladimir led an expedition against Chersun in the Crimea, a town where the Christian Church was well established, and which was of some importance to the Empire (p. 139 above). The reason may have been, as Minns suggested, that it was held by rebels at the time, so that Vladimir was both helping Basil and displaying his own strength;[1] possession of the town would have been a valuable bargaining factor in his dealings with the Greeks. The attack was apparently from the sea after the fleet had been brought down the Dnieper, and Vladimir besieged the town until it is said that an arrow was shot from inside the walls carrying a message telling how to cut off the water supply. Another version[2] is that the man who sent the message was a Varangian called Sigbiorn (Zhidibern), who warned Vladimir that he must cut the road by which supplies were reaching the town from merchant ships. Either tradition could be reliable if Vladimir's attack was in the area of the modern Quarantine Bay, since the water-supply entered the town on the north-east side and ships could have brought in supplies to North Bay. The arrow story is admittedly a conventional motif, found in Polyainos and other ancient writers, but this does not necessarily mean that the tradition is wholly fictitious; Vladimir may have received a message from someone in the town, where the population was very mixed, giving him essential information leading to the taking of Chersun. He is said to have celebrated his marriage with the Emperor's sister there and presented the city to the Emperor as a present from the bridegroom. One tradition says that he was also baptised there, although it seems more likely that his baptism took place at Kiev. He agreed to accept Christianity as early as 987, while the Chersun expedition was in the summer of 989, the date being based on references to a comet and an earthquake in Greek records. On the whole the long delay seems unlikely, especially since the Greeks appear to have insisted on baptism before they would agree to the marriage taking place.[3]

During Vladimir's reign there were several attacks by the Pechinegs on Kiev and other towns. One story aims at showing

[1] Minns, 537.
[2] Ibid. 536. Part of the story resembles the Ragnheid one, since Vladimir is said to have raped the daughter of the ruler of Cherson and then to have married her to Sigbiorn.
[3] Vlasto, 257 ff.

their stupidity and follows a well-known pattern: when they were besieging Belgorod, a small town on the Irpen not far from Kiev, the townspeople had used up almost all their supplies and an old man advised them to pour their last remaining stocks of porridge and honey into tubs, which were placed in pits in the ground. They told the Pecheneg messengers that they could rely on constant supplies of food from the earth, and gave them porridge and mead made from the honey, and the Pechinegs were so impressed that their prince gave up the siege. This belongs to a series of 'strategy' tales of cunning ruses employed in war, of which a considerable number occur in Greek and Roman writers. Stender-Petersen suggests that such tales were brought into Russia from the Varangians in Byzantium, where they were likely to be popular in the army. The deceiving of the enemy over supplies is found in stories by Frontinus and Polyainos, although the details of porridge and honey and the custom of storing it in pits have evidently been brought in to suit conditions in Kievan Russia.

Another tale told of the Pechinegs is that they challenged the Rus to produce a wrestler to meet their own champion, a man of huge strength, and offered to keep peace for three years if anyone could defeat him. Stender-Petersen emphasises the influence here of the biblical story of David and Goliath, both in this story and others attributed to this period.[1] In the Pecheneg story there are obvious resemblances: the two armies faced one another, no one could be found for some time to volunteer to fight the champion, who was of great size, until at last an old man suggested his youngest son, whose four brothers were serving in the army. This youth had so powerful a grip that he could tear a hide to pieces with his hands, and when tested against a fierce bull he tore off part of its skin, just as David claimed to have overcome a lion and a bear which came after his flock, and to have slain the lion with his hands. Vladimir sent the boy out against the wrestler, and although inferior in size he crushed his opponent to death, and the Rus chased the Pechinegs from the field. The episode concerning the bull resembles that told of the Icelandic hero Thorstein Oxleg, found in *Flateyjarbók*,[2] and possibly here the Goliath motif has

[1] Stender-Petersen (1934), 158 ff.
[2] *Flateyjarbók*, *Óláfs Saga Tryggvasonar*, 213, 261; translated J. Simpson, *The Northmen Talk* (London 1965), 212 ff.

been linked with another traditional tale about a strong man; it certainly seems unreasonable to assume that all the stories of single combat associated with the court of Vladimir, of which there are several, are derived from the Bible, since both Germans and Scandinavians had their own native traditions in which duels between two champions as the means of deciding a battle played a considerable part.[1]

One of the duels said to have been fought at Kiev comes in the Icelandic saga of Biorn, Champion of Hitdale, which although of little literary merit belongs to a group of early sagas and was thought by Braun to have been largely based on oral tradition.[2] Biorn was a poet who came to Russia to serve under Valdimar (Vladimir), at a time when the King had been challenged to a duel by his kinsman Kaldimar for his kingdom. Kaldimar was a famous swordsman and the King was seeking someone to take his place, as he had little hope of victory. Biorn had gone to Gardar to win fame, and he volunteered to fight, saying that it was unfitting that his lord should be left without support. The battle was long and hard, although no details are given except that the men fought with swords and that Biorn finally struck down Kaldimar, but was himself severely wounded. A tent was set up for him, since he was too weak to be moved. The main interest of this incident to the saga-teller seems to be that the duel delayed Biorn's return to Iceland until the girl he loved was married to another man. Indeed the whole episode is clumsy, and the poem said to have been composed by Biorn after the fight is inconsistent with the prose account: Biorn says that he is sleeping with other warriors in a tent, and that Ingibiorg would wish to be with him if she knew that he was so near, but he is in Russia while she is out in Iceland. It seems as if the episode of a wounded man left in a tent has been brought in here as an excuse to introduce the poem.

Thus there is no evidence in Biorn's verses to confirm the tradition of the duel, and none of the examples of single combat referred to in the Russian sources correspond with his story. The slaying of Yaropolk, Vladimir's eldest brother, was carried out by Varangians, who stabbed him in the ribs from either side as he came into the hall for a meeting with his brother; this took place

[1] Davidson (1962), 193 ff.
[2] Braun (1924), 172–3.

about 980, about nine years before Biorn was born. The duel between the Pechineg and the unnamed youth was a wrestling match, dated 992 in the *Primary Chronicle*. Later in Yaroslav's reign there was a duel between his half-brother Mstislav and Redeya, prince of the Kazogs; this also was a wrestling match, but Mstislav, when almost overcome, stabbed his opponent after being thrown.[1] There are also a number of duels attributed to the hero Starkad in Saxo's *History*, some of which are associated with Russia.[2] The first was against a champion called Wisinnus, who lived on a rock in Russia called *Ana-fial*; he was a great duellist and could blunt swords by his gaze, but Starkad overcame him by covering his blade with a thin skin. He then defeated a Byzantine champion called Tanna, and 'drove him to flee as an outlaw to unknown quarters of the earth', which seems to be an elaborate way of saying that he killed him. His next opponent was a certain Waska or Wilzla in Poland. Then he met a Saxon champion Hama, who had challenged King Frode of Denmark; Starkad declared that it was not fitting for kings to fight those of lower rank and took Frode's place. Both champions were escorted to the place of the duel by their countrymen and, when they met, Hama thought his opponent too old to be taken seriously and flung him to the ground, but Starkad then drew his sword and killed Hama. This has some resemblance to the Mstislav story, since a wrestling match ends with the man who has been thrown stabbing his opponent, and Stender-Petersen suggested that this also was a Russian story which Saxo, in accordance with his practice, transferred into the realm of the Saxons nearer home. It does not seem possible to decide which, if any, of the various duel stories are likely to be genuine traditions of some famous fight, or what the possible links between them can be. It is interesting, however, to find so many stories of this kind linked with Vladimir's court, and such tales might have been carried back by Varangians to Scandinavia, as Braun suggested. Certainly at this period the *Primary Chronicle* seems to be relying largely on tales of a popular type, which could owe something to oral traditions among the Varangians. The Prince himself, it may be noted, is no more than a figure-head, in striking contrast to his predecessor Svyatoslav.

[1] *Primary Chronicle*, 1022, 134.
[2] Stender-Petersen (1934), 171 ff.; Saxo VI, 187-8, 229-31.

After the death of Vladimir bitter conflict broke out once more among the sons born to various wives before his conversion, and his eventual successor Yaroslav does not emerge from the accounts as a particularly heroic figure. In the *Primary Chronicle* it is his Slav counsellors and the people of Novgorod and Kiev who are represented as having the upper hand. He is said to have had large forces of Varangians in Novgorod, but the townspeople objected to their unruly behaviour and killed many of them in an attack on the 'court *Poromoni*', which Cross translates as 'market-place', suggesting that it comes from the Norse *farmanna* (of the men from abroad) and refers to the part of the city which belonged to the Varangians.[1] Yaroslav was angry at this, but could do nothing, since he relied on the townspeople to support him against his brother Svyatopolk, who had established himself at Kiev. For three months the armies of Yaroslav and his brother faced each other across the Dnieper, and the leader of Svyatopolk's forces mocked at the men of Novgorod and called them carpenters, and taunted Yaroslav with his lameness. Once the river was partially frozen, however, Yaroslav and his men crossed it and his followers pushed out the boats which brought them so that there could be no retreat. The attempt was successful; Svyatopolk's men were driven on to the thin ice and defeated, and Yaroslav took Kiev.

Two years later Svyatopolk returned with his Polish father-in-law, Burislav, who is described as a large, stout man. Yaroslav's foster-father Budy mocked at him, declaring 'We shall pierce your fat belly with a pike', but this was a premature boast, for the invaders made a sudden attack and drove Yaroslav out of the town. He made up his mind to leave Russia, but once more his Slav general and the men of Novgorod took control, insisting that he should fight another battle; they even destroyed his ship so that he could not escape. They set out to collect tribute in skins from surrounding districts, in order to pay fresh forces to support them. Meanwhile Svyatopolk had quarrelled with his father-in-law Burislav, and when the battle took place he was finally defeated, although it was a bitter conflict, described as the most terrible struggle which ever took place in the land of Rus. The soldiers are said to have fought hand to hand; 'three times they

[1] *Primary Chronicle*, 1015, 130; note 124.

clashed, so that blood flowed in the valleys'. This sounds like the echo of an heroic poem, and the fate of Svyatopolk might also have been taken from some heroic narrative: his army was dispersed and it is said that he fled to Poland and died a madman, terrified by invisible pursuers.

The next opposition came from another half-brother, the same Mstislav who fought the duel against the Kazog prince (p. 155 above). He is described as a big man, red-faced, with large eyes, a bold warrior, who was also merciful and famed for his generosity towards his followers, to whom he begrudged 'neither treasure nor food nor drink'. He was a Christian; nevertheless he appears to belong to the old heroic tradition in contrast to the cautious and wavering Yaroslav. Mstislav had been ruling in Tmutorakan in the south-east, and there he built a church in honour of the Holy Virgin as a thanksgiving for his victory over the Kazogs. Yaraslav and Mstislav met at night in a storm, and once more the account of the battle sounds like a quotation from a poem: 'The lightning flashed, the weapons gleamed, and the thunder rolled, and the fight was violent and fearful.'

Evidently the Varangians played an essential part in these conflicts. Yaroslav is said to have had a Norwegian prince, Hakon, on his side, an outstanding figure in a gold-ornamented cloak. In some of the best manuscript readings, he is called *slepu*, 'blind', which was thought by Braun to be a slip for *s'epu*, 'handsome'.[1] However, there are cases in Saxo's tales where old warriors whose sight was failing are described as 'blind'. one of these being Harald War-tooth at the Battle of Bravellir, and this may simply be an indication that Hakon was an ageing man.[2] Mstislav was the victor in this battle, but he generously allowed his elder brother to retain Kiev while he held Chernigov and the land round it, with the Dnieper as the boundary between them. To this Yaroslav agreed but chose to remain in Novgorod instead of Kiev. The brothers appear to have remained on good terms until the death of Mstislav, who was evidently far more popular than his brother. We know little about him, but he seems to have kept up contacts with Scandinavia, since he married a Swedish princess, Christina,

---

[1] Braun (1924), 159 suggested that he was a member of the royal family.
[2] M. Wistrand, 'Slaget við Bråvalla', *Arkiv f. nord Filologi*, 85 (1970), 215.

daughter of King Ingi, and had a daughter Malmfrid who married the Norwegian King Sigurd the Crusader.

The general unpopularity of Yaroslav seems to have been partly due to meanness towards his followers, and especially towards his Scandinavian mercenaries. This accusation is levelled in one of the most detailed of the Icelandic stories dealing with events in Russia at this period, the Tale of Eymund, included in the Saga of Olaf the Holy in *Flateyjarbók*.[1] Reference is often made to this source, but it is seldom examined in detail, and it seems worth while to pay some attention to it here. It had been suggested that the story is based on traditions carried to Iceland by men of Eymund's company,[2] and certainly it implies considerable knowledge of relations between Yaroslav and his Varangian troops, even if it may not be historically accurate. The hero Eymund was the son of a Norwegian king in Hringariki and a great-grandson of Harald Fairhair, while he was also a close friend of Olaf Haraldson (the Holy) in boyhood. He left Norway because of the treachery of his brother Hraerek against the king and went to the court of Yaroslav in search of fame, since he had heard that there was fighting among the sons of Vladimir for the kingdom. The three sons who come into the story are called Burizlaf, Jarisleif and Vartilaf; the first, holding Kiev, must be Svyatopolk; Jarisleif, holding Novgorod, is evidently Yaroslav; Vartilaf has been identified with the nephew of Yaroslav who ruled Polotsk, although he bears some resemblance to Mstislav. Eymund offered Jarisleif support against his brother in Kiev and arrived in Novgorod with his foster-brother Ragnar and several hundred Scandinavians. Jarisleif is represented as a capable king, but somewhat weak and mean, while his queen, Ingigerd, was a fine and generous lady. They welcomed Eymund and he gave them news of Norway.

Eymund offered to defend the kingdom against the King's enemies in return for payment in gold and silver, good clothes for his men and their own living quarters. The King hesitated and asked what pay they required. Eymund stipulated that a hall and food must be provided, together with an ounce of silver for every man in the company and an extra half-ounce for each steersman (the captain of a ship), since they had brought their own ships with

---

[1] *Flateyjarbók* II, *Óláfs Saga ins helga*, 118 ff.
[2] Braun (1924), 179 ff.; Cross (1929), 186 ff.

them. In case of war they were to be under the command of Jarisleif and he must provide his own army. Eymund explained that part of the pay could be in beaver or sable skins and 'other things easy to obtain in your land', while they would provide sufficient booty to produce the stipulated amount. Finally the King agreed to a twelve-month contract, and the Norwegians beached their ships and made preparations for fighting. They were satisfied with the accommodation and the food they received.

Before long a demand came from Burizlaf for certain towns and villages near the border, declaring impudently that it would suit him very well to collect revenue from them. Jarisleif consulted Eymund in alarm; Eymund warned him that if he gave way now more demands would follow; he concluded: 'I do not know why you hold a foreign army here if you are not going to rely on us.' Jarisleif accordingly refused Burizlaf's demands; Burizlaf guessed that his brother must have obtained support and was told that there were 600 Norsemen in Novgorod. The two armies confronted each other on either side of a river, where the banks were wooded. For four days Jarisleif hesitated and his men began to drift away, until Eymund offered to take his ships along the river and attack from behind the enemy position. This proved successful and there was great slaughter among Burizlaf's followers, 'so that it would take a long time to write down their names', and Jarisleif obtained much booty.

The Norsemen were greatly praised, but they did not receive their payment on the allotted date, since the King thought that his brother was dead and all his troubles over. Eymund at last told him bluntly that Burizlaf was alive, had spent the winter in Biarmaland and was advancing with an army of Biarmians, which would attack in about three weeks' time. The King then made arrangements with the Scandinavians for another year's service from them, and Eymund ordered his men to cut down trees and fortify the town with a log stockade, the logs pointing outwards so that the enemy could not get near enough to shoot over the wall. Outside the stockade he dug a deep ditch and covered it with wood, and then put some gold rings on a pennant worked with gold and fastened it to a pole beside the gate [1] in order to tempt the Biarmians who

[1] Such rings were used to fasten a pennant to a lance: P. Paulsen, *Alamannische Adelsgräber von Niederstotzingen* (Stuttgart 1967), 107 ff., Abb. 58.

were always greedy for gold. The invaders saw the rings and thought that they had caught Yaroslav unprepared; they made for the gate and many fell into the ditch and were killed. Then Burizlaf led a second fierce attack with the main army, forced a way into the town and was only driven out when Eymund came to the aid of Jarisleif, who was wounded in the foot. Burizlaf's men fled to the woods and many were killed.

When the King still delayed payment, Eymund accused him of dishonesty, since they had brought him ample booty. He reminded the King that many of his men had been wounded and must now be fed and tended; he declared that if they did not get compensation for their injuries, he and his men would leave: 'They will not serve for food alone, and we would rather go to the realm of some other king and seek renown there.' Jarisleif had found his brother's standard after the battle and assumed that he must be dead, but Eymund now told him that Burizlaf had escaped once more and was advancing with an army of Turks, black men [1] and 'all kinds of heathen', prepared to give up Christianity if he could win the kingdom. Ragnar wanted to abandon Jarisleif to his fate, but Eymund declared that they would be disgraced if they left at a time of crisis. When the King begged his help, he offered to deal with the invaders without calling on the people of Novgorod, who might be unwilling to turn out for another battle, and he asked the King if he were prepared to have his brother killed. Jarisleif replied that if he sent them out against Burizlaf he could not object to his brother's death.

Eymund and Ragnar hid in the woods where they expected Burizlaf to pitch his tent, beside a great oak in a clearing. Eymund tied the branches down with rope, and when Burizlaf's tent was set up under the tree, a rope was fastened to the golden weather-vane on the central pole by one of Eymund's men hidden in the branches. When all were sleeping, they cut the ropes holding down the tree and the tent was lifted up into the air. Eymund had discovered where the King lay, for he had visited the camp disguised as a beggar the night before, and in the general confusion he slipped up to the King's bed and cut off his head.

Jarisleif reddened with anger when Eymund took him the head of his brother and clearly resented his deed. However, he agreed

[1] Probably certain nomadic tribes. See p. 61 above.

that Eymund should return and bury the dead King, whose followers had fled in panic when they discovered his death. Jarisleif now ruled both Novgorod and Kiev, but he still gave no payment to Eymund's company and some of his court began to grumble because Burizlaf had been slain. Finally Eymund announced that he was going to join the third brother, Vartilaf; he and his men went to their ships. Queen Ingigerd realised her husband's folly and went after them with her kinsman, Jarl Rognvald. Eymund met her on the river bank in spite of Ragnar's warnings; he only narrowly escaped death when she drew off her glove as a signal to her men to surround and kill him. Eymund leapt back and his men jumped ashore and pushed the Queen and her party down the bank into thick mud, where they were unable to move. Ragnar would have carried Ingigerd off, but Eymund preferred to keep her friendship and let her return in peace

He offered the same terms to Vartilaf as he had previously arranged with Jarisleif. Vartilaf explained that he had no authority to decide for himself, but he consulted his people and they urged him to accept. His power, he said, was less than that of Jarisleif in Novgorod, but he promised to discuss plans openly with Eymund and to see that the Norsemen were promptly paid. When Jarisleif's demand came for certain towns and villages to be handed over, Eymund warned the King that 'a greedy wolf is ill to deal with', and that more demands would follow if these were granted. So once more the two armies faced each other across a river, but this time Eymund counselled delay. He and Ragnar slipped away to a path leading to Jarisleif's camp, and as the Queen came along it with a small party they stabbed her horse and carried her off before her companions realised what had happened. Eymund brought the Queen to Vartilaf and proposed that she be invited to mediate between the brothers; Vartilaf agreed. Ingigerd declared that Jarisleif should continue to hold Novgorod, 'the best kingdom in Gardariki', while Vartilaf should hold Kiev, 'second in value for tribute and dues', and Eymund himself should rule Vartilaf's town of Polotsk and return it to the brothers if he died without an heir. Eymund was to be responsible for the defence of the land, and the King would provide armies as needful. This agreement worked well, although after three years Vartilaf died and Kiev returned to Jarisleif.

The last settlement resembles that made between Yaroslav and Mstislav in the account in the *Primary Chronicle*, and part of the story may be based on conflict between the brothers in the early part of Yaroslav's reign. The most interesting feature, however, is the relationship between kings, townspeople and the Scandinavian mercenaries, which is made very clear. In Novgorod Jarisleif had power to decide peace or war, but he depended on the townspeople to raise an army; in Polotsk Vartilaf had less power than Jarisleif and had to consult his people before making important decisions, such as the engagement of mercenaries. The Norsemen came to seek wealth and fame in Russia, bringing their own ships with them, and in return for loyal support and fighting power received accommodation in their own hall, provisions, compensation for injuries received in fighting, and an annual payment in silver or furs, while the booty gained in battle went to the king. In the case of large-scale warfare, the king and townspeople provided an army, and the king acted as leader, while the Scandinavians gave support. According to this story, contracts with mercenaries were made for a year at a time. Skins were still used as an important source of revenue, and could be offered in part payment if silver were short.

It is noteworthy that the rulers of Kiev and Novgorod are no longer represented as Scandinavian, although they clearly had close contact with the royal families of Norway and Sweden and their courts served as places of refuge for those who had to leave Scandinavia for a while. Ingigerd and Rognvald were Swedes, and we know that Mstislav had connections by marriage with Sweden and Norway. It was clearly not always easy for the fighting companies to get payment for their services, and one episode in the *Primary Chronicle* represents Vladimir as behindhand in paying his Varangians, so that many of them quitted his service (p. 149 above). On the other hand, he is said to have commented that while gold would not secure him a retinue, his retinue would bring him treasure, as his father and grandfather had proved. Accordingly when they grumbled about eating with wooden spoons, he had silver ones provided for them: [1] 'for Vladimir was fond of his followers, and consulted them concerning matters of administration, wars and government.'

[1] *Primary Chronicle*, 994–6, 122.

There must have been many sagas about the adventures of the Varangians, and the opening section of *Yngvars Saga* alludes to the story of Eymund supporting Jarisleif, and evidently from a different version to that in *Flateyjarbók*, since Burizlaf is said to be captured and blinded and brought to the King, while Eymund took rich booty. There was clearly great interest in Iceland in the court of King Vladimir and King Yaroslav, and information was still reaching the west until the end of Yaroslav's reign, although by the eleventh century the centre of interest was already shifting from Russia to Byzantium.

CHAPTER 6

The Last Links with Scandinavia

One immediate link between Gardar and Scandinavia in the reign of Yaroslav was the presence of Ingigerd in Novgorod. Yaroslav's queen was the daughter of Olaf of Sweden and she played a major part in the *Tale of Eymund*, where she is represented as an attractive, generous but rather ruthless queen, who did much to decide the policies of a weak and cowardly king. Indeed in Icelandic sources Ingigerd developed into something approaching a romantic heroine, continuing to love Olaf Sigurdson of Norway whom her father would not permit her to marry. The facts of the story are established, but the further implications found in a number of sources and developed in particular by Snorri Sturluson in his saga of Olaf the Holy are part of a general saga tradition, and their authenticity is doubtful.[1] *Ágrip* gives a straightforward account of Olaf of Sweden refusing to let his daughter marry his Norwegian namesake and then arranging for her marriage with Yaroslav. It seems that the proposal of marriage was taken to Sweden by the Icelander Hjalti, who was spending a year at the Norwegian court, and that some of the King's poets accompanied him on the journey to Uppsala. The Swedish King was most unwilling to come to any agreement with Norway, although according to *Ágrip* his daughter favoured the match, and Snorri makes the landowners at the Thing at Uppsala speak out roundly against the King's anti-Norwegian policy (p. 24 above). When Olaf of Norway came to southern Sweden, however, to meet his

[1] Braun (1924), 182 ff. A. M. Arent has analysed Snorri's development of the story of the wooing in a paper on 'Snorri Sturluson's Mirror of the Thirteenth Century' given at the Saga Conference at Reykjavik in 1973, not yet published.

bride, the Swedish party never arrived, for Ingigerd's father had declared in fury, according to Snorri, that she should never marry the Norwegian king, 'in spite of all the great love which you have set on that proud man'.[1] Ingigerd sent warning to her kinsman Jarl Rognvald that her father was still hostile and asked him to let Olaf of Norway know of this. Olaf was 'angry and sick at heart, and for some days no man could get speech with him', and his only comfort was in talking to men like Sigvat the Poet about Ingigerd. Then Yaroslav asked for Ingigerd in marriage, and Rognvald suggested that her sister Astrid should be betrothed to the Norwegian king without her father's consent being asked. Ingigerd agreed to marry Yaroslav on condition that Jarl Rognvald should go with her into Russia and be allowed to rule in Aldeigjuborg, since she wanted to protect him from her father's vengeance.

Braun argued that interest in affairs at Yaroslav's court and knowledge about the proposed marriage which came to nothing must have been due to Icelanders like Hjalti Skjeggason, who were in Norway with King Olaf when the matter was discussed. Hjalti returned to Iceland in 1019, and after this court poets like Sigvat and Hallfred kept up an interest in Russia because Olaf II fled there with his young son Magnus in 1029. He is said to have been warmly welcomed by Yaroslav and Ingigerd (now presumably meeting for the first time the man whom she had wanted to marry), and they offered to give him the rule of Bulghar on the Volga, while Olaf himself considered journeying to the Holy Land. However, in the end he returned to Norway against their advice; Yaroslav supplied him with horses and provisions and his young son Magnus was left in Ingigerd's care while Olaf returned to fall at Stiklastad.

Two prose versions of the saga of Olaf the Holy, in *Ágrip* and *Flateyjarbók*, include the comment that Ingigerd was unwilling to let Magnus go when men came to fetch him home after his father's death. In the version of the saga in *Morkinskinna* Yaroslav is said to have been provoked into striking his wife when she disparaged his new hall, saying that it was not as fine as that of Olaf. This resembles a story in *Ágrip* and *Fagrskinna*, where Ingigerd insults her father by comparing his gains during the morning's shooting expedition with Olaf's victory over a number of kings in one day; She so angers him that he declares she shall not marry Olaf after

[1] *Heimskringla, Óláfs Saga ins helga*, 89 ff.

all. We can see in such anecdotes the tendency to turn historical events into fiction, so characteristic of Icelandic story-tellers when certain characters come into the tale. Interest in Ingigerd was natural after the excitement stirred by the proposed marriage in 1018, while her generous and determined character may be a genuine tradition based on her reputation in Sweden and Novgorod. The romantic emphasis on her ill-fated love for a man whom she had never met seems, however, to have grown as the story was told, and interest in idealisation of Olaf the Holy gave it additional popularity. In Russian sources we hear nothing of all this. Ingigerd is called Irene, and only her death in 1050 is recorded, together with the fact that she had six sons.

The contests between the brothers in the story of Eymund are presumably based on a sketchy knowledge of affairs in Russia after Yaroslav came to the throne. Svyatopolk's enmity towards him and his attempts to get the whole kingdom from his brother are corroborated by the *Primary Chronicle*. The form in the Icelandic story which the attacks took and the final death of the Prince at the hands of Eymund are likely to be fiction. Whether the tradition of the elaborate schemes to take his life could have been linked in some way to the Russian tradition that he died a madman, believing that he was pursued by invisible assailants, can only be a matter for speculation with our present limited knowledge. The third prince, Vartilaf, might be Bryacheslav, son of Izaslav, of Scandinavian descent on his grandmother's side (p. 150 above), who ruled Polotsk after his father and died in 1044. He fought against Yaroslav in 1021, and is said in the *Primary Chronicle* to have been defeated, but immediately after this comes the attack by Mstislav, who defeated Yaroslav and then agreed to a division of the kingdom as in the Icelandic story. The plot of *Eymund's Tale* could thus have included a combination of these two encounters with rival claimants in Yaroslav's family. No corroboration has been found for Eymund's rule over Polotsk. The wound to Yaroslav's foot, said in the story to have been caused by a wound in one of the battles with his brother, was evidently intended to account for the prince's lameness, which is mentioned in Russian sources but which appears to be a condition going back to childhood.[1]

Another saga which preserves memories of a Scandinavian

[1] *Primary Chronicle*, 1016, 131 and note 129.

prince who visited Yaroslav's court is *Yngvars Saga Víðforla*, which is the only surviving Icelandic saga with a Swedish hero. The saga has come down in a somewhat muddled form, and includes some fantastic adventures, which led its editor to undervalue it when it was first published in Copenhagen in 1912. We have good reason, however, to accept it as based on a genuine tradition of a famous expedition in eastern Russia undertaken by a member of the Swedish royal line in the eleventh century. Braun thought that Ingvar, the hero, was a member of the old royal dynasty at Uppsala which was dispossessed after the conversion, several of whose members made an attempt to regain power.[1] He is said in the saga to have been the grandson of Eirik the Victorious, and Braun thought that he was probably the son of Emund, from information derived from a number of runic inscriptions which refer to his famous journey to the east. There is no doubt that the expedition was an important and costly one, for as many as twenty-six stones in Sweden mention men who perished with Ingvar.[2] No other expedition of this size has been recorded on the memorial stones of the eleventh century in Sweden.

The inscriptions in four cases mention Serkland as the place where the men lost their lives. In the early Viking Age this usually meant the southern area beyond the Caspian, but later it was used loosely for the area occupied by Muslim peoples east of Gardar (p. 60 above). Ingvar's journey was clearly an ill-fated enterprise; twelve of the inscriptions use such phrases as 'was slain', 'fell', 'ended his life', and no one is recorded to have returned or to have died at home. Some are said to be steersmen of the ships which went out with Ingvar. The purpose of the expedition is not clear from the inscriptions, although one from Gripsholm states that: 'They went out far, valiantly, after gold, and gave meat to the eagles in the south, in Serkland.'

The men named on the stones came from one particular area in Sweden, that around Lake Mälar, with three exceptions from north Uppland, Västmanland and north-east Östergotland. Wessen notes that the stones form a separate group with distinctive style and ornament. The date given in the saga for Ingvar's death is 1042, eleven years after the fall of Olaf the Holy, and this agrees

[1] Braun (1910), 99 ff.
[2] Ruprecht, 55 ff.; Wessen, 30 ff.

reasonably well with the estimated dates for the inscriptions. It agrees also with the date given in three series of Icelandic annals,[1] although we do not know whether these were all taken from some earlier source or whether they are the result of learned speculation based on a knowledge of the saga. On the whole Wessen is inclined to accept it as an old and reliable tradition.

As far as can be ascertained from information about the families of the men commemorated on the stones, those taking part are older than might be expected on an ordinary raiding or military expedition. Some inscriptions are incomplete, but out of those which are well preserved no less than eleven are provided by a son or daughter to record a father's death, and nine of the men mentioned are married; only two mention parents and two a mother only. Ruprecht estimated that at least as many as twelve out of the twenty-six were older men. He thought that Ingvar's company may have been one of those seeking service with Yaroslav, but it is possible that the purpose of the expedition was to re-open the old trade route down the Volga, and that therefore a number of experienced men were invited to take part. The saga presents the voyage as one of exploration, and though they were not entering unknown territory, as Wessen points out, there would probably be little exact information available about conditions of travel further down the Volga, while in any case changes in the movements of the nomadic peoples in this area would need to be taken into account. The collapse of the Khazars must have made a considerable difference to conditions in this area.

According to the saga story, Ingvar had won fame in his youth by his successes in winning tribute from the Semigaller in the east Baltic. Olaf of Sweden would not grant him any land of his own, so he left the country when he was twenty and went to Yaroslav's court, where he spent three years studying languages. Then he set out to explore the largest of three rivers in the east of Gardariki, which would presumably be the Volga. He desired to find where it led, and this no one could tell him. He and his four friends and their followers had very strange adventures, winning a silver cauldron from a giant, seeing a shining mound covered with snakes, and meeting a flying dragon; a number of his men were lost on the way. The first winter was spent at the court of a beauti-

[1] *Annales regii, Lagmansannalerna* and *Flateyjarbók*.

ful queen called Silkisif, whom Ingvar instructed in the Christian faith. Then they passed a number of rapids on the river (p. 87 above) and spent a second winter at the court of Heliopolis, ruled by a heathen king who spoke Greek. He told them the river led to the Red Sea, but warned them of various perils which they might encounter on the way. In the next stage of their journey they pulled down the house of a giant, causing his death, and carried his huge foot away with them.[1] Next they encountered a fleet of ships equipped with Greek fire, but Ingvar used fire-arrows which a bishop had blessed and got the better of the encounter, though one of his ships was burnt (p. 277 below). The giant's foot came in useful in their next adventure, since it distracted a dragon so that they could rob his mound. At last they came to the point where the river descended over a cliff into the sea, and here there was a hall haunted by evil spirits, where King Harald of Sweden had perished long ago; Ingvar found the King's standard and took it back with him on the return journey. There was a curse on the hall because of the terrible things which had happened there, and on the way back many men perished; finally Ingvar himself died of sickness. The remainder of the saga, which seems to be a postscript, deals with the adventures of Ingvar's son who went on the same journey and married Silkisif.

Some of the incidents in the saga, such as the account of the rapids and the encounter with Greek fire, are convincing in their details and seem likely to be based on some knowledge of conditions in the eastern region. If the purpose of the expedition was indeed to find a way down to the Caspian Sea for trade purposes, now that there was no longer opposition from the Volga Bulgars or the Khazars to be reckoned with, then an explanation may be found for the strange episode of the haunted hall. It could refer to the terrible defeat on the Lower Volga in the previous century (p. 128 above), when many of the Rus army are said to have perished in the river. The account in the saga is not very clear, but a demon explains to one of Ingvar's men who had entered the hall that Harald, King of the Swedes, had once followed this road before:

'... and he perished in the whirlpool of the Red Sea with his

---

[1] This strange incident might conceivably be based on the acquisition of part of a great statue in the Greek area of south Russia.

company, and now he has come here on guard, and as a proof of my story there is his banner preserved in the hall, and Ingvar can take it with him and send it to Sweden, so that they are not left in ignorance of the fate of their king.'

The various stories of giants, dragons and the like in the saga are characteristic of tales of the eastern region in the legendary sagas; they may also be compared with the tales heard by Ibn Fadlan when he was on his way up the Volga in the early tenth century, travelling to the court of the Bulgar king.[1] Strange stories of wonders and perils must have been brought back from this region, some of which in a distorted form seem to have found their way into the saga literature. The saga-writer in this case probably knew little of the facts of Ingvar's expedition, but filled up his plot with popular tales of this kind. However, as Wessen suggests, he may also have drawn on oral tradition brought to Iceland from Russia. The saga says that only one ship out of the thirty which set out returned to Gardariki, and that Garda-Ketil, Ingvar's friend, carried the news of the Prince's death and the loss of many men back to Sweden; Ketil then took the story back to Iceland. Although this may be the conventional way of inventing authority for a wild story, the number of rune-stones which refer to the expedition show that the tale must have been widely known.

Evidently this last attempt on the part of Swedish adventurers to find a source of wealth in the eastern region by the old methods, which may have had state backing from home, came to nothing. There was another failure in the last part of Yaroslav's reign, when the last Rus raid on Constantinople took place. The date given in the *Primary Chronicle* is 1043, and there is good corroboration from Greek sources in accounts by Cedrenus and Michael Psellus,[2] the latter claiming to have watched the defeat of the invading ships as he sat with the Emperor looking over the Bosphorus. Psellus declares that the barbarian nation of the Rus had always hated the Empire and used any pretext for attack, a not unreasonable claim in view of the series of earlier attacks over the Black Sea. They had accomplished nothing, he declares, in the reign of Basil II, who was a strong ruler, but after his death and

[1] Canard, 108 ff.
[2] Psellus, *Chronographia* (translated Sewter), VI, 91, 199 ff.

that of Romanus III they decided on another attempt. A great fleet was prepared by building many boats, large and small, and this was on the point of sailing when the Emperor, Michael V, was deposed; it was this unpopular Emperor who had refused to make use of the Varangian Guard (p. 221 below) and during whose brief reign Harald of Norway had been in prison. Whether this had anything to do with the renewed enmity of the Rus is not known, but according to Cedrenus they were angered by some event in Constantinople, and he gives as a reason the slaying of a Rus of noble birth during an attack on Rus merchants in the capital. Psellus also emphasises that the Rus had no grievance against Constantine IX, Michael's successor, but rather than waste all their preparations they proceeded with the attack. The fleet arrived in the Bosporus, and the Rus began by giving the Greeks an opportunity to buy them off, but their terms were so excessive as to be out of the question. Psellus gives the amount demanded as a thousand *stater* for every ship, and Cedrenus as three pounds' weight of gold for each sailor, the money to be counted out on one of their own ships. Naval forces in the capital were once more below strength, but the Emperor collected together the few triremes available, together with transport vessels and some old ships refitted, and had them all equipped with tubes for sending out Greek fire. They were then assembled in the harbour, while the Rus were anchored on the opposite shore. In the morning the Rus ships advanced, and ranged themselves in a line across the Bosporus, so that the way was blocked, and they presented a terrifying sight for the Greeks. Psellus himself watched from a hill, and in the afternoon he saw the triremes which the Emperor had sent out against the enemy leaving the harbour. Several of the Rus ships advanced to surround them, and their crews tried to damage them below the water-line with long poles. The Greek vessels were manned with pikemen, stone-throwers and hurlers of Greek fire, and they attacked the Rus vessels until the crews were so helpless before the fire that they threw themselves into the water. More Greek ships advanced, and the Rus began to withdraw; then a sudden storm blew up, and some of the enemy ships sank while others were driven ashore or captured by the triremes and towed to land. Cedrenus records as many as 15,000 corpses washed up on the shores of the Bosporus, and among the damaged vessels was that of the leader, Prince Vladimir, the son of Yaroslav.[1] He was obliged to board another vessel, and he and his bodyguard withdrew northwards towards the Bulgarian coast, and succeeded in attacking some of the triremes which were pursuing them, and even in capturing four of them. The Slav commander, Vyshata, then announced that he was going to take the land route home with his soldiers, which he thought gave them better chance of survival. Near Varna, however, they were attacked by a local force and lost many men, and about 800, including Vyshata himself, were sent to Constantinople and many blinded; Vyshata got back to Kiev three years later. The storm which dispersed the enemy ships must have added to the legend of the good luck of the Emperor Constantine, to which Psellus refers. This is the last attack on the Byzantine capital in the Kievan records.

From this time the campaigns of the Scandinavian leaders in Russia and the companies of mercenaries can no longer be traced in detail, and there are no Norse records to help us to trace the ending of the Varangian story. The emphasis instead shifts to Constantinople itself, where Norsemen in increasing numbers were entering the Emperor's service, and their adventures there left an imprint on Icelandic literature.

This is the end of a stirring chapter, much of which must have been remembered in Swedish tradition but never have reached Iceland. It is clear from sources outside Scandinavia that there was ample material for heroic poetry and saga in the doings of the eastern Vikings, of which only faint and scattered echoes have reached us. Tales of fights and alliances and diplomacy over a wide area in eastern Europe give us further indication of the breadth and variety of contacts which were made in the course of over two hundred years with the nomadic peoples and the Muslims. Because we are considering for the most part the movements of relatively small companies under individual leaders and not large armies equipped for mass movement, the opportunities to gain knowledge of the life of these alien peoples, and to absorb something of their customs and traditions, must have been considerable. The persistence of Scandinavian infiltration into the dangerous regions along the eastern road indicates its rich rewards and possibilities, and the effects cannot be limited to economic gains alone, important

[1] Cedrenus, 759, 553.

though these were. Explorers like Ǫrvar-Odd and Ingvar and the forgotten leaders who took their boats to the Black Sea and the Caspian were followed by many lesser adventurers, some of whom must have spent the better part of their lives in the eastern region, so that the way was kept open for ideas as well as silver coins to travel back to Sweden and Norway. When we add to this the encounter with the wealth and splendour of Byzantium and its store of ancient lore and modern technical knowledge, the picture of the eastern road takes on new richness and diversity.

PART THREE

Norsemen in Byzantium

1. *The Vikings threaten attack*
A crew of seamen waving their swords shown on a memorial stone of the Viking Age from Lärbro, Stora Hammars, Gotland (from cover design for the Catalogue to an Exhibition, The World of the Vikings, organised by the Statens Historiska Museum, Stockholm; copyright: Prof. Hans-Jürgen Spohn, Berlin, 1972).

2 (*overleaf*). *Wall paintings in St Sophia, Kiev.*
a. A mural dated 1113–25 in the tower of the church of St Sophia at Kiev. The Emperor stands in the Imperial Box to the right of the picture, while his suite are in the open gallery, and members of his bodyguard look out through windows in the stone wall below (from V. Lazarev, *Old Roman Murals and Mosaics*, London, 1966; copyright: Phaidon Press).

b. Part of an elaborate group painting of Yaroslav and his family in the church of St Sophia at Kiev. The prince and his eldest son and Irene and her eldest daughter were shown on either side of the seated figure of Christ on the west wall of the central nave; the four younger sons were on the north wall and the group shown here on the south wall. Three daughters, Elizabeth, Anna and Anastasia, married kings, and since they wear no crowns here they were presumably painted in 1045. It is not known which of these figures represents Elizabeth, the wife of Harald Hardradi (from V. Lazarev, *Old Roman Murals and Mosaics*, London, 1966; copyright: Phaidon Press).

3. *The Rider and the Woman on stones from Gotland and Thrace*
a. A memorial stone from Halle Broa, Gotland, of Viking Age date (from Lindqvist, *Gotlands Bildsteine*; copyright: Kungls. Vitterhets Historie och Antikvitets Akademien, Stockholm).
b. Votive stone to Heros Manimazos, from Tomis, Romania. (Copyright: Institute of Archaeology. Academy R.S.R. Bucharest.)

4. *The Rider to the Other World.*
a. Top panel of memorial stone from Alskog, Gotland, of Viking Age date. showing a rider on the eight-legged horse of Odin received by a woman with a cup. The rounded shape on the left is thought to represent the hall of the dead. (Copyright: A.T.A. Sweden.)

b. A stone from Ziatna Panega, Bulgaria, dated to the 2nd.–3rd. century A.D. showing the Hero God or Thracian Rider. (Copyright: National Archaeological Museum, Sofia.)

CHAPTER 1

The Varangian Guard

Much of the history of the Vikings in the East is concerned with their attacks on the Byzantine capital of Constantinople. However, their relations with the Empire were by no means entirely hostile, and the tradition of service in the Byzantine forces in the tenth, eleventh and twelfth centuries must now be considered in its turn. The history of Scandinavians serving in Constantinople and on various campaigns abroad has been carefully traced by Sigfus Blöndal in his valuable study, *Væringjasaga*, a work all too little known because it was published in Icelandic. His indefatigable researches into Norse and Greek sources reveal the wide experiences open to those who entered the Emperor's service, especially to those in the Varangian Guard in close contact with the imperial family and with the rise and fall of dynasties in the heart of the Empire. It has been claimed that the work needs extensive revision, because of Blöndal's tendency to assume that Icelanders were present on many occasions when the evidence is doubtful.[1] However, his full and careful documentation and ability to draw from a wide range of sources render it a formidable achievement, something which needs to be taken into account by any serious student of the history of the Varangians.

The tradition of reliance on barbarian troops from outside the Empire was as old as the city itself, for Constantine showed great honour to the Cornuti for the part which they played in the Battle of the Milvian Bridge in AD 312. Not only are these Germanic warriors depicted clearly on the Arch of Constantine standing close to the Emperor, but the emblem of curving horns ending in animal heads worn on their helmets was incorporated into the Roman army, together with the Germanic battle-cry, the

[1] Benedikz, 24.

barditus.[1] Crack regiments were formed from the most valuable barbarian recruits, like the Bucellari and the Foederati. From the earliest history of Constantinople there were certain picked companies whose duty was to guard the city and palace, and the person of the Emperor; these formed part of the *Tagmata*, the section of the army stationed in and around the capital.[2] The companies known as the Schools (Candidati), the Excubitors and the Arithmos were included in this from very early days, and the Hikanatoi were added as a fourth cavalry company by Nicephorus I in the early ninth century. There were also two infantry companies, the Numeri and the Optimati, who guarded the walls. Other special companies were created from time to time, especially in the eleventh century.

Of these the most important was the Schools, a cavalry troop of young Greeks living in the capital, who could go home when not on duty. They wore white trappings over their armour, and played a major part in public ceremonies in which the Emperor was involved. The Excubitors carried out police duties and made arrests; they had a garrison in the capital and others in various towns in Asia Minor, and used to accompany the Emperor on his campaigns. The Arithmos were responsible for guarding the palaces at night. It was possible for Scandinavians to find a place in such regiments once contact with the capital was established in the ninth century, for it was about this time that the guard was enlarged and mercenary troops admitted into it in large numbers. The presence of the Rus in the imperial forces is recognised as early as 911 in the treaty drawn up at this time (p. 92 above). Vikings might serve along with Germans, Hungarians, Goths, Lombards, Normans and Pechinegs, and there were also two separate contingents of Turks from Central Asia known as the Pharangians, and a company of Khazars. There seems little doubt that from the tenth century onwards the development and use of the Tagmata became increasingly flexible, and it was no longer wholly restricted to the capital.

The Imperial Bodyguard proper was known as the Hetaireia, divided into two sections, the Great and the Little Hetaireia; there

[1] Alföldi, 173 ff.
[2] Bury (1911), 47; (1912) 227 ff.; Ennslin, 40 ff. For the separate companies see Guilland (1967), and for a detailed summary see Glykatzi-Ahrweiler, 24 ff.

The Varangian Guard

seems for a time to have been a third 'Middle' division as well. The intention behind the division may have been to keep Christians and non-Christians, or men from very different backgrounds, apart.[1] The Captain of the Guard was the Grand Hetairearch, an office probably created by Michael III in the mid-ninth century. It was a position of great responsibility, since among the Captain's duties was that of preserving the Emperor from treachery, which was no easy task in plot-ridden Byzantium. He was usually a member of some aristocratic Greek family, possibly a kinsman of the Emperor.

No separate band of Varangians seems to have been formed until 988, when Basil II received a large contingent of 'Scythians' at the time of Vladimir's baptism. There appear to have been earlier attempts to persuade Olga to send mercenaries to the capital (p. 253 below). The force sent in 988 was to support the Emperor and his brother against the rebellion of Bardas Phocas, according to Yahya of Antioch, a reliable source.[2] This was part of the agreement by which Vladimir received the Emperor's sister Anna in marriage, and his capture of Cherson may have helped to ensure that the Byzantines kept their part of it (p. 152 above). According to Greek sources, as many as 6,000 men were sent to assist the Emperor,[3] and Psellus tells of their arrival from the Taurus (Russia), and of the effective use made of them:[4]

'These men, fine fighters, he [Basil] had trained in a separate corps, combined with them another mercenary force divided by companies, and sent them out to fight the rebels. They came upon them unexpectedly when they were off their guard, seated at table and drinking, and after they had destroyed not a few of them, they scattered the rest in all directions.'

This encounter formed part of the Battle of Chrysopolis, fought in the summer of 988, and the use of picked foreign soldiers in this way was a counter-offensive against Phocas, who had been using young Iberians:[5] 'the finest fighters . . . in the flower of

[1] Blöndal (1954), 57. [2] Minns, 536–7.
[3] References are listed by F. Dölger, *Regesten der Kaiserurkunden des oströmischen Reiches* (Munich 1924), I, 771, 99.
[4] Psellus I, 12, 34–5 (Sewter's translation).
[5] Ibid. I, 16, 36.

their youth, tall men and men of equal height as though they had been measured with a ruler.'

It is clear that Vladimir's adoption of Christianity marked a turning-point in the history of the eastern Vikings; there must now have been many bands under Scandinavian leaders eager to seek wealth and fame in some new field now that the great armies of Svyatoslav had been defeated and disbanded. It was often difficult for them to obtain their pay from the princes of Gardar (p. 149 above), and no doubt the marvels of life in Byzantium and the opportunities for fighting there with good pay had been much talked of since Olga's visit to the capital in 958. The emperor was always ready to recruit reliable companies of fighting men, and Basil II was a fine warrior leader, likely to appeal to the Varangians. Evidently it was part of this 'Scythian' force from Russia which he used in his own bodyguard, since, as Psellus puts it, he was 'well aware of disloyalty among the Romans'.

In Greek sources the Varangians are sometimes referred to as Tauro-Scythians (although this term may have been used fairly loosely) and sometimes as the 'axe-bearing barbarians', or those who 'dangle their swords from their right shoulders'. Such was the picture which they presented to the Greeks, since their technique was to fell their opponents with their axes, and then despatch them with their swords.[1] Every Emperor could, however, arrange his bodyguard as he himself wished, and the unpopular Michael V (1041-2) according to Psellus preferred to make use of young Scythian eunuchs whom he had bought as slaves and who were probably Slavs or Pechinegs.[2] On the other hand it is clear that he did not disband the existing Guard.

The Varangians continued as a mainly Scandinavian company until the second half of the eleventh century, when after the Norman Conquest English as well as Danish nobles who decided to leave England were absorbed into it. Our evidence for this change is rather vague, and Blöndal thought that it had been exaggerated, and that Scandinavians remained in the majority until 1204, when after the sacking of the city by the Crusaders the guard virtually ceased to exist.[3] Anna Comnena writes of 'barbarians from Thule'

[1] Buckler, 367.   [2] Psellus V, 15.
[3] Blöndal (1954), 366; (1939/2), 145 ff.; Dawkins (1947), 39 ff.; C. Fell, 'The Icelandic Saga of Edward the Confessor', *Anglo-Saxon England*, 3 (1947), 179 ff.

in the late eleventh century, but this might refer to Scandinavia or north Russia as well as to England. According to Saxo, Danes were in the forefront in the early twelfth century (p. 257 below) and the Emperor appears to have gained new recruits from Scandinavia from those who came as pilgrims under the leadership of Sigurd of Norway and Rognvald of Orkney. There seems no doubt that through the eleventh and twelfth centuries the duty of guarding the Emperor's person at home and on campaigns abroad fell chiefly on the Varangians and Vardariots, a body of Christian Turks from Macedonia. The period of the Varangian Guard was comparatively brief, but it was a tradition of which the Icelanders were extremely proud, and its impact on saga literature of the twelfth and thirteenth centuries has caused echoes in romantic fiction of late times, and tends to be exaggerated in popular books on Byzantium.

It was not as easy to get into the Imperial Guard as the sagas tend to imply in such statements as: 'They were well received as soon as it was known that they were Norsemen',[1] although there were probably no obstacles in the way of fighting men who wanted to enter the army or navy. There appears to have been a system for recruiting men from other regiments or from the fleet if they showed outstanding qualities, and some Scandinavians probably served in their own ships and were later promoted to service in the Guard. There was an entrance fee to be paid by a new member,[2] and this was a considerable sum; possibly the treasury helped with loans, since it was known that the money earned in the Guard was good and included rich gifts to the imperial household. The rate of pay is difficult to calculate, because of various unknown factors involved. One pound in gold was equal to seventy-two gold coins, and in the *Book of Ceremonies*[3] there is reference to sixteen pounds being the entrance fee for the Great Hetairia, ten for the Middle Hetairia, and seven for the companies of Pharangians and Khazars, two bodies of foreign guardsmen. The pay seems to have been as much as forty gold coins a year for the Little Hetairia and forty-four for the Greater, so that the original entrance fee would

---

[1] *Grettis Saga*, 86.
[2] For the principle of the *roga*, which complicated the award of offices in the tenth and eleventh centuries, see Lemerle (I owe this reference to Professor Grierson).
[3] *Book of Ceremonies* (ed. Niebuhr, Bonn, 1829), I, 692-3.

be recovered after some years in service.[1] In addition to the salary, there were special gifts like those given at Easter, gifts at the coronation of an Emperor, and a share in the booty taken on campaigns. There is a tradition that Harald of Norway was accused of not giving up the correct amount of booty to the Emperor (p. 222 below), while Snorri has the puzzling statement in *Heimskringla* that after an Emperor's death the Varangians had the right to go through the palace 'where the taxes were hoarded' and take what they could for themselves.[2] He has interpreted the term *pólútasvarf* as 'palace spoils', but he may be in error here, since it appears to come from a Slav word for the collection of tribute (p. 51 above). A good deal of money came in at the accession of a new Emperor, when donations were sent, while landowners had to pay dues for the support of foreign mercenaries, and it is conceivable that Harald was concerned with the collection of this. Snorri believed that he had been in Constantinople for the crowning of three emperors and that this proved most profitable for him. Harald also won an enormous amount of booty on his various campaigns and sent large sums home to Yaroslav, his future father-in-law (p. 227 below). The impression of the good pay received by the Guard made on visitors to the palace is shown by Liutprand's comment in *Antapodosis*:[3] 'The palace at Constantinople is guarded by numerous companies of soldiers in order to secure the Emperor's safety, and every day a considerable sum of money is spent upon these men's pay and rations.'

Scandinavians could hold various offices in the Guard, although the highest ranks were likely to be reserved for members of noble Greek families. Blöndal thought it possible that Nabites, leader of the Guard under Alexius I, could have been a Scandinavian;[4] the name is not Greek, and could conceivably be formed from some Scandinavian nickname such as 'Near-Biter'. A certain Ragnvald from Uppland in Sweden, commemorated on a runic stone, is said to have been leader of the war-troop in the land of the Greeks and may have held some office in the Guard in the eleventh century

---

[1] Bury (1912), 228; he reckoned that the salary represented an annuity of about $2\frac{2}{3}$ to 4 per cent.
[2] *Heimskringla, Haralds Saga Sigurðarsonar*, 16.
[3] Liutprand, *Antapodosis*, I, 12, 42 (Wright's translation).
[4] Blöndal (1939/2), 145 ff.

(p. 238 below). Harald Sigurdson himself officially held the rank of Manglabites and later as a reward for his services in the Bulgarian campaign he was given that of Spatharocandidatus. The duty of the Manglabites was originally to walk before the Emperor in procession, carrying a jewelled whip on a belt, used to restrain the crowd; the man holding such an office was entitled to wear a sword with a gold hilt. The rank of Spatharocandidatus has been compared with that of colonel, although it was not necessarily a military rank. Among the wives of officials who welcomed Olga of Kiev on her visit to the palace, the wives of Spatharocandidati are ranked sixth, and the appointment evidently comes fairly high in the list of fourteen grades of court officials. All were originally associated with important offices, but by the tenth century they had degenerated into mere titles to mark the rank of the recipient.[1] A Byzantine general writing between 1075 and 1078 [2] warned the emperor against promoting foreigners to high offices at court, stating that neither Romanus III nor Basil II had ever promoted a Frank or Varangian to a higher rank than Spatharius. He mentions Harald Sigurdsson as a Northerner who rose to such a rank and was quite contented with it. This implies that in the late eleventh century some Varangians at least may have risen to higher office in the Guard. There were certainly a number of sections in the Guard itself, so that a man might rank as a leader without holding command of the Imperial Guard as a whole. Harald's position on his campaigns was presumably that of the commander of a company of Scandinavians under a Greek general.

The Imperial Guard had its quarters in the Great Palace and seems to have occupied part of the buildings originally reserved for the Schools and Excubitors, but they may have been lodged in different places at different times. The buildings for troops were on the east side in the tenth century, reached through the Brazen House, before proceeding to the Palace of Daphne. When the Varangian Guard was fully established, it probably took over some of the duties of the Excubitors and shared their quarters, which in Icelandic sources are said to be in *Skipt*.[3] There was an Icelandic

---

[1] Ensslin, 19; Ostrogorsky (1968), 367–8.
[2] *Cecaumeni Strategicon* (ed. Vasilievskii and Jernstadt, Petrograd 1896), 246, 97; Ostrogorsky (1968), 317–18.
[3] Guilland (1969), 14 ff.

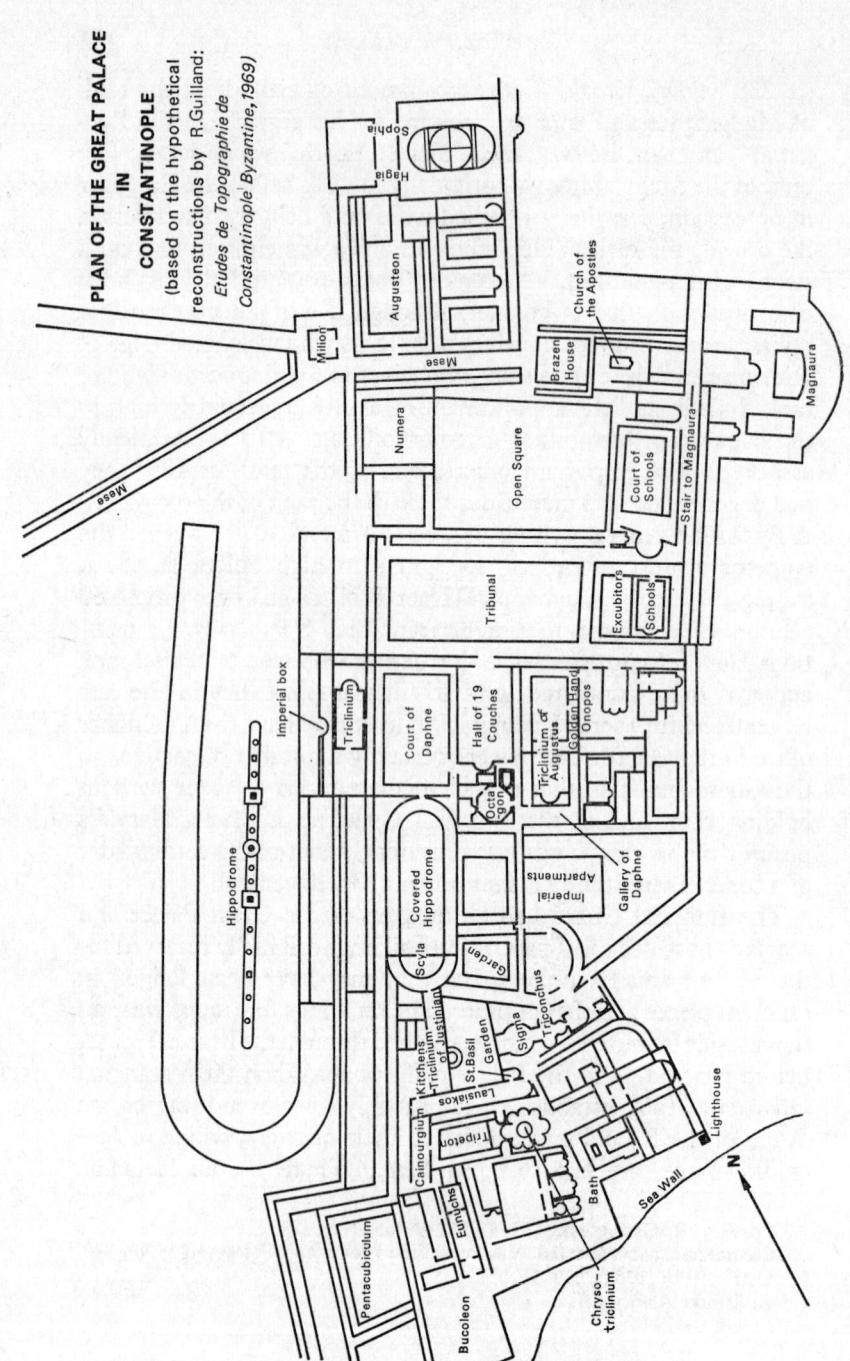

MAP 6

tradition that Harald Sigurdson and his men were lodged on an upper floor:[1]

'In Constantinople there are two suites of rooms in the palace occupied by the Imperial Guard, one above the other... the Greek soldiers and Varangians disagreed about these rooms and the matter was settled by drawing lots; Nordbrikt (Harald) and the Varangians obtained the upper rooms, and from that time it has been the rule that these upper rooms have been occupied by Norsemen.'

At one time they seem to have been lodged in Numera, a building near the Hippodrome used as a prison in the ninth and tenth centuries, where again they were on an upper floor. Michael Glykas was said to have been imprisoned there, and he left a poem referring to the noise made by the Varangians at night, which disturbed him greatly, while he complained that Numera, deep underground, was smoky, evil-smelling and 'worse than Hades'.[2] The buildings occupied by the Guard in the palace are thought to have been arranged round a large courtyard with porticos, the court either open or roofed in to provide more room for those off duty. In a story of Liutprand telling how the Emperor Leo tested his guard, they are said to have been lodged twelve in one room.[3] Carvings of shields on the wall where the palace of the Bucoleon once stood, near the sea wall, led to a theory that the Varangians were quartered there, but the idea that the shields were marked in some cases with Scandinavian bind-runes appears to be a mistaken one.[4]

The Emperors valued the Varangians above all for their loyalty and courage, their fighting qualities and ability to carry out commands efficiently and without question. It is somewhat unrealistic to accuse them of acting as thugs and assassins;[5] in an age of considerable ruthlessness and in the records of Byzantine history in particular, their actions do not stand out as particularly brutal, and a strong Emperor obviously had to have a reliable force of men

[1] *Fornmanna Sǫgur, Haralds Saga Sigurðarsonar*, 6, 147–8.
[2] Guilland (1969), 41.
[3] Liutprand, *Antapodosis*, 1, 12.
[4] Blöndal (1954), 360.
[5] As does Benedikz, 24.

behind him to protect himself from the kind of treatment meted out to the unfortunate Nicephorus by his wife's lover. There is no doubt that the Guard was respected and feared. We have the vivid picture by Anna Comnena of the effect of such tough guardians of the Emperor's person on a man who had been plotting treachery. When John Solomon was found to have been taking part in a plot against Alexius I and he was brought before the Emperor, she describes the scene thus: [1]

'The soldiers who from of old were his appointed bodyguard came to the Emperor's tent first, some wearing swords, others carrying spears or their heavy iron axes on their shoulders, and ranged themselves in the form of a crescent at a certain distance from his throne, embracing him, as it were; they were all under the sway of anger . . .'

When Solomon was threatened with torture if he did not confess, he

'looked fixedly . . . at the barbarians standing in a circle round the Sebastokrator, brandishing their one-edged axes on their shoulders, and forthwith fell to trembling and revealed everything'.

Anna emphasises the loyalty of the Guard and this cannot be put down to mere romantic idealism on her part, since she gives it as a valid reason why her father Alexius, when not yet Emperor and plotting to gain the throne from the aged Nicephorus III, did not venture to attempt to win them over.[2] He was warned that they would not listen to any talk of treachery and that their loyalty was equal to that of the Immortals, the finest regiment in the army, a special company of picked Greeks formed by Michael VII to fight the Turks, and called after the famous warriors of Darius the Persian:

'The Varangians too, who carried axes on their shoulders, regarded their loyalty to the Emperors and their protection of the imperial persons as a pledge and ancestral tradition, handed down from

[1] Anna Comnena (translated Dawes), 9, 231.
[2] Ibid. 2, 64.

father to son, which they keep inviolate, and will certainly not listen to even the slightest word about treachery.'

Alexius went by this advice and turned instead to a company of German troops for support. This was in 1081, when the Guard is thought to have included many recruits from England, but it is interesting to find Anna assuming considerable continuity among its members and a tradition of loyalty passed down from father to son. The loyal Varangian, however, must have found himself in difficulty on many occasions in the troubled history of the capital, when the successful overthrow of an emperor took place, and it must have been hard to see where his duty lay. One example of this was the deposition and blinding of the cruel and foolish young Emperor Michael V in 1042, although as he had chosen his own special bodyguard the Varangians were presumably not pledged to support him (p. 221 below). Another was in 1057, when Michael VI was forced to abdicate in favour of the general Isaac Comnenus, and Varangians fought on both sides; four of them are said to have attacked Isaac at once, but he was a fine swordsman and managed to defend himself from his horse and beat them off (p. 243 below). When Nicephorus II was murdered by John Tzimisces in 969, the conspirators, aided by his faithless wife Theophano, forced their way into his bedroom and there found the Emperor asleep on the floor in his purple robe. By the time the bodyguard came to his defence, it was too late to save him, and in the fierce fighting seventy of them are said to have fallen. This was before the time of the Varangians and the gruesome story may have been in the mind of Basil II when he formed his new company not long afterwards. Revolts and conspiracies were frequent in Byzantium, and in the mid-eleventh century Nicephorus Bryennius (either the father or the grandfather of the husband of Anna Comnena) and his brother John, two popular leaders, tried to win over the guard to revolt against the Emperor, Nicephorus Botaniates, but failed. It seems, according to Attalaleiates, that some Varangians joined them, but the main body refused and sent one of their number to remonstrate with the rebels, whereupon John ordered that his nose should be cut off. Alexius, then a Domestic of the Schools, put down the revolt, and Bryennius was captured and afterwards blinded, although both brothers were later pardoned. Some time afterwards the Varangian who had been mutilated is said to have met John Bryennius and killed him; what his fate was has not been recorded.[1]

Discipline in the Guard had to be preserved and the men are represented as having their own laws and power to impose penalties on those who broke them, unless the Emperor intervened. Cedrenus has a story of one of the Varangians seducing a woman during a stay in Asia Minor, in the area later known as Lydia, where the Guard were on winter quarters in 1034 during a campaign. She killed him with a 'foreign sword', which may have been the man's own weapon, and when this was known the Varangians met together and decided that the woman should inherit the possessions of the dead man, while his body was treated as that of a suicide and thrown out with no burial rites.[2] There are two stories in the Icelandic sagas of vengeance killings by Icelanders of members of the Guard; they may be fiction, but could possibly be based on some incident which happened at Constantinople. The more convincing is that in *Grettis Saga*,[3] the account of the avenging of Grettir the Strong, killed with his younger brother in 1031. The deed was carried out by another brother, Thorstein Asmundarson, known as *drómundr*. This nickname does not seem to be understood by the saga-writer, who says that it means 'slow in movement', but Thorstein must have taken the name from a type of Greek ship known as *drómundr* in Old Norse (p. 264 below), and perhaps was so called because he served in the Greek navy. According to the saga, Thorstein followed Grettir's slayer, Thorbiorn Angle, to Norway, but found he had left for Constantinople and taken a place in the Guard under the Emperor Michael Katalak. Thorstein left his property in Norway and set out in pursuit of the man whom he had never met. He also obtained a place in the Guard, but did not find Thorbiorn until one day there was a 'Weapon-Thing', by which is meant a check on the weapons each men possessed before they left on a campaign. Thorbiorn produced the short sword which he had taken from the dead Grettir, a much prized possession, and it was admired by those standing round, who asked how it had got a nick in the blade.

[1] Blöndal (1939/2) takes this version from Attaleiates and Scylitzes. Another version is that the Varangian attacked Nicephorus and so precipitated the revolt.
[2] Cedrenus II.
[3] *Grettis Saga*, 86.

Thorbiorn then boasted how he had slain the great champion Grettir the Strong and cut off his head. On hearing this, Thorstein asked to see the weapon, and when he had it in his hand he struck at Thorbiorn and cut into his head down to the jaw, so that the man fell dead. At this the palace steward, called *gjaldker*, arrested Thorstein and asked why he had committed such an act of violence at the 'holy Thing'. This phrase is based on Icelandic tradition, but it is a suitable one in the context, since violence in the palace would constitute a breach of the peace as serious as if committed during the Icelandic Thing or Assembly. Thorstein then told his story, and was supported by many persons there:

'... saying that the deed was excusable when a man had come as far from home as Thorstein had done in order to take vengeance. The councillors there admitted that this was reasonable, but as there was no one present who could verify what Thorstein said, their law stipulated that anyone who slew a man was bound to forfeit his life, with no alternative.'

The rest of the tale, telling how a rich woman called Spes fell in love with Thorstein and paid a ransom for him, deceiving her husband with a false oath and later marrying her lover, is a well-known popular tale, possibly suggested by the Tristram story but probably of eastern origin.[1] Whatever its source, the story is clumsily worked into the last part of the saga, and is given a serious ending, since Thorstein and Spes finally separate in order to live holy lives, which has a somewhat incongruous effect. The part of the story where Thorstein is rescued by a woman who hears him singing in his dungeon may have been suggested by the story of Harald the Ruthless, well known in Iceland (p. 223 below). The incident where Thorstein escapes through a trap-door in a room built over the sea so that he is not found with Spes also resembles a tale told of Harald escaping from a room of a similar kind where he had been with the Empress's sister Maria in *Morkinskinna*.[2] However, this does not detract from the interest of the first part of the tale, which seems to show some knowledge of life in the Guard, and which is not in itself improbable.

[1] One version is a Sanskrit one; see Schlauch (1934), 87 ff.
[2] *Morkinskinna*, 12, 79.

The second tale of vengeance is found in *Heiðarvíga Saga*, which survives in an incomplete form.[1] According to the original version, retold from memory by Jón Óláfsson, Gest Thorhallarson killed Viga-Styr in 1007, under considerable provocation, and the dead man's son pursued him to Constantinople. When a wrestling match took place among the men of the Guard, Thorstein wrestled with Gest and then wounded him with a short sword which he had hidden under his cloak, but the wound was not serious. The Varangians separated them and, as in the other tale, the penalty for such an action was death. The ending, however, is a different one, for Gest himself intervenes, offering half of his earnings together with half those of Thorstein as a ransom, and explaining why the latter felt bound to avenge his father. Several men there knew Thorstein's family and supported his plea for mercy, which was finally granted. Gest gave Thorstein some money for his journey home, and he himself stayed in Constantinople and never returned to Iceland. Again the story seems to show some knowledge of conditions in the Guard and mentions both Varangians and Norsemen as taking part in the wrestling.

The Greek historian Attaleiates has a tale of how the Emperor Nicephorus Botaniates (1078–81) and his secretary were once attacked on a staircase by some drunken Varangians.[2] The Emperor defended himself well and was helped by some members of the court until men from a Greek company came to his aid. The ring-leaders were not put to death but sent away to distant garrisons outside the city, and most of the soldiers were pardoned, which says much for the Emperor's generosity. According to Psellus, the Emperor before Nicephorus, Michael VII, also let some members of his bodyguard remain unpunished when they had been intending to injure him, although no details are given.[3] Perhaps they too were drunk; there is no doubt that there was much drinking in the Guard, as we can see from the admonition given to the Danes serving the Emperor by King Eirik of Denmark (p. 258 below). In this connection the story of one of the Varangians' famous exploits has a ring of truth about it. This tale is placed in a number of different contexts in Icelandic sources,

[1] *Heiðarvíga Saga* (*Íslenzk Fornrit* 3, Reykjavik 1938), 11, 243.
[2] Attaleiates, 294–6.
[3] Psellus (Michael VII), 2.

being found in several versions of the kings' sagas;[1] it is confirmed in Greek sources, in the works of the historians Cinnamus and Nicetas. The incident in fact took place in the reign of John II Comnenos, son of Alexius I, near Esk Zagna in Macedonia about 1121, during the final battle against the Pechinegs who had caused so much trouble to the Empire, but in some of the Icelandic accounts it is placed in the reign of King Kirjalax, or Alexius I, and in one case associated with Harald the Ruthless.[2] According to Cinnamos, the Pechinegs defended themselves vigorously against the Byzantine troops, and entrenched themselves with their wives and children behind their wagons covered with ox-hide. The Greeks were unable to break through, and at the moment of crisis the Emperor was forced to call on his 'axe-bearing Britons, a people who of old had been in the service of the Emperor', while according to Nicetas he called upon his Guard, armed with long shields and double-bladed axes, and they won the victory, whereupon the Emperor instituted a festival of thanksgiving, said to be kept up until the writer's own time. In the sagas it is said that troops of Greeks, Franks and Flemings failed to pierce the Pechineg defence, until the Emperor grew angry. His men told him that he ought to make use of his 'wine-bags' (*vinbelja*), by which they meant his Varangians. In *Flateyjarbók* this insulting term is replaced by the more innocuous 'friends', but three versions retain 'wine-bags'.[3] The Emperor retorted that he did not intend to waste his jewels, and then Thorir Helsing, said to be the grandson of the Icelander Ketil *jambi* but not known elsewhere, declared that they would gladly leap into the fire if it would please the Emperor. The Varangians then called on St Olaf for help, promising to build him a church. After this the Pechinegs saw a small company of men approaching, led by a rider on a white horse (a typical Byzantine motif), and they were unable to resist the attack.

Dawkins' illuminating study shows how tangled are the sources dealing with the Varangians in the sagas, but also how, behind the

[1] Dawkins (1937) gives the various prose sources where the tale can be found, but omits the poem *Geisli* (*Skjaldedigtning*, B1, 52 ff.) where it is also included.
[2] *Morkinskinna*, 65–6.
[3] *Óláfs Saga ins helga* (Copenhagen 1825–37), 5, 136; *Saga Óláfs konungs* (Christiania 1853), 242; *Heimskringla, Hákonar Saga Herðibreiðs*, 21, where the story is given along with that of King Olaf's sword, both taken from *Geisli*.

various versions connected with different periods and historical characters, there may be a substratum of historical truth. As he concludes, it shows how 'perfectly true incidents in Greek history could be made use of by the writers of the sagas'. The tradition that a church was built by the Varangians and dedicated to King Olaf, which is linked to this story, appears to be another example of oversimplification and of bringing in a favourite saga motif whenever possible. It would scarcely have been possible for the church to have been built after this battle (p. 205 below), and in any case the church of the Varangians appears to have been dedicated to the Holy Virgin and not to St Olaf, although there may have been relics of the King kept there. Yet the part played by the Varangians at a crucial point in the battle and the existence of a church associated with them in the capital are both corroborated by Greek evidence.

CHAPTER 2

Life in Miklagard

Part of the duty of the Emperor's bodyguard was to accompany him on his round of ceremonials and festivities; thus they visited various palaces and churches, stayed on door duty when important visitors were presented or lined the way along which they passed to the Emperor's presence, and guarded the ruler when he passed through the streets or entered his box in the Hippodrome. Constantinople was the richest city in the Mediterranean world, and its sophistication, luxury and advanced technology must have amazed men arriving from the Scandinavian North or the small settlements of Gardar. Miklagard, the Great Town, as they called it, had perhaps a million inhabitants, although the exact population is difficult to estimate.[1] It was equipped with street lighting, drainage and sanitation, and had hospitals and orphanages, enormous public baths, aqueducts, huge water cisterns, libraries and luxury shops, like the 'House of the Lanterns' where the superb Byzantine silks were sold and which was lit up at night. The city was surrounded by twelve miles of towering walls to defend it from attack, the remains of which are still impressive today. Its great harbours were frequently filled with war-ships, and on a promontory within the palace enclosure was the Pharos or Lighthouse, while a chain of beacons linked the city with Asia Minor across the Bosporus and enabled messages to be sent rapidly to distant parts of the Empire.

Inside the huge fortress, doubly protected by walls and water, was a cluster of splendid buildings, palaces and churches, filled with sacred relics and treasures from many parts of the world. The area of the Great Palace, like the Kremlin in Moscow, formed a city within a city. It held seven palaces, including the residence of

[1] Teall, 105, 134; Miller, 119.

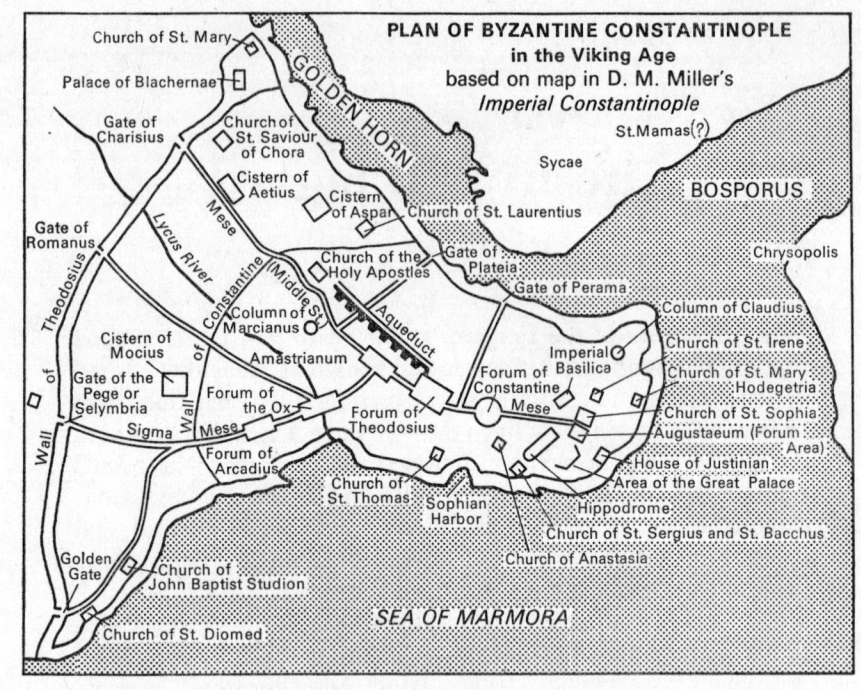

MAP 7

the Emperor and his family, and many halls and official buildings where affairs of state were conducted. These were set in gardens and pleasure-grounds with superb views over the Sea of Marmora and the Golden Horn, and within the walls were the Emperor's private polo-ground, his zoo and aviary. The palace area was entered through bronze gates unlocked at dawn and closed to the public later in the day; Liutprand in the tenth century says they remained locked from nine in the morning until three in the afternoon.[1] Here business was transacted, foreign visitors were entertained and ambassadors received, while for a large part of the day the imperial family could lead their own lives in comfort and privacy. The emperors could, if they chose, spend much of their lives inside the Palace precincts, apart from visits to the Hippodrome and to various churches, and many of the courtiers entered the palace in

[1] Liutprand, *Antapodosis* V, 21, 190. cf. Ebersolt (1917), 14 ff.

the morning and returned to their homes at night; as for the great majority of the citizens, they probably never set foot in the palace at all. The ladies of the court seldom went outside the walls, although the Empress might visit Hagia Sophia and even went to the Hippodrome on state occasions, wearing a kind of military tunic based on that worn by a Roman general.[1] By the eleventh century, however, the emperors preferred to use other palaces outside the enclosure, particularly the Blachernae Palace, near the walls in the north-east sector, which had fine marble courtyards and a great central hall of porphyry. Alexius I and after him Manuel I used the palace a great deal, and it was here that Eirik the Good of Denmark was lodged in 1102 (p. 257 below).

The splendour of the setting in which the emperors functioned was the wonder of the western world. The Trichonchus Palace, built in 738, which the Varangians must have known well, was roofed with gold. In the adjoining hall, Sigma, there were fountains which could flow with wine, and doors of silver and polished bronze. In the state throne-room where foreign visitors were received in the tenth century there were jewelled organs, and the great throne of the Emperor, based on the description of that of Solomon in the Bible; it was guarded by two great lions of gilded bronze, while before it stood a metal tree with many birds in the branches. These were two of the far-famed automata of the imperial court (p. 274 below), and we have a first-hand description of them from Liutprand, who visited Constantinople in 948 on his first diplomatic mission there.[2] He disliked the Byzantines and was to find them even more unpleasant on a later visit; consequently he tried hard to remain unmoved by their magnificent ostentation, but even so his account of what he saw is an impressive one:

'Before the Emperor's seat stood a tree, made of bronze gilded over, whose branches were filled with birds, also made of gilded bronze, which uttered different cries, each according to its varying species. The throne itself was so marvellously fashioned that at one moment it seemed a low structure and at another it rose high into the air. It was of immense size and was guarded by lions, made

[1] Haussig, 188.
[2] Liutprand, *Antapodosis* V, 5, 207–8 (Wright's translation). For the automata, see Brett, 477 ff.

either of bronze or of wood covered over with gold, who beat the ground with their tails and gave a dreadful roar with open mouths and quivering tongues. Leaning on the shoulders of two eunuchs I was brought into the Emperor's presence. At my approach the lions began to roar and the birds to cry out, each according to its kind; but I was neither terrified nor surprised, for I had previously made enquiry about all these things from people who were well acquainted with them. So after I had three times made obeisance to the Emperor with my face upon the ground, I lifted my head, and behold, the man whom just before I had seen sitting on a moderately elevated seat had now changed his raiment and was sitting on the level of the ceiling. How it was done I could not imagine, unless perhaps he was lifted up by some such sort of device as we use for raising the timbers of a wine press.'

In this last supposition the practical Liutprand may have been correct, but it may be noted that he makes no attempt to give any explanation of the metal automata. The Byzantines, benefiting from the considerable advance in technology made in Alexandria, achieved great success in this field. Such magnificent toys were much valued at eastern courts; there is record of another tree with singing birds in the court of the Caliph of Baghdad, and one with jewelled fruits at Samarkand. Liutprand also describes a banquet held in the 'House of Nineteen Couches', where the Emperor and his twelve most privileged guests reclined round a table in a group intended to symbolise the Last Supper of Christ and his disciples, while other guests were arranged at tables of twelve throughout the hall. The dinner service was of gold, and the final course of fruit, served in three huge golden bowls, was swung from gilded ropes above the tables and moved by a device in the ceiling, since the bowls were too heavy to carry. Liutprand witnessed an outstanding acrobatic entertainment at the banquet, when two boys balanced on high poles which a man carried on his head. During the visit of Olga of Kiev in 959, she was received with much ceremony and entertained by the choirs of the two main churches of the city accompanied by organ music, as well as by dramatic performances (p. 251 below). Such splendours and marvels were the daily background of the Varangians, since as members of the bodyguard they were on door duty or attendance on the Emperor at functions of this kind.

They took part also in the ceaseless round of ritual and ceremonial which formed part of the Emperor's duties as the shepherd of his people and representative of Christ in the city 'guarded of God'. They would accompany him to the great racecourse, the famous Hippodrome, used not only for chariot races but also for animal shows, fights, games and boxing, fireworks, and various acrobatic and musical entertainments.[1] Here there were representations of the hunt up to the twelfth century, although fights with wild beasts had been prohibited long before this, while in interludes between races there were entertainments by mimes and clowns, often satirical in character. Popular scandals could be exposed in this way, and indeed the Hippodrome was a place where considerable freedom of speech was permitted and where the Emperor came into direct contact with the common people, who at times showed a good deal of hostility towards their rulers. Usurpers and traitors, even those of high birth, were exposed in the Hippodrome, and deserters placed there to be booed by the populace, while the heads of executed rebels and enemies of the state might be exhibited there. The greatest humiliation possible was to be paraded in women's clothes, facing backwards on an ass, like an unfortunate Patriarch in the eleventh century.[2] Prisoners of war and booty were also displayed in the Hippodrome, and it was there that the leaders of the Bogimil heresy were burned alive, as vividly described by Anna Comnena. The Imperial box could be entered directly from the palace enclosure, and here the Emperor appeared in state robes, carrying the lighted candle which had been used at prayer in his private chapel that morning. When all was ready he blessed the huge audience and dropped a white handkerchief as a signal for the race to begin. The Empress might be present on special occasions, or could watch with her ladies from a private upper apartment somewhere in the palace enclosure.[3] The symbolism of the triumphant Emperor at the Games formed an important part of Byzantine ritual tradition, and it is significant that it was painted on the staircase of St Sophia of Kiev about 1037

---

[1] Guilland (1966), 289 ff.
[2] Schlumberger II, 280–1; cf. Miller, 128 ff.
[3] Vogt II (Commentary), 119 ff.

by a Byzantine artist.[1] Charioteers waiting at the gates, gladiators in animal masks and an artificial hunt are shown, and the Emperor is depicted about to start the race. The Church condemned 'satanic' circus games, and the purpose in showing them here must be a symbolic one (see Plate 2a).

Although varied and elaborate entertainments were staged in the Hippodrome, the main attraction was undoubtedly the races for four-horse chariots, which aroused passionate excitement among the citizens. As Miller points out,[2] the success of the winning charioteer was identified with the victorious Emperor and the luck of the city, so that 'in every crowned athlete the imperial crown was vindicated'. On the low wall or *Spina* which divided the course there were figures of classical gods and heroes, and these seemed to the Scandinavians like characters from their own mythical and heroic past: 'Many kinds of ancient doings were depicted there, Aesir and Volsungs and the sons of Gjuki wrought with much skill in bronze and metal, so that they seemed to be alive, and it appeared to men that they too were present at the games.'

This account comes from *Morkinskinna*,[3] as part of the description of the visit of Sigurd the Crusader to the Emperor Alexius early in the twelfth century (p. 262 below). The Emperor offered his visitor either six pounds in red gold or an entertainment in the Hippodrome, which the King learned would be just as costly a gift. The visitors were much impressed by the elaborate entertainment which accompanied the races: 'It seemed as if men were riding in the air, and there was also Greek fire and some music. There was all kinds of singing also, psaltery, organ, harps and fiddles and every kind of stringed instrument.' When the races took place, the Emperor backed one team and the Empress the other, and the Emperor's won; this was welcomed as a good omen for success in his next campaign.

The races took place between the two great factions in the city, the Blues and the Greens. There had originally been four, but the Reds and Whites had become of little account by the tenth century. These divisions originally represented the four quarters of the city,

[1] A. N. Grabar, *L'Empereur dans l'art byzantin* (Paris 1936), 71 ff.
[2] Miller, 30.
[3] *Morkinskinna*, 164, 350.

and at one time showed signs of developing into powerful political
parties, but their rights were skilfully curtailed until they were
little more than sporting associations or clubs. Some vestiges of
their former importance survived: they still played a part in the
city's defence, provided choirs for rituals in which the Emperor
took part, and acclaimed him at his coronation. Since the Hippodrome was used for political meetings, the races preserved something of the excitement of a political contest as well as of a major
sporting event. There were many high-born men in the factions,
and the charioteers might be from good families; they were
immensely popular, idolised by the people and in high favour with
the Emperor, who on occasion acted as godfather to their children.
There was nothing in all Europe to equal the splendours of the
Hippodrome and the wonders of the games, and the Guard would
play an important part in attendance on the Emperor, since the
people might take the opportunity to express their indignation at
some unpopular move by their rulers.

Of great importance also were the processions which formed a
large part of the Emperor's duties. The magnificence of these
comes out in a description by Harun b. Yahya in the tenth century,
who watched the long procession from the palace to Hagia Sophia
at one of the main festivals.[1] The street was spread with mats and
strewn with leaves and branches, and the walls of the buildings
hung with silk. There were large numbers of Greeks in silk robes
of red, white and green, and then a company of 'servants' in sky-
coloured silk, with gilded axes, who were presumably the Guard.
Then came eunuchs, pages and patricians, and finally the Emperor,
preceded by the silentarius, who hushed the crowd. The Emperor
wore his crown and splendid robes, but held a golden box which
contained a handful of earth; his chief minister walked behind
and at every two steps reminded the Emperor to 'Think on
death', whereupon the Emperor opened the box and kissed it,
weeping.

After the victorious campaign the Emperor would enter by the
Golden Gate at the western end of the walls and proceed along the
broad straight road, the Mese or Middle Way, which bisected the

---

[1] Vasiliev (1932/2), 159; Izedin, 55 ff.; Ebersolt (1917), 40 ff. It seems as if the
numbers must have been exaggerated. For a more jaundiced account, see
Liutprand, *Embassy to Constantinople*, IX, 240 ff.

capital and formed a sacred triumphant path to the Milion, the symbolic *omphalos* or central point of the city from which all measurements were taken. Here a gilded column was set under a triumphal arch bearing the figures of Constantine and Helena supporting the Cross, in the midst of the great forum of the Augusteon. The Mese led to the cathedral of Hagia Sophia, into which captured insignia were brought after a victory to be laid on the altar. On 11 May each year there was a great procession to celebrate the founding of the city, while at mid-winter the Emperor and Empress took part in the ceremony of the *procypsis*, adapted from the rites of the pagan sun-god. They appeared on a brightly illuminated balcony along with the princes and nobles, the Emperor in his coronation robes, and were suddenly revealed against the darkness after a parade by the Palace Guard and the singing of the hymn 'Christ is born, He who hath crowned thee, O Emperor'.[1]

By the time the Scandinavians were serving in the Guard the coronation of a new Emperor usually took place in Hagia Sophia,[2] and this was an impressive occasion in which the Varangians took a leading part. A hundred of them followed the new Emperor, carrying their axes, and were followed by a procession of young Greek noblemen. The Guard surrounded the Emperor as he put on the insignia of power, the sword and sceptre, purple mantle and shoes. After the crowning there was a long procession to do homage, and the Varangians, along with other foreigners serving in the Palace Guard, were permitted to express themselves in their own language. On feast days and solemn occasions the servants of the Emperor again did homage, and on the week before Palm Sunday there was a long ceremony which Liutprand in the tenth century was allowed to watch.[3] The recipients advanced in order of precedence, beginning with the Marshal of the Palace, the Commander-in-Chief of the Army, and the Lord High Admiral of the Fleet. Bags of money and cloaks, presumably the coveted lengths of silk, were waiting for them on the long table, and the ceremony occupied the Emperor from six to ten in the morning for three days on end, while lesser officials who received less than a

[1] Haussig, 193.
[2] Ebersolt (1917), 24 ff.
[3] Liutprand, *Antapodosis*, VI, 10, 211. Lemerle, 79, shows some doubt on the figures given by Liutprand.

pound in gold took their gifts from the chief chamberlain during the week following.

The Varangians had their part to play in the elaborate ritual of the Church's year. Before Palm Sunday one of their duties was to strew the floor with boughs of myrtle, laurel and olive, and to strip the Brazen House, on the way from the Palace to Hagia Sophia, of all its treasures in preparation for Holy Week. They would share in the ceremonial at marriages of members of the imperial family, including that of the Emperor himself; this involved the coronation of the new Empress, and such pagan symbolism as the bride's procession to the bath on the third day after the ceremony, when she was accompanied by waiting-women carrying red apples, the symbol of love and fertility.[1] When the Emperor died, his body was laid in state in the Hall of Nineteen Couches, clad in the imperial robe and purple shoes which no one had the right to wear until his successor was crowned. Members of the court came to pay their respects to the dead, and solemn dirges were sung, until the cry came from the Master of Ceremonies: 'Depart O Emperor, for now the King of Kings and Lord of Lords summons you', repeated three times. Members of the bodyguard had the duty of carrying the dead man into the Brazen House and are said in the *Book of Ceremonies* to 'do what was usual', which probably means mounting guard over the Emperor while lesser officials and the people of the city filed past the couch on which he lay.[2] Then came the summons again: 'Depart O Emperor', and the eunuchs bore him out for burial, usually to the Church of the Apostles. Finally the crown was lifted from his head and a purple circlet put in its place before the closing of the coffin.

Besides such special occasions, there were services on most days for the Emperor to attend and some of the Guard accompanied him; they frequently escorted him to the church on foot and then rode back with him to the palace while the singers in the choir followed in carriages.[3] There were many services in the great church of Hagia Sophia, built by Justinian in the amazingly short period of six years and completed by 527. It formed one of the glories of the city, not only on account of its superb proportions

---

[1] Vogt II, 50, 21; Ebersolt (1917), 32.
[2] Vogt II, 69, 84 ff.; Commentary, 96.
[3] Wellesz, 135.

and the beauty of the great dome, but also because of its rich mosaics and numerous holy relics. Procopius wrote of it thus :[1]

'So the church has become a spectacle of marvellous beauty, overwhelming those who see it, but to those who know it only by hearsay altogether incredible. For it soars to a height to match the sky and as if surging up from amongst the other buildings, it stands on high and looks down upon the remainder of the city . . . as from a watchtower. . . . The upper part . . . seems somehow to float in the air without firm basis. . . . The huge spherical dome . . . seems not to rest on solid masonry, but to cover the space with its golden dome(?) suspended from heaven.'

The beauty of the building of Hagia Sophia may still be appreciated, but comparatively few of the mosaics in gold, coloured glass and polished marble which once filled it still remain. The powerful effect of these depended largely on the generous supply of candles and oil lamps in Byzantine churches, as Robert Payne has pointed out in a perceptive essay.[2] Massed banks of candles gave the figures the appearance of constant movement, while the light enhanced their colours and the glint of gold, creating shadows to increase their mysterious beauty. The flickering light had a numbing effect on the beholder, and the rich and apparently animated figures transformed the interior into something which the worshippers could feel was a foretaste of the glories of heaven. Many of the services in Hagia Sophia were held at night and went on till dawn so that the mosaics would shine out against the darkness. The idea of filling the inside of a church with a number of figures leading up to the dominating face of Christ above the altar, while the exterior remained plain, was something new in the conception of a holy place. The Byzantine artists, moreover, were skilful in eliminating the optical accidents of space, and figures which seem long and narrow when photographed on a level were correctly proportioned to fit into the curved surfaces and create an illusion when viewed from below. The church itself was designed as an image of the cosmos, the dome symbolising heaven, the upper section paradise,

[1] Procopius, *Buildings* (Loeb edition VII, 1, 27–8), 12 ff.
[2] D. H. Gary and R. Payne, *The Splendours of Byzantium* (London 1968), 9 ff.

or the Holy Land during the life of Christ, and the lower the terrestrial world.[1]

The period from the late ninth to the late eleventh century, when the Varangians were in Byzantium, was the classical period for mosaic decoration, and the majority of surviving figures are ninth-century work.[2] The effect of the decoration and the services of the Byzantine churches is well expressed in the *Primary Chronicle*, in the section concerned with the conversion of Vladimir, even though this may be a late insertion.[3] It is said that Vladimir, moved by the sermon of a Christian scholar, sent messengers to report on the worship of God among the Volga Bulgars, who had tried to win him over to Islam, and also in the churches of Germany and Constantinople. They reported thus to the Prince on their return:

'When we journeyed among the Bulgars, we beheld how they worship in their temple, called a mosque, while they stand ungirt. The Bulgar bows, sits down, looks hither and thither like one possessed, and there is no happiness among them but instead only sorrow and a dreadful stench. Then we went among the Germans, and saw them performing many ceremonies in their temples; but we beheld no glory there. Then we went to Greece, and the Greeks led us to the edifices where they worship their God, and we knew not whether we were in heaven or on earth. For on earth there is no such splendour or such beauty, and we are at a loss how to describe it. We only know that God dwells there among men, and their service is fairer than the ceremonies of other nations. For we cannot forget that beauty.'

While it is improbable that any simple test of this kind was ever carried out by Vladimir, he must have considered the possibilities of the various faiths open to him, and there is a tradition of an attempt to attract him to the Islamic faith (p. 151 above). The description seems to be inspired more by real love and knowledge of the unearthly beauty of the Byzantine churches than by mere propaganda for Byzantium against Rome. Certainly the influence of Hagia Sophia can be seen in the church of the same name at Kiev,

[1] Demus, 9 ff. [2] Mango (1967), 47 ff.
[3] Cross (1953), 245, notes 92, 93; 987 in the *Primary Chronicle*.

with its eleventh-century mosaics and wall-paintings. It was in direct imitation of the famous Byzantine church, just as the Golden Gate at Kiev was a copy of the celebrated way of entry into Constantinople.

A somewhat startling reminder of the presence of Scandinavians in the church at Hagia Sophia is the discovery of a Norse name cut in runes on the marble screen of the south gallery, first noticed in 1964.[1] It is one of many inscriptions in various languages and alphabets and has been read as the name Halfdan, possibly late eleventh century in date, although some have dated it earlier. There is no means of knowing whether it was carved by one of the Varangians, or by a merchant or pilgrim.

Hagia Sophia and the other churches of the capital, such as St Irene, whose battered remains still stand to the north of the cathedral, the Church of the Apostles, pulled down when the Blue Mosque was built, and St Mary of the Blachernae, in the northeastern sector of the city, were all filled with priceless relics, which the Byzantines valued above gold and silver and would go to any lengths to obtain.[2] It was firmly believed that the safety of the city depended on relics like the robe and girdle of the Virgin, kept in her church at Blachernae, and the famous icon of the Hodegetria, 'Pointer of the Way', which showed the Mother of God with her son on her arm, and was so huge that it took four men to carry it. Other precious relics were fragments of the Cross, the holy lance which pierced Christ, the trumpets of Jericho and the rod of Moses, the 'image of Christ not made with hands', which was imprinted on linen, the crown of thorns, the shroud from Christ's tomb, and the towel used to dry the feet of the disciples before the Last Supper. There were also remains of some of the great figures of the early Church, brought from their graves in other countries, including Luke, Andrew and Timothy, while the head of John the Baptist and the foot of St Paul were preserved in elaborate shrines. There were many relics of later saints, and some bizarre items, including a letter said to have been written by Christ himself. Some of the most valuable relics were brought out in times of acute danger, as during the Rus attack of 860 (p. 121 above), and they were often carried with the Emperor on campaigns abroad. It was

[1] Svärdström, 247 ff; Liestøl (1970), 126.
[2] Ebersolt (1951), 17 ff.

this dazzling array of relics, some of which, although by no means all, were carried off by the greedy Crusaders in 1204, which brought so many pilgrims to Byzantium.

The Varangians had their own special church in the twelfth century. In the sagas it is called the church of St Olaf, but according to Greek sources it was dedicated to the Holy Virgin of the Varangians. In some accounts it is claimed that it was built after John II won the Battle of Stara Zagora against the Pechinegs with Varangian help (p. 191 above). In one version of the saga of Olaf the Holy [1] the church is said to have been in honour of the Mother of God and the Holy Olaf, and it may have had some special association with the cult of the king. It appears to have stood behind the chancel of the church of Hagia Sophia, and it may have been destroyed in the sack of the city in 1204. However, there is a reference under the year 1361 to a small monastery dedicated to the Virgin of the Varangians in the *Acta Patriarchatus Constantinoppolitani*, when it was apparently occupied by a convent of nuns.[2] This church of the Varangians was the place where the sword of St Olaf, recovered after his last battle in 1030, was said to have been placed over the altar in the reign of Alexius I. The account of its discovery is given in the poem *Geisli* by Einar Skulason, which was solemnly recited by the poet in the Cathedral at Trondheim on St Olaf's Day (29 July) in 1153. Eindridi the Younger, who spent some time in the Emperor's service (p. 263 below) and was killed in 1162 in Norway, is said to have brought the story to the North. He declared that he had talked with Varangians who had been in the famous battle against the Pechinegs, and who still spoke the Norse tongue. Although he himself did not witness the sword miracle, he evidently believed it to be true.

This story is included in both *Heimskringla* and *Flateyjarbók*.[3] King Olaf is said to have dropped his sword Hneitir when he fell wounded, and a Swede who had broken his own weapon picked it up and fought with it. He kept it all his life and it afterwards passed to his son and other members of his family, each of whom was told its name and history. One of this man's descendants came to Constantinople with the sword in the time of Alexius I. One

---

[1] *Bergsbók* (*Óláfs Saga ins helga*, edited Johnsen and Helgason), 834.
[2] Blöndal (1954), 224 ff.
[3] *Heimskringla, Hákonar Saga Herðibreiðs*, 20; *Flateyjarbók* II, 377.

summer he was on campaign with other members of the Guard and they were keeping watch in turn over the Emperor's tent. Between watches they slept in their helmets with their shields hanging above them; each man laid his hand on his sword hilt and kept his weapon under his pillow. In spite of this the owner of Hneitir found on three successive nights that his sword was gone when he awoke and that it lay out on the open ground some distance away. At first he thought that his companions had played a trick on him, but when they too were astounded at this happening, he told them the story of the sword. The account reached the ears of the Emperor. He gave the owner of the sword three times its normal worth in gold and placed the weapon over the altar in the church of St Olaf, 'which the Varangians held'.

There is little doubt that to the Norsemen who learned to know the city well, Constantinople must have appeared a place of mysterious and stirring events, and of mystical power which could be evoked in time of need. There was much superstition abroad in the capital, and the statues of an earlier epoch, since sculpture was no longer being produced in the ninth and tenth centuries, were viewed with particular awe. There were many prophecies and legends which linked them to the city's approaching doom, and these were, strangely enough, remembered in the time of its greatest prosperity.[1] The Cross at Milion, the centre of Constantinople, was surrounded by a chain which was kept locked; it was said that as long as this remained intact no enemy could take the capital and that the key was buried under the column. Strange inscriptions in other languages on monuments in the Hippodrome and the Forum were said to foretell the city's destruction by the Rus, while the statue of a rider brought from Antioch and set up in the Bull Forum had scenes carved on it which were said to show this attack taking place. The *Patria*, a tenth-century work concerned with the magic powers of statues, refers also to images in the Hippodrome which would give birth to monsters and devour men.[2] So strong was the belief that there are references to the deliberate mutilation of certain statues by the Emperor, and these, though unlikely to be true, furnish additional evidence for this strange preoccupation with doom hanging over the city, and with the belief in the sinister influence of these monuments.

[1] C. Diehl, *Byzantinische Zeitschrift*, 30 (1929–30), 192–6.   [2] Miller, 159 ff.

CHAPTER 3

A Norwegian Prince in Byzantium

We know the names of many Scandinavians who are said to have served in the Varangian Guard, but the outstanding one is that of Harald Sigurdson, known as the Ruthless (*inn harðradi*), who returned from Constantinople to rule Norway from 1046 to 1066 and has been called the last of the great Viking leaders. The early part of his life has been recorded in a number of Icelandic sagas. One was written by Snorri Sturluson and is part of the *Heimskringla*; another is included in *Morkinskinna*, a defective text of the thirteenth century with much later material interpolated, forming a racy account with many stories which Snorri omitted. The saga of Harald in *Fagrskinna* makes duller reading, but the writer was probably working about 1220 and clearly knew earlier sources and much valuable skaldic verse. The account in *Flateyjarbók* is close to that in *Morkinskinna*.

The information in these sagas and in the poems concerned with Harald's stay in Byzantium is of great value for our knowledge of the employment of Scandinavians there, even though the experiences of a prince must have differed from those of less important mercenaries from the North. It shows also how the adventures of so famous a leader inevitably absorb current tales and traditions, so that the hard core of fact behind the stories is not easy to establish. We are fortunate that Halldor Snorrason was with Harald in Byzantium and appears to have carried many stories back to Iceland (p. 230 below). We have some of Harald's own poems about his exploits, and those of other Icelandic poets who served him in Norway. Snorri includes fifteen quotations from the King's poets in his account of Harald's early adventures, using the work of the King himself and of six of his skalds.[1]

Harald's favourite poet was Thjodolf Arnorsson, who died soon after the King was killed at Stamford Bridge in 1066, and Thjodolf's brother Bolverk also served under him. Another of his poets was Stuf the Blind, grandson of Gudrun, Osvif's daughter, the heroine of *Laxdæla Saga*; an amusing account of his first encounter with the King is given in *Stuf's Tale*.[2] Others were Thorarin Skeggjason, the brother of Markus, poet and Lawspeaker, from whom Snorri's mother was descended, and two other men of whom little is known, Illugi of Bryndale and Valgard of Voll. Snorri Sturluson trusted the information given by these court poets, although he may have occasionally misinterpreted them; he himself shrewdly points out that [3] 'they would not dare to tell the King about his own deeds if all those who listened knew that what they heard was nonsensical and untrue, and he himself was aware of this. That would be mockery rather than praise.'

We have a most valuable account of Harald's career in Byzantium in an anonymous Greek work called *Advice to an Emperor*,[4] the manuscript of which was discovered in the church archives in Moscow in 1881. It forms part of the so-called 'Strategicon' of Cecaumenus, a collection of admonitions and anecdotes apparently written during the reign of Michael VII (1071–8). The author claims to have served with Harald in the Bulgarian campaign, and his description of the Prince, which must have been written after his return to Norway, runs as follows:

'Harald (Aralíes) was the son of an emperor of Varangia, but had a brother, Olaf (Ioulavos), who, after the death of his father, took the ancestral empire and appointed Harald, his brother, to be second with him in the empire. Even though he was young, (Harald) chose to go and do obeisance to the Emperor, Lord Michael the Paphlagonian, of most blessed memory, and to come

---

[1] For Harald's poets, see Turville-Petre (1966).

[2] *Stúfs Þáttr*, *Íslenzk Fornrit* V (Reykjavik 1934), 281 ff.

[3] Prologue to *Heimskringla*, referring specifically to the events of Harald's life.

[4] *Cecaumenus Strategicon*, 266, 97. The translation given here is by Charlotte Roveché, to whom I am most grateful for help with this passage.

and see the Roman establishment. He brought with him troops as well, five hundred valiant men, and entered (the city), and the Emperor received him suitably, and sent him, with his troops, to Sicily; for the Roman army was there, attacking the island. He departed and demonstrated great deeds. When Sicily had been conquered, he returned with his troops to the Emperor, and he gave him the title of *manglavite*. After this, the revolt of Delianos took place in Bulgaria. Harald also went on a campaign with the Emperor, with his own troops, and demonstrated deeds against the enemy worthy of his nobility and valour. When the Emperor had subdued Bulgaria, he returned. I, too, was there exerting myself on behalf of the Emperor, to the best of my ability. When we came to Mesinopolitis, the Emperor, rewarding him for his exertions, gave him the title of *spatharocandidate*. After the end of (the reigns of) the Lord Michael, and of his nephew, the ex-Emperor, in the reign of Monomachus, (Harald) wanted and requested to go away to his land, and was not allowed to, but departure was difficult for him. However, he got away by stealth, and ruled in his land instead of his brother Olaf. He did not grumble because he had been given the title of *manglavite* or *spatharocandidate*, but instead, even when he was ruling, he kept faith and friendship towards the Romans.'

This account shows considerable knowledge of Harald's history. He left Norway at fifteen, when his half-brother Olaf Haraldson (the Holy) was killed at Stiklastad in 1030. According to the poet Thjodolf, Harald was forced to leave the dead Olaf, whom he had supported valiantly, 'in order to save his own head'. This implies flight with the other fugitives, although *Morkinskinna*, perhaps in order to justify Harald's escape, has an elaborate story, shortened in Snorri's account, of how he was borne off the field severely wounded, and taken by Rognvald Brusason of Orkney to a remote farm in a forest to be healed of his injuries. We have a verse by Harald himself describing his flight in more realistic terms:[1]

> 'I creep from wood to wood
> with little honour now;
> yet who knows if I may not
> win far-flung fame hereafter?'

---

[1] *Skjaldedigtning*, B1, 328, 2.

Next summer he was in Russia, as Thjodolf's brother Bolverk tells us:[1]

'Next year, warlike prince,
you were out East, in Gardar.'

Harald seems to have spent three or four years, from 1031 to 1034 or 1035, in the service of Yaroslav, and we are told that he commanded a company defending the Prince's kingdom along with Eilif, son of Rognvald of Orkney. Thjodolf declares that they fought against the East Wends and the Laesi, and forced on them 'the discipline of the company' (*liðmanna rettr*). *Laesi* is a name for the Poles, so that the campaign in which Harald took part probably formed part of that recorded for the year 1031 in the *Primary Chronicle*, under Yaroslav and Mstislav (p. 157 above). Snorri does not tell us why Harald decided to go to Constantinople, but other versions of the saga indicate that it was because of his desire to marry Yaroslav's daughter Ellisif (Elizabeth) who is believed to be one of the four young princesses shown in the wall painting of about 1054 in St Sophia at Kiev (Plate 2b). The figures of their mother Ingigerd and her eldest daughter have disappeared, and it has not proved possible to identify the separate figures, but this portrait of members of Yaroslav's family, painted at about the time of Ellisif's marriage to Harald, is of great interest.[2] At first, however, Harald was presumably told that in spite of royal birth and kinship with King Olaf he must achieve greater things before permission could be given for the marriage. We know also that Harald was both ambitious by nature and greedy for gold, so that the attraction of service with the Emperor is easy to understand. In some of his verses he refers to the rebuff by Ellisif's family: alluding to his achievements in Sicily, he remarks sarcastically that this was no place where a mere layabout would choose to go, and ends with the bitter refrain, repeated in each stanza:

'Yet the bracelet-goddess in Gardar
still stands aloof from me.'

After leaving Russia Harald sailed with his company to Constantinople, probably by way of the Black Sea.[3] Bolverk has a verse

[1] Ibid. B1, 355, 1.
[2] V. Lazanev, *Old Russian Murals and Mosaics* (London 1966), 47 ff.; 236.
[3] *Morkinskinna* says that he went via Rome, but this seems unlikely.

referring to his arrival, when the cold wind drove the black bows of his ships towards land, and the fine vessels were borne on by their sails, till from the prow the Prince beheld the 'metal of Miklagard'.[1] Some editors have interpreted this as iron towers or even ships, but *malmr* is frequently used of gold, and the glittering roofs of the capital must have been an impressive sight as the travellers came up the Bosporus and neared the Golden Horn. Harald reached Constantinople about the time of the death of the Emperor Romanus III (1028–34), who was succeeded by Michael IV, second husband of the Empress Zoe. Michael is referred to in the sagas by what was presumably a popular nickname, *Katalak*. This is found in Greek sources in the form *Parapinakes*, 'clipper of the currency'; Michael came from a family of silversmiths, and the nickname also refers to his policy of devaluing the currency.[2] Under him Harald evidently first served with his ships in the Greek navy, and then fought under the brilliant Greek general Georgios Maniaces. Snorri calls him Gyrgir, but *Fagrskinna* gives his name in both Greek and Norse forms: 'The army of the Greek king was then commanded by George, a kinsman of the queen, whom Northmen called Gyrgir.' There is no evidence for his relationship with the Empress, since Maniaces came from Central Asia. But this idea may have been suggested by the favour shown him by Zoe, and the fact that generals were often members of the imperial family, as was Stephanis, the Admiral of the Fleet at this time. Under Maniaces Harald was evidently in command of his own company of Varangians, for according to Snorri many already in the East had now joined him. He is represented as unwilling to co-operate with his superior; he preferred to act independently, which is in keeping with what we know of his character and later career. All sources except Snorri include the story of Harald keeping his royal birth secret, because it was not usual for a man of such high rank to serve in the forces, and using the name of Nordbrikt. An Icelander called Mar, who also led a detachment in the army, tried to discover Harald's true identity from Halldor, but without success.[3] The secret is said to have come out later, at

[1] *Skjaldedigtning*, B1, 355, 2.
[2] e.g. *Grettis Saga*, 86. Information about the Greek form of the name was given by Charlotte Roueché.
[3] *Morkinskinna*, 59–60.

the time when Michael V became Emperor and Harald fell out of favour.

Harald was renowned for his determination, his clever strategies, his firm discipline and his ability in winning plunder for himself and his men; such characteristics won him the nickname *Harðráði*, which can be translated as 'ruthless' or 'tough dealer'.[1] Snorri gives us a vivid picture of the Prince's appearance and character at the close of his saga:[2]

'Harald the King was a handsome man, of some presence, with fair hair and beard and long moustache. He had one eyebrow higher than the other. His hands and feet were large but well-proportioned, and he was five ells in height. He was grim towards his enemies and severely punished all opposition. . . . King Harald was eager for power and wealth. He was very generous to those of his friends who were dear to him. . . . King Harald never fled from battle, but often when the odds were against him he found some way to avoid a confrontation. All who followed him in battle or on raids said that when he was in a dangerous position he would choose a course of action which everyone afterwards realised was that most likely to succeed.'

Here Harald is said to be exceptionally tall, over seven feet; although possibly when Snorri wrote the Icelandic ell may have been somewhat less than seventy-nine centimetres (eighteen inches).[3] The story of Harald of Wessex offering the Norwegian King 'seven feet of English ground, or more, since he is taller than other men'[4] is well known, and this might account for Snorri's estimate, if he took the 'seven feet' to refer to Harald's height and not to the normal length of a grave. Certainly the King was taller than most men and generously built. In the sagas he is a forceful character, self-willed, courageous, far-seeing, greedy for wealth, attractive to women, and a ruthless enemy. He was said to have been sought after by the Empress Zoe herself, and according to *Morkinskinna* survived unscathed when he returned a rude answer

---

[1] Turville-Petre (1966), 3. The nickname is given in *Fagrskinna*, 106.
[2] *Heimskringla, Haralds Saga Sigurðarsonar*, 99.
[3] *Íslenzk Fornrit*, 28 (Reykjavik 1951), 199.
[4] *Heimskringla, Harald's Saga Sigurðarsonar*, 91.

to her request for a lock of his hair.[1] He is also said to have won the heart of her sister Maria (a fictitious character), whom he carried off when he finally left the city, but put her ashore again with her attendants in order to show the Empress that he could have taken her with him had he so wished. He had a series of quarrels with Maniaces over matters concerned with precedence and loot, and is represented as getting the better of the Greek general on several occasions. When for instance they disputed as to whether Varangians or Greeks should have first choice of camping ground and the right to set off first on a campaign, Harald cheated by a schoolboy trick over the drawing of lots, marking his token with the same sign as his opponent and then throwing the token he had drawn into the sea before anyone caught sight of it. He is also said to have given Maniaces little support in battle, but to have made vigorous efforts when with his own men so that they always took the victory. He was always on the look-out for booty and many young Greeks were anxious to serve with him for this reason. No doubt there is some truth in the picture of rivalries between Varangians and Greeks, and in the delineation of Harald as independent, shrewd and ruthless, but such stories may be accepted as part of a pattern, showing how a man of Harald's type might be expected to behave, rather than a factual record. The Greek account of Harald's career indicates that he acquitted himself well both in Sicily and Bulgaria and received promotion for his services, so that his opposition to Maniaces must have been kept within reasonable bounds.

In addition to stories of Harald's relations with the Empress and Maniaces, Snorri has four accounts of the taking of towns, in some cases where Maniaces had given up hope of success. One was by the strategy of fastening incendiary devices (fir chips, melted wax and brimstone) on to birds, so that they flew back to their nests in the eaves and set the houses alight; a second by digging a tunnel under the walls, so that Harald's party emerged in a hall where the townspeople sat drinking and sent them fleeing in terror; a third by organising sports outside the walls and lulling the suspicions of the besieged; and a fourth by giving out that Harald was dead and getting permission to bring his coffin into a church for the funeral. Clearly, as Snorri himself recognised, Harald attracted many

[1] *Morkinskinna*, 60.

current tales to himself. It is claimed in *Heimskringla* that much has been omitted because the evidence was doubtful:[1]

'Harald was stronger and handier than other men with weapons, as has already been stated. There is however a great deal more about his famous deeds which has not been recorded. This is due partly to our lack of information and also because we do not want to set down in a book tales for which we have no witness. Even though we have heard many matters talked of or mentioned, it seems better that these should be added later rather than for it to be necessary to take them out. Many tales about King Harald are found in the verses which Icelanders recited to him or to his sons, and because of this he remained a good friend to them.'

It may be noted that episodes concerning Zoe, Maniaces and the taking of cities by means of tricks are not referred to in the verses of Harald's poets. Evidently Snorri was critical in selecting material and liked to claim witnesses for what he used, yet he accepts these tales. However, one of the Icelanders accompanying Harald was Halldor Snorrason (p. 230 below), from whom Snorri himself was descended,[2] and some of the tales may have been known in his own family traditions. Halldor was a close friend of Harald, and yet a number of quarrels between him and his prince are recorded in the tales and insulting words attributed to Halldor. When Harald became king, Halldor left his service and returned to Iceland. He evidently brought back stories of Harald's adventures, and we are told that he was famous for his stories [3] and that when he told of his exploits abroad to Berglot, Jarl Hakon's daughter, many people gathered round to listen. There is also a story in *Morkinskinna* [4] of a young Icelander at Harald's court who told stories every evening until his material gave out just before Yule. The King discovered that he had one story left, that of Harald's own adventures in the south, which he was afraid to tell. Harald, however, encouraged him to do so, and then praised the tale, asking where he learned it. The young man replied that he had

[1] *Heimskringla, Haralds Saga Sigurðarsonar*, 36.
[2] For Halldor's genealogy, see *Laxdæla Saga, Íslenzk Fornrit* V (Reykjavik 1934), introduction lxxxv.
[3] *Halldórs Þáttr* I, *Íslenzk Fornrit* V, 252.
[4] *Morkinskinna*, 72–3, 199.

listened to Halldor Snorrason telling it at the Althing each summer, until he learned it by heart. 'Then it is not surprising that your knowledge is good,' was the King's comment. Such stories may be fiction, but they show that Halldor was remembered for his accounts of Harald's adventures. De Vries suggested that some of Snorri's tales may thus not be late additions to the saga, but early traditions which were first related by Halldor himself; this would account for the part played by Halldor in some of them, and particularly for the blunt speeches which he makes on occasion. However, the tales of Harald's military strategies must still be suspect, particularly since some of these are related of other leaders in classical or medieval sources.

One of particular interest is that of the incendiary birds, who have lighted tinder or brimstone fastened to their bodies and fly back to their nests in the eaves to set houses on fire in a besieged town. De Vries thought that this idea might arise from the use of carrier pigeons to take messages, said to have been a practice among the Saracens, and certainly used by the Romans.[1] It may also be noted that the substances Snorri mentions, fir chips, melted wax and brimstone, were used in incendiary mixtures, fastened to arrows or javelins and shot at buildings.[2] We have plenty of information about such devices in Greek and Roman writers, and the subject was of interest to the Byzantine Greeks on account of the use of Greek fire as a weapon (p. 276 below). The story of the birds could well have been popular in Constantinople and among the Byzantine forces, regarded as an amusing fantasy by the more knowledgeable and perhaps taken seriously as an ingenious strategy by Scandinavians and Normans fighting with them. It is significant that the motif appears in a number of early sources in medieval French and Scandinavian literature. Snorri's account of the use of birds is close to that of Saxo, where the hero Hadingus fastens *fungos* (presumably some kind of touchwood which would ignite easily) under the wings of birds and sets fire to Duno in the eastern Baltic.[3] Saxo refers to the same strategy on two other

---

[1] De Vries (1931), 66, footnote. A reference to carrier pigeons is in Malterra, *De Rebus Gestis Rogerii Cimitis et Roberti Guiscardi*, II, 42. There is evidence for their use by the Romans: J. Toynbee, *Animals in Roman Life and Art* (London 1973), 258–9.

[2] Partington, 1 ff.

[3] Saxo I, 24, 30.

occasions, and the king of the town, Handvanus, is once said to have cleared all tame birds out of his town to prevent a repetition of the same trick, which suggests pigeons as a possibility.[1] The device is referred to in an English source, attributed to a Scandinavian leader Gurmundus, the Danish Guthrum who fought in England in the ninth century and was said to have used sparrows to capture Cirencester, so that it was known as Sparrowcester.[2] Guthrum's capture of this town is given in the *Anglo-Saxon Chronicle* under the year 879, and much earlier there is a reference to the same town being taken by the Saxon leader Cerdic; this may be why the sparrow story is told of him also by several medieval writers. The device is also attributed to Princess Olga of Kiev (p. 135 above). It is found similarly in medieval French and Anglo-Norman sources, told of the Norman hero Robert Guiscard who was fighting in south Italy at about the same time as Harald. Wace and Layamon use it in the eleventh century, and thus it could have found its way into Geoffrey of Monmouth and the medieval French romances.[3]

Other tales are told of both Harald and Robert Guiscard. One of these is of the mock funeral, when the coffin, said to contain the dead body of the leader, was carried into a besieged town for a funeral service, and so the troops were able to enter the town and capture it. Another is the use of walnuts for a fire when fuel was lacking, included in Wace's account of Robert's pilgrimage to Jerusalem [4] and told of Harald when he was trying to impress the Greeks by a grand banquet.[5] It is reasonable to suppose that such stories were current in Byzantium in the eleventh century, particularly in areas where Scandinavians and Normans were fighting side by side, as in Sicily in 1040. The fact that men were prepared to take even the unlikely manœuvre of the incendiary birds seriously is shown by its appearance in the Essex Hundred Rolls of 1274, where a threat to burn down London by using cocks in this way is solemnly recorded.[6]

[1] Ibid. II, 41, 49; IV, 120, 147.
[2] H. Cam, 'The Legends of the Incendiary Birds', *English Historical Review*, 31 (1916), 98–101.
[3] De Vries (1931), 66 ff.
[4] Wace, 8257 ff.
[5] *Morkinskinna*, 66.
[6] Cam, op. cit., 101.

The tale of the mock funeral appears twice in Saxo, told of Frodo I capturing Polotsk in Russia and later London.[1] On the first occasion the death of the leader was announced and a mound raised for him, so putting the townspeople off their guard, and on the second his men were permitted to enter the town to choose a new leader after surrendering. The same story is told of Hasting's capture of Luna in Dudo and Wace.[2] It was known in classical times and occurs in the story of the capture of Magnesia by Callicratidas;[3] it is likely to have been current in Byzantium.

Another familiar theme is that of the tunnel under the walls, told of many campaigns in different periods, but since this was a practical device in warfare it is hardly possible to decide whether Harald himself ever employed it. All three tales would fit in with the character of the Scandinavian leader, who was sagacious and brave, and delighted in ingenious methods of outwitting the enemy. A point in support of De Vries's theory that such tales were taken back to Iceland by Halldor Snorrason is that the names of historic people such as George Maniaces and the Greek emperors are included and that one emperor is remembered by his nickname. The tradition that Harald was in Byzantium for the death or dethronement of three emperors could also be correct if he entered the Byzantine forces while Romanus III was alive and witnessed the death of Michael IV and the dethronement of Michael V. The discovery of the Greek account of Harald's career in Byzantium has indeed indicated that there was more historic foundation for the Icelandic traditions than had been thought probable.

One of Snorri's four tales of capturing cities is of a somewhat different kind from the rest. It is recorded by him only, although the incident at the end where Halldor taunts his leader with cowardice is included by *Morkinskinna* in the tale of the mock funeral.[4] This account is more circumstantial than the other three, makes no claim to the marvellous or improbable, and makes use of no hackneyed device; it does not glorify Harald unduly and indeed reminds us of the heavy price which his men often had to pay on his campaigns in search of plunder. According to this story,

[1] Saxo II, 41, 49; 50, 61.
[2] Dudo, 132 ff; Wace, *Roman de Rou*, 643 ff.
[3] Polyaenus, *Stratagemata*, VII, 11, 5.
[4] *Morkinskinna*, 10, 76; *Flateyjarbók*, III, 302.

Harald was unable to capture a rich town, well defended by earthworks, and the townspeople mocked at him from the walls, deliberately unlocking the gates and shouting that the Varangians were no better at fighting than hens. Harald told his men to ignore these insults, since if they rushed at the gates the defenders had weapons ready and could shut them in when they chose and slaughter them inside the walls. He proposed instead that they should mock at the townspeople in turn by organising sports outside, out of the range of arrows, to show how little they cared for the threats of the enemy. The games went on for some days, and the Varangians took part unarmed:

'... We have the names of Icelanders who went out with Harald: Halldor, son of Snorri *Góði* – he brought this tale back to Iceland – and also Ulf, son of Ospak, son of Osvif the Wise. Both were men of great strength, very valiant with weapons, and dear to Harald. They both took part in the games. When these had gone on for some days, the townsmen wanted to show even greater hardihood. They went unarmed up on the walls and let the town gates stand open. Now when the Varangians saw this, they went one day to the games with swords under their cloaks and helmets beneath their hoods. After taking part in the games for a while, they saw that the townsmen were off their guard, and they swiftly seized their weapons and ran towards the gates. At this the townspeople came out against them with their weapons, and there was fighting round the gates. The Varangians had no shields, and could only wrap their capes round their left arms. Some were wounded, some fell, and all were in desperate straits. Harald and his force from the camp came up to the support of his men, but the townsmen had now got up on the walls and shot at them and pelted them with stones. As Harald reached the gate, his standard-bearer fell. He called out: "Halldor, take the standard." Halldor answered him rashly: "Who wants to carry the standard for you, when you have been so slow following us up?" These were words of anger rather than truth, for Harald was the boldest of men in battle.'

The town was finally captured, and Halldor in the fighting received a wound on the face which left him with a permanent scar. In *Morkinskinna* Halldor's taunt comes in the funeral tale, where there is no obvious reason why he should be so bitter against his leader, and his words are even more insulting: 'The Lord can carry the standard for you, you coward!' or in *Hrokkinskinna,* 'Trolls take the standard for you, you coward!' It seems likely that this story was based on an actual incident taken from Halldor's own narrative, part of a family tradition to account for the scar on his face.

The towns which Harald is said to have captured are given no names, neither is their position defined. All the saga accounts are vague concerning Harald's movements, but in one of Thjodolf's poems we are told that he took eighty towns in Serkland before leaving for Sicily.[1] By Snorri's time, the name Serkland could be used for the coast of North Africa, and there is a reference to Africa in his narrative, which may have been suggested by a mention of a 'king of Africa' in one of the poems.[2] The Emperor had given support to an Arab chief, the Emir Akhal Abulaphar, against his brother in Sicily, and the Emir's men were commonly known as 'Africans'. Later on the Caliph of Tunis and Kairwab, Muizz Ibn Badis, sent an army to Sicily under his son. However, the towns referred to are more likely to have been in Asia Minor, which was also known as Serkland, an excellent region for plunder, and there was campaigning there in 1034, in which Harald could have taken part. The number eighty given in the poem seems to be a traditional number for the capture of many cities (p. 140 above).

It could have been during this first period of campaigning that Harald visited Jerusalem, before he left for Sicily in 1038. The poet Stuf says that he went from the land of the Greeks to lay Jerusalem under his power [3] and that the country came into his possession unburned. There is no evidence for any campaign in the Holy Land, and the Caliph was on good terms with the Emperor at this time, but soldiers were sometimes sent to escort Christian pilgrims, and in 1036 there was an agreement with the Caliph that the Emperor should restore the Church of the Holy Sepulchre after it had been burnt.[4] If the Byzantine craftsmen were sent under a special military guard, Harald may have been responsible for this.

---

[1] *Skjaldedigtning,* B1, 339, 2.
[2] Ibid. 340, 3.
[3] Ibid. 373, 2.
[4] Schlumberger III, 204.

He is said on his visit to have given generous gifts at the Holy Shrine and to have bathed in the river Jordan.

It has been suggested more than once that the 'town in the south', mentioned in one of Harald's poems, was Athens, and that he was responsible for capturing it and for the runic inscription on the great marble lion from the Piraeus, now in Venice. Some scholars have even sought for a reference to 'Harald the Tall' in the runes.[1] Unfortunately the runes are now so worn that it is impossible to interpret them, but there is no evidence to associate them with Harald; they appear to be of later date, and indeed the type of ornament used indicates that they were cut by Swedes.[2] Of the various readings made in the past, that of Brate has met with most acceptance.[3] The town captured by Harald in the south could be in Asia Minor or more probably in Sicily.

In 1040 there was a Bulgarian rising, led by an escaped slave who claimed to be Peter Delean, grandson of the former ruler Samuel.[4] Harald took part in this campaign, on the evidence of *Advice to an Emperor* (p. 209 above), although there is no reference to it in the Icelandic sources; however, the title of 'burner of the Bulgars' given to Harald by Thjodolf in a poem [5] was presumably prompted by his activities in this region. There is a reference in Greek sources to a valiant division of the Tagmata, the 'Tagmata of the great-hearted', winning a victory at Thessalonica in 1040,[6] and it has been suggested that this might refer to Harald and his followers, but it is doubtful whether they were there so early. Michael began his campaign in 1041. The slave who began the revolt was replaced by Alousan, son of a former Bulgarian ruler and a man greatly respected, who fled in disguise from Constantinople, had the impostor blinded and took over the leadership. However, when he failed to take Thessalonica in 1040 he gave up the revolt and surrendered to the Emperor, who pardoned him and sent him home, and the unfortunate Bulgarians, now without any leader, were

---

[1] e.g. Peter Levi, *The Times Literary Supplement*, 31 March 1972, 349.

[2] Kendrick, 176 ff.; E. V. Gordon, *An Introduction to Old Norse* (2nd ed., Oxford 1951), 192–3, 264.

[3] E. Brate, 'Pireus-lejonets runinskrift', *Antikvarisk Tidskrift för Sverige*, 20 (3) 1919, 1–48.

[4] Runciman, 234.

[5] *Skjaldedigtning*, B1, 339, 1.

[6] Blöndal (1954), 134–5. For the Tagmata, see p. 178 above.

defeated by the Greeks. Harald must have taken part in this fighting and on his way back to Constantinople he won commendation from the Emperor for the part he had played. Michael Hendy argues convincingly that a rare gold histamenon, struck for Michael IV in Thessalonica, formed part of the reward which Harald received for his services in the Bulgarian campaign.[1] This coin must have reached Lund in Sweden, since its design has been carefully imitated on a Danish silver penny of Svein Estridson, about 1047 in date. The histamenon formed part of a limited issue, and Harald, who must have travelled back through Thessalonica to Constantinople, could have received it there from the Emperor and then contrived to send it out of the country with his other gains, so that it ultimately reached Scandinavia (p. 227 below).

Harald had presumably now been accepted in the Emperor's Guard, and on his return to the city he became part of the Palace Guard, taking a number of his followers with him, and received the rank of Spatharicandidatus. Not long after his return Michael IV, knowing that he had not long to live, abdicated and withdrew into a monastery. Harald was now under a new emperor, Michael V, the nephew of his predecessor, who had been pushed into prominence by his uncles, the brothers of Michael IV. Psellus disliked this young man intensely, describing him as a duplicit character, ruthlessly ambitious and capable of great cruelty, ready to destroy members of his own family or loyal followers if they stood in his way. He began by opposing the eunuch John Orphanotrophus, the outstanding man among his uncles and the power behind the throne in the previous reign, in favour of another uncle, Constantine. He and Constantine found a way to send John into exile, and Michael then took over full control. He chose to make little use of the Varangian Guard, preferring to use eunuchs (p. 180 above), and this no doubt explains why the Guard showed him little loyalty. Psellus claims that even the Tauro-Scythians were unable to restrain their anger at the Emperor's actions,[2] and remarks also that when a rising took place not even the Emperor's mercenaries could be relied on to obey him, while some were openly hostile. Harald's former general, Maniaces, was in prison owing to a regrettable incident when he struck the Lord High Admiral

[1] Hendy, 187 ff. I owe this reference to Charlotte Roveché.
[2] Psellus V, 26, 30.

Stephanus with a whip in fury at learning that he had allowed the Arab fleet to escape. Although Stephanus was the father of the Emperor, Michael decided to release Maniaces, who was an excellent commander, and sent him back to Italy. At about this time Harald himself was thrown into prison, together with Halldor and Ulf, his two right-hand men.

The reason for the imprisonment is not known, but it seems to have been due to some accusation that Harald had wrongfully appropriated wealth belonging to the Emperor. This could have been a trumped-up charge made by his enemies, but at least one quarrel over the taking of plunder is included in the account of Harald's campaigns in *Morkinskinna*,[1] when Harald insisted on retaining what he had won after capturing a city and refused to send the booty back to the capital; it is said that Maniaces reported to the Emperor that Harald wanted all that he took for himself. The precise regulations as to loot taken on campaigns are not clear. According to Snorri, Harald was bound to pay one hundred marks to the Emperor for every ship which he captured and could keep the rest of his gains. Snorri also hints that Harald was accused of misappropriation of money at the death of an Emperor. The poems make no mention of Harald's imprisonment, and Snorri's account is far from clear, since he makes it take place after the rebellion against Michael was over and Zoe's new husband, Constantine, became Emperor, and attributes it to Zoe's anger at an affair between Harald and her sister Maria. It seems, however, that Harald must have been imprisoned during the earlier period, either after the release of Maniaces, or possibly when Michael became Emperor and showed his distrust of the Varangians by making no use of them as a bodyguard. The Rus are said to have had a grudge against some action by Michael V (p. 171 above) and as a result they made their attack on the city in 1043, although by that time Constantine had succeeded Michael; and imprisonment of Harald would have been a possible reason for the expedition.

The account in the sagas is not a realistic one. Harald and his two friends were said to be imprisoned in a cold and unpleasant dungeon near the Chapel of the Varangians, which might suggest Numera (p. 185 above). In the account in *Flateyjarbók*, however, there is a reference to a tower over the prison, which was pointed

[1] *Morkinskinna*, 68 ff; 77.

out to visitors from Scandinavia as the place where Harald had been a captive.[1] In the dungeon was a huge serpent, in some versions a dragon, which Harald killed by stabbing it while Halldor and Ulf held on to its head and tail. This story seems to be widely known, since in *Halldor's Tale* there is reference to a rhyme which an ill-wisher made against Halldor, taunting him with having done no more than sit on a serpent.[2] Saxo also gives an account of the exploit, as it was told to King Valdemar of Denmark, and declares that the King much enjoyed the story and used to retell it himself; he also had in his possession a knife said to be that which Harald used to kill the serpent, now so rusty that it would hardly cut at all.[3] His account makes no reference to Harald's Icelandic companions, but tells how he was accompanied by a faithful slave. The Prince was lowered into the dungeon in his shirt, while the slave was naked, and Harald used his shirt as a weapon by filling it with the bones of dead men lying in the dungeon. He then jumped on the dragon's back and stabbed it in the belly with a knife which he had kept concealed when they removed his possessions, while the slave battered the creature's head with the bag of bones. When the Emperor learned of Harald's exploit, he pardoned him and gave him gold and a ship so that he could leave for home.

It seems likely that this tale was suggested by the familiar motif of a hero or heroine imprisoned in a snake tower, one of which was said to be shown to pilgrims in Westphalia in the twelfth century.[4] Krappe has collected a number of such traditions; it seems probable that they were current in south-eastern Europe and were among the traditions associated with Harald and carried back to the North. There is no doubt that varying versions of the fight between Harald and some creature in the dungeon were widespread and popular; William of Malmesbury for instance knew of one where he did battle with a lion,[5] which he was condemned to fight as a punishment for carrying off a noble lady of the Greeks. Snorri evidently thought that the tradition was not a reliable one, and omits the episode. In his account Harald's release was due to

[1] *Heimskringla, Haralds Saga Sigurðarsonar*, 14; *Flateyjarbók* III, 305.
[2] *Halldórs Þáttr* (*Íslenzk Fornrit* V, Reykjavik 1934) I, 253; cf. *Morkinskinna*, 79.
[3] Saxo XI, 3.
[4] Krappe, 23 ff.
[5] *De Gestis Regum Anglorum* III (Rolls Series II), 318.

the intervention of a woman, after King Olaf had appeared to her in a dream and directed her to go to the prison and let Harald out.[1] It seems possible that his escape may have come about during the rebellion against Michael which is described in Psellus, when a number of buildings were destroyed and the mob for a time took control.[2]

This revolt, which shook Constantinople, took place in April 1042, after Michael and his uncle Constantine foolishly tried to get rid of Zoe by accusing her of poisoning and other crimes. She was sent to the Isle of Princes, where her hair was shaved off and she was forced to become a nun. At the same time the Patriarch was directed to retire to Stenon Monastery, and sent there in the charge of some Varangians, who had orders to kill him. However, he won over the Guard, who had no reason to be faithful to Michael, and returned to the city to ring the church bells and rouse the people. There was a widespread revolt in favour of the Empress Zoe, in which, according to Psellus, women and girls as well as men took part, all demanding her instant return and making violent demonstrations. Many of the Guard joined the rebels, and Constantine had to cut his way through the furious mob in order to reach the palace.

He sent a ship to bring back Zoe, but this was not sufficient to content the mob; they insisted on sending for her sister Theodora, who had long been banished to a nunnery, and on making the two women joint Empresses. On 20 April the palace was attacked from three sides, from the Hippodrome, the Forum, and the place of the ball game. Michael and his uncle Constantine fled to the church in Studion in monks' robes and clung to the altar, while the crowd set fire to the House of the Archives. Blöndal suggests that a verse by the poet Valgard, quoted by Snorri, might refer to this occasion:[3]

> 'The flames, furiously raging
> burst out from the soot;
> smoke columns rose in the air
> above the crumbling buildings.'

The context, however, is unknown, and the description may refer to some exploit in Sicily or Asia Minor. He also attempts to explain

[1] *Heimskringla, Haralds Saga Sigurðarsonar*, 14.
[2] Psellus V, 26 ff; 138 ff.
[3] *Skjaldedigtning*, B1, 360, 2; cf. Blöndal (1939), 120 ff.

a verse (in which Harald is said to have lessened the number of Varangians by causing some men to be hanged) by linking it with the same occasion, on the grounds that some of the Varangians supported the Emperor and others were on the side of the mob, including Harald himself, but this again is uncertain. We know that the Emperor and his uncle were torn from the altar and taken out to be blinded; according to the unanimous tradition of the Icelandic poets, the leader of the party sent to blind him was Harald himself. Thorarin Skeggjason declared that the Prince obtained gold, and 'the enthroned King of the Greeks became stone-blind with terrible hurt',[1] while Thjodolf states that Harald caused both eyes of the King to be taken out: 'He left a grisly mark on the bold King.'[2] Snorri's comment was that if the deed had been done by someone else, the poets would have known of it, since the story of the blinding was brought home by Harald himself and those who accompanied him. Psellus claims to have been present in the church when the mob and the soldiers entered. He states that a 'newly-appointed official' arrived with more soldiers and citizens and announced that by order of Theodora the two men were to be removed; he promised that no harm should be done to them, but they refused to leave, until finally the mob dragged them out. Theodora's supporters feared that Zoe might restore Michael to the throne rather than consent to share power with her sister, but they were unwilling to kill the Emperor outright, and so 'bold, resolute men', according to Psellus, were sent to the church with an executioner, with instructions that the fugitives were to be blinded as soon as they were brought into the street. From the evidence of the Icelandic poets it seems probable that the leader of the 'bold, resolute men' was no other than Harald himself. The Emperor lost his nerve utterly when he learnt his fate, although his uncle showed courage and offered himself as the first victim, asking the men to whom the job had been entrusted to make the crowd stand back. He lay flat on the ground and made no move while his eyes were gouged out, but Michael was overcome with hysterical terror and had to be bound. Once the blinding was over the mob was satisfied, and Michael (and presumably Constantine also) was taken to a monastery to live out the remainder of his life.

[1] *Skjaldedigtning*, B1, 368.
[2] Ibid. B1, 340, 6.

It seems probable that Harald was paid by Theodora's supporters to carry out this unpleasant task. Snorri is wrong in assuming that the Emperor who was blinded was Zoe's fourth husband, Constantine Monomachus, who ruled 1042–5, but this is an understandable error, since no name is given to the man who was blinded by the poets who describe the episode. He took the blinding to be Harald's vengeance for his imprisonment and makes his escape from the city follow immediately. Norse sources agree with the statement in the *Advice to an Emperor* that Harald asked leave to go back to Norway and was refused, and that he succeeded in getting away secretly. Snorri describes how he took his own ship successfully over the chain which closed the exit to the Bosporus, but that the second ship failed to clear it and many of its crew were lost. There is evidence for the use of a chain across the Golden Horn; Leo the Deacon described this as a very heavy chain of iron attached to the tower Centenarion and resting on what seem to have been enormous floats.[1] This barrier was removed during the day and replaced at night, and its use was first recorded against the Arab fleet in 717–18, again in the time of Michael I (820–9) and in 969. It seems that there was also a chain across the Bosporus, but there is some uncertainty as to whether it was there in Harald's time, and Snorri may have been misled here. Stender-Petersen thought the story was fiction, imitated from an anecdote in Frontinus,[2] but many harbours had chains of this kind and there is no doubt that Mohamet II was forced to take his ships over the land at the Golden Horn in 1453 because the chain was then in position. Saxo's account makes no mention of it, but states that the Emperor gave Harald a ship; it may be that he contrived to row secretly up the Bosporus to the Black Sea, avoiding the chain which closed the Horn.[3] If Harald were taking gold back with him, it would be essential to avoid the customs, as its export was forbidden.

After leaving Constantinople Harald returned to Kiev and married Yaroslav's daughter Ellisif, to whom a number of his poems are addressed. He is said to have taken back much wealth, and had sent back considerable amounts of treasure to Yaroslav on

---

[1] Guilland (1969), II, 121 ff.
[2] Stender-Petersen (1934), 98.
[3] *Gesta Danorum* (edited Holder, Strassburg 1886), XI, 3.

earlier occasions. After the marriage he went back to Norway and shared the rule of the country with his cousin Magnus. There is no doubt that Harald's gains from his Byzantine service were considerable. Snorri declares that the amount of gold sent back to Russia was so huge that 'no one in the northern lands had seen its equal in the possession of any one man'.[1] Later in the saga there is an account of how Harald displayed his enormous wealth. He had a number of chests brought in, together with bundles of clothes, weapons and other valuables, and declared that he was ready to share all this with King Magnus:[2]

'Then Harald had a large ox-hide spread out and emptied on to it the gold out of the chests. Scales and weights were brought and the wealth weighed out into two parts, and all who saw it wondered greatly that so much gold could have been brought together into one place in the northern lands. It was however in reality wealth belonging to the King of the Greeks, for all men say that there are buildings there filled with red gold.'

Harald offered Magnus an ingot of gold the size of a man's head, and Magnus responded by giving him all the gold which he himself owned, consisting of one arm-ring. To another man, Thorir of Steig, Harald presented a bowl of maple wood, hooped with gilded silver and with a gilded silver handle, filled with newly-minted silver coins, as well as two rich gold arm-rings and a cloak of purple with white fur inside. A certain Thorgils, son of the Lawspeaker who died in 1201, had, according to Snorri, seen an altar-cloth made from this cloak, while the maple cup had been described to him by Gudrid, granddaughter of Thorir of Steig. These are in fact typical mementos of Byzantium: the new coins could have been part of Harald's legitimate pay, while the gold could well be plunder from the cities of Asia Minor or southern Italy; the cloak was presumably of Byzantine silk, and the description of it as 'brownish-purple' (*brúnn purpuri*) distinguishes it from the special imperial purple which might be worn by the Emperor alone.

The fame of Harald's wealth travelled far. An addition to Adam of Bremen's History even suggests (improbably) that he took it

[1] *Heimskringla, Haralds Saga Sigurðarsonar*, 16.
[2] Ibid. 24.

with him to England on this final expedition, so that the wealth, which weighed so much that 'twelve young men could hardly lift it to their shoulders', fell into the hands of William the Bastard.[1] Philip Grierson has shown good reasons for believing that the surprising number of copies of Byzantine coins produced in Denmark in the eleventh century resulted from the money brought back by Harald;[2] the dates of the coins copied range from the reign of Basil II to Constantine IX, and these are what might be expected if we assume that the originals formed part of Harald's acquired treasure.

We are told in the *Advice to an Emperor* that Harald kept on friendly terms with Byzantium after he became King (p. 209 above) and that as a result Greek priests were sent from Constantinople into Norway. The tradition of what could be Byzantine priests reaching Iceland has been preserved in Icelandic sources; bishops from abroad are said to have arrived in Iceland, offering more lenient doctrines than those in the Icelandic Church, and they were finally banned by Archbishop Adalbert of Hamburg.[3] *Islendingabók* mentions three Armenians (*ermskur*) among them, called Petrus, Abraham and Stephanus, and five others called bishops who accompanied them. In the *Grágás* bishops ignorant of the Latin tongue, either Armenians or Greeks, are forbidden to consecrate churches or confirm children, but Harald evidently defied Adalbert, since he was reproached by Pope Alexander II for having several unconsecrated bishops with him. Thus it seems possible that members of the Byzantine Church visited Scandinavia as a result of Harald's links with Constantinople.

Selma Jónsdóttir deals with this question in her study of the fine Icelandic carving of the Last Judgement, fragments of which survived in a farmhouse in northern Iceland.[4] It is possible, as she points out, that *ermskur* may not necessarily mean Armenian; other suggestions have been that these are men from Ermland (Pomerania) or hermit monks from Italy, where Basilian monks from the Greek Church had set up communities. She herself favours the connection with Italy, because of close resemblances

[1] Adam of Bremen III, 52, Schol., 83.
[2] Grierson (1966), 124 ff.
[3] *Hungrvaka* (*Altnordische Saga Bibliothek* 11, Halle 1905), 2, 92; *Íslendingabók* (*Íslenzk Fornrit* I, Reykjavik 1968), 8, 18; Macler, 239 ff.
[4] Selma Jónsdóttir, 79 ff.

between the motifs and style of the Last Judgement theme in the carving and those associated with Monte Cassino in Italy. The Greek monks, from whatever country they came to Iceland, must have brought with them some painting or ivory of the Last Judgement to use when they preached to the northerners, and the picture was copied by an Icelandic woodcarver of considerable skill and set up in the large hall built at Flatatunga in the eleventh century. The existence of this fine piece of work, although in a fragmentary state now owing to neglect in the last century, is a striking confirmation of continued links between Scandinavia and Byzantium during the period of Harald's rule in Norway.

CHAPTER 4

In the Service of the Emperor

Apart from the towering figure of Harald of Norway, a number of Scandinavians are mentioned in Icelandic prose sources as having served in Byzantium, and a number are said to have won honour in the Guard there. Reference has been made (p. 214 above) to the outspoken Halldor Snorrason, who seems to have had a love-hate relationship with his prince. He was born in the first years of the eleventh century, of distinguished parentage on both sides; his father Snorri Thorgrimsson was the famous Snorri *goði* of the sagas, who married as his third wife Hallfrid, Einar's daughter, and Halldor was the son of this marriage. He is described as a huge man, powerful and handsome, who could remain unperturbed through sudden reversals of fortune, losing neither sleep nor appetite.[1] He talked little, but could on occasion be outspoken, blunt and obstinate, so that he was not a very popular companion. Halldor returned to Iceland about 1051 and played an important part in spreading stories about the King's doings abroad. Ulf Ospaksson, who remained with Harald until he died, also fought with him in Byzantium, and is described along with Halldor in *Heimskringla*. He was a man of good family, a descendant of the famous Ketil Flatnose, the important landowner in Norway who was among the first settlers in Iceland; Ulf was also the brother of Gudrun, the heroine of *Laxdæla Saga*. He is said to have been wise, capable and eloquent, a loyal and honourable follower of the King. When they returned to Norway, Harald gave him the rank of *Stallari* (Marshal), and Ulf married Jorunn, the sister of Harald's second wife Thora. Ulf died shortly before Harald him-

[1] *Heinskringla, Haralds Saga Sigurðarsonar*, 36.

self fell at the Battle of Stamford Bridge in 1066. Only one verse attributed to him survives, which seems to recall early adventures with the King; it was said to have been composed at the end of his life, when he heard people declare that the house-carls of the English King were so brave that one of them could deal with two of Harald's best warriors. Ulf retorted that in that case there would be little point in the King's marshals going aboard his longship, but that 'in my youth it was otherwise'.[1] As he stood beside Ulf's grave, the King lamented him with the words: 'There lies he who of all men was most loyal and true to his lord.'

It could have been the example of his uncle Ulf which led Bolli Bollason, Gudrun's son, to go abroad to Byzantium. His return from Miklagard is described in *Laxdæla Saga* (p. 105 above) and the neighbourhood was said to be much impressed by his magnificence. It is stated here that he was the first Northman known to have served in the Guard and to have won gifts and honours there. The dating of Bolli's stay in the south is not easy to work out. He was born in 1006 or 1007, and married Thordis, daughter of Snorri *goði*, before Snorri's death in 1031.[2] According to *Eyrbyggja Saga* the marriage seems to have taken place in 1024 or 1025, and Bolli went abroad the following year, leaving his little daughter Herdis to be fostered by her grandmother Gudrun. According to *Laxdæla Saga* he returned home while Snorri was still alive, but this leaves him very little time to win a place in the Guard, since he is said to have spent some time in Norway and Denmark before going on to Constantinople. Blöndal suggested that the journey did not take place until after Snorri's death, and that he spent a number of years in Byzantium, returning home a wealthy and sophisticated man.[3] This would fit in with the statement in the *Tale of Snegla-Hall*[4] that he was among the followers of Harald the Ruthless; when the King heard that two of his old followers, Hall and Bolli Bollason, had died in Iceland, he said of Bolli: 'The champion has bowed before the spears.' If Bolli were serving under Harald in the 1130s, a period in which the Prince was amassing

---

[1] Ibid. 79.
[2] *Laxdæla Saga*, 70; for the dating, see *Íslenzk Fornrit*, 5, introduction section 4.
[3] Blöndal (1954), 324 ff.
[4] *Snegla-Halls Þáttr, Flateyjarbók* IX, 295.

much plunder, this would fit in with what is known of his life and would account for the fact that he returned home with a great deal of wealth.

Bolli could hardly have been the first Northerner to serve in the Guard, but there could have been a family tradition that he was the first to go out there direct from Iceland, since most of the early Varangians had been fighting in Russia. We have a few names in the sagas of men said to be in Constantinople before 988, but the evidence for these is not very convincing. In *Hráfnkels Saga* two men are mentioned who would have been in Greece before 950 if the tradition were reliable, but since little trust is now put in this saga as a historical record and there is no confirmation of their existence from elsewhere, this need not be taken very seriously.[1] One is Thorkell Thjostarson, who helped Einar's old father to avenge him, and who is said to have returned to Iceland after six years of service under the Emperor. The second is Eyvind Bjarnarson, the brother of Hrafnkel's opponent Sam, who is said to have been seven years abroad and to have been much favoured by the Emperor. Such statements are probably based on the general assumption that to visit Byzantium was the expected thing for a brave man to do if he wanted to win wealth, the equivalent in the late Viking Age to raiding in the Baltic in earlier times.

Another doubtful claim is made for Finnbogi the Strong.[2] According to his saga, he was sent by Jarl Hakon to Constantinople to collect a debt from a merchant called Bersi who owed the Jarl twelve marks. Finnbogi went by sea, greeted the Emperor in his hall and was offered quarters for the winter. The King admired his strength and asked in what he set his trust, and Finnbogi made the conventional reply of the pagan Viking, saying that he trusted in himself. In the spring the Emperor saw to it that Bersi paid his debt and himself generously added the interest due to the Jarl. He then asked Finnbogi for a demonstration of his strength, and the hero picked up the throne and carried this and the Emperor on his shoulders. This does not strike one as a very realistic account, and since the historical Finnbogi was born about 925 and came into

---

[1] *Hráfnkels Saga*, 4 and 3; Cross (1950), 50 refers to Thorkell as the first Scandinavian to take service in Byzantium, but this is misleading.
[2] *Finnboga Saga*, 19.

contact with the men of Vatsndale[1] he would be an unusually early visitor to Constantinople if it were reliable. However, at least the theme of the recovery of the debt is a practical one and not usually found in stories of visits to Constantinople, so some genuine tradition might lie behind this part of the story; the recovery of debts for those residing in the capital is specifically mentioned in the agreement of 911 (p. 92 above). The Emperor's name is given as John, which would make him John Tzimisces, who reigned from 969 to 976.

Hallfreðar Saga contains a character called Gris Saemingsson, the husband of Kolfinna, who was pursued by the hero Hallfred. Gris is a middle-aged, short-sighted man, but both brave and magnanimous. He is said to have owned a spear which he claimed that the king of Miklagard had given him, and he could remember how the Byzantine ruler had honoured him in his youth, and how 'it seemed a terrible thing to me when I lost my lord'.[2] Gris married Kolfinna about 980, so the Emperor whose death he mourned would have been the same John who died in 976 and was a popular leader, if this tradition were correct.

The brother of the famous Gunnar of Hliderend, in *Njáls Saga*, Kolskegg Hamundarson, is said to have left Iceland for Byzantium when the brothers were outlawed and Gunnar at the last moment refused to honour the agreement and stayed behind. Kolskegg sailed for Norway, declaring that he would never return, since Gunnar was certain to be killed. After a stay in the Danish court, Kolskegg is said to have had a dream of a shining figure who commanded him to journey south and become a Christian, a favourite motif in many saints' lives, and he was baptised and journeyed through Russia to Constantinople: 'the last that was heard of him was that he married there and became a leader in the Varangian company and remained there until he died'.[3] However, although there are several references to Gunnar's family in the sagas and *Landnámabók*, there is no mention of Kolskegg; it had been suggested that his name ('Blackbeard') was a nickname for Gunnar's brother Helgi, but the evidence for Kolskegg's presence in the

[1] Ibid. *Íslenzk Fornrit*, 14 (Reykjavik 1959) introduction, section 6.
[2] *Hallfreðar Saga*, 3; 4; 10.
[3] *Brennu-Njáls Saga*, 81. See also *Íslenzk Fornrit*, 12 (Reykjavik 1954) introduction, section 2.

Varangian Guard must be regarded as doubtful. Gunnar was born about 945, so if Kolskegg existed he could have served in the campaigns of Basil II.

The slayer of Víga-Styr, Thorgest or Gest Thorhallarson, is said to have reached Constantinople after the slaying, about 1007, and he could have been there in the reign of the same Emperor (976–1025). The attempt to kill him made by Víga-Styr's son has been referred to earlier (p. 190 above). The hero of the saga in which this story episode, Bardi Gudmundarson, is also said to have ended his days in Byzantium, after a divorce from his wife, and to have served in the Guard: [1] 'All Northmen there set great store on him, and he was most popular among them. He defended the King's realm valiantly whenever there was need of fighting for three years.' He is said to have fallen when the Guard were manning the galleys during an attack by an invading force about 1025.

Thorstein *drómundr*, the brother of Grettir the Strong, was also said to have travelled to Constantinople for an act of vengeance (p. 188 above). It is possible to judge from his nickname that he served in the fleet, and he would have been there about the same time as Harald, since Grettir's death was in 1031. The saga says that he killed Thorbiorn in the reign of Michael Katalak, that is Michael IV, who began his reign in 1034.[2]

Morkinskinna mentions Mar Hunrodsson as leader of a company of Varangians in Sicily at the time when Harald joined the Guard (p. 211 above). Mar's son, Haflidi, was a famous Icelander who died about 1130, so that it is just possible that Mar was in contact with Harald if his son lived to be a very old man. Munch believed that Haflidi married the niece of Halldor Snorrason.[3] Another man mentioned in *Morkinskinna* and in *Ljósvetninga Saga* [4] is Thormod, son of either Eindridi or Asgeir, who escaped from Norway after killing Hall Otryggsson, a member of King Harald's bodyguard, about 1061; he would have lost his life had not Harald's son Magnus helped him to get away. According to a

[1] *Heiðarvíga Saga*, 41.
[2] *Grettis Saga*, 86.
[3] P. A. Munch, *Samlede Afhandlinger* (edited G. Storm, Christiania 1873) I, 509.
[4] *Morkinskinna*, 92, 233–4; *Ljósvetninga Saga*, 20; *Íslenzk Fornrit*, 10, Reykjavík 1940, introduction xxxiv.

story in *Flateyjarbók*, he impressed the Emperor with his strength, since although he was a small man he was able to lift a bull.

Beside the Icelanders named in the sagas, there is a distinguished Dane who may have fought under Basil II in the early eleventh century, Eilif Thorgilson Sprakalegg, whose brother Ulf married the daughter of Svein Estridson of Denmark and was thus connected with the royal line. Eilif took part in the invasion of England in 1009, and was one of the earls appointed by Knut to govern the country; his name appears on a number of English charters between 1018 and 1024.[1] Blöndal thinks that the tradition in *Jómsvíkinga Saga* that he died fighting for the Emperor may be trustworthy,[2] but if he ended his life as a member of the Guard, he must have left England after 1024; he would have presumably have taken a number of his followers with him, and there is mention of a large Danish contingent which had been established for a long time in the Guard in the account of Eirik of Denmark's visit in the twelfth century (p. 257 below).

In the twelfth century the Norwegian Thorir Helsing is mentioned as a leader in the Guard in the story of the attack on the Pechinegs (p. 191 above) and in the poem *Geisli* it is stated that 450 Norsemen were concerned in this attack, although the leader is not named.[3] Eindridi the Younger, who brought home the story of St Olaf's sword (p. 205 above), is said in *Orkneyinga Saga*[4] to have spent a long time in the Emperor's service before visiting Orkney in 1148 and persuading Jarl Rognvald to make his pilgrimage to the Holy Land (p. 263 below). He parted company with the other travellers during the voyage, and when they reached Constantinople they found him in high favour with the Emperor; this is said to have been in the reign of Menelias, Manuel I, who reigned 1143–1180. Eindridi came home to be killed by his old enemy Jarl Erling Crickneck,[5] and the account of his doings is thought to come from a lost saga of Jarl Erling;[6] he is represented as an important man in Norway, but his family is unknown.

---

[1] F. M. Stenton, *Anglo-Saxon England* (1947). 410.
[2] Blöndal (1954), 319–20; cf. *Flateyjarbók* I, 165, 205; *Fornmanna Sgǫur* VII, 34.
[3] *Skjaldedigtning* B1, 441, 55.
[4] *Orkneyinga Saga*, 85.
[5] *Heimskringla, Magnúss Saga Erlingssonar*, 14.
[6] Taylor, 82 ff.

Blöndal has some additional names on his list of men said to have visited Byzantium; some of these were pilgrims and will be mentioned later; others seem to be mere inventions, like a man called Eldjarn who made up an insulting verse in *Morkinskinna*[1] or another called Erlend whose wife was cured through Harald Sigurdsson of an illness caused by a demon.[2] There is little reliable evidence for any known Icelanders in the Guard before Harald's time, and most of those whose backgrounds can be traced were there in the second quarter of the eleventh century at the earliest. Emperors mentioned in the sagas are John Tzimisces, Michael IV and V, Constantine Monomachus, Alexius I and Manuel I.

It must be remembered also that when the sagas refer to a man serving the Emperor, it does not follow that he was a member of the Varangian Guard; even if the tradition is a reliable one, he may have taken part in one of the many campaigns led by Emperors abroad, on land or on the sea. Relatively few Icelanders are likely to have found places in the Guard; there would be more Norwegians and still more Swedes among its members, and evidently a number of Danes, some of whom may have come from England in the eleventh century. Evidence of a different kind is provided by the memorial stones from Sweden recording the deaths of men abroad or of those who returned from a journey to die at home. Wessen and Ruprecht have done important work on these runic inscriptions, showing that memorial stones were evidently erected as an established custom in certain areas from which many men went abroad, raised as evidence of death either by the next of kin or by comrades who returned from a trading or military expedition. A number of the men commemorated may be presumed to be young, since the stones were erected by their parents and there is no mention of wives or children. In Uppland and Södermanland a large number of stones mention journeys to Russia or the land of the Greeks, and forty-two stones from Uppland record a journey eastwards as against eleven westwards (fifteen could belong to either category). There are smaller numbers from Västergotland, Östergotland and Smaland, and a few from Denmark. Fifteen stones from Uppland record the journey of Ingvar and his company into southern Russia (p. 167 above). It has been estimated that the

[1] *Morkinskinna*, 148, 325.
[2] Ibid. 60–2.

number of married men increases in the northern provinces, rising to forty-five per cent in Västergotland and sixty-four per cent in Uppland. The old terms *þegn* and *dreng*, familiar in heroic poetry, still appear, and it seems likely that *þegn* was used to refer to a married man who possessed land, while *dreng* was a bachelor who had not yet settled down and was attached to a warrior leader who led expeditions abroad.[1] The men mentioned on the stones evidently belonged to a farmer-warrior class. When the word *svein* is used it seems to denote one of lower rank, possibly a servant; on the other hand 'housekarl' is a term of honour.[2]

There is a heroic ring about several of the more elaborate inscriptions, and some fall into metrical form, and might be quotations from funeral poems recording the achievements of the dead. A stone at Turinge Church, Öknebo, Södermanland,[3] is in memory of a certain Thorstein and his sons and includes lines of verse:

'To the best in the land
the brothers belonged,
holding well the housekarls
in the warrior host.
Fighting he fell
East in Gardariki,
loved leader of the war-band,
among the land's best.'

Another from Djulefors [4] declares that Olaf, the man commemorated by his kinsman,

'ploughed east with his prow
and lies dead among the Langobards.'

Olaf could have been one of the many who died fighting in Italy in the mid-eleventh century. Askil from Bogsta, Södermanland, is said to have fallen 'on the east way', where he fought till 'the leader of the folk was forced to fall'.[5] Such epitaphs imply the existence of heroic narrative poems in the alliterative style rather than complex skaldic verse, and its use in Sweden in the eleventh

[1] Ruprecht, 62 ff.
[2] Ibid. 67.
[3] Ibid. 79 (140-1).
[4] Ibid. 88 (143).
[5] Ibid. 71 (139).

century is consistent with the continuation of heroic traditions among those who went east which has already been noted.

A number of the stones record deaths 'in the East' without details of where the men fell, so that they might have died either in Russia or Byzantium.[1] One mentions a man who found death 'in the south'.[2] Two brothers from Västergotland, Asbiorn and Joli, are called most able champions, and they are said to have found death in the East 'with the warrior company'.[3] They could have been members of the Varangian Guard, but could also have been fighting as mercenaries in Russia. One man called Ragnvald, who himself had the runes carved on a stone from Kyrkstigan in Uppland, is described as having been leader of the war-troop in the land of the Greeks,[4] and this suggests that he held a post in the Guard. The word for troop is lið, and a man called Lið-Bofi from Östergötland was presumably a member of some fighting band, although we do not know where he died.[5] Two men are said to have reached the land of the Greeks and to have shared out gold; one was Olaf of Råby, Södermanland, whose stone was probably erected before 1051,[6] and the other Hedin from Grinday in the same region.[7]

References to men who died among the Greeks come from Västergotland,[8] Smaland,[9] Östergötland (two),[10] Södermanland (three)[11] and as many as twelve from Uppland.[12] We have no means of knowing whether they were fighting men, traders or pilgrims.

Most of the inscribed stones belong to the eleventh century, and those which can be dated more exactly appear to belong to the middle of the century or a little later. A few come from the first half of the century, including one from Östergötland which might

[1] Ibid. 28 (N. Jutland); 63 (Östergötland); 94 and 96 (Södermanland); 119, 153, 154, and 167 (Uppland).
[2] Ibid. 127 (150).
[3] Ibid. 39 (132).
[4] Ibid. 174 (159).
[5] Ibid. p. 77.
[6] Ibid. 90 (143).
[7] Ibid. 81 (141).
[8] Ibid. 34 (131).
[9] Ibid. 51 (135).
[10] Ibid. 58 (136); 60 (137); the first doubtful.
[11] Ibid. 70 (139); 99 (145); 110 (147); the last doubtful.
[12] Ibid. 111 (147); 116 (148); 118 (149); 133 (151); 134 (152); 138, 140, 142 (153); 151, 152 (155); 157, 159 (156).

be as early as 1010 [1] and which is erected in memory of five sons, one of whom died among the Greeks, while there are a few from the last years of the century.[2] Thus the inscriptions may be said to belong to the period in which interest in Byzantium is shown in the Icelandic sagas, a period when there was ample opportunity to win riches and renown in the Byzantine forces. Before the time of Basil I (976–1025) Norsemen would be more likely to be fighting against the Empire than in its defence, although John Tzimisces, the leader who defeated Svyatoslav in the Bulgarian campaign, also led expeditions into Mesopotamia, Syria and the Holy Land in 974–5. But it was under his successor Basil II that opportunities for military service were most tempting, and during his reign some thousands of Varangians were sent by Vladimir to assist him against a revolt in Asia Minor, which led to the establishment of the Varangian Guard (p. 179 above). Basil had a long series of campaigns, moving with unremitting vigour from one corner of the Empire to the other, and often spending winter with his troops far from the capital. He fought in Bulgaria, gradually gaining control over that unhappy land and finally achieving the victory of the Kleidon Pass in 1014, sending a ghastly procession of blinded Bulgarians staggering home to spread terror into every town and village. In 1071 he captured the Bulgarian capital Achrida and took possession of a great treasure hoard, the riches and heirlooms of the Bulgarian royal house; he is said to have given a huge collection of gold coins to be shared out among his troops.[3] He is also said in this campaign to have divided his prisoners into three companies, one to be kept for himself, one for his Greek soldiers and the third for the Varangians. On the way home after this victorious expedition, he marched through Thessaly and then halted at Athens, giving thanks to the Holy Virgin of the Parthenon; unfortunately it is too early, if the runologists are correct, to attribute the runes carved on the marble lion of the Piraeus to a group of Swedes returning from this campaign (p. 220 above).

Basil was also kept busy in the eastern regions of the Empire, where he won new territories. In 994 he sent an army against

[1] Ibid. 61 (137).
[2] Ibid. 115 (148) from Uppland, now in Oxford; and 94 (144) from Södermanland.
[3] Schlumberger II, 386.

MAP 8

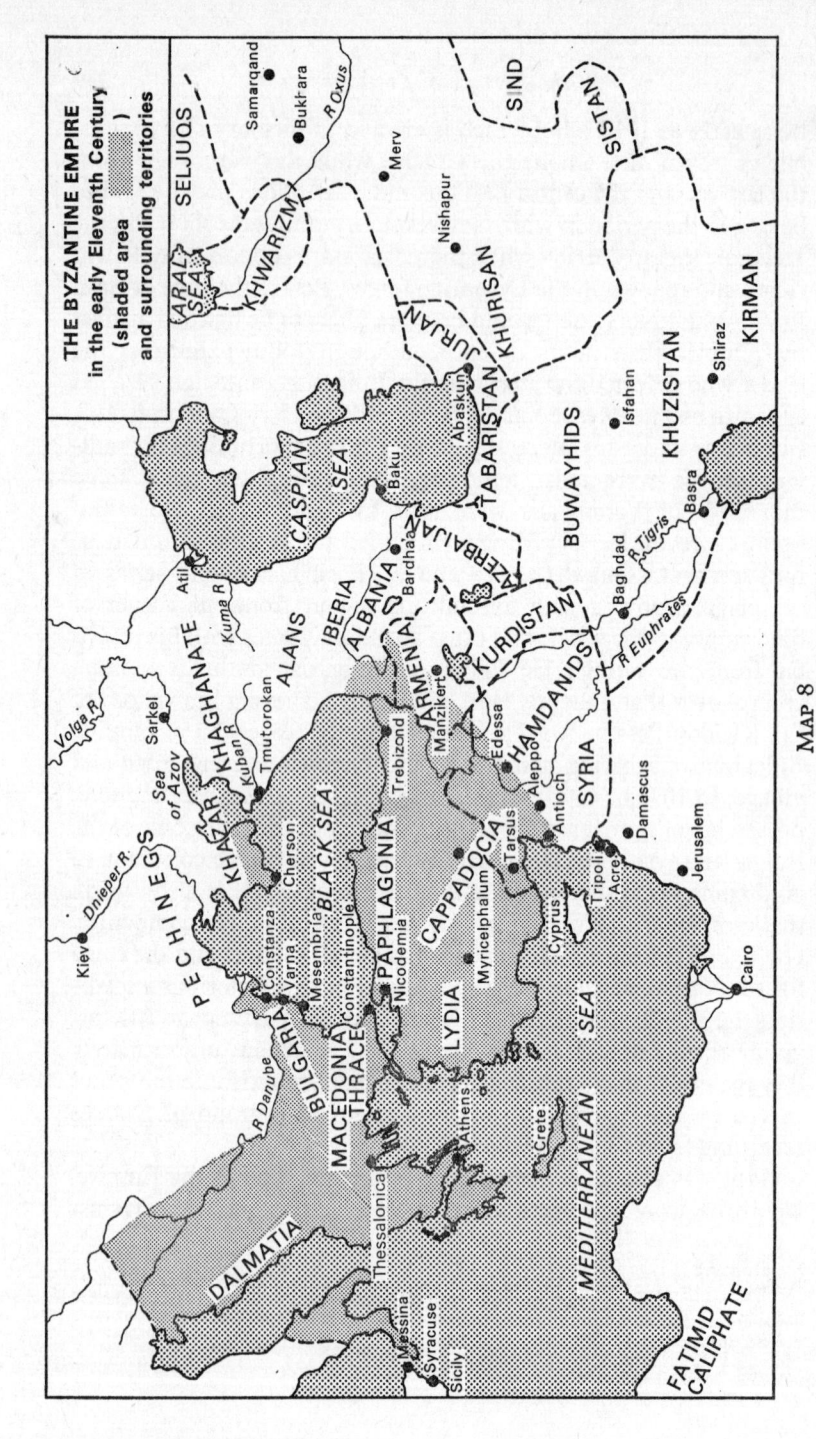

Based on a map in the *Cambridge Medieval History*.

Antioch, and when this was defeated went himself to win a decisive victory and take the city. He reached Tripoli, burning and pillaging on the way, and in 999 was back in Syria and wintered in Tarsus. Then after the death of King David of Georgia he moved in to claim lands which the King had promised to the Empire. All this time the Varangians were with him, and Arisdagus, a Georgian historian, describes the fierce fighting which took place when there was a meeting with the Georgian rulers and nobles. One of the Varangians was said to have been taking hay to his horse when an Iberian took it from him; a second Varangian came to his support and then fighting began, until a large number on both sides were involved. The Varangians outnumbered the Iberians, and many of these were killed, including some of the princes. The Rus and Iberians had met before, and in 988 the Iberians had been on the side of the rebel Bardas Phocas, so there may already have been bad feeling between them.

In 1001 Basil was near Ararat and the source of the Euphrates, set up garrisons and posts in Armenia, and led his forces home through Cappadocia, ending with a triumphal entry through the Golden Gate after two years' absence from the capital. In 1016 he sent an imperial fleet against the Khazars. In 1020 he moved back to Georgia, since the ruler Keorki insisted on defying him; Basil gave him many opportunities to submit and then set his troops to create a reign of terror in the peaceful region of Ogoni. Many of the people were moved over the mountains into the Trebizond area, and neither women, children nor old folk spared; Arisdagus particularly mentions the Russian Varangians as showing great ferocity. An exceptionally cold winter forced the army to retreat to Trebizond, and most of Armenia was later annexed without bloodshed. Just when Keorki surrendered, a new revolt broke out in Cappadocia, led by Nicephorus Phocus, the son of Bardas. His murder prevented a dangerous situation developing, but Keorki again revolted in Georgia. Basil dealt a final crushing blow against the Georgians, and again the Varangians are said to have distinguished themselves, attacking before the rest of the army had engaged and putting the rebels to flight on 11 September 1022.[1] So many of the enemy were killed that Basil is said to have paid a

[1] *Historie de la Georgie* (translated M. F. Brosset, St. Petersburg 1849–54), 308.

gold coin for every head brought in from the battlefield, and to have stacked this grim booty along the road as a warning against future resistance.

This great and ruthless military leader must have attracted many men to follow him and he left the Empire more firmly established than it was ever to be again. After him Romanus II (1028-34) benefited from the generalship of the brilliant George Maniaces (p. 211 above), who rose from the ranks and remained unpopular with the Byzantine military aristocracy; he had outstanding successes, as when he drove back the Muslim forces threatening Antioch and took Edessa in 1032. Then came a threat from the west, when the Pechinegs crossed the Danube and Peter Delean began his Bulgarian revolt (p. 220 above). This was put down by Maniaces with the help of Harald of Norway and his Varangians, and he also defeated the Saracens in the Mediterranean and took Messina and Syracuse before he was recalled, owing to his quarrel with the Admiral, and put into prison. He regained his Mediterranean command under Constantine IX, and when he returned to Macedonia, where his own estates were under attack, he was proclaimed Emperor by his followers. He had won one battle against imperial forces sent against him when he was killed by a stray arrow, and his head was carried into the capital in 1043. It was just after this that the Rus made their attack on Constantinople, to be driven off by Greek fire (p. 170 above) and Harald left for Russia about the same time.

In the Balkans the Pechinegs were still making trouble, owing to a fierce and destructive feud between two sections of their people. The Emperor brought a number of them into his army, hoping to use them in the East, but John Scylitzes gives a dramatic account of how a number broke away, swam their horses across the Bosphorus and returned to join their own people. They defeated some Norman mercenaries and appeared at Adrianople to win a victory over the imperial troops. Forces from the Schools drove them off and, as they were still threatening the capital, John the Philosopher collected all the mercenary troops available, together with the Imperial Guard, and fell on the Pechinegs when they were lying drunk after a banquet, taking back many of their heads to the palace. They were surprised a second time by Nicephorus Bryennius and lost large numbers of men. But lack of supplies caused the

Greeks to retreat, and all that could be achieved while a new army was being collected, including the Varangians and whatever forces could be spared, was a truce made with the Pechinegs a short time before the death of the Emperor in 1055. The leader of the Varangians had meanwhile been collecting yet another army to push back the Turks in the east, and this force assembled at Caesarea.

Then the generals revolted against the weak leadership from the capital and Michael VI abdicated in favour of Isaac Comnenus. Varangians seem to have been fighting on both sides in a battle near Nicaea (p. 187 above). Isaac won the battle, and he defended the eastern frontiers, beat off the Hungarians in the Balkans and kept the Pechinegs under control. The chief threat now came from the Seljuq Turks, who had overcome the Alans and taken Baghdad; they stormed Caesarea in 1067 and overran Asia Minor. Romanus IV led an army of mercenaries against them in 1071, but after some initial success his army was wiped out at Manzikert and he himself captured. He was ransomed and returned home only to be blinded and deposed.

At this critical time a young man of statesmanship and determination, Alexius I Comnenus, was acclaimed Emperor. We know that he was unable to call on the Varangians for support (p. 186 above), but he was helped by other mercenaries to take over power. The position was grim: the Turks held Asia Minor, the Normans under Robert Guiscard threatened the capital, and in 1090 the Pechinegs advanced, supported by the Emir of Smyrna. Once more mercenaries were collected, and Alexius managed to hold his own, calling in the Cumans and defeating the Pechinegs decisively at Mount Levunion. He even won back some towns on the Asian coast, and so the Empire survived at his death. His son John II carried on his work for a while, defeating the Pechinegs again with the help of his Varangians in 1122 (p. 191 above) and recovering Antioch in 1137. Unfortunately he was killed in 1143 before he could embark on a major campaign in the East. Under his successor Manuel I there was trouble from the crusading armies, whose enmity against Byzantium increased. The Sicilian Normans were powerful in the Mediterranean, and although Manuel's sovereignty was acknowledged in a triumphal procession into Antioch, with the King of Jerusalem riding meekly behind him and the Prince of

Antioch holding his stirrup, this merely postponed disaster for a while. The Seljuq broke their agreement at Myriocephalon, fell upon Manuel's army and destroyed it utterly.

The lamentable story of the disruption of the Empire does not concern us here. The relevant point for the study of Scandinavians in the East is the ample opportunity afforded them in the eleventh and twelfth centuries of hard fighting and a chance to gain wealth on many frontiers where mercenary troops were in demand, from the time of the campaigns of Basil II to the defeat of Manuel in Asia Minor. The troubles of the harassed Empire absorbed and used up quantities of the warlike companies which had been built up in Russia in the tenth century, and men from the North must have fallen on many battlefields against Christian and pagan opponents. No doubt the Imperial Guard also was stretched to the limit in repeated attempts to build up fresh armies to meet the threats from every side. The Emperor's men fought in Asia Minor and the Near East, round Antioch and in the Holy Land; they terrorised the Caucasus area in Georgia and Armenia, spent winters in Trebizond and Caesarea in Asia minor, campaigned in northern Greece and the Balkans, and fought by land and sea round Sicily and southern Italy.

There is much written evidence for the presence of Scandinavians in eastern Europe, and a new piece of archaeological evidence has come to light in Rumania, in a chalk quarry near Constanza on the Black Sea coast.[1] Excavations carried out in 1957–60 revealed that chalk was dug out here in the tenth century AD, and that a number of small chapels, some of them used as burial places, had been cut out in the chalk, together with galleries, caves and living quarters. The chapels seem to have been in use for a short while only, and their walls are covered with graffiti and inscriptions in many languages, some of them in types of writing not yet deciphered. Those in Old Slavonic may have been made by the monks who once used the chapels; there is for instance a pathetic inscription in Chapel B4, a quotation from St John's Gospel: 'Smite the shepherd and the sheep will be scattered'. There are also a number of crosses and some drawings with a Christian significance, like the stylised picture of Christ's Nativity and a figure with a nimbus in chapel E3, the most richly decorated,

[1] Barnea (1962), 187 ff.

Fig. 3. Dragons of Scandinavian type, drawn on the walls of a chapel and a burial chamber in a chalk quarry, c. A.D. 1000, at Constanza, Romania. (after Bilcuirescu, *Cahiers Archéologiques* 13, 1962).

with a sanctuary and altar. There are also many drawings of horsemen and one of a ship with a curved prow, as well as various animals and some obscene sketches. Among the large number of drawings there are some which are believed to be Scandinavian in origin, in particular some figures with dragon heads and interlaced bodies, found on the walls of C1 and E5 (Fig. 3).[1] One short inscription on the wall of E3 is in runes which appear to be Scandinavian in type.

It would not be difficult to account for the presence of Scandinavians in this area, at the approximate date of the inscriptions, which according to a Greek inscription in one of the chapels was about 992; at this period the Byzantine army was likely to be occupied in the region, and it has been suggested that the cutting of chalk was due to work in strengthening the fortifications nearby.[2] The yearly voyages down the Dnieper in the tenth century (p. 81 above) may have brought the Rus to this part of the Black Sea coast before they made the final crossing to the capital. After Svyatoslav's campaign, Cedrenus states that the Emperor left an army behind to protect Constanza and other cities which had submitted, and a new city was built on an alluvial island in the Danube in the early eleventh century, perhaps intended as a naval base. There was evidently a very mixed population here, which helps to account for the mixture of cultures and languages represented on the chapel walls. The army also brought men of many nationalities together, while the area was an important one for trade. Whoever cut the runes in the chapel could then have been either a member of the Byzantine army or one of the Scandinavians engaged in trading, and these carvings, like those on the marble lion from Athens, and the inscription in Hagia Sophia, bear witness to the links between Scandinavia and the Balkan area in the eleventh century.

---

[1] Ibid. 208.
[2] Barnea and Diacanus, 181 ff. cf. Barnea (1962), 206.

CHAPTER 5

The Holy City

Pilgrimage has been defined as 'a journey undertaken from religious motives to a sacred place'.[1] One aspect of Constantinople which must not be forgotten is that it was an important place of pilgrimage for the men and women of the North. The image of Constantinople, never wholly abandoned by her rulers and people in spite of obvious anomalies, and continually emphasised by the elaborate ritual of Byzantine life, was that it was the city 'guarded by God'. The figure of the Emperor, whether born in the purple or reaching the throne from some humble beginning by dubious means, was accepted unreservedly as the representative of Christ on earth.[2] In the early days of the city the pursuit of relics was carried out untiringly, with the result that the churches and palaces there were treasure-houses, containing the greatest collection of holy things in Europe (p. 204 above), many of them obtained from the cities of Asia Minor in which the early churches were established.[3] The people turned to these instinctively in times of crisis, when the city was threatened with attack. Moreover, Constantinople formed a convenient stopping-place for those who travelled by the eastern road to visit the Holy Land.

In his account of pilgrimages made by Scandinavians to the Holy Places, published as long ago as 1865 and all too little known, Paul Riant pointed out that the assumption that the northern lands remained largely outside the great pilgrim movement of the tenth and eleventh centuries was wholly untrue. He found much information in the Icelandic sagas and elsewhere to prove his point. Indeed, some of those mentioned on runic stones in Sweden

[1] T. Kollek and M. Pearlman, *Pilgrims to the Holy Land* (London 1970), 10.
[2] For the role of the Emperor, see Miller, 21 ff. and Guerdan, 17 ff.
[3] Ebersolt, 17 ff.

as having died out East or in the land of the Greeks may well have been on pilgrimage.[1] One stone from Broby in Uppland bears the inscription: 'Estrid had this stone raised for her husband Osten; he went to Jerusalem and died abroad in the land of the Greeks'. Another lost inscription recorded near Stockholm was made for a woman who hoped to journey east to Jerusalem and recorded this intention on a runic stone. These were inscriptions of the eleventh century. The obvious route from Sweden to the Holy Land was that followed by merchants and fighting men, down the river route to the Dnieper and to the Black Sea. Alternatives were the 'south' or 'Rome' road, through Germany to Rome and then by sea to Palestine, which was one often taken by the Danes. There was also the 'west' road by sea round Spain and through Gibraltar, used by some Norwegians travelling in large companies, but only men of means were likely to attempt so long a voyage.

Among the first of the Northerners who made the journey to Constantinople for religious as well as political reasons was Helga or Olga of Kiev, who was also the first royal visitor of Scandinavian race to visit the city. She came there in 957 and may have been baptised there, although there is also a tradition for an earlier baptism in Kiev itself.[2] Cedrenus states that the baptism was in Constantinople, and so does the *Continuator Reginonis*, believed to be Adalbert of Trier. He knew Olga well, since he was the first Christian bishop in Kiev and should have known what happened on this important occasion. James, a monk of Kiev writing about 1075, mentions the baptism as taking place in Constantinople, but also states that Olga had been a Christian for fifteen years when she died in 969. This would mean that she was converted as early as 954, three years before she made the journey. This may account for the dating of the visit to Constantinople in the *Primary Chronicle* as 955.

There is, however, no doubt as to the correctness of the 957 dating, since we have full details of the arrival of Olga in the *Book of Ceremonies*, and the exact dates of the receptions held in her honour.[3] Olga brought her own chaplain with her and she may have spent a considerable time after her conversion receiving

[1] Wessen, 45.
[2] Cross (1953), 239–40; Vlasto, 250 ff.
[3] *Book of Ceremonies* II, 594, 15 ff.

instruction in the faith, and been 'prime-signed' only, according to the procedure followed by Scandinavian converts at the courts of Christian rulers. Olga at this time was ruling Kiev for her little son Svyatoslav and must have been well aware of the great political and trading advantages to be gained from a Byzantine alliance; nor would she underestimate the acceptance of Christianity as a bargaining factor. The baptismal ceremony may therefore have been deliberately postponed until it could take place in Constantinople, and it may be significant that she received the Christian name of Helena, which was that of the Empress at the time of her visit as well as that of the mother of Constantine, the founder of the city.

The elaborate series of receptions and banquets held for Olga, who is referred to throughout by her Scandinavian name of Helga, are recorded fully in the *Book of Ceremonies* of Constantine Porphyrogenitus, who was her host. Four important receptions for foreign visitors at this period are mentioned. The first was in May 946, when emissaries of the Emir of Tarsus came to exchange prisoners and make peace; the second was in August of the same year, when other representatives of the Arabs arrived; the third was in October 948-9, for ambassadors from Andalusia; and finally we have Olga's visit, the longest of those recorded, beginning on 9 September 957 and ending with a banquet on 8 October. The length of the visit might be accounted for if a baptismal ceremony formed part of the proceedings, but this is not mentioned in the *Book of Ceremonies*. In his discussion of these court receptions in the reign of Constantine Porphyrogenitus,[1] Toynbee emphasises the frenzied preparations which went on to make an impressive spectacle for the distinguished guests: hangings, chandeliers, wreaths and other decorations were borrowed from the city churches; the imperial standards were paraded; the silver organs of the Blues and Greens were brought in to accompany choirs from the two chief churches, Hagia Sophia and the Holy Apostles. Fine silk draperies, rich Persian carpets, ample floral decoration, leaves of laurel, ivy, myrtle or rosemary strewn on the floor, or rose petals when in season, and fine silverware from the treasures of the palace, were all included in the display on such occasions. Those taking part wore splendid official robes of bright colours, often of a

[1] A. Toynbee, 499 ff.

richer type than they were by rank permitted to wear, and were carefully arranged in groups so that the colours made a pleasing pattern. These entertaining details come mostly from the account of the earlier reception for the Muslim ambassadors in the Magnaura, but we are informed that when Helga and her retinue arrived the arrangements were similar in every respect to those on the previous occasion.

However, since the Princess Helga was a woman she was received by the Empress in the long hall known as the Justinianos, or the Triclinium of Justinian.[1] To get to this point, she and her retinue had to pass through a considerable section of the palace and their progress is carefully recorded (see plan, p. 184). On entry through the Brazen House, they were met by an official who formally asked their names: [2]

'On the ninth of September, Wednesday, a reception took place, similar in every respect to the previously described reception (i.e. of the ambassadors) on the arrival of Helga, the Princess of Rhos, and the Princess herself entered with her own related princesses and more important ladies-in-waiting, she preceding all the other women, they following one after another in order, and she stood in the place where the *logothete* usually makes the interrogations. Behind her entered the envoys and agents of the princes of Rhos, and stood lower down, by the entrance.'[3]

We are told that the Princess proceeded through the Palace of Daphne and through several halls to the Onopos (Ass's Foot) which formed the vestibule of the palace, and into the Golden Hand, a narrow passage which may have taken its name from a mosaic showing a hand as a symbol of the imperial authority, marking the entrance to the precincts of the Emperor and his family.[4] Helga sat down to wait in the Augusteos, and after a time was conducted through the Apsis, joining the old and new parts of the Palace,[5] and then to the Hippodromium, which was probably

[1] Janin, 116–17.
[2] There is no available translation in English of this passage, and I am much indebted to Charlotte Roueché for the one given here.
[3] The place of entry where two door-keepers ushered visitors in and out; it may have been closed by curtains.
[4] Janin, 113; Vogt II, 42, 186.   [5] Janin, 117.

a small roofed race-course for private entertainments, to wait again in the Scyla which led to the Triclinium of Justinian. Here the Empress was seated on the throne of Theophilus, on a dais covered with purple silk, and beside the throne was a gold chair on which sat the Empress' daughter-in-law.

First the household of the Empress was brought up one by one to be formally presented in order of rank: these were ladies who were the wives of magistri, patricians and others holding high official rank at court. Next came the turn of the visitors, and once more the Princess gave her name as she entered with the ladies of her company. After this she returned to the Scyla, while the Empress moved on to her own apartment by way of the Cainourgium, the room to which the ladies of the court came bearing gifts when a son was born to an Empress. The Empress' apartment was in the section of the palace reserved for women and eunuchs [1] and the Princess Helga now passed through the Lausiacos, a long hall set with columns, to the Tripeton,[2] where stood one of the famous palace clocks (p. 275 below). This led into the Cainourgion, where the Emperor joined the Empress and the imperial children in her apartment, and Helga was summoned to join them: '... and at the demand of the Emperor sat down and talked, on whatever she wished, to the Emperor.'

Later in the same day there was a banquet for the ladies in the same Triclinium which had been used for the reception. The Empress sat on the throne and Helga stood beside her. Members of the visiting company were presented once more in order of rank and made obeisance. The Princess herself was not required to prostrate herself or even to take the half-kneeling position required for ambassadors presented to the Emperor, since we are told:

'The princess bowed her head slightly where she stood, and sat down at a separate table, with the women of 'belted' rank, according to the custom. Know that the singers of the Church of the Apostles and of Hagia Sophia were present at this banquet, singing imperial songs. They also performed all (sorts of) theatrical performances.'

[1] Vogt II, 181.
[2] Janin, 103.

Meanwhile the men from Kiev were being entertained at a second banquet, in the Chrysotriclinium, not far away, except for the less important members of the party, who presumably ate elsewhere. Afterwards all received gifts of money; there is mention of Helga's nephew, eight of her 'close companions', twenty envoys, forty-three agents, her priest Gregory and two interpreters; also the men of her son Sphendoslav (Svyatoslav), six attendants on the envoys, and the interpreter of the Princess. The amounts given ranged from thirty miliansia to her nephew to three miliansia each to the attendants on the envoys. Dessert was served in another room, as was the usual custom, and the Princess was then permitted to join the imperial family:

'After the Emperor had got up from the banquet, there was dessert on jewelled dishes of cast metal, and the Emperor sat down with Romanus the Porphyrogenitus and their imperial children and daughter-in-law and the Princess, and 500 miliansia were given to the Princess on a gold and jewelled dish, and to her close female companions twenty miliansia each, and to her eighteen ladies-in-waiting, eight miliansia each.'

It is interesting to note that Helga was permitted to remain upright, and one may speculate as to the possible arguments which went on before this compromise was reached. She came as an ambassador, but was also recognised as a ruler in her own right, and was in the unusual position of a woman received with high honour in the imperial court, She did not, however, share a table with the imperial family, but like the Muslims on a former occasion ate at a separate one, accompanied by the women whose husbands held high rank at court. The gift she received was of the same amount as that given to each of the Tarsan ambassadors.

The last banquet for Helga was held on Sunday, 18 October, and once more the women of the party dined with the Empress, this time in a different hall, the Pentacubiculum, joined to the oratory of St Peter and St Paul, beyond the apartments of the women and the eunuchs.[1] The Emperor and the men of Helga's company were in the Chrysotriclinium as before. This time Helga received 200 miliansia as a gift, her nephew twenty, and other

[1] Ibid. 117.

members of the retinue corresponding amounts in order of rank.[1]

We are not told where Helga's party were lodged, but the two formal occasions must have given her opportunity to see and to marvel at many of the splendours of the palace. The Chrysotriclinium, where the Emperor banqueted, was the great domed throne-room which had become the centre of the palace at this period; his throne was set in the apse, in which there was a mosaic of Christ enthroned, and the room contained a huge chandelier and many precious objects, including the imperial crowns and jewels, two golden jewelled organs and the tree of gold set with mechanical singing birds. The long hall, where the women dined on the first occasion, was ornamented with mosaics and had a floor of coloured marble slabs. Helga had the chance on this occasion of a frank discussion with the Emperor, as informal as anything in the Byzantine court was likely to be. There is no mention of an entertainment at the Hippodrome, such as was provided for the ambassadors, but since court ladies were not normally present in the imperial box this would hardly be suitable.

In the *Primary Chronicle* there is a more ingenuous account of the visit, which Obolensky suggests may have come from some Varangian saga current at Kiev.[2] According to this the Emperor was amazed at the beauty and wisdom of the Princess and declared that she was worthy to reign over his city, even proposing that she become his wife. However, since at her request he had acted as godfather at her baptism, he was forced to agree that this was impossible and he gave her many gifts of gold, silver, silk and vessels. In spite of this it is implied that Olga was far from satisfied at her reception. After she returned home, the Emperor is said to have sent a message to remind her of these gifts and of her promise to send slaves, wax and furs in return, together with mercenary troops to support him. Olga sent a somewhat cold reply, saying that when she arrived at Byzantium her ships had had to remain at anchor some time before she and her retinue were allowed to enter the city; this is quite possible, since we know that stringent

---

[1] Toynbee (505) notes slight inconsistencies here. There is no mention of Helga's interpreter the second time, and two additional envoys and one agent are now included in the list.
[2] Obolensky (1971/1), 190.

measures were usually taken before any potentially dangerous
company of foreigners was permitted inside the city walls. She went
on to say that if the Emperor were willing to spend as long on the
Pochayna, the stream flowing past Kiev, as she had had to spend on
the Bosporus, then she would accede to his requests. No doubt we
have to allow for considerable exaggeration here, but it is significant
that Olga sent to Otto I, asking for priests and a bishop from the
Christian church in the west to come to Kiev, and this is how
Adalbert of Trier became the first bishop there. Pagan opposition
proved too strong for him, however, and he left in 962. Thus Olga
finally rejected the alliance with Byzantium through the eastern
church, although its influence is shown in the first church of St
Sophia which she built in Kiev and which survived until 1017.

It was some time before any royal visitor from the North
followed in the footsteps of Olga. Less exalted travellers arrived,
however, seeking spiritual inspiration, and among them an Icelander, Thorvald the Far-travelled, a missionary who had been
converted by a Saxon bishop, Frederick, and who had tried to
preach the new faith to his countrymen in 981.[1] Not surprisingly,
Thorvald found it difficult to avoid hitting back at those who
opposed him. He had been a distinguished Viking before his conversion, although he is said to have refused to profit from much of
the booty he took, returning objects of special value and children
from good families to their homes. After he had killed two poets
who made mocking verses about him and a man who opposed his
preaching, Bishop Frederick withdrew his support.

In 990 Thorvald made a pilgrimage to Jerusalem and the Holy
Places, and then journeyed through Syria to Byzantium. We are
told that the Emperor received him with honour and gifts, and that
he was praised by the bishops of Greece and Syria for his work in
spreading the faith. He was specially renowned on the east road,
and the Emperor sent him into Russia as a leader of a missionary
party, with power over all kings there and in Gardariki. This tradition probably refers to the time of Basil II, after the conversion of
Vladimir, when many priests and bishops were sent among the
Rus, so that it may not have been so distinguished a commission
for Thorvald as is implied in the saga. He is said to have died in

---

[1] *Þáttr Þorvalds ens Viðfǫrla* (edited B. Kahle, Halle, 1905), 9. See also introduction, 2.

The Holy City

Russia at Drofn or Drafn, where a monastery bore his name.[1] Thorvald was accompanied on his pilgrimage by another Icelander, Stefnir Thorgilsson of Kjalarnesss, who was baptised in Denmark; he was a descendant of Ketil Flatnose and also a poet, although little of his work survives.[2] Olaf Tryggvason sent him on another expedition to convert Iceland, but it did not meet with much success.

Here we have two examples of northern converts seeking to learn more about the faith by visiting the Holy Land and then coming to Constantinople, after their first attempts at missionary work proved disappointing. Both these men were said to have been in contact with Olaf Tryggvason, and a series of legends links Olaf himself with Constantinople, although there is no historical foundation for his visit there. One tradition [3] is that he was prime-signed there before baptism, and that he begged a bishop named Paul to accompany him back to Gardar to preach, so that he was largely responsible for Vladimir's conversion. This has not been taken very seriously by historians, although Vlasto suggests that Olaf might have been one of those responsible for negotiations with Vladimir.[4]

After Olaf's disappearance in the sea-battle of the year 1000, a series of tales tell how he escaped by swimming under water and was picked up by a small boat manned by Wends and taken to the south Baltic coast. His sister-in-law Astrid was said to be responsible for his rescue, and to have kept him in Stettin until he recovered from his wounds. She wanted him to get back the kingdom, but he insisted that it was God's will that he should retire from the world, and set out for Rome dressed as a merchant. Some years later an impressive old man in a monk's habit was said to have been seen by a number of Scandinavian travellers in Syria; he sent gifts and messages back to Norway and was held to be Olaf himself. The truth of this was said to be proved by the presence of his sword and helmet in Antioch and his coat of mail in a Jerusalem monastery, and this offers a clue to how these stories may have begun. Edward the Confessor was said to have had a book record-

---

[1] In *Kristnisaga* 13 he is said to have died near Polotsk. The reference to Drafn comes from a poem attributed to Brand.
[2] *Skjaldedigtning* B1, 146; cf. *Þáttr Stefnis þorgilssonar* in *Flateyjarbók* I, 238–9, 285 ff.
[3] *The Great Saga of Olaf Tryggvason*, 76.
[4] Vlasto, 258–9.

ing Olaf's journey to Palestine read aloud in his court, and also to have announced Olaf's death in 1036. Riant gives a full account of the popular tales of Olaf's survival,[1] but he and other historians have found themselves unable to accept these as historical evidence. They form an interesting link, however, between Scandinavia and the Near East, and show the importance of relics of famous northern heroes, as well as those of saints and apostles, as an attraction for travellers and pilgrims from the North. They also illustrate the growth of folklore around historical persons, and this group of legends about Olaf may be compared with a group of equally persistent traditions about the survival of the Russian Czar Alexander I after his alleged death at Taganrog in 1825.[2] The Czar was also said to have been taken away in a boat, in this case an English yacht on the Sea of Azov, and to have gone out of Russia, while the dead body of a courtier was substituted for the funeral ceremony. A number of historians have accepted the claim that Alexander later appeared in Siberia in the form of a mysterious hermit, a man of distinguished appearance and manners, whose identity has never been revealed.

The sword of Olaf II was said to have been kept in the Varangian church in Constantinople (p. 206 above) and there was a story of how he, like his predecessor, had always intended to visit the Holy Land. However, in 1014 he was prevented from sailing there by the western route by a dream of a tall man who ordered him to return when he was about to pass through the Straits of Gibraltar.[3] The basis of this seems to have been the huge statue of a man with his arm pointing towards the west which stood near Cadiz on the remains of one of the pillars of Hercules; Arab sources mention two other statues, one pointing east and the third pointing at himself, but these had disappeared by the tenth century. When Olaf II was driven out of Norway to Russia, he considered retiring to the Holy Land, it is said, but was told by Olaf Tryggvason in another dream

---

[1] Riant, 108 ff.

[2] For two points of view, see M. Paleologue, *The Diplomatic Czar* (translated E. and W. Muir, London 1938), 303 ff.; and E. M. Almedingen, *The Emperor Alexander I* (London 1964). I am indebted to Stephanie Dee for these references. See also Davidson, 'Folklore and History', *Folklore* 85 (1974) 85 ff. for further discussion of these traditions.

[3] Riant, 76. The figures are described by a twelfth-century Spanish author, al-Zuhri.

to go back to his kingdom. It was claimed that those responsible for his death at Stiklastad became pilgrims out of remorse, and that even the unscrupulous Thorir Hund (p. 36 above) went to Jerusalem and never returned.

The reasons taking Harald of Norway to Constantinople were, as we have seen, unconnected with religion, although he is said to have visited the Holy Land (p. 219 above). More royal pilgrims came from Scandinavia, however, one of them a Danish king, Eirik the Good, who started on a journey to the Holy Land, though he never reached it, and called at Constantinople in 1103. A detailed account of this visit is given in the twelfth book of Saxo Grammaticus [1] who was writing not long after and is a reasonably reliable witness for this period. Eirik followed the east road through Russia and came across the Black Sea to Constantinople; he had made a previous pilgrimage to Rome and set up two hostels for Scandinavian pilgrims in Italy. When he arrived at the Byzantine capital, he was at first denied access by the Emperor, Alexius I, who suspected that his huge company might be a threat to the city. He was permitted only to camp outside the walls, for Alexius was apprehensive lest he might win over the Danes in the Varangian Guard and use them against the Emperor. Saxo states that at this time the Danes were 'in the foremost place' in the Guard, and were in high favour with Alexius, who entrusted his life and safety to them. Eirik accepted the refusal, but humbly asked leave to visit the city churches, since it was love of religion alone, he said, which had brought him there. Then the Danes who served the Emperor asked permission to greet their king, and Alexius consented on condition that Eirik met them in small groups and did not address the whole company together. He sent spies who understood Danish to report what the King said.

Eirik spoke most properly to the members of the Guard, encouraging them in their loyalty to the Emperor, and his words as reported by Saxo are consistent with what we know of the traditions of the Varangians from other sources: [2]

'Those Danes who had been in Greek service had over a long period gained great renown by their deeds. Although they were

[1] *Magnúss Saga góða*, 11.
[2] Saxo, *Gesta Danorum*, XII, 6, 1 ff.

foreigners here, yet they were treated nobly and given power over the people of the land, and far better treatment here abroad than they would have received in their own country. Moreover, the Emperor had entrusted his life to their loyal defence, an honour due not so much to their own merit as to the deeds performed by those in service with the Greeks before them. Therefore they should as far as possible endeavour to lead a sober life and not give themselves up to drunkenness; they would give better service if they did not fill themselves with wine and cause the Emperor anxiety by slackness in duty, or readiness to stir up bickering and strife when they were not within the bounds of temperance. He impressed on them also that when they had to engage the enemy they should value courage above the preservation of their lives, and should not try to save themselves by taking to flight before they were hurt. For when one day they returned to Denmark he would reward them for their loyal service here with his favour, while he promised that if they lost their lives fighting manfully in battle he would show honour to their kinsmen and friends.'

When this was reported to the Emperor he was greatly impressed and admitted that he had misjudged the Danish King. He then had the city decorated for a great procession and carpets laid down in the street, and he walked hand in hand with his royal visitor when Eirik entered through the gates. He allowed the King to stay in one of his palaces, and according to Saxo no Emperor lived there afterwards, since it would not have been fitting. This could be a misunderstanding based on the fact that the Great Palace was abandoned as a residence in this period in favour of other palaces in the city. When the Danish King was leaving, the Emperor asked him what he would wish to receive as a gift, and Eirik asked for holy relics only; he was given the body of St Nicholas and a fragment of the True Cross, and these he sent home to Roskilde and to a church at Slangerup which he himself had built. He was also offered a large sum in gold and this after some protests he consented to accept; Blöndal suggested that it may have been part of an agreement by which some of his large retinue stayed behind in the Emperor's service, as happened later in the case of Sigurd of Norway, since Eirik would not need so many men for the

The Holy City

remainder of his journey by sea.[1] In return Eirik presented gifts to the Emperor.

Some gaps in this account may be filled from *Knytlinga Saga*, which confirms Saxo's story.[2] Here it is said that Alexius welcomed Eirik and gave him a splendid reception, offering him either a sum in gold or an entertainment in the Hippodrome, but since the first part of his journey had proved very costly he chose the gold. Alexius is also said to have given him clothes, by which must be meant the celebrated 'cloaks' or lengths of Byzantine silk which were so highly valued, and fourteen warships. The saga quotes a verse from Markus Skeggason,[3] and the information about the gifts evidently comes from this. Markus composed his *Eiríksdrápa* soon after the visit, and this tells how the shrine and the cross were borne out of the city with singing and the sound of bells; this evidently refers to St Nicholas' shrine and the piece of the True Cross which is mentioned in Saxo. It is also said in the verse that the king received *skrúð*; this is a term used of hangings in a church or for certain kinds of good quality cloth, and could here be used to refer to silk. There is also mention of half a *lest* or cargo of red gold, and fourteen warships. This poem on Eirik's death was composed soon after he left the city, since he never reached the Holy Land; he fell ill of a fever and died in Cyprus, where he was buried in the church at Baffa, where according to the Abbot Nicholas in 1150 there was a Varangian garrison.[4] The rest of the Danish company went on, but in Palestine Queen Bodhild also died.

The attraction of Constantinople as a place of pilgrimage and a goal for those who wanted to grow rich in the Emperor's service was still strong later in the twelfth century, as Snorri tells us in *Magnússona Saga*:[5]

'When Magnus' sons were accepted as kings, those who had gone abroad with Skopti Afmundson came home again, either from Palestine or Miklagard, and had a great deal to tell; the information which they brought made many men in Norway eager

---
[1] Blöndal (1954), 211–12.
[2] *Knytlinga Saga* (Copenhagen 1919–25), 81, 192.
[3] *Eiríksdrápa*, *Skjaldedigtning* B1, 419, 29; Markus died in 1107.
[4] Riant, 161.
[5] *Heimskringla*, *Magnússona Saga*, 1.

to make such journeys. It was said that Norsemen prepared to enter military service in Miklagard received much wealth. These men urged that one of the Kings, Eystein or Sigurd, should go out there and be the leader of a company of men who desired to make the journey. The Kings agreed to this, and shared jointly in preparations for the voyage. Many great men, those holding office and rich land-owners, took part in the expedition. When all was ready it was decided that Sigurd should go, and Eystein should rule the land on behalf of them both.'

Sigurd at this time was about nineteen years of age. He and his company journeyed by the west route, sailing round France and Spain into the Mediterranean with various adventures on the way, battles with Vikings on the sea and fights with Arabs in Spain. They won much booty in the Balearic Islands, where they took a rich treasure by letting men down in ships' boats to a cave in a cliff held by the heathen. Sigurd was welcomed warmly by Roger of Sicily and then went on to the Holy Land, where he was received by Baldwin of Jerusalem. There is a reference to his arrival in the *History* of Fulcher of Chartres, recording the Jerusalem expedition from 1095 to 1127.[1] This tells how certain Norwegians arrived in Joppa with fifty-five ships (other sources say sixty) at a crucial point in the campaign, when Acre was under siege by the Saracens. Their leader is described as a very handsome youth, a kinsman of the King of Norway. There is also a reference to the meeting of Baldwin and Sigurd in the *Chronicle* of Albertus of Aix.[2]

We are given another detailed account of the visit in the *Fornmanna Sǫgur*.[3] Here it is said that the Egyptian fleet retired from Akrborg (Acre) when the Norwegian ships appeared and Sigurd entered the city. Baldwin begged him to stay for a time and help with the conquest of the Holy Land, and Sigurd replied that this was why he had come, but that he also wanted to visit the Holy Places. Baldwin then took him to Jerusalem, where clerics in white robes led a procession to the Holy Sepulchre. The King of Jerusalem is said to have ordered the road leading to the city to be

---

[1] Fulcher of Chartres, *A History of the Expedition to Jerusalem 1095–1127* (translated F. R. Ryan, University of Tennessee, 1969) II, 44, 199.
[2] Albertus Aquensis XI, 7.
[3] *Fornmanna Sǫgur, Sigurðar Saga Jórsalafara*, 7.

covered with rich red cloth and to have told the people that a great king was coming, and

'... it is fitting that we give him great honour and treat royally a prince who had already supported the divine church of Christ by his great exploits against the pagans. We will judge of his power and worth by the way in which he behaves. If he comes straight into the city and does not seem to notice the rich materials spread out to do him honour, we must assume that he is used to such luxury at home....'

Not surprisingly, Sigurd is said to have ignored the trappings, and his company rode over them without comment, for he had warned them that whatever extraordinary things they might see they should never show surprise. Baldwin took his guest to all the Holy Places, and they picked palms and visited the Jordan, where it would seem that Sigurd swam over, as was the custom, and recorded his crossing by tying a knot in the brushwood on the other side, or so he claimed later. Then the King asked Sigurd what he most desired to have, and Sigurd asked for a piece of the True Cross. After some discussion with the patriarch and bishops, this was agreed to, on condition that it was placed beside the shrine of St Olaf in Norway. After this Sigurd supported Baldwin in the siege of Sidon.

He left in the winter of 1110 and went on to Cyprus, where no doubt he visited Eirik's tomb. He is said to have stayed a month at Aegilsness waiting for the right wind, because he wanted to display his ships with silk coverings on their sails as he advanced into the harbour at Constantinople. The spirit of one-upmanship is very clear throughout this account, and the bargaining of Sigurd for a piece of the Cross, in order to equal Eirik's earlier achievement, is in keeping with the account of Sigurd's doings in Constantinople. We may discount many of the details, some of which echo stories about Harald the Ruthless and other famous western leaders of earlier times, although no doubt the arrogant young King did his best to impress the Emperor of this magnificent city and to show himself not unworthy of other Scandinavians whose visits had become the subject of poems and stories in the North. With his splendid sails he moved slowly down the coast, past strongholds, castles and villages, and people came down to the shore to watch his fleet sail by. Alexius directed that *Gullvarta*, the Golden Gate, should be opened for him and the name used here appears to be a Russian form, evidently in use among the Varangians.[1] Then the street was covered with silk, and Sigurd and his men rode over this to the palace; in order to impress the Greeks further, he even fitted gold shoes to his horse and arranged that one should drop off on the way and that no one should attempt to retrieve it. He was met by singers and musicians, and ushered into the palace, where the Emperor sent him purses of gold and silver; these, however, he instantly handed to his men. Then followed coffers of gold, which he treated in the same way, and finally a robe of purple silk and two chests of gold with gold rings, and the robe and rings Sigurd deigned to accept, making a speech in Greek to thank the Emperor. After his stay he was offered the same choice between a gift of gold and an entertainment in the Hippodrome as had been made to Eirik; since Sigurd was on his way home and had won much booty already, he chose to see the games. An account of these has been given (p. 198 above). Then Sigurd invited the Emperor to a feast, and again we hear of walnuts being used when ordinary fuel could not be obtained (p. 216 above). When he left to return by the east road, he presented his ships with golden figure-heads to the Emperor, and these figure-heads are said to have been placed in St Peter's Church, which might mean the old monastery of St Peter, not far from the harbour. There is a legend that one of these, a gilded dragon, was taken to Belgium when the city was sacked and set up in the tower of the Town Hall in Ghent; however, the dragon there appears to be the work of local craftsmen of the thirteenth century.[2]

Both the story of the walnuts and that of the silk sails has been used before; Oleg of Kiev was said to use sails of silk (p. 124 above), although it is conceivable that some rich material obtained in the Holy Land was used to impress the Greeks, and silk would be a suitable material for sails. The scorn of gold and silver is also stressed in stories of Harald the Ruthless and other heroes, and the gold horseshoe left in the road was a gesture attributed to Robert of Normandy.

[1] Liden, 358 ff.
[2] Blöndal (1954), 216.

Such stories, whatever their origin, were clearly inspired by the awe and envy felt by the Scandinavians for the riches and luxuries of the Byzantine world, and a desire not to fall short of the standards of this new and bewildering city. Sigurd's journey was evidently a profitable one, from the words attributed to him after his return to Norway: [1] 'I fought many battles in Serkland, and in all of them I won the victory and got much rich booty, the like of which has never come into the land.' The very wording of this boast, however, recalls the great achievements of Harald the Ruthless and the wealth he brought home; the pattern for a Norwegian king visiting the East has now been firmly established and must be suitably sustained by the story-teller.

The last Northern leader recorded as visiting Constantinople was Jarl Rognvald of Orkney, no longer a young man, since when he left home he was in his mid-forties, but nevertheless a leader who could more than hold his own with the great Viking champions of the past. The account of his voyage to the Holy Land and back by way of Constantinople is given in *Orkneyinga Saga*, and is thought to have been derived from a separate tale or *þáttr*, based partly on the verses of the Jarl himself and other poets in his company and partly on oral tradition. Much of the narrative in *Orkneyinga Saga* at this point, however, probably belonged to a lost saga of Erling Crickneck, the Norwegian jarl who played a large part on the expedition.[2] Eindridi the Younger was supposed to have persuaded the Jarl to undertake the pilgrimage, and he offered himself as guide (p. 235 above). Elaborate plans were made and the preparation took two years. New ships were built in Norway for the enterprise, and it was agreed that the Jarl himself, the leader of the party, should be the only man to have an ornamented ship with a dragon figure-head. His vessel was built at Bergen, and in the spring of 1150 the Jarl went to collect it. It is described in the saga in some detail: 'The ship had 35 thwarts and was a work of fine craftsmanship, decorated all over; the figurehead and poop and weather-vane were inlaid with gold, and the rest of the ship carved from stem to stern. It was the most splendid vessel of its kind.'

In spite of the agreement, Eindridi made himself unpopular by

[1] *Heimskringla, Magnússona Saga*, 21.
[2] Taylor, 82 ff.

arriving at Bergen in the same summer with a dragon war-ship of his own, with gold inlay on prow and poop and painted bows; this ship, doubtless to many people's satisfaction, was lost off Shetland.[1] After the ships had been manned, the company returned to spend the winter in Orkney. Several Norwegians of rank took part in the expedition and their names are given: Erling Crickneck and Aslak Erlendson were kinsmen of Rognvald, and there was also Guttorm Mjola-Pali, a chief from Halogaland, and Eindridi the Younger, Sweyn Ronaldson from Caithness, and from Orkney Magnus Havardson and Jon Fot Petuson, the brother-in-law of Rognvald, while Bishop William of Paris acted as interpreter. There were also four poets in the company: Thorgeir Scotpoll, Odd the Little, Thorbjorn the Black and Armod. During the winter in Orkney the weather was bad and the company seems to have been difficult to keep under control; it may have been at this time that a visit was made to Maeshowe, the great prehistoric burial mound with a megalithic grave-chamber on the Orkney mainland. Runes were cut in the chamber stating that 'Jorsalamen' (pilgrims) broke in, and that a treasure had been carried out, although whether this refers to discoveries made at this time or earlier is not clear.[2]

Finally, in 1151 the fifteen ships set out, Eindridi having now procured a new vessel to replace the one he had lost. The voyage down the east coast of England and round France and Spain was an exciting one, with some fighting on the way and chances to gain booty. After passing through the Straits of Gibraltar Eindridi left the expedition, confirming their suspicions that he had played them false during an attack on a castle. Near Sardinia they encountered two dromunds, huge high merchant ships 'such as men have in this part of the world', which they at first took for islands because of their enormous size. Although the Bishop warned them that if they tried to board them, hot pitch and brimstone could be poured on them from above, they decided to make the attempt. They took some of their ships so close that missiles and burning liquid fell clear of them into the sea, and while they sheltered behind their shields, bowmen from the other ships shot at the dromund. Those

---

[1] Ibid. 85.
[2] *Royal Commission of Ancient Monuments of Orkney and Shetland* I, 47; II, 307 ff. cf. Liestøl (1965) 55 ff.

close to the vessel's side then made a hole through the hull and so got on board. Much of the valuable cargo, however, was lost, as they set fire to the ship before they discovered it and could not rescue it from the burning vessel.

They sailed to Crete and the Holy Land, arriving at Acre, where a number of the company died of sickness. They visited the Holy Places, and Rognvald and Sigmund Fishhook swam across Jordan and tied knots in the brushwood on the other side as Sigurd had done. Then they composed verses, evidently in sport, in which they referred to the stay-at-homes and those who had not made the journey, perhaps aiming taunts at Eindridi. Sigurd's own words to his brother Eynstein after he returned home,[1] when he indicated that he had tied a knot for Eynstein across the Jordan, and that unless his brother went and untied it he could not escape a curse laid upon him, are evidently a reference to the old association between a knot and a magic spell, the spoken words being valid until the knot which secures their power is untied. It seems as if the Northmen turned a familiar custom, that of swimming the Jordan as a proof that the pilgrim had accomplished his vow, into a boast and challenge to those who had not proved themselves their equals on a dangerous pilgrimage. Indeed, it becomes apparent that the Christian kings and jarls from the North on pilgrimage were not so different after all from those earlier Vikings who sought out Constantinople as the place where they might win wealth and renown and establish their superiority over those who had remained at home.

Of the visit to Constantinople itself we are told little except that they were delayed at Aegilsness and then 'sailed in as they knew Sigurd the Crusader had done', the saga-writer being anxious that Rognvald should not fall behind his illustrious predecessors. They were well received by the Emperor Manuel I (1143–80), who offered to take them into his service if they wished to stay in Byzantium. Rognvald's own verse, quoted below, implies that this had been the original plan. The Emperor is also said to have given the jarl a gift of money, probably the allowance to support them during their stay. It may be that the presence of the treacherous Eindridi, now in high favour with the Emperor, helped to dissuade them from accepting the offer of entry into the Guard, and they

[1] *Heimskringla, Magnússona Saga*, 21.

left in the spring. They sailed to Bulgaria and journeyed overland by way of Rome, Germany and Denmark. On their return we are told that all passed for men of greater renown after this expedition.

The rhyming verse composed by Jarl Rognvald calling to his companions to sail to Miklagard forms a fitting ending to a chapter on the links between Scandinavia and Byzantium. Once more we see the great city as the goal of the adventurer, the place where rich rewards awaited the bold traveller, and where there was opportunity to fight under the banner of a distinguished leader and great emperor. Although the goal of famous shrines and holy relics was supposed to have been the inspiration for their journey and they claimed to have undertaken it for the greater glory of God, it would seem that in fact little had changed. Rognvald's words are significant: [1]

'Let us ride on the sea-king's steed;
no plough from the field shall we need;
our soaked prows shall furrow the sea,
and to Miklagard go we.
Serve the prince for our pay and so
into clash of conflict we go,
to redden the wolf's jaws and bring
back gold from the glorious king.'

[1] *Skjaldedigtning* B1, 486, 31.

PART FOUR

Ideas from the East

Introduction

In their expeditions eastwards for trade and tribute, or to enrol as fighting men under the princes of Gardar and the Byzantine Emperor, the Scandinavians made contact with many peoples and races. They had a long association with the Lapps and Finno-Ugrian tribes of the northern Baltic and arctic Russia, including the mysterious Biarmians, and encountered other Finno-Ugrian and Balt peoples, as well as the western Slavs of the south Baltic, as penetration eastwards continued. Later came contacts with the eastern Slavs, with the Turko-Tatar peoples of the Middle Volga, the Pechinegs and other nomads, and the Bulgars of the Danube. There were dealings both friendly and hostile with the Jewish Khazars, who themselves ruled a kingdom of mixed races and religions, with the Muslim peoples of the Caliphate, and with Arabs encountered in the course of trading. Finally there was a relationship of long standing with the Greeks of Byzantium and their subject peoples, culminating in the employment of Scandinavians in the Imperial Guard. Those who fought for the Emperor might move far afield, visiting Asia Minor, the Caucasus, the Holy Land and the eastern Mediterranean. Some of the contacts were brief and hostile, but many undoubtedly lasted over several centuries.

It is to be regretted that few sources from the Viking Age survive in Sweden, the region from which so many men moved eastwards. We know more of Denmark and Norway, but it is from Iceland that our written sources are mainly derived. However, the Icelanders were great travellers, always greedy for stories and information from abroad, some of which they incorporated with great skill into their prose sagas. We have the evidence too of their travelling poets, who returned from service in the courts of kings not only with material gain but with poems and stories; some had first-hand experience of expeditions eastwards, described in their vigorous, pithy but unfortunately often ambiguous verses. Court poetry has been called one of Iceland's invisible exports,[1] and it acted also as an invisible import, bringing in traditions from the eastern world. Moreover, in the northern mythology of the Edda poems and the *Prose Edda* we have a rich picture of the imaginative world of the late Viking Age, and certain features stand out from what we know of the myths of other Germanic peoples in pre-Christian times. It may fairly be asked how far this is due to symbols and concepts derived from the eastern region which have acted as inspiration to poets and story-tellers.

Two influences worked on the Vikings on their eastern journeys: first, that of a society far more advanced and sophisticated than their own, that of the Byzantine Empire and particularly its capital; and secondly that of the customs and traditions of the various barbarian peoples with whom they came into contact. Here the problems of eastern influence will be considered in three separate studies. First, there is the question of possible effects on Scandinavian literature and mythology from the link with Byzantium; secondly, that of shamanistic elements in Old Norse literature, which might be due to contacts with nomadic tribes practising shamanism in eastern Europe; and thirdly, that of eastern characteristics in the cult of Odin as expressed in the art and literature of the late Viking Age. Each of these contains its own complex problems, and the intention is to suggest paths for future work rather than to give any definite answer. Many different disciplines and languages are involved, and there is urgent need for more co-operation between scholars if further progress is to be made. Peter Buchholz has said that it seems as if a history of Germanic religion could only be written as a collaborative undertaking,[2] and this is particularly true as regards the rich traditions of the Viking Age recorded in Iceland in the Christian period.

---

[1] M. Magnusson and H. Palsson. Introduction to *The Vinland Sagas* (Penguin Classics, 1965), 14.

[2] Buchholz, 'Perspective for historical research in Germanic Religion', *History of Religions*, 8 (1968–9), 111.

CHAPTER 1

Marvels and Portents

When the Northmen reached Constantinople, there was much to impress them: the splendid palaces and monuments and churches, the elaborate processions and the ostentatious wealth of the city, the great walls and the gilded roofs. When the community of the gods, Asgard, is described as a series of gleaming palaces within an encircling wall, built by a giant, the model for such descriptions could well be the Great City. In the Edda poem *Grímnismál* the dwellings of the gods are seen as halls roofed with precious metals, thatched with silver, set with pillars of gold and gleaming from afar. Adam of Bremen's description of the temple at Uppsala with its golden chain on the roof may be compared with such imagery, and seems likely to be based on literary rather than realistic traditions.[1]

Association of the gods of Asgard with Constantinople is no mere supposition. When Sigurd the Crusader visited the Hippodrome (p. 198 above) it was said that the figures of gods and heroes on the *spina* made it seem as if the Aesir and the great heroes were themselves present at the games. The fame of the Hippodrome was great in Europe and inspired the frescoes at Kiev in the eleventh century (p. 197 above). Olsen suggested that the picture of Valhall in *Grímnismál*, with hundreds of doors through which Odin's warriors could pour out on the last day, was based on the Roman Colosseum,[2] reminding us that other memorable buildings outside Byzantium may have caught the imagination of the Northern poets. But the Hippodrome, still featuring in the twelfth century as a place of lavish entertainment and the centre where

[1] Adam of Bremen, IV, 26, Sch. 139 (possibly an addition by another writer).
[2] M. Olsen, 'Valhall med de mange dörer', *Acta Philologica Scandinavica* 6 (1931–2), 151 ff.

technological marvels like fireworks were displayed, must have bulked large in the tales of travellers. So also must the Great Palace, with its complex series of buildings, galleries and passages, also without equal in Viking Age Europe.

The idea that Byzantium, with its many statues of gods and heroes, could represent the ancient home of the northern deities was in accord with antiquarian speculation about the Aesir under their leader Odin coming from south-eastern Europe. Snorri suggests this in the *Prose Edda* and in *Ynglinga Saga*, where the Aesir are said to come from Asaland or Asaheim, east of the Don. The same idea is found in other Icelandic sources,[1] and it was linked with that of the Trojans moving northwards after the fall of their city. Saxo implies that Odin dwelt in Byzantium, in his tale of a golden image of the god sent there by the northern kings as a token of homage.[2] Snorri tells us that Odin had great possessions in the land of the Turks, that is, Asia Minor, and journeyed up through Gardariki and Saxland to Denmark, into the realms of Gylfi of Sweden, the figure who asks questions concerning the gods in the first section of his *Prose Edda*. In *Ynglinga Saga* it is Gylfi who came to terms with the new arrivals, knowing that he could not contend against the folk of Asaheim; and so Odin settled in Sigtuna, while Njord, Freyr, Heimdall, Thor and Balder all had their own dwellings and served him as temple priests.

The obvious basis for a link between the Aesir and Asia is similarity of name. In the same way Vernadsky argued that the Aesir were to be linked with the Asii who merged with the Alans, or with the Rukh-As (p. 60 above). Icelandic scholars believe, however, that the name Aesir is to be linked with the *Anses*, whom Jordanes described as dead kings or heroes worshipped by the Goths, and with the Anglo-Saxon word *Ós* for 'god'; the same root is found in names from early runic inscriptions.[3] But in the legends of Asaheim scholarly speculation blends with travellers' tales of the marvels of the eastern regions, supported by the notion that the gilded figures of ancient deities in Constantinople represented the old gods of the North, and by euhemeristic theories that the

[1] Baetke, 22 ff.
[2] Saxo I, 25, 30–1.
[3] De Vries, *Altnordische Etymologisches Wörtebuch* (1961) under *Áss*; cf. Bosworth and Toller, *Anglo-Saxon Dictionary*, under *Ós*; Krause (1937), 438, no. 39; 550, no. 59.

heathen gods once lived on earth, fashionable among scholars of the eleventh and twelfth centuries.

The pageants and processions and brilliant mosaics in the Byzantine churches may have helped to inspire accounts of elaborate temples and figures of the northern gods with rich robes and jewels standing in temples decorated with gold and silver. It is now generally felt that such traditions in the written sources are due to literary convention and not based on realistic accounts of pre-Christian worship in the North. When goddesses like Thorgerd *Hǫlgabrúðr* [1] appear in the air over a battlefield shooting arrows to assist Jarl Hakon against his enemies, there is considerable resemblance to popular stories about the Blessed Virgin and the saints who appeared to give help to the Emperor's forces, current among the Byzantines. The sense of doom which hung over Constantinople even in the time of its prosperity, and which was associated with the statues in its streets and squares (p. 206 above) may also have left its influence on northern myths concerning the destruction of Asgard, the city of the gods, whose bright treasures were found among the grass in later days to bring back memories of its former greatness.

The idea that some of the plots of the later Icelandic sagas may have been brought back by Icelanders from Constantinople, put forward by Leach in 1921,[2] has not so far been justified. Further work on romance literature has revealed the tangled complexities of the motifs found in the popular stories and their rapid distribution through many countries of western Europe. However, some features in the *Fornaldar Sǫgur*, in particular the restoration of lost princes and princesses and the recital of their adventures, show a marked resemblance to prevailing fashions in Byzantine fiction.[3] There are also certain motifs in tales of the heroes suggesting an eastern origin, such as that of the hero meeting his death in a snake-pit. This could only have originated in eastern countries or in North Africa, where snakes abound, and such a method of execution is known to have been used by a king of Tunisia in the nineteenth century.[4] Nordland may be right in emphasising the

[1] *Flateyjarbók* I, 155 and other versions of Olaf Tryggvason's Saga. There is a reference to this legend in the twelfth-century poem *Buadrapa*.
[2] Leach, 268; 384.   [3] Schauch (1934), 55 ff.
[4] Dronke, 65 ff.; Krappe, 24 ff. Cf. O. Nordland, *Viking*, 13 (1949), 92, and Magoun, 211 ff.

influence of Christian vision literature and the conception of the grave as a pit of serpents, but the motif of the man surrounded by snakes is found on the Gotland stones in a pagan context,[1] and again on the Oseberg wagon; it may well have come from the eastern region with other traditions associated with the heroes of Odin. Krappe has found parallels in Greek, Macedonian and Mongol tales.

In the opening chapter of one of the later sagas, *Dámusta Saga*, a singularly dull story is given a setting in Constantinople.[2] The Emperor of the tale is said to live in a fortress with a great minster, the mother of many churches in the city, called *Aegisif*, the Icelandic name for Hagia Sophia. We are told that the walls of the city were so high and steep that only a bird might pass over, and that at Stolpasund (the Golden Horn) there was a narrow strait, where iron pillars stood with iron gates between, and beyond was an inlet where many warships could lie at anchor. These details seem to have been taken from some description of Constantinople such as might be found in a guide book for pilgrims. Here memories of the walls and the chain over the harbour have impressed the traveller, and the impressive showmanship in the Great Palace must have helped to give the Byzantines a reputation for secret knowledge and even magical power. The great throne with its mechanical devices, as Liutprand describes it (p. 195 above), is one example of Byzantine technology, and mechanical clocks and gold and silver organs were displayed to important visitors. In belittling such effects as childish ostentation, Arnold Toynbee speaks from the standpoint of our own scientific age [3] and surely underestimates the effects of the ingenious working models on those who could have had no notion of the principles involved. The Byzantines were not in themselves great inventors, but benefited from scientific work which had been going on in Alexandria for centuries and from the technology of their Arab neighbours; this was put to direct use in the heating, lighting and drainage of their city, as well as in the devices and entertainments with which they hoped to impress their visitors.

We have no detailed accounts of how the automata worked. Liutprand suggested that the raising of the throne may have been

[1] Lindqvist (1941), Klinte Hunninge I and Ardre VI, figs. 128, 139.
[2] *Dámusta Saga*, edited L. F. Tan Havarhorst (Haarlem 1939), 1.
[3] A. Toynbee, 498.

on the same principle as a wine-press, while it seems that the singing birds worked by means of either air or water pipes.[1] It is scarcely likely that Liutprand, with his scorn of all things Byzantine, exaggerated what he saw. The metal tree was perhaps inspired by one ornamented with jewels at the court of Baghdad, visited by Byzantine envoys in 917. Some of the clocks were probably water ones, and simple mechanism only would be needed to strike the hours, but when figures appeared in doorways when the hour struck, as in the case of the clock described by Harun b. Yahya in the tenth century, these must have been worked by weights, rollers and pulleys in the manner of the automatic puppet theatre.[2] Such clocks were probably made by Muslim craftsmen, and were sometimes sent as gifts to Christian monarchs; their basic principle was that of a float suspended in a basin of water which was filled or emptied by the regulating mechanism.[3] Seven clocks are recorded in Constantinople, including the famous one in the palace and one in Hagia Sophia. The organs, also described by Harun b. Yahya, may have been worked by bellows or by one or two compression cylinders, with a central wind chamber in which water acted as a pressure-stabilizing device;[4] they were quite small instruments, which could be moved about as needed.

The claim has often been made that the automata influenced descriptions of marvels in western romance literature, but there is little evidence for this in Icelandic works. Whether the description of figures of youths blowing horns, worked by the wind, in the account of the hall of Hugon in the *Pèlerinage de Charlemagne* and its many imitations was based on two figures on the gate of the Bucoloen seems doubtful; there is a description of them in a work attributed to Georgius Codinus [5] but there is no reference to such figures in early sources.[6] Literary descriptions of Hugon's palace have clearly influenced that of the hall of Raudulf visited by Olaf the Holy in a tale in *Flateyjarbók*,[7] though here there is additional

[1] For the wine-press, see Usher, 124; for the automata, Brett, 477 ff.
[2] Vasiliev (1932); cf. Izedin, 59; Janin, 103–4; for the puppet theatre, Usher, 140 ff.
[3] Ibid. 142 ff; 188 ff.
[4] Ibid. 136 ff.
[5] Schlauch (1932), 500 ff.
[6] Neither Gulland (249 ff.) nor Janin (120 ff.) mentions evidence for them.
[7] Schlauch (1934), 157 ff.

material about the study of the heavens not found in the French source; but this need not have come direct from Byzantine sources.

Certainly one of the technological marvels of Byzantium which must have had a devastating effect on the Scandinavians who encountered it was Greek fire, used in sea battles against ships attacking Constantinople. Here we are dealing not with literary models but with the direct world of experience. The development of this fire weapon by the scientists of Byzantium and its efficient distribution for use in the navy from the seventh century onwards was certainly an outstanding achievement, which I have discussed more fully elsewhere.[1] It continued to be a powerful secret weapon until the thirteenth century, when the discovery of the importance of saltpetre led to work on explosives rather than incendiary weapons. By this time the Arabs had developed incendiaries to such a point that the Byzantines no longer held the outstanding advantage they had once possessed, while their naval organization was no longer as efficient as it had been. There is no doubt that the essential ingredient of the fire was a compound containing petroleum, in the form of either crude oil or a distilled fraction, and in the latter case probably thickened with resins to produce a sticky liquid which would continue to burn over a long period.[2] Many incendiaries were in use in the ancient world by nations within reach of the natural oil seepages in Persia and the area round the Caspian, but the great advantage of the Byzantine fire was its efficient control: we are told that it could be projected either to the left or right, and made to fall from above.[3] The effects of this terrifying weapon are described by Anna Comnena in her account of a sea battle near Rhodes in 1103:[4]

'The barbarians now became thoroughly alarmed, firstly because of the fire directed upon them (for they were not accustomed to that kind of machine, nor to a fire which naturally flames upwards but in this case was directed in whatever direction the sender desired, often downwards or laterally), and secondly they were much upset by the storm, and consequently they fled.'

[1] Davidson (1973/1), 61 ff.
[2] For objections to other theories, see Partington and Forbes (1959, 1964).
[3] Described in *Tactica* in a passage which Partington discusses in detail (15 ff.).
[4] Anna Comnena (translated Dawes) XI, 292–3.

Liutprand tells us that in 941 the Greeks were able to use the fire because the Lord helped by lulling the winds and calming the waves, 'for otherwise the Greeks would have had difficulty in hurling their fire'.[1] On a calm sea there could have been no adequate defence by the small wooden ships, and men who plunged overboard ran the risk of being burned by the fire on the water. Our knowledge of modern flame-throwers gives us some idea of the frightfulness of this weapon, and since the Viking method of attack necessitated drawing close to the enemy ships in order to board them they were especially vulnerable.

The fire was again used against the Rus in 1043 (p. 170 above). Psellus [2] tells us that when the attack was made, naval strength in the capital was low, but a few triremes equipped with devices for using the fire had an immediate effect on the line of Rus ships drawn up across the Bosphorus. The mere threat of the fire could act as a valuable deterrent, as when in 971 Svyatoslav's forces found their way down the Danube blocked by the Greek fireships, and were unable to escape from Dristra when their position became desperate (p. 145 above).

The method of discharging the fire was by tubes set in the sides of ships. In *Tactica* it is said to have issued forth with a noise of thunder and with fiery smoke, and it is clear that the flame could travel some distance. It was used also in land battles and against siege weapons, but its main value to the Greeks was in fighting at sea. There is a clear reference to Greek fire in *Yngvars Saga*, the account of a famous expedition down the Volga by a party of Swedes in the eleventh century (p. 167 above). Ingvar had received warnings about Greek fire, and he and his men realised what was happening when it was flung at them by ships hidden in the reeds.[3] They heard the noise of bellows, and the men on the ships '... began to blow with smiths' bellows at a hearth with fire in it, and there was a great roar from this. There was a tube of bronze (*eirtromba*) and from it much fire flew against one of their ships, so that in a short time nothing was left of it but ashes.' Ingvar retaliated by using a fire-arrow kindled by a tinder-box which a bishop had blessed, and set the enemy ship alight in its

[1] Liutprand, *Antapodosis* 5, 15, 186.
[2] Psellus VI, 94–5.
[3] *Yngvars Saga*, 21.

turn. He continued to shoot his arrows whenever he heard the noise of bellows, and in the end gained a victory over 'the devil's folk'. Such arrows were certainly used in war,[1] but it is hardly likely that a Swedish prince in the eleventh century would have them ready to hand, or that ships with Greek fire manned by a heathen crew would have been waiting for him on the Volga. However, this passage shows a knowledge of how the fire was used, and the mention of the bellows fits in with other evidence from Greek sources for the heating of the inflammable liquid ejected from the tubes.[2]

The moral effect of the fire was enormous, and the terror and excitement which it aroused may be compared with our own reactions to the atomic bomb. Many thought it a supernatural weapon, and in the *Primary Chronicle* it is said that when the Rus returned home in 941 [3] '... each recounted to his kinsfolk the course of events and described the fire launched from the ships; they related that the Greeks had in their possession the lightning from heaven, and had set them on fire by pouring it forth, so that the Rus could not conquer them.' This terror was deliberately exploited by the Byzantines. Anna Comnena recounts that Emperor Alexis himself visited the shipyards to instruct the workmen and directed that animal heads should be fixed to the ends of the metal tubes discharging the fire, so that they had [4] '... the head of a lion or other land animal made in brass or iron with the mouth open and gilded over so that their mere aspect was terrifying. And the fire which was to be directed against the enemy through tubes he made to pass through the mouths of the beasts so that it seemed as if the lions ... were vomiting the fire.' Supernatural fire issuing from the mouths of fierce beasts is a wonderful image of power and terror; Alexis knew exactly what he was about. The emphasis on the fire-spitting dragon in early medieval literature as distinct from that of the serpent or the flying dragon may well owe something to confused memories of fierce dragon-heads projecting fire from Greek ships, while the horror of the incendiary attacks may account for the vividness of the description of the fiery dragon in

[1] e.g. *Aeneas on Siegecraft* (edited L. W. Hunter, Oxford 1927), 33, 90 and examples given by Partington.
[2] Davidson (1973/1), 71 ff.
[3] *Primary Chronicle*, 955–41, 72.
[4] Anna Comnena (translated Dawes), xi, 292.

the Anglo-Saxon poem *Beowulf*. In this way an ancient symbol gained life from the realities of technological warfare and the reputation of the Byzantine defences.

Methods of production were kept secret and the policy proved so effective that we are still told that the secret of the fire has been irretrievably lost. In the tenth century Constantine Porphyrogenitus forbade his son in a solemn and eloquent passage to reveal to any other nation the secret of the 'liquid fire which is discharged through tubes'.[1] This, together with the imperial vestments and diadem of the Emperor, was to be regarded as a sacred trust, the gift of an angel to the first Emperor Constantine. He says concerning the fire: 'We are assured by the faithful witness of our fathers and grandfathers that it should be manufactured among the Christians only, and in the city ruled by them, and nowhere else at all, nor should it be sent nor taught to any other nation whatsoever.' Anyone who failed in this trust, even should it be the Emperor himself, must be expelled from his position and put to death. There is a warning story of a military governor bribed to hand over Greek fire to an enemy, who was himself consumed by fire from heaven when entering a church. In fact, there were lapses, as when thirty-six siphons and the fire to use in them fell into the hands of the Bulgarians in the 814 campaign, while petroleum was being put to very effective use by the Arabs. However, possession of the Byzantine fire would be of little use to an enemy without the necessary skill and organisation to manufacture large quantities by a reliable formula and to keep up a constant supply to the navy. The preparation, packing and despatch of the liquid, said to have been the responsibility of one particular family in Constantinople, were carried out over a long period with impressive efficiency.

The techniques employed against incendiary devices may also have added to the reputation of the wise men of Byzantium. Use of asbestos fabrics was apparently known in the ancient world, since Strabo, Pliny and other writers refer to napkins made from it which could be cleansed in fire.[2] Pliny claims that this special cloth was used to wrap the bodies of the dead before cremation, so that

[1] *De Administrando Imperio*, 69 ff.
[2] Laufer, 301 ff. The mineral used was probably chrysolite, differing from modern asbestos (J. W. Evans, *Mineralogical Magazine*, 14 (1904–7), 143–8).

the calcined bones would be kept together. Asbestos carpets were used by the Arabs in the Viking Age, and soldiers trained to hurl petroleum wore asbestos coats for protection.[1] Ploss [2] discusses the widespread tradition of garments of invulnerability in medieval Germanic literature, and offers as an analogy the tunics worn by American soldiers in the Korean War, made of glass fibres woven with nylon; although a single fibre is fragile, many heated together form a material which is both flexible and virtually impenetrable. If asbestos and silk were woven together in medieval times, this would form a protective garment against fire and weapons, and Ploss quotes Anna Comnena's reference to mailcoats and helmets of grey silk resembling metal in colour, worn by Alexius' soldiers at the battle of Lebunion in 1191, when there was insufficient iron for all.[3]

The shirt of invulnerability is a favourite motif in Norse literature. In the account of the death of the hero Ragnar Lodbrok, he wore a shirt which weapons could not pierce, and this protected him for a while in the snake-pit. When, however, he went out earlier in his career to slay the dragon, he took practical measures to guard against its fiery breath: he chose woollen cloth of coarse quality, heated it in tar until it was matted and impregnated with resin, and then rolled it in sand to give it a hard surface.[4] In Saxo's account we are told that the hero intended [5] '... to use a dress stuffed with hair to protect himself, and also took one that was not unwieldy that he might move nimbly.' Here, however, the point of the protection against fire is lost, since only the poison of the dragon is mentioned, and Ragnar's method of hardening the cloth by plunging it into cold water and letting it freeze on his body is not a sensible one. In *Beowulf* the aged king prepared a protection against the fire of the dragon by having a huge iron shield made, large enough for two men to shelter behind; while at the same time he wore his special 'battle-shirt', which Grendel's mother had been unable to pierce with her knife.[6] The emphasis in the poem

[1] R. J. Forbes, *Studies in Early Petroleum History* (1958), introduction.
[2] Ploss, 26 ff.
[3] Anna Comnena VIII, 5, 203.
[4] *Ragnars Saga Loðbrókar*, 2.
[5] Saxo IX, 302, 365.
[6] *Beowulf* 2337–41; 2523–4; the term 'battle-shirt', *heresyrce/hieroserce*, is used only on these two occasions.

on the fire raining from the air and flowing in a liquid stream out of the dragon's lair, 'hot with battle-fire',[1] as well as on the terrible effects of burning on the warriors who encounter the monster, raises the question of whether here we may discern Swedish influence, based on some knowledge of Greek fire used in warfare.

Ploss noted that Ragnar's protective shirt was obtained from Aslaug, the daughter of Sigurd the Volsung, who fought as a valkyrie, and that it is described as a grey garment, the gift of the gods.[2] Such a garment is found in a number of stories connected with the Volsung cycle, and is associated with Brynhild, Dietrich and Wolfdietrich in Germanic tradition. The earliest mention of this tunic is in the Icelandic poem *Hamðismál*, when Hamdir and Sorli wear garments to protect them from wounds, and Jormunrek accordingly calls on his men to stone them.[3] They are said to pull on their 'well-woven' garments as they draw near the hall of the King. In another account of this tragic expedition, in *Guðrúnarhvǫt*, Gudrun is said to provide her sons with 'ample mailcoats' when they set out. Ursula Dronke doubts whether the idea of the coat which protected the wearer from wounds formed part of the original story, although the point is emphasised in both the *Prose Edda* and *Vǫlsunga Saga*.[4] But she also notes a hint in the earliest source, a ninth-century poem by Bragi, which describes the heroes as *hrafnblair*, apparently referring to the dark clothes or armour which they wore, and uses the term *saums andvanar*, 'without a join', suggesting a protective garment with no weak places. Thus it is possible that in the earliest tradition Gudrun's sons wore tunics of outstanding quality, giving protection against wounds, and that later on the story of a magic garment inevitably crept into the account. Emphasis on the dark colour of such garments recalls Anna Comnena's mention of the silk tunics of metallic shade worn by the soldiers, and it is interesting that in the *Icelandic Sagas* we find the convention that men going out to kill wear a dark garment.[5] One further example of strengthened silk is found by Ploss in the realm of myth: the cord Gleipnir used to bind the wolf is said in the *Prose Edda* to be a smooth silk ribbon impossible to break.

[1] Ibid. 2545–9.
[2] Ploss, 21 ff.
[3] *Hamðismál*, verses 16, 25.
[4] Dronke, 179–80.
[5] Ibid. 209, note 3.

Indeed the silk of Byzantium possessed an almost supernatural aura in itself. The finest quality silk was a state monopoly, used for the robes of the Emperor, and might not be purchased (p. 94 above). This, along with Greek fire, was something which must not be allowed to fall into enemy hands. The slippers of purple silk which the Emperor wore had enormous symbolic value, and his robes, made of rich silk with elaborate designs, sometimes ornamented with gold and lined with fur, were among the greatest treasures of the state. There were also special silk robes of various colours worn by the different ranks at court on state occasions and festivals.[1] Gifts of lengths of silk made to foreign diplomats or members of the household were greatly valued, and these were the greatest honour which could be bestowed on western rulers. Something of this is reflected in the Icelandic sagas in the emphasis on clothes of scarlet silk, like those worn by Bolli and his men on their return from the East (p. 105 above).

Thus although there is little evidence of direct literary influence from Byzantine sources on Norse literature, there is influence of a different kind to be discerned. Knowledge of Byzantium results in a kind of scholarly speculation, mingled with folklore and what might be called science fiction. This enriches the myths of the gods in literature of the late Viking Age, and the tales of heroes and marvels in the period following. But there is influence also from the Eastern regions of an independent kind, associated with the world of barbarians rather than Greeks, as we may see in the two following chapters.

[1] Ebersolt (1917), 50 ff.

CHAPTER 2

The Role of the Shaman

As increasing interest has been shown in shamanism during recent years, it has been recognised that there is a strong shamanistic element in Old Norse myths and tales of magic. Striking resemblances between certain rites and symbols in Old Norse literature and those recorded among peoples of northern Europe and northern and central Asia who have practised shamanism in recent times have been pointed out more than once. In particular the behaviour of the god Odin has been claimed to show marked shamanic characteristics.

Mircea Eliade commented on this in his detailed study of shamanism first published in 1951.[1] He took as the essential quality of the shaman ability to enter into a state of ecstasy and to journey in spirit to other regions. He compared the myth of Odin hanging on a tree to gain knowledge with tales of shamans enduring the torments of initiation before gaining full powers. He noted that Odin rode on his eight-legged horse to the Land of the Dead, and that he could take on bird and animal form; he could gain information from the dead, while he had a following of berserks, dedicated warriors who fought in a state of ecstatic fury, rendering them impervious to wounds. Other Norse supernatural beings could take on bird or animal shape, while the accounts of the type of magic known as *seiðr* appear to fit into the characteristic background of shamanism as practised in Siberia.

As to whether this evidence means that shamanism was developed among the Germanic peoples in pre-Christian times,

[1] *Le chamanisme et les techniques archaiques de l'estase* (Paris 1951). Revise English translation by W. R. Trask (London 1964). For the section on Odin see (1964), 380 ff.; cf. Davidson (1964), 141 ff.

Eliade remains cautious.[1] Vajda, in a later paper on shamanism,[2] argues that ecstasy may be present without involving shamanism in the true sense, but his list of requisites is generally covered by Eliade's summary of the characteristics of Odin. Some scholars nevertheless remain unconvinced, and Fleck, in a study of *Grímnismál* [3] where Odin sits in torment between two fires and reveals hidden wisdom, argues that the characteristics listed by Eliade could be related to other sides of the religious tradition, and particularly to that of sacral kingship. This is a fair criticism, but Fleck ignores other work on shamanistic elements in Old Norse literature, and in particular that of Strömbäck.[4]

Strömbäck concentrated on *seiðr*, a particular ceremonial associated with divination or magic which appears to differ from what we know of early Germanic paganism. *Seiðr* is carried out on a *hjallr*, a platform or scaffold, sometimes described as a high seat. On this a woman usually sits (it is mainly though not invariably women who play the main part is such rites), and may be assisted by helpers singing spells. After the ritual, she appears to emerge from a state of trance, and then reveals hidden information about the future, either of the community as a whole or of individuals present.

In his detailed examination of passages where the term *seiðr* occurs, Strömbäck shows that many of these are late additions, some imitations of earlier passages, and some influenced by literary models outside Norse literature. Some, however, appear to be derived from early traditions, in particular the tale of the *seidkona* Heid in *Hrólfs Saga Kraka*, found also in Saxo, who was possibly using a more reliable form.[5] Here a king who has seized the kingdom from his two young nephews consults a sorceress in order to discover where the boys are hiding so that he may put them to death. In order to avoid betraying them, the woman cuts the ceremony short; in Saxo's account she falls down as if senseless, and in the saga account she leaps down from the platform. Another tradition which may be early is that of the Lapp woman

[1] Eliade (1964), 375 ff.
[2] Vajda, 456 ff.
[3] Fleck, 49 ff.
[4] An English translation of the Swedish study (Lund 1935) is in preparation, and is to be published by the Folklore Society.
[5] Strömbäck, 79 ff.; Saxo VII, 217–18, 262.

working *seiðr* in *Ǫrvar-Odds Saga*,[1] a story which has been referred to in an earlier chapter (p. 38). This *seiðkona* is also called Heid, and she is invited to the hall of a landowner named Ingjald living in northern Norway. She is assisted by a choir of youths and girls singing spells, and with this company goes out at night 'to perform *seiðr*'. No details are given of this ritual, but next day the woman prophesies concerning the destinies of a number of those present including Odd, although the young hero is very hostile towards her. The earliest manuscripts of this saga are of early fourteenth-century date, and it may go back to about 1300 in its written form. Strömbäck believes that this account influenced the story of a Lapp woman entertained at the hall of another Ingjald in *Vatns-dæla Saga*.

The most detailed and arresting account of *seiðr* is that in the saga of Eirik the Red.[2] Consultation of the seeress Thorbjorg takes place in Greenland, and she is called a *spákona*: that is, a woman with power to foretell the future. She is also 'the little *vǫlva*', or seeress, and we are told: 'She had had nine sisters, and all were *spákonur*, but she was now the only one left alive'. During the winter it was the custom of Thorbjorg to go to feasts, and men would usually invite her to visit them when they were anxious to learn their future for the coming season.' When she was invited by Thorkell in this way, it was in order to find out whether the severe famine from which the district had been suffering was likely to cease. The seeress arrived in the evening, and what is described as a high seat had been made ready, with a cushion which had to be stuffed with hens' feathers. Her appearance is described in detail:

'She had on a blue cloak, set with stones all over the skirt; she had glass beads round her neck, and a hood of black lamb's fur on her head, lined with white catskin. She had a staff in her hand with a knob at the end; it was bound with brass and stones set round the knob. She had on a girdle of touchwood, and on it a large skin purse, in which she kept the charms needed for her magic; she had hairy boots of calf-hide, with long thongs and big knobs of tin at the ends. She had on gloves of catskin, white and furry inside.'

She had a meal with the rest, but special dishes had been made

[1] *Ǫrvar-Odds Saga*, 2.   [2] *Eiríks Saga Rauda*, 4.

ready for her: 'Gruel of goat's milk was prepared for her, and for meat the hearts of all living creatures available. She used a brass spoon and a knife with a handle of walrus ivory, with two rings of copper, broken at the point.' After this she was asked if all was as she wished, and if she thought that she could find out what they desired to know. She replied that she was unable to tell until next morning, after she had slept.

The main ceremony was on the following evening, and she asked for women with knowledge of what was needed for the *seiðr*, who could sing a spell called *Varðlokur*: [1] '... but no such women were to be found. Inquiries were made round the farm to see if anyone knew it. Then Gudrid said: "I am not skilled in magic nor a wise woman, but my fostermother Halldis out in Iceland taught me a song which she called *Varðlokur*."' At first Gudrid, who was a Christian, was unwilling to sing, but she was finally persuaded. The women then formed a ring round the platform (*hjallr*) and Thorbjorg sat on top. Gudrid sang the song so well that those present thought they had never heard more beautiful singing. The wise woman thanked her warmly, saying that many spirits (*náttúrur*) have now come, thinking the music fair to hear, 'those who before wished to keep away and not to listen to us'. Many things were now revealed to her, she said, and she told them that the famine and epidemic from which they were suffering would end. She then foretold the destiny of Gudrid herself.

The date of the saga is probably late thirteenth century, but it may go back to the twelfth century in its original form. Traditional sources are used, some from *Landnámabók*, but it has been thought that the account of the ceremony was the work of a reviser with considerable interest in magic of this kind, perhaps writing from first-hand knowledge, or else with access to a written account by someone who had witnessed such a ceremony. A traditional portrait of a seeress, handed down from pagan times, is hardly likely to be so detailed, and the account gives the impression by details like the broken knife that it is from an eye-witness. It seems improbable that such a rite could have taken place in Greenland or even Iceland, but it could have been based on something witnessed in northern Norway, or further east. The saga-writer was obviously anxious to bring in the prophecy of the glorious future of Gudrid's

---

[1] For possible meanings of this word, see Strömbäck, 124 ff.

descendants, among whom were three Icelandic bishops, and to place her in the centre of the stage. He could have picked on the traditional motif of the foretelling of the future by a wise woman, and made use of this detailed account to elaborate his setting.

The resemblances, however, are not so close to what we know of shamanism among the Lapps as that among the peoples further east. One important feature is the costume. It has often been pointed out that the shaman's costume emphasises his association with the animal world, its main parts consisting of head-covering, decorated robe or cloak, gloves, boots and staff.[1] Here we have a hood, decorated cloak, fur gloves, leather boots and staff. The glass beads and the 'stones' on the cloak are in keeping with the ornaments, all of a symbolic nature, adorning the costume of a Siberian shaman. The cloak in the saga account is called *tuglamǫttul*, 'cloak with straps', and the term has usually been interpreted as a cloak with straps for fastening; but no other examples of this are known, and it may indicate a garment hung with thongs, straps or bands in the manner of the shaman's cloak in Siberia and elsewhere. A modern shaman of the Enets wore boots of deer hide with the fur inside, the fur closely trimmed and the soles of sheared deer fur.[2] Fur gloves formed an important part of the costume, although not worn on the hands but fastened to the sleeve.[3] Birds' feathers were frequently used, and here it may be significant that they were used inside the cushion on which the *vǫlva* sat. The symbolic meal of animals' hearts is another link with the animal world, and it may be noted that the receiving of a piece of reindeer heart was part of the ritual of an Evenk shaman,[4] which also included the calling of spirits to attend the ceremony, as in the Icelandic account; this indeed is a frequent feature of shamanistic ceremonies.

A second parallel is found in the form of the rite of divination. First the *vǫlva* answers questions concerning the community as a whole and then makes individual prophecies about the futures of those present, answering individual questions. A similar feature is found among shamanistic ceremonies of the Chukchees: the shaman first sings and beats his drum, and then goes on to foretell

[1] Harva-Holmberg (1927) 514 ff. and (1938) 499 ff.; Eliade (1964) 145 ff.
[2] Prokofyeva. 143.
[3] Ibid. 135 ff.
[4] Anisimov, 104.

the future, speaking to those present one at a time: [1] 'When he was through with one case he would stop for a while, as if recovering himself, and then after several deep-drawn sighs, would pass on to the next applicant.' In the ceremony witnessed among the Evenks in 1931 by Anisimov, the long and exacting performance ended with questions being put to the shaman, his answers here being obtained with the use of a rattle and a reindeer's spatula on which he laid burning coals.

It can hardly be expected that the saga account should agree in every detail with any single description of ceremonies from one particular region several centuries after the saga was written, but the detailed parallels are so impressive that it seems reasonable to suppose that some first-hand knowledge of shamanistic ritual lies behind the account. On the other hand, there are significant omissions. We find no mention of either a drum or a dance being used, although there is nothing to rule out the possibility that the *vǫlva* passed into an ecstatic trance before gaining her knowledge about the future. Strömbäck suggested that an obscure passage in *Lokasenna* may refer to Odin beating on a lid when he performed *seiðr*,[2] while comparison has been made with the berserks beating on their shields, but there is no clear evidence in the literature of association of *seiðr* with any rite of this kind. Also *seiðr* appears in the sagas either to be a divination ceremony or a piece of harmful magic.[3] There appears to be no association with the search for the spirit of a sick person, or for the conducting of the spirit of a sacrificed animal to the Other World, as is usual in Lapp or Siberian shamanism. Again the use of a high platform is the main feature of the *seiðr* ceremony, and this is not the case in Lapp or Siberian shamanism, although a low symbolic platform of wood is noted in the account of the Evenk shaman,[4] and the Eskimo shaman commonly sat or lay on a sleeping platform for the ceremony.[5] Kiil has suggested that the *seiðr* platform symbolises that on which the dead man was placed, and suggests that we may see such a structure depicted on the tapestry from the Oseberg ship burial of ninth-

[1] M. A. Czaplicka, *Aboriginal Siberia* (1914), 193–4, from Borgoras, *The Chukchee* (Memoirs of the American Museum of Natural History VI, 1904–10).
[2] Strömbäck, 32.
[3] Davidson (1973/2) 36 ff.
[4] Anisimov, 86.
[5] E. Holtved, *Studies in Shamanism*, 26.

Fig. 4. Part of the ninth-century tapestry from Oseberg, showing a structure which has been interpreted as a divination platform (after Kiil, *Arkiv f. nordisk Filologi* 75, 1960).

century date.[1] He also identifies the *seiðhjallr* with Odin's seat from which he could see into all worlds, and again with the structure 'resembling a door' erected for the funeral ceremony of the Rus on the Volga (p. 66 above), when the slave girl was lifted up to look over it into the world of the dead. It is interesting to compare with this the door symbol of parallel or crossed pieces of wood set up for the Evenk shaman, symbolising the blocking of the way into the lower world,[2] and the occasional practice of leaving the body of a dead shaman on a wooden platform in the forest.[3] However, the evidence of *seiðr* from the texts hardly seems to justify the claim that here we have examples of shamanistic practices carried out by the Scandinavians in Iceland in pagan times, the memory of which has passed into the literature of the twelfth and thirteenth centuries.

Strömbäck's conclusions were that by the thirteenth century and later comparatively little was known of the practice, but memories of ceremonies on a high platform and consultation of those skilled in divination had left their mark on both prose and poetry and were associated in particular with the god Odin. He believed that the main inspiration for this came from northern Norway as a result of association with the Lapps. In several cases the *vǫlva* is a Finn (? Lapp) woman, and there are cases of Finn men also being consulted in this way. In *Vatnsdæla Saga*[4] three *Finnar* are consulted by Ingimund in Norway and call themselves *semsveinar*: this word must come from the name used by the Lapps of themselves (modern *Samek*).[5] However, in this case they do not work *seiðr* from a platform but retreat into a hut, remaining there until they have discovered what Ingimund desires to know; it is said that their spirits have travelled over the sea to Iceland and back.

Although there is no mention of the drum in Icelandic literature, an early thirteenth-century story from the Latin *Chronicon Norwegiae*[6] describes its use by Lapp shamans for healing purposes. Two Norwegian merchants had visited the home of a Lapp,

[1] Kiil, 85 ff.
[2] Animisov, 88 ff.
[3] M. A. Czaplicka, *Aboriginal Siberia* (1914), 156–7, 161.
[4] *Vatnsdæla Saga*, 12.
[5] Buchholz, 180.
[6] Karsten, 74 ff. For the original, P. A. Munch, *Symbolae ad historiam antiquarum rerum norwegicarum* (Kristiania 1850), 4–5.

and while they were having a meal their hostess suddenly collapsed. A 'diviner' was then called in, and he spread out a cloth, seated himself beneath it, and lifted up an object like a sieve in shape, on which were depicted a whale, a reindeer drawing a sledge and a boat with oars, objects said to help the spirit of the diviner on his spirit journey. He danced and chanted incantations for a long while, but finally collapsed, black in the face; his belly burst open and he died. A second man expert in such arts was summoned, and after he had danced for a while, the woman on the floor regained consciousness and told them what had happened. The first shaman had journeyed in the form of a whale, whereupon an enemy spirit had taken on the form of a pointed stake and speared the whale, so that the injury appeared on the body of the shaman. This account is in keeping with later descriptions of shamanism among the Lapps, but differs from accounts of *seiðr* in the absence of a platform and the use of the drum. Also the shamans are both men, as was usual among Lapps, although women might help by singing spells. We are told nothing of the shaman's costume, but it might be noted in passing that the animals represented in the costume of the Greenland seeress are not those likely to be found among the northern Lapps.

Peter Buchholz has shown that there is a good deal of additional evidence to be taken into account for the knowledge of shamanistic ritual and imagery in Icelandic literature.[1] He has collected material for the use of animal spirits and for the taking on of animal form both by supernatural beings and by men and women, and also for the travelling of the spirit away from the body. He also notes the tradition for a series of worlds, both horizontal and vertical, through which the spirit passes, and that of a long and dangerous journey to the Other World. He surveys in detail evidence for the ecstatic state, the mantic trance, and the torment endured by those seeking hidden knowledge, including Odin's sufferings hanging on the tree or seated between two fires. He notes, too, the association of such practices with a change of sex, a characteristic found among the shamans of Siberia,[2] as well as the

---

[1] *Shamanistische Züge in der altisländischen Uberlieferung*, doctrinal thesis, University of Münster, Saarbrücken 1968.

[2] This aspect has been emphasised by Soviet scholars; see Rank, 'Shamanism as a Research Subject' in *Studies in Shamanism*.

concept of healing by supernatural beings who appear in dreams. There are frequent cases of the covering of the head of someone entering into a state of trance, as in the Norwegian account, and also of the deliberate sending out of the spirit to gain information, associated with the term *gandr*. This is a word of Germanic origin found in the sagas, and was in use among the Lapps, who according to accounts by earlier missionaries used to keep flies in a *gand*-box to harm men and cattle.[1] It seems at one time to have been associated with the idea of the guardian spirit in both human and animal form. This detailed investigation of imagery, vocabulary and literary motifs is of great importance for any study of shamanistic elements in Icelandic literature.

Further evidence may be sought in tales of witchcraft in the sagas; I have discussed this elsewhere,[2] noting how besides familiar magic practices such as control of the weather, physical harm brought on enemies, the blunting of weapons and the use of evil runes, there are also examples of harmful magic which can be paralleled from tales of shamanistic lore. These tales could well be based not on accounts of adventures in the ordinary world, but on the exploits of shamans in the spirit world, and some of them are accounts of conflicts between supernatural beings like that in the Norwegian story quoted above. We have an example in a series of tales about *sjónhverfing*, where a man is concealed from his pursuers by a special type of magic, the 'deceiving of the sight'. A light-hearted story in *Eyrbyggja Saga* is an example of this. An objectionable character called Odd was concealed by his mother, Katla, a dangerous woman skilled in magic. When his pursuers entered the house they saw Katla spinning; beside her stood Odd, but all they could see was a distaff. After they had left the house they suspected that they had been tricked and came back. Katla was combing her son's hair in the entrance, but they thought she was grooming her goat. A third time they returned to come upon Odd lying in the ash-heap, but all that they could see was Katla's tame boar stretched out there. Then they were joined by a woman skilled in magic, Geirrid, and when Katla saw her approaching in a blue cloak she declared that *sjónhverfing* would now be of no avail; she hid Odd under the dais, but Geirrid went straight to his

[1] Lid (1927), 331 ff. cf. *Nordisk Kultur*, 19 (1935) 34–9; Karsten, 87.
[2] Davidson (1973/2).

hiding-place, and he and his mother were put to death. There are a number of stories of this kind, although less detailed, and it is instructive to compare them with shamanic myths like one recorded among the Chukchee: [1]

The Moon desired to carry off a girl, and she was warned of this by a great bull reindeer in her father's herd. He offered to help her and dug in the snow with his hoof; then he told her to sit down, and she appeared to be a little heap of snow: 'The Moon came, looked for the girl, walked round but could not find her. The top of her head was visible to be sure, but it looked like a hillock.' Moon went away, and the reindeer took the girl home. They discussed what should be done to disguise her when Moon came back: '"Perhaps a stone block?" "He will know it." "Well, a hammer?" "He will know it." "Well, a hair in the bed curtain?" "He will know it, he will know it." "You know what, I shall turn you into a lamp." "Good, good."' Moon searched the house, but left the lamp alone because it was dangerous for two fires to come together. As he was leaving, the girl called to him, and he went back. This happened three times, until Moon shrivelled and grew weak, and the girl bound him. He agreed to create the seasons of the year for the people and to stay in the outer sky. The story thus accounts for the moon's waning and is a type of creation myth.

Deceiving magic of this kind is associated with the eastern people in Scandinavian literature. Thorir Hund, said to be skilled in Finn magic, uses it to hide his party from the Biarmians (p. 37 above), while Saxo attributes it to the Lapps,[2] and Gunnhild learned such arts from Lapp teachers.[3] The most famous example of *sjónhverfing* was that practised on the god Thor by Utgard-Loki, and there are links between this figure and the giant Svyatogor in the Russian *byliny*.[4]

Another significant group of tales resemble those told of shamans fighting one another in animal form. In a story in *Hjálmðers Saga* [5] there is a sea-battle between a number of characters skilled in magic. One lies down under a heap of clothes and forbids anyone to utter his name; he then appears in the sea in

[1] Anisimov, 216–17.
[2] Saxo V, 165, 204.
[3] *Heimskringla, Haralds Saga ins Hárfagra*, 32.
[4] Chadwick (1964), 243 ff.
[5] *Hjálmðers Saga ok Ǫlvés*, 20.

the form of a sword-fish. The princess escaping from her wicked father does the same, and appears as a porpoise. Her father is pursuing the ship in the form of a walrus, and the others attempt to drive him off, aided by two supernatural helpers who appear as vultures in the air. When the man, Hord, awakes from his trance he is seen to be wet, as if he had been in the sea, while the princess is found unconscious and weak and has to be revived with wine.

In another story from *Sturlaugs Saga*, much of which is set in the eastern region and where some *seiðmen* are found in a cave near Aldeigjuborg, a contest takes place between a youth and a Finn wizard; they do battle first as dogs, then as eagles in the air tearing at one another 'so that blood fell to the earth'.[1] This type of battle is found as a folktale motif in later times, but is also frequent in shamanistic lore; Vasja and others point out that this is an essential part of shamanistic tradition. Czaplicka [2] refers to one such battle between a Samoyed and a Yakut shaman, said to have gone on for years, where the scene of strife passed from the earth to the sky, then to the sea and finally to the depths below. Lapp shamans were said to fight in the form of reindeer spirits. It is not always clear whether it is the shaman himself who takes on animal form or the shaman's animal spirit which appears as a reindeer, but this ambiguity is characteristic of the adventures of shamans in the Other World; Hultkranz for instance notes that among the North American Indians no clear distinction is made between the shaman and his guardian spirit and that the shaman may journey in his guardian spirit's form.[3] Sometimes the animal spirit indeed is called one of the souls of the shaman.[4] In the story from the *Chronicon Norwegiae* the shaman was in the form of a whale and a hostile spirit took on the form of a stake to pierce his body.

Another story from the sagas which bears a close resemblance to some of those collected from shamans is the tale of the enchanted bull in *Eyrbyggja Saga*, a 'dapple-grey' animal, born to a cow after she had licked the ashes of the fire on which the dead body of the

---

[1] *Sturlaugs Saga Starfsama*, 12.
[2] M. A. Czaplicka, *My Siberian Year* (1916), 212.
[3] Hultkranz, 36.
[4] Anisimov, 101 ff. refers to the *khargi* or animal double which the Evenk shaman sends into the lower world.

evil Thorolf Lamefoot had been burned to stop him walking after death.[1] A shamanic tale recorded from the Yakuts in 1925 [2] tells of two brother shamans pursued by their enemies. One went back to the camp of the previous night to look for a lost mare and found her licking the ashes of the fire. He struck her with a willow-switch, whereupon she suddenly turned into a bull, which gored the shaman with his horns. He managed to return home to his brother before he died, and when the other man heard how his brother had been attacked by an evil spirit sent by their enemies, he turned himself into a great bull with huge horns. Letting out a loud bellow he went in pursuit of the enemy spirit, and they met in their bull forms on a holy mountain, where the shaman gored out his adversary's lung. The vanquished bull promised that he would never appear to any of the shaman's family again, but at the end of the victorious shaman's life, he met the same bull again in battle, and was defeated. His human body was found by his kindred dead upon his couch.

In the story in *Eyrbyggja Saga* the bull calf born after the cow had licked the ashes had a very loud bellow, and an old woman with second sight declared: 'That is the voice of a troll and not of a living creature.' She urged Thorodd to slaughter the calf, but he only pretended to have done so, and the calf grew into a bull of enormous strength and size, manageable only by Thorodd. At five years of age he got loose in a hay-meadow and Thorodd went to chase him out, but was attacked. He was carried round the field on the back of the bull, which finally tossed him into the air and gored him. The animal then ran away and plunged into a bog. Thorodd, like the shaman, was found dead in his bed when the men who had chased the bull returned home. Animals of this particular grey colour (*apalgrár*) are usually supernatural creatures in the sagas, and the shade is equivalent to the 'dapple-grey' of the Siberian story. The colour of Thorodd's bull, its great size and tremendous bellow, as well as the unrealistic nature of the story, suggests that a shamanic legend has inspired it. It could, however, hardly be a Lapp tale, since in Lappland the spirits fought as reindeer; it would have to come from a cattle-breeding area further south.

Finally there is a group of tales relating to supernatural foster-

[1] *Eyrbyggja Saga*, 63.
[2] Friedrich and Buddruss, 109 ff.

mothers.[1] In these the hero is adopted by a being usually called a giantess and has a strange relationship with her, being at once husband and foster-child. He stays with her for a while, but in general no children are born of this union, or else they come to an untimely end. Eventually the hero returns to the normal world and marries a human wife, but the giantess may continue to be his protectress and guardian spirit, coming to his help if he summons her, and she may give him magic weapons or come to him in bird or animal form. One of these stories concerns Ǫrvar-Odd, who had long connections with the eastern regions (p. 38 above). In the course of his travels he visited the fair giants of Risaland, and the giant's daughter Hildigunn put him into a cradle with her baby brother and treated him like an infant. Later, however, he became her husband and left Hildigunn with child. Other versions of the same motif are found in a number of the *Fornaldar Sǫgur*.[2] It also plays a major part in *Bárðar Saga Snæfellsáss* which is set in western Iceland; here the giant Bard is the 'god' of an Icelandic mountain, a conception similar to that found among the Lapps. He has nine daughters who live with him in a cave, and sometimes brings a young man to spend the winter there to be instructed in law and genealogies, and to contract a marriage with one of the daughters. The eldest of these, Helga, is said to spend much of her time roaming about the country, living in caves and hills and sometimes hiding in a house, lying in a curtained bed and playing the harp through the night; she declares that her dwelling is 'not in any one place'.[3]

The same motif occurs in Saxo's story of Hadingus,[4] which includes a short commentary on what is meant by a giantess. Hadingus, like his father, married the daughter of his *educator*, the equivalent of the foster-father of the sagas. She is called Harthgrepa, the daughter of the giant Vagnhoftus to whom he was sent as a boy to be fostered and instructed. She could be of giant size, but sometimes took on human form, and her own description of this change of form seems to have been suggested to Saxo by the

---

[1] Ellis (1942), 70 ff.
[2] *Hálfdanar Saga Brǫnufóstra; Illuga Saga Gríðarfóstra; Sǫrla Saga Sterka* and *Hjálmðers Saga ok Ǫlvés*.
[3] *Bárðar Saga Snæfellsáss*, 7.
[4] Saxo I, 20, 24 ff.

passage in Boethius where the figure of Philosophy is described.[1] However, there is little reminiscent of the instructress of Boethius in Harthgrepa, except that she acts as a supernatural helper and guide. She accompanies him dressed as a man, teaches him how to gain information from the dead, and when they are threatened by a hand of enormous size Harthgrepa swells to giant strength and grasps it so that Hadingus can cut it off, but she is afterwards torn to pieces by supernatural beings.

Close parallels to such stories may be found among the numerous traditions of female protective spirits who become the 'wives' of Siberian shamans. There are particularly good examples among the Golds, in a number of accounts collected by Sternberg.[2] The spirit wife of the shaman is called an *ayami*, and he was told: 'There can be no shaman without an *ayami*. What assistant spirits will come to him without one? The *ayami* is the shaman's teacher, he is like a god of his. A man's *ayami* is always a woman, and a woman's [is] a man, because they are like husband and wife. Some shamans sleep also with their assistant spirits, as with a woman.' He records a story of a shaman called to his vocation by a beautiful woman who came to him when he was ill; she was like a human being, but only seventy-one centimetres tall: [3]

'She said: "I am the *ayami* of your ancestors, the Shamans. I taught them shamaning. Now I am going to teach you".... Next she said: "I love you. I have no husband now, you will be my husband and I shall be a wife unto you. I shall give you assistant spirits. You are to heal with their aid, and I shall teach you and help you myself".... I felt dismayed and tried to resist. Then she said: "If you will not obey me, so much the worse for you. I shall kill you." ... She has been coming to me ever since, and I sleep with her as with my own wife, but we have no children. She lives quite by herself without any relatives in a hut on a mountain, but she often changes her abode. Sometimes she comes under the aspect of an old woman, and sometimes under that of a wolf, so she is terrible to look at. Sometimes she comes as a winged tiger. I mount it, and she takes me to show me different countries.'

[1] *Consolation of Philosophy* I, 1.
[2] Sternberg, 487.
[3] Ibid. 476 ff.

Another outstanding shaman from the Amyr region told Sternberg that he had three such spirit wives, and also a human wife, a girl of about eighteen, who was devoted to him. Similarly, among the Buryats a young shaman's spirit was said to visit the god of the Middle World, who lived with the nine daughters of Siboni, the god of the dawn, a special deity of the shamans. The young man might woo these maidens, and later would take a spirit of the sky as his own wife; a public marriage ceremony was held to celebrate this, although he had a human wife as well.[1] Shamans among the Teleut, a Turkish tribe, were said in tales and poems to journey to heaven to meet the nine daughters of Ulgen in the fourteenth heavenly sphere. They too could win wives in the spirit world, and the spirit wife would aid the shaman at critical times throughout his life and carry away his spirit at death.[2]

Here we have strong resemblances to the foster-mother stories in the sagas, and particularly to the strange material in *Barðar Saga*, where the relationship between the giant's nine daughters and the young men who visit them is similar to that between the shamans and their spirit wives. Another set of tales relating to the fair King Gudmund and his many fair daughters and the dark King Geirrod, whose kingdom lies next to that of Gudmund, also fit into the same general pattern and resemble those of the black and white shamans and their spirit helpers. Gudmund's kingdom is known as Glasisvellir, and as the Land of the Not-Dead; it is visited by human heroes who become the lovers of his daughters, and one of these returned to King Olaf's court as a blind man, because Gudmund's daughter plucked out his eyes in anger when he left her.[3] The journey to Gudmund's realm is long and difficult, through intense darkness and cold, like that to the cave of Bard, and this is in keeping with the shamanic tradition of the long and difficult voyage to the spirit world.

Some of this shamanistic lore, as it indeed appears to be, could have reached northern Norway and Iceland through contacts with the Lapps, but it seems reasonable to assume that much of it came into Norse tradition as a result of contacts with the peoples of eastern Europe. The Finno-Ugric tribes of the north, the Turko-

[1] Ibid. 485 ff.
[2] Ibid. 487 ff.
[3] *Þáttr Helga Þorissonar* in *Flateyjarbók* I, 293, 359 ff.

Tatar people of the Volga area, and nomads like the Pechinegs and other tribes moving westwards across the steppe in the period from the ninth to the twelfth century are all known to have practised forms of shamanism. Some of the tales of magic and adventure heard among them may have been brought back to Iceland, and it may be noted that the *Fornaldar Sǫgur*, particularly rich in such motifs, have many references to the eastern region. Anisimov [1] notes traditions among Siberian shamans of an earlier time when the military leaders of their tribes were themselves shamans, and we may recall certain figures like the famous Ogmund who was the arch-enemy of the hero Qrvar-Odd; he was a magician dressed in a costume of black felt, with his face almost covered, and was a great warrior as well as an adept in all kinds of magic. Indeed many of the fantastic elements in the sagas become comprehensible if they are seen as part of a background of shamanistic lore. Sometimes they were skilfully incorporated into a realistic Icelandic setting, but we know that this was often done when making use of tales from abroad.[2]

Such traditions may also have influenced the mythological world of the North. There is a close link between the giant foster-mothers and other female guardian spirits in the literature, the *hamingjur*, *fylgjur* and valkyries. It would appear that Germanic beliefs of considerable antiquity have here merged with new ideas and imagery brought in from the East, and consequently the old pagan memories have been charged with new power, and survive in stories of Christian times. This is particularly true with regard to traditions surrounding the god Odin, who will be considered in the following chapter.

---

[1] Anisimov, 118–19.
[2] e.g. The tale of Hroi the Fool in *Flateyjarbók*: see Strömbäck, *Sixth Viking Congress*, Uppsala 1969, 28 ff.

CHAPTER 3

Odin in the East

We have seen how important a part was played by the island of Gotland as a stopping point on the various routes between Scandinavia and the East. It is not always recognised how rich a body of evidence this island has preserved for the mythology of the Viking Age in its collection of sculptured stones. The stones were raised in large numbers as memorials for the dead,[1] and perhaps intended, like the runic stones of Sweden, to provide an official record of death (p. 236 above). No doubt many stones commemorated those who died in the East, but since there are few runic inscriptions there is no way of discovering this. The practice of raising memorial stones continued from the early sixth century to the Christian period, and some of the memorials are of great size, with traces of colouring, so that the scenes portrayed must have once stood out like sections of a great oil painting. We are left now with only the outlines of the decorated panels, depicting scenes of action, which may be compared with the lively pictures on narrow strips of tapestry from the Oseberg ship and from Bayeux in Normandy.

In the earliest series of stones the outstanding motifs are those of a round whirling disc and beneath it a ship manned by rowers. The ship is thought to represent the journey of the dead, and parallels to both ship and disc may be found on tombstones and altars of the Roman period.[2] In the stones raised in the Viking Age, however, only the ship is retained while the disc is replaced by one or more scenes with human figures. Some appear to be incidents

---

[1] Stones discovered before 1942 have been published by S. Lindqvist, *Gotlands Bildsteine* (Stockholm 1941–2). Later discoveries have appeared in the journal *Götlandskt Arkiv*.
[2] Gelling and Davidson, 142 ff.

from heroic stories, and parallels to them have been suggested from tales in the *Fornaldar Sǫgur*. For instance, on a stone from Stora Hammars there is a scene of sacrifice, with a tree pulled down and a man attached to it by a rope, so that he will be hanged when it is released. This recalls the tale of the sacrifice of King Vikar in *Gautreks Saga*.[1] He had intended the hanging to be no more than a dramatic ritual, in order to gain a favourable wind from Odin, but the warrior Starkad caused it to become a grim reality. On the other hand, the scene may be intended to show the hanging ritual associated with Odin's cult and not any specific story. It is hazardous to identify such pictures with tales surviving in literature many centuries later in date, but there seems no room for doubt that there is a close link between the carvings and the traditions of the heroes of Odin, men like Sigurd, Starkad, Ragnar Lodbrok and the like. Symbols of Odin are frequently found on the stones: his eight-legged horse, the eagle, spear and *valknut* (the knot symbol associated with the god) as well as figures of valkyries, and warriors fighting and feasting.

One scene occurs frequently on stones of all sizes, generally placed in the upper panel and often found in conjunction with the ship. This is a warrior on horseback facing a woman who holds up a horn. Lindqvist gives twelve examples of this scene,[2] as well as others where the stones are damaged and it is impossible to tell if the woman is there or not. There are also stones showing the warrior alone,[3] and occasionally the woman with the horn is there without the warrior.[4] There can be little doubt that this scene represents the dead hero entering the realm of Odin and welcomed by a valkyrie with a drink of mead. Scenes where a woman or a line of warriors hold up rings (possibly influenced by Roman figures of Victory) also seem to indicate the hero's welcome.[5] Such a scene is described in two tenth-century poems, one, *Eiríksmál*, commemorating the death of Eirik Bloodaxe, who fell in battle in Stainmore in northern England in about 954, and the other, *Hákonarmál*, on the death of Hakon the Good in Norway after his last battle in 961. They refer to the preparation of the hall of

[1] *Gautreks Saga*, 7.
[2] Lindqvist, figs. 78, 83, 85, 86, 104, 105, 128, 134, 137, 141, 175, 182.
[3] Ibid. figs. 64, 103, 139.
[4] e.g. Stenkyrka, ibid. 515; cf. 128.
[5] Ibid. figs. 83, 86

Odin for the arrival of the princes from the battlefield, the washing of beakers for the banquet, the bringing of mead by the valkyries, and the sending out of two famous heroes to greet the new arrivals. Valkyries are described escorting the dead king to Valhall. It seems that here we have an established tradition of the king entering Odin's hall, although these poems belong to a time of transition, and Hakon was known to be a Christian. Possibly such poems were recited at the funeral feast.

The rider on the horse may represent the dead king journeying to Valhall, but there is some ambiguity here, since Odin himself can be represented by such a figure, as on the Vendel helmet plate of the seventh century, and the rider with a spear is found frequently on Germanic territory;[1] the question then remains open whether this may sometimes be the god, particularly when on three of the stones he appears on an eight-legged steed.[2] It certainly seems that myths concerning Odin are pictured on the stones, for when an eagle is shown instead of the rider on a stone from Lärbro Stora Hammars[3] this surely represents the myth of the magic mead being brought by the god back to Asgard. Other details confirm that the main subject of the stones is the entry into Odin's realm. The drinking scenes emphasise the importance of feasting; the battle scenes, either between hosts[4] or separate warriors, are in keeping with the Valhall theme. The figure of a dog or wolf[5] could be the creature guarding the entrance to the world of the dead of which we hear in the poems. The stylised representation of a hall with a curved roof, as at Ardre,[6] could signify the hall of the warrior god, and at the same time suggest the burial mound. A figure with a spear hovering in the air over a battle scene[7] would presumably be a valkyrie presiding over the field, ready to escort the dead to Odin (see Plate 4).

The two figures of the welcoming scene, the rider and the

[1] e.g. on the stone from Hornhausen: see Stelzer, 401 ff.; Holmqvist, 79 ff.; Kuhn, 95 ff.
[2] Lindqvist, figs. 86, 137, 139; cf. Davidson (1967), 125.
[3] Ibid. fig. 84.
[4] Of particular interest is the scene where two warrior hosts meet: ibid. figs. 81 and 97.
[5] Ibid. figs. 128, 137.
[6] Ibid. fig. 139.
[7] Ibid. figs. 137, 139 (? 134).

woman with a horn, are found as small amulets in graves from Birka and Öland[1] (Fig. 5), confirming the popularity of this concept in eastern Scandinavia, on the route across the Baltic to Russia. Although one carving of the woman carrying a horn has been found as far afield as Sockburn-on-Tees in Yorkshire,[2] no examples so far have been found in Norway or Denmark, and no representations of the eight-legged horse of Odin outside Gotland. While some of the motifs on the stones, such as the ship and the warrior with a spear, link up with earlier pagan traditions in the North, the welcoming scene has striking parallels in south-eastern Europe.

There is another rich series of carved stones in Bulgaria, Romania and Yugo-Slavia, erected in the Roman period, large numbers of which have survived into our own times. These depict the figure known as the Thracian Rider. Kazarov published a corpus of such stones in Bulgaria in 1938, and gave 1,128 examples, and there are large numbers in museums in the other Balkan countries, while new finds continue to be made. It seems as if at one time every village must have erected a stone to this popular deity, and shrines such as that at Batkun (with 301 stones) and Glav Peneja[3] contained numerous stones dedicated to him. Some of the carvings are crudely done, as if for simple country folk, but it may be noted that as in Gotland many of the stones had originally been painted.[4] They were set up in high places, near springs, inside caves or on rock walls, or sometimes in graves, while the Rider might be displayed in houses or on city gates as a protective emblem.[5] They served both as votive offerings to the deity and as memorials to the dead. The god was identified either by inscriptions or attributes with a number of different Greek and Roman deities, in particular with Apollo, Dionysius, Aesculapius, Silvanus and Pluto. This might be taken to imply the existence of a pantheon of Thracian gods, but Venedikov reached a different conclusion, namely that there was one outstanding Thracian deity in the Roman period whose powers included the granting of inspiration, ecstasy, healing and fertility, who was associated with the under-

[1] Davidson (1967), 130.
[2] Lang, 141 ff.
[3] Venedikov, 154 ff; 161.
[4] Vulpe, 336; Kazarov (1938), 5.
[5] Benoit, 92; Will, 60–1.

world and with hunting scenes. The purpose behind the erection of such carvings seems to have been twofold: heroisation of the dead and the making of votive offerings to the Divine Protector who could help during life and lead men to the Other World after death. Pettazzoni believed that this god developed out of the native Thracian deity identified by Herodotus with Hermes, the god worshipped by the aristocratic class in Thrace and regarded as their divine ancestor.[1] These men were warriors, with heroic traditions; they had elaborate funeral customs and believed they would join their ancestors after death, while the god called Hermes was evidently a psychopomp who conducted them to the realm of the dead. By the Roman period this cult had clearly become a popular one, and most of the stones were set up between the second and fourth centuries AD. The god was a versatile figure who invited identification with a number of different deities of the classical world when he came to be depicted in human form in the manner of the Greeks and Romans.

The Thracian god rides on a horse, sometimes standing still, sometimes trotting or galloping. Kazarow divides the stones into three main classes: in the first the Rider approaches some object or figure on the right, a tree with a serpent round it, an altar, or a woman with hand extended or holding a bowl; in the other two classes he is shown as a hunter, either holding a spear or lance with one or more dogs running beside him, or returning from the hunt with his spoils.[2] Although small additions may be made, the most striking characteristic of these stones is their uniformity. One main rider dominates the scene, standing or rearing up his horse before some figure or object, or taking part in a hunt. He usually has his face turned to the spectator and is a young unbearded man, with flying cloak and short tunic, although he may appear as a warrior, wear trousers, or be shown naked; occasionally he has two or even three heads.

One source of the Rider scene must be the Greek tombstones which show a man or woman on horseback.[3] The hunting scene has a long history, and is found on Roman sarcophagi and gravestones, frescoes and mosaics, as well as on carvings of the Mace-

[1] Pettazzoni (1954), 83 ff.; 89.
[2] For criticism of his divisions, see Will, 66 ff.
[3] Pettazzoni (1956), 178 ff.

donian rulers.[1] Benoit emphasises its religious significance: it is essentially a divine effort against supernatural adversaries and perhaps against death itself, which may be symbolised as a boar.[2] As on the Greek monuments, the Rider may represent the heroic dead, but he is certainly in many cases a divine figure, as we can see from the identification with other deities; in the Christian period he was often regarded as St George and the stones preserved as icons of the saint.[3] The figure may have been originally derived

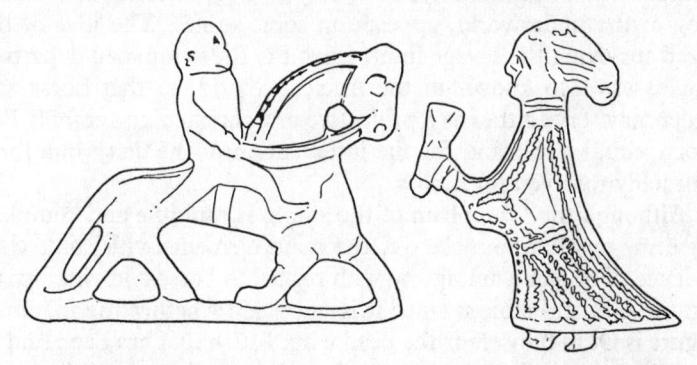

Fig. 5. The Rider and the Woman, two amulets in silver found in Viking Age graves at Birka and Klinta, Öland, 3.2 cm and 2.7 cm high respectively.

from an early riding god of Anatolia,[4] and the style of dress and modification of the oriental way of depicting a galloping horse suggest that this tradition reached Thrace by way of Greece, from the hellenistic rather than the classical world.[5] It is not likely that he originated from the Egyptian Horus, as was once suggested, since the riding deity was taken from Anatolia to Egypt in the second century BC.[6]

The Rider, particularly in Kazarow's Class I, appears at times to represent the dead man, and it might be argued that he was shown

[1] Benoit, 56 ff. An example in Roman funereal art is the stele of Artemidorus (J. Toynbee, *Death and Burial in the Roman World* (London 1973), 250).
[2] Benoit, 57–8.
[3] Kazarov (1953), 137; Will, 83 ff.
[4] Will, 104 ff.
[5] Will, 88 ff.
[6] Benoit, 52.

at his favourite occupation of hunting or as riding into battle, with the horse indicating his status. However, when the name of the dead is given and the title of Hero added, the dead must be appearing in his heroic aspect, and Will claims that in many cases the stones represent a heroic death.[1] But the Rider is an ambiguous figure, as is also his horse: at times this certainly represents the journey to the Other World, but it may also identify the rider with his divine protector.[2] The battle scene and the hunt can both be of Other World significance, and it may be noted that Cerberus, the dog of the underworld, appears on some stones. The idea of the dead surviving the savage hunt, when the Rider pursued departing souls, was also known to the Ancient World, so that horse and rider may serve either as a protective or a threatening symbol. The horse could also stand for the intervention of the deity in a form normally reserved for heroes.

Although the symbolism of the stones is multiple and complex, it seems possible to make out the main elements with some confidence. The same ambiguity with regard to horse and rider exists on the Gotland stones, since it is uncertain whether the mounted figure is Odin himself or the dead man. Much that has been said of the Thracian Rider could apply directly to Odin: use of the horse as an Other World symbol, identification with the heroic dead, the association with battle, ecstasy, and the journey to the underworld. The ship on the Gotland stones adds a further ideogram, for this could be at once a symbol of the last journey, a status symbol, and a link with the divine powers. This symbol appears also on Roman and hellenistic gravestones, and on one stone from Tomis in Romania it is shown in association with the welcoming scene where the Rider meets a woman, so that the total effect is very close indeed to that of the Gotland stones. The figure of the woman facing the Rider is found on a number of Thracian stones[3] and recalls that of the valkyrie with the horn (see Plate 3).

The Thracian god, like Odin, was a psychopomp; he was presumably linked with inspiration and ecstasy, since he could be identified with Apollo and Dionysius; he was originally worshipped, if Pettazzoni is right, by aristocratic warriors, and was

[1] Will, 79.
[2] Benoit, 19.
[3] e.g. Kazarov (1938) figs. 169, 205, 240, 253, 301, 396, etc.

seen as the ancestor of kings: we may note that all these characteristics apply to Odin. He was a god of the chase and Odin was remembered as leader of the Wild Hunt long after the pagan period.[1] It seems indeed possible that there were links between this powerful Thracian deity and the Germanic Wodan, ancestor of kings and god of death and magic in the Roman period, identified with Mercury by the Romans. However, when we find the impressive collection of stones erected in Gotland to the glory of Odin and the memory of the heroic dead, this strongly suggests that the Scandinavians who went eastwards were themselves struck by the resemblance between their god and the Thracian Rider on the carved and painted stones of the Balkan region, so that they were inspired to introduce the same type of memorial into Gotland. The Gotland stones emphasise the importance of Valhall, and this symbolism in turn could have had an effect on the literature of the ninth and tenth centuries, and the rich imagery associated with the realm of Odin, as well as the lively interest in the god and his heroes which survived the conversion to Christianity.

There are other aspects of Odin's cult where the evidence is less striking, but still noteworthy. One of these is the emphasis on the voluntary suicide of a faithful wife or concubine at a warrior's funeral. The element of suttee is not easy to establish from archaeological evidence; Shetelig in his investigation of double interment in Norway found nothing conclusive, and it is always necessary to allow for an epidemic or an accident in which husband and wife perished together. However, he pointed out that double burials were almost unknown before the Viking Age and that the custom of interring a second person in the grave, as in the case of the Oseberg ship-burial, increased during this period. Two excavations of mounds of Viking Age date provide evidence strongly suggesting the sacrifice of a woman at a warrior's funeral, one in the Isle of Man and one in Orkney,[2] the woman in both cases having apparently been killed at the funeral and her body placed over the man's grave. However, the Orkney woman was thought to have been about fifty and in poor health, and this may

[1] De Vries (1956) I, 449–50.
[2] Bersu and Wilson, 9; 47; 91. There was a second body, which could have been a woman, in the ship burial at Ballatoole also. The Orkney burial was excavated by Norwegian archaeologists from Bergen in 1968.

have been the sacrifice of a slave, not a voluntary death of a wife or concubine. We have two cases at Birka of a woman's body apparently thrown into a woman's grave, and the same is true of a double burial at Sowerby in Yorkshire.[1]

In Russia, and particularly in the region round Kiev, there are cases of double interments, with a woman placed in a man's grave.[2] One impressive burial at Chernigov, the *Chernaya Mogila* 'royal' tomb, of the mid-tenth century, contained a warrior buried with a woman and a youth in a timber grave-chamber like a house under a mound; there were rich gravegoods, including weapons, armour, drinking horns, two horses and signs of other animals killed at the funeral.[3] We face the usual problem of whether such graves could belong to Rus leaders, perhaps with Slav wives, or whether they are those of the Slav aristocracy. The Arab geographers tell us that Rus wives or slave-girls were put to death at the funerals of important men, their bodies being either buried or burned. Ibn Rusteh in the early tenth century (p. 63 above) stated that a Rus man was placed in a wooden grave 'as big as a house', with clothes, ornaments, food, drink and wealth, and that finally his favourite wife was placed in the tomb, and the door was shut, so that she was left to die.[4] He has also a reference to suicide by Slav women; if a dead man had more than one wife, she who claimed to love him best set up two posts with a beam across them, fastened a rope to the beam and attached it round her neck, and then hanged herself by standing on a bench which was taken from under her, and after her death men burned her body.[5]

According to St Boniface,[6] a missionary on the Frisian coast in the eighth century, a virgin among the Old Saxons who disgraced her father's house by taking a lover, or a married woman who committed adultery, was sometimes forced to hang herself, and when her body was cremated her lover was hanged over her pyre. He says also of the Wends, 'a most degraded and depraved race', that

[1] *Medieval Archaeology* 4 (1960), 137; there seems no reason to assume, as Wilson does (*supra* 130, p. 91), that the Sowerby grave is evidence for suttee.
[2] Blifeld, 155.
[3] Gimbutas (1971), 159 ff.
[4] Ibn Rusteh, *Les Atours précieux* (Cairo 1955) (translated Wiet), 165.
[5] Ibid. 161.
[6] Letter of Boniface to Aethelbald of Mercia, 746–7, *Anglo-Saxon Missionaries in Germany*, edited and translated C. H. Talbot (London 1954), 123.

Odin in the East

nevertheless they '... have such high regard for the bonds of matrimony that when the husband is dead the wife refuses to live. A wife is considered deserving of praise if she dies by her own hand, and is burned with her husband on the same funeral pyre.' A voluntary death by strangling and burning was recorded of the slave-girl who died at the funeral of a Rus leader on the Volga in 921 (p. 63 above). The *Hudud al-'Alam*, evidently drawing on the same early sources as Ibn Rusteh, declares that among the Slavs, when a man died his wife killed herself if she loved him [1] while Al-Istakhri stated that among the Rus girls were burned to death when a man died, if they consented.[2] Al-Mas'udi gives more details, but it is not clear whether these refer to the Slavs or the Rus: he says that the dead are burned with weapons, animals, birds and wealth, and that [3] 'when someone dies, his wife is burnt alive with him. But when a woman dies, the husband does not share the same grave. If an unmarried man dies, they let him celebrate his marriage after death. The women earnestly desire to be buried with their husbands, in order to follow them to Paradise'. This is very close to Ibn Fadlan's account, possibly based on it. Canard [4] suggested that the slave-girl's death on the Volga was preceded by a marriage ceremony in which she became the wife of the dead man: this explains the sexual intercourse between the girl and the kinsmen of the dead, her reference to members of her family in Paradise, where they would presumably be assembled for the wedding celebrations, and her allusion to her dead master as her husband. In one version she is strangled not by a cord but with a veil, which he suggests is that of the bride.

Thus there is evidence for a practice resembling suttee among both the eastern and western branches of the Slavs, and it seems possible that the Rus learned the custom from them. The ceremony witnessed by Ibn Fadlan, incidentally, was conducted by an old woman, who was most unlikely to have been a Scandinavian. If the slave-girls of the Rus were Slav women, this may account for the practice among the Swedes on the Volga; they would already have been familiar with the idea of killing a slave at a

[1] *Hudud al-'Alam*, 158; 428; 436.
[2] Dunlop, 99.
[3] Al-Mas'udi, translated Dunlop, 205–6; cf. Abu al-Fida' in the fourteenth century (*Geography of Abu al-Fida*, translated Reinauld, (Paris 1848), 305).
[4] Canard, 130; 133.

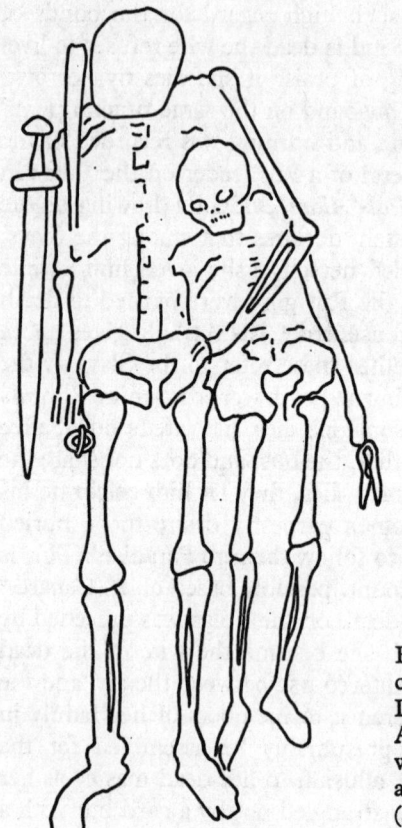

Fig. 6. Plan of a grave in the cemetery of Shestovtsi in the Dnieper area of Russia, of Viking Age date, excavated in 1925. The woman lay beside the warrior and a horse was included in the grave (after Blifeld, *Sovetskaya Archeologiya* 20, 1954).

funeral, but the new element appears to be the emphasis on marriage and the sacrifice of a wife or concubine by her own choice. This is the tradition found in comparatively late literary sources in Scandinavia,[1] an outstanding example being the story of Hagbardus and Signy in Saxo,[2] which offers a parallel to the types of ritual suicide mentioned by Boniface. Hagbardus was hanged because he had been Signy's lover without her father's consent, but Signy chose to die with him and set fire to the house in which she and her maids were confined, and then strangled herself and per-

[1] Ellis (1943/1), 50 ff.
[2] Saxo VII, 234, 281 ff.

suaded them to do likewise. Hagbardus saw the flames as he was about to die and uttered a triumphal poem in which he rejoiced because of the faithfulness of his betrothed, and declared that their love would bring them happiness in the Other World. Sometimes, it may be noted, this custom is associated with Sweden: Jarl Valgaut of Gautland, on leaving his wife to visit King Olaf, told her to burn herself on a funeral pyre if he did not come back;[1] while we are told concerning Sigrid the Proud, probably a fictitious character, that she left Eirik the Victorious before he died because it was the law in Sweden that at the death of the king the queen should be laid in the how beside him, and Sigrid had no desire to end her life so soon.[2] There are references also to such voluntary suicides in the Edda poems; Brynhild killed herself so that she might be burned on a pyre at Sigurd's funeral and follow him to the Other World, and Sigrun in the Helgi poems enters the gravemound of Helgi Hundingsbani.

It seems possible that the inspiration behind such literary traditions has come from the east into Sweden; there seems no reason to suggest that the influence went the other way and that the tradition was carried by the Scandinavians into Russia, as ship-funeral appears to have been. The origin of the sacrifice of the wife might be traced back to the Scythians in southern Russia at a much earlier period,[3] and the practice of suttee may have reached India from the same central area.[4] In both India and Scandinavia there is emphasis on the honour which such a sacrifice brought to the woman and to the dead man.

As to whether the conception of women warriors, also associated with Odin and his heroes, might have originated in the eastern region, the evidence here is inconclusive. Such a tradition was known among the Sarmatians in the third century BC, when girls were said to fight along with men and to be required to slay an enemy before they could be given in marriage.[5] There is confusion here, however, with the many legends current about the Amazons,

---

[1] *Fornmanna Sǫgur* (Copenhagen 1825–37) V, 327 ff.
[2] *Flateyjarbók* I, 63, 88; for Sigrid the Proud, see introduction to *Heimskringla*, Íslendzk Fornrit 26 (Reykjavik 1941), cxxv.
[3] T. Talbot Rice, *The Scythians* (1957), 88 ff.
[4] For reference to suttee at various periods, see *Hobson-Jobson*, edited Yale and Burnell, London 1903 ('suttee').
[5] T. Talbot Rice (*supra*), 48.

and again with the traditions of the valkyries sent to the battlefield by Odin. Women warriors are also found in early Celtic tradition.[1] Thus, though John Scylitzes stated that women's bodies in fighting attire were found among the dead in Svyatoslav's forces after a battle on the Danube (p. 114 above), and the tradition of women fighting in battle is certainly prominent in the *Fornaldar Sǫgur*, it would be unwise to assume eastern influence without stronger evidence.

There is, however, no doubt that certain aspects of the Odinic tradition which were current in the late Viking Age are strongly associated with symbols and practices to be found in the eastern region. The link between the Gotland stones and those in the Balkan countries is easily accounted for, as there is plenty of evidence, as we have seen, for Scandinavian penetration in this part of the world over a considerable period, both under Syvatoslav and then in the service of the Byzantine Emperor. Moreover, in the picture built up from many sources of the fierce and dedicated warriors fighting among the Rus, we find a tradition fully in keeping with the cult of Odin, as depicted in the literature of the Viking Age and later. A warrior cult already flourished in the Scandinavian North in the pre-Viking period, when part of its vigour and lively symbolism appears to have been derived from the Roman army. During the Viking Age it evidently took on new life under the conditions in the eastern region, where many warrior bands took part in campaigns over the whole area, making alliances with many barbaric peoples, or fighting as mercenaries for various princes; the cult of a battle-god would be encouraged and strengthened by the customs of the nomads and the many warring peoples whom the Scandinavians encountered there. This could account for the richness and vigour of the Odinic stones in Gotland, for the increase of human sacrifice which is suggested by archaeological evidence in Scandinavia, and for the enthusiasm with which the cult of Odin was still presented in literature of the Christian period.

---

[1] A. T. Hatto, 'On the excellence of the Hildebrandslied', *Modern Language Review*, 68 (1973), 831.

Conclusion

No doubt there are further paths which might be profitably pursued concerning possible eastern influences on Scandinavian mythology. A number of scholars have pointed out resemblances between Iranian concepts of the end of the world and the account of the destruction of gods and men at Ragnarok in the poem *Vǫluspá*. Early this century the possibility was explored by the Danish folklorist Axel Olrik, and later by two German scholars working on the Iranian side, Reitzenstein and Peuchert.[1] Since then the case has been taken no further, on the grounds that although the parallels were interesting there was no obvious route by which Iranian concepts could have reached the pre-Christian North, and resemblances might be due to a shared background of Indogermanic religion.[2] It would, however, be quite possible for such traditions to have reached Scandinavia in the Viking Age or even in the early Christian period, since we have evidence for contacts with Russia, the Balkans and the regions round the Caucasus. Peuchert, moreover, suggested that some Manichean ideas could have been brought into Iceland in the eleventh century by the so-called 'Armenian' priests (p. 228 above). The evidence, however, is too complex to be dealt with here and I hope to discuss it fully elsewhere.

Another possibility deserving consideration is that the traditions

[1] For Olrik, the fullest account is *Ragnarok: die Sager von Weltuntergang*, translated Ranisch, Berlin and Leipzig 1922; Reitzenstein, 'Die nordischen, persischen und christlichen Vorstellungen vom Weltuntergang', *Vorträge der Bibliothek Wartburg* 1923–4, Berlin and Leipzig 1926, 142–69; also W. E. Peuchert, 'Germanische Eschatologien', *Archiv für Religionswissenschaft*, 32 (1835) 1–37.

[2] De Vries (1956–7) II, 402–3. A recent study on Ragnarok by J. S. Martin (Melbourne Monographs in Germanic Studies 3, Assen 1972) ignores this problem.

about Loki as a bound giant in Icelandic literature owe something to legends of the giant warrior of Mount Elbruz in the Caucasus region. Olrik collected a vast amount of material, both literary and oral, to show how this powerful figure was associated with one particular peak, Elbruz, from very early times, and known to the Greeks in the form of the Prometheus legend. Folklore about the giant was still current in the last century, and English travellers in 1868 coming down from the mountain were asked if they had seen him. The bound figure was that of a giant or hero, sometimes given the name of Amiran or Abrskil, who might be described as an old bearded man or as a nameless warrior. Out of the enormous mass of legends and folklore a clear pattern emerges, that of a supernatural figure who offends the supreme god and is bound to a mountain peak or in a cave near it until Judgement Day. Sometimes he tries to reach a sword just beyond his grasp, or a dog endeavours to lick through his chain, but the fetters are always renewed just when escape seems possible. Occasionally a human being discovers him, but always fails to give him the help needed because the time for the world to end is not yet come. Olrik shows how Christian and Muslim elements have attached themselves to the tradition in different areas in the course of time, while stories of the same type have sometimes been linked for a while with other peaks, such as Mount Ararat, but the association of the bound giant with Elbruz has continued for over a thousand years. So vigorous a tradition must have been encountered by Scandinavians who penetrated into the Caucasus area, and it certainly seems to have been carried into Russia, from parallels with the legend of the giant Svyatogor in the *byliny*,[1] who had the power to pull down the heavens and drag up the earth from its foundations. He in turn has clear links with the strange figure of Loki of Utgard, the enormous giant skilled in deceptive magic who outwits Thor in the tale in the *Prose Edda*, and who is described as a giant bound in a cave in Book VIII of Saxo's history. Eastern influences here might account for the puzzling reference to Utgard (the realm beyond), to distinguish this Loki from the more familiar trickster of Asgard. The breaking loose of the bound Loki, punished for his part in the death of Balder, is linked up with the tradition of Ragnarok in some of the Edda poems.

[1] Chadwick (1964), 243 ff.

There are resemblances, too, between the accounts of the creation of the world as given in Snorri's *Prose Edda* and certain Iranian legends. Schier has pointed out parallels in the coming together of cold and heat to form life, and in the creation of the world from the body of the giant Ymir.[1] In stressing these, he added that it was difficult to see how and when such ideas from the Near East could have reached Scandinavia. As with the conception of the last great battle, however, there is no real difficulty if we assume that the time of transmission was the Viking Age. The parallels certainly need to be taken seriously in any future study of the beginning and end of the world in Norse literature.

We know that the eastern road of the Vikings took them into strange lands and brought them into contact with cultures very different from their own. For all their apparent isolation, the Scandinavians were continually looking outwards and exploring far afield; otherwise it would be hard to account for the richness of Icelandic literature in the thirteenth century and the complexity and vigour of the northern myths. The Viking Age is usually held to have ended in the eleventh century, when the military raids and the land-taking ceased, but the Viking type of exploration and activity was by no means over in the East. Companies of Scandinavian fighting men continued to be absorbed into the Byzantine forces until the sacking of Constantinople in 1204 brought the long period to a close. Those who sought trade, fighting and plunder had plenty of opportunities in south-eastern Europe in the twelfth century, and Christians could find excitement and perhaps wealth on pilgrimage journeys. Once the Tatars invaded Russia, however, the old river routes no longer remained open to adventurers and pilgrims.

The influences giving new vigour to Icelandic tales, poems and legends did not all come by way of manuscripts reaching secluded scholars in their monasteries. Some of the lore from the eastern regions must have arrived in the form of oral tradition, brought home by poets and story-tellers; new motifs and patterns were stored in the minds of returning travellers and might be re-expressed in a northern idiom in literature and art. There were also

---

[1] K. Schier, 'Die Erdschöpfung aus der Urmeer und die Kosmogonie der *Vǫluspa*', *Märchen, Mythos, Dichtung* (Festschrift Friedrich von der Leyen, ed. H. Kuhn and K. Schier), Munich 1963, 304 ff.

antiquarians and geographers who seized on information about voyages down the Russian rivers, or shamans beyond the Baltic, and were ready to link it with strange lore about the wonders of Scythia in ancient writers. The runic memorial stones from eleventh-century Sweden suggest that funeral poems about men who died abroad may have been one source of information concerning the Baltic, the Volga and the Dnieper. It was known that northern princes went to Miklagard to be received by the greatest ruler of the Christian world, and stories of their achievements were enriched from the common stock of travellers' tales and fanciful interpretation of poems about their exploits. There was room here for national pride, wonder and curiosity, and for humour as well as envy in the portrayal of a world so fantastically different from the small settlements and homely markets of the north. The great expanses of arctic Russia, the huge areas of tundra and forest and steppe ending at the Urals and the Caucasus, provided a background for tales of fantasy and adventure, to set beside those from the fashionable romances of the west. Confused memories of the barbaric customs of nomad and Muslim peoples and impressive funeral rites of pagans became part of the tales of heroic leaders in the east whose names were distorted or forgotten, while the marvels were still remembered. We do not know how long the Scandinavians in Kiev or Novgorod held their own at the courts of Slav princes, but merchants and mercenary war-bands appear to have kept their own halls for a considerable period in the Slav cities, where tales could be told and gossip exchanged with travellers. Little enough of all this has survived, but confused traces remain in the literature of the Middle Ages.

The assumption that myths and legends recorded after the close of the pagan period must be the result of vague memories of pre-Christian traditions in the Germanic North may not always be correct. There is a freshness and a strength of conviction about the tales of Odin and his heroes which suggest new inspiration keeping the old traditions alive and helping to shape them anew, and the eastern regions are the direction from which one might expect such inspiration to come. The Vikings were exposed to ideas from many different cultures, and the influence of the Celtic west must not be discounted, but certain features in the myths point east rather than west, and the importance of Sweden as a seat of pagan culture after the general acceptance of Christianity in western Scandinavia must be borne in mind. Long controversies about the historical and cultural effects of Scandinavian penetration on Russia have led scholars to neglect the traffic in the opposite direction, which must have gone on for some hundreds of years. The range of the Gotland carvings, unequalled in the vigour of their mythological impact, is a reminder of the importance of such influences. Their existence must have had a powerful effect on the folklore and legends of the early Middle Ages, and we may remember also more perishable but portable productions in wood and tapestry which could help to preserve tradition and to carry new motifs from one region to another.

The Vikings have left us much treasure on the eastern road, but the effort of extracting it is not easy; we need help from many directions, and co-operation from scholars in different disciplines. The characteristic possessions of these eastern Vikings were ships, swords and the little balances in which they weighed out their broken silver, and these three together form a fitting symbol of the life they led. They played a vital part in building up the economy of their homelands and contributing to the imaginative life of their age. Odin was the god of warriors, but also of merchants, the *Mercurius Mercator* of Germanic tradition, and *Farmatýr*, the God of cargoes. There could be no more fitting patron for these tough merchant-adventurers. Odin was also the god of poets, and poetry and saga helped to keep memories of their doings alive into the Christian period. Even when the new patrons of the Varangians, the Blessed Virgin and St Olaf, took over, the old spirit of the shrewd god of inspiration lived on, for luck and keen weapons were still needed on the eastern road. The story was to end, like the career of Odin in the northern myths, in tragedy and destruction, when the coming of the Tatars and the sack and ultimate capture of the Great City closed the eastern road from Scandinavia to Byzantium for ever.

Bibliography

Adam of Bremen   *History of the Archbishops of Hamburg and Bremen*, translated F. J. Tschan, Columbia University, 1959 (Dept. Historical Records of Civilisation, Sources and Studies 53).

Alföldi, A.   '*Cornuti*, A Teutonic Contingent in the Service of Constantine the Great', *Dumbarton Oaks Papers* 13 (1959) 171–9.

Al-Mas'udi   *Les Prairies d'or*, translated Maynard and De Courteille, Paris, 1962.

Anna Comnena   *The Alexiad of the Princess Anna Comnena*, translated E. A. S. Dawes, London, 1928.

Anisimov, A. F.   'The Shaman's Tent of the Evenks' and 'Cosmologinal Concepts', *Siberian Shamanism* (see below) 84–123, 157–229.

Arbman, H.   (1939) *Birka, Sveriges äldsta Handelsstad* (Från forntid och medeltid 1) Stockholm, 1939.

(1940) *Birka* 1, Stockholm, 1940–3.

Arrhenius, B.   (1968) 'Ett Traddragninstrument fran Birka', *Fornvännen* (1968) 288–93.

(1970) 'Knivar fran Helgö ond Birka', ibid. (1970) 50–1.

Artsikhovsky, A. V. and Kolchin, B. A.   *Materials and Researches on the Archeology of the USSR*, nos. 55, 65, 117, 123 (Works of the Novgorod Expedition), in Russian: English summary by M. W. Thompson.

Avdusin, D. A.   'Smolensk and the Varangians', *Norwegian Archaeological Review*, 2 (1969), 52 ff.

Baetke, W.   'Die Götterlehre der Snorra Edda', *Berichte über die Verhandlungen der sächsischen Akademie der Wissenschaften zu Leipzig* (Phil. hist. Klasse) 97, 3 (1950) 1–68.

Barnea, I.   (1955) 'Byzance, Kiev et l'Orient sur le Bas-Danube du Xe. au XIIe. siècle', *Nouvelles Études d'histoire, présentées au X congrès du sciences historiques, Rome*, 1955, 169–80.

(1962) 'Les monuments rupestres de Basarabi en Doubroudja', *Cahiers Archaéologiques* 13 (1962) 187–208.

(1967) (with others) 'Nouvelles recherches sur le *limes* byzantin du

Bas-Danube au Xe–XIe siècle', *Proceedings XIII International Congress of Byzantine Studies* 1966 (Oxford 1967) 179–93.

Benedikz, B. S. 'The Evolution of the Varangian Regiment in the Byzantine Army', *Byzantinische Zeitschrift* 62 (1969) 20–4.

Benoit, F. 'L'héroïsation équestre', *Publ. des Annales de la Faculté des Lettres* (N.S. 7) Aix-en-Provence, 1954.

Bersu, G. and Wilson, D. *Three Viking Graves in the Isle of Man* (Society for Medieval Archaeology, Monograph Series 1) London, 1966.

Birkeland, H. *Nordens historie i middelalderen etter arabiske kilder* (Det Norske Videnskaps-Akademi Skrifter II, Hist. Filos. Klasse) Oslo, 1954 (2).

Blake, N. F. *The Saga of the Jomsvikings*, translated with introduction and notes, London, 1962.

Blifeld, D. I. 'A historical appreciation of the Burials of the Prince's Retinue in Wooden Chamber Graves of the 9th–10th centuries in the Dniepr Region' (in Russian) *Sovetskaya Archeologiya* 20 (1954) 148–62.

Blindheim, C. (1960) 'The Market-place in Skiringssal', *Acta Archaeologia* (Copenhagen) 21 (1960) 83–100.

(1969) Kaupangundersøkelsen avsluttet', *Viking* 33 (1969) 5–38.

Blöndal, S. (1939/1) 'The Last Exploits of Harald Sigurdson in Greek Service', *Classica et Medievalia* II (1939) 1–26.

(1939/2) 'Nabites the Varangian', ibid. 145–67.

(1954) *Væringjasaga*, Reykjavik, 1954.

Boba, I. *Nomads, Northmen and Slavs: Eastern Europe in the Ninth Century* (Slavo-Orientalia II), The Hague, 1967.

Bolin, S. 'Mohammed, Charlemagne and Ruric', *Scandinavian Economic History Review* 1 (1953) 5–39.

Book of Ceremonies edited Niebuhr, Bonn, 1829.

Brate, E. 'Pireus-lejonets runinskrift', *Antivarisk Tidskrift för Sverige* 20 (3) 1919, 1–48.

Braun, F. (1910) 'Hvem var Yngvarr enn Viðfǫrli?' *Fornvännen* (1910), 99–117.

(1924) 'Die historische Russland im nordischen Schrifttum des X–XIV Jahrhunderts', *Festschrift Eugen Mogk*, Halle, 1924, 150–96.

Brett, G. 'The Automata in the Byzantine Throne of Solomon', *Speculum* 29 (1954) 477–87.

Bromberg, E. 'Wales and the Medieval Slave Trade', *Speculum* 17 (1942) 263–9.

Buchholz, P. *Schamanistische Züge in der altisländischen Überlieferung* (Doctrinal Thesis, Münster 1968).

Buckler, G. G. *Anna Comnena*, London, 1929.

Bury, J. B. (1911) 'The Imperial Administrative System in the 9th Century', *British Academy Supplementary Papers*, London, 1911.

Bury, J. B.   (1912) *A History of the Eastern Roman Empire from the Fall of Irene to the Accession of Basil I*, London, 1912.

Canard, M.   'La Relation du voyage d'Ibn Fádlan chez les Bulgares de la Volga', *Annales de l'Institut d'Études Orientales* 16 (1958) 41–146.

Cedrenus   *Compendium Historium*, edited Niebuhr, *Corpus Scriptorum Historiae Byzantinae*, Bonn, 1839.

Chadwick, N.   (1946) *The Beginnings of Russian History: an enquiry into sources*, Cambridge, 1946.

 (1964) 'The Russian Giant Svyatogov and the Norse Utgartha-Loki', *Folklore* 75 (1964) 243–59.

Charles, B. G.   *Old Norse Relations with Wales*, Cardiff, 1934.

Cleve, N.   'Jungereisenzeitliche Funde von der Insel Berezan', *Eurasia Septentrionalis Antiqua* 4 (1929) 250–62.

Cross, S. H.   (1929) 'Yaroslav the Wise in Norse Tradition', *Speculum* 4 (1929) 177–97.

 (1953) *The Russian Primary Chronicle, Laurentian Text* translation with notes, with O. P. Sherbowitz-Wetzor (Medieval Academy of America Publications 60) Cambridge, Mass., 1953.

Davidan, O.   'Contacts between Staraja Ladoga and Scandinavia', *Varangian Problems* (below) 79–94.

Davidson, H. R. E.   (1962) *The Sword in Anglo-Saxon England: its archaeology and literature*, Oxford, 1962.

 (1964) *Gods and Myths of Northern Europe* (Pelican Books), Harmondsworth, 1964.

 (1965) 'The Significance of the Man in the Horned Helmet', *Antiquity* 39 (1965) 23–27.

 (1967) *Pagan Scandinavia* (Ancient Peoples and Places 58) London, 1967.

 (1972) *The Battle God of the Vikings* (University of York Medieval Monographs 1) York, 1972.

 (1973/1) 'The Secret Weapon of Byzantium', *Byzantinische Zeitschrift* 66 (1973) 61–74.

 (1973/2) 'Hostile Magic in the Icelandic Sagas', *The Witch Figure* (Folklore Essays in honour of Katherine M. Briggs, edited V. Newall) London, 1973.

Dawkins, R. M.   (1937) 'An Echo in the Norse Sagas of the Patzinak War of John II Komnisos', *Mélanges Émile Boisacq, Annuaire d'Institut de Philologie et d'Histoire Orientales et Slaves* 5 (1937) 243–9.

 (1947) 'The Later History of the Varangian Guard' *Journal Roman Studies* 37 (1947) 36–46.

Demus, O. F.   *Byzantine Mosaic Decoration: aspects of monumental art in Byzantium*, London, 1948.

Dronke, U. *The Poetic Edda*, vol. I (Heroic Poems), edited with translation and commentary, Oxford, 1969.

Dunlop, D. M. *The History of the Jewish Khazars* (Princeton Oriental Studies 16) Princeton, 1954.

Ebersolt, J. (1917) 'Mélanges d'histoire et d'archaéologie byzantines', *Revue de l'histoire des Religions* 76 (1917) 1–123.

(1951) *Constantinople: recueil d'études, d'archaéologie et d'histoire*, Paris, 1951.

Ekblom, R. 'Roslagen, Russland', *Zeitschrift für slavische Philologie* 26 (1957) 47–58.

Eliade, M. *Shamanism and Archaic Techniques of Ecstasy* (revised edition), translated W. R. Trask, London, 1964.

Ellis, H. R. (Davidson) (1942) 'Fostering by Giants in Old Norse Saga Literature', *Medium Ævum* 10 (1941) 70–85.

(1943) *The Road to Hel: a study of the conception of the dead in Old Norse literature*, Cambridge, 1943.

Ensslin, W. 'The Byzantine Army', *Cambridge Medieval History* IV (ii) 1967, 35 ff.

Falk, K. C. 'Dneprforsarnas Namn i Kejsar Konstantin VIIP orfyrogennetos '*De Administrando Imperio, Lunds Universitets Arskrift*, N.F. 46 (1951).

Flateyjarbók Edited G. Vigfusson and C. R. Unger (3 vols.) Christiania, 1860–8.

Fleck, J. 'The Knowledge-Criterion in the *Grímnismál*: the case against Shamanism', *Arkiv för Nordisk Filologi* 86 (1971) 49–65.

Floderus, E. 'Vastergain', *Fornvännen* 19 (1934) 65–83.

Foote, P. G. and Wilson, D. M. *The Viking Achievement*, London, 1970.

Forbes, R. J. (1959) *More Studies in Early Petroleum History, 1860–1880*, Leiden, 1959.

(1964) *Studies in Ancient Technology* I (2nd edition) Leiden, 1964, 100 ff.

Fornaldar Sǫgur Edited V. Asmundarson (3 vols.) Reykjavik, 1884–89.

Formanna Sǫgur Edited S. Egilsson and others (12 vols.) Copenhagen, 1825–37.

Friedrich, A. and Buddruss, G. *Schamangeschichten aus Siberien*, translated from Russian (*Weisheitsbücher d. Menschheit*) Munich, 1955.

Geijer, A. 'Die Textilfunde aus den Graben', *Birka Untersuchungen und Studien III* (Kungl. Vitterhets Historie och Antikvitets Akademien), Stockholm, 1938.

Gimbutas, M. (1963) *The Balts* (Ancient Peoples and Places, 33) London, 1963.

(1971) *The Slavs* (Ancient Peoples and Places, 74) London, 1971.

Glykatzi-Ahrweiler, H. 'Recherches sur l'administration de l'Empire byzantin aux IXe.–XIe. siècles', *Bulletin de Correspondance Hellenique* 84 (1960) 1–91.

Gregoire, H. (1937) 'La Legende d'Oleg et l'expedition de "Igor"', *Bulletin de L'Academie Royale de Belgique* (Classe des Lettres, 5) 23 (1937) 86–94.

(1954) 'Les Invasions Russes dans le Synaxaire de Constantinople', *Byzantion* 24 (1954) 141–5 (with P. Orgels).

Grierson, P. (1959) 'Commerce in the Dark Ages', *Transactions Royal Historical Society* (Series 5) 9 (1959) 123–40.

(1966) 'Harald Hardrada and Byzantine Coin Types in Denmark', *Polychordia, Festschrift Franz Dölger* (*Byzantinische Forschungen* I), Amsterdam, 1966, 124–38.

Guerdan, R. *Byzantium, its triumphs and tragedy*, translated D. L. B. Hartley, London, 1956.

Guilland, R. (1966) 'Études sur l'hippodrome de Byzance', *Byzantinoslavica* 27 (1966) 289–307.

(1967) *Recherches sur les institutions byzantines* (Deutsche Akad. d. Wissenschaften Berlin, Berliner byzantinistische Arbeiten 35) Berlin, 1967.

(1969) *Études de Topographie de Constantinople Byzantine* (Berliner Byzantinistiche Arbeiten 37) Berlin, 1969.

Haegstad, A. 'Ha Al-Tartuschi besøgt Hedeby (Slesvig)?', *Aarbøger nordisk Oldkyndighet og Historie*, Copenhagen, 1964, 82–92.

Harva-Holmberg, U. (1927) *Mythology of All Races IV: Finno-Ugric, Siberian* (Archaeological Institute of America) Boston, Mass., 1927.

(1938) *Die religiösen Vorstellung der altaischen Völker*, Folklore Fellows Communications, 125, Helsinki, 1938.

Haussig, H. W. *A History of Byzantine Civilization*, translated J. M. Hussey (2nd edition revised) London, 1971.

Heller, R. *Literarisches Schaffen in der Laxdæla Saga* (Saga 3) Halle, 1960.

Hendy, M. F. 'Michael IV and Harald Hardrada', *The Numismatic Chronicle* (series 7) 10 (1970) 187–97.

Hensel, W. *Anfänge der Städte bei den Ost- und West-Slawen*, Bautzen, 1967.

Holmqvist, W. 'Zu Herkunst einiger germanischen Figurendarstellung der Völkwanderungszeit', *IPEK* 12 (1938) 78–95.

Hudud al-'Alam Regions of the World, translated V. Minorsky (E. J. W. Gibbs Memorial Series 11) Oxford, 1937.

Hultkranz, A. 'Spirit Lodge, a North American Shamanistic Seance', *Studies in Shamanism* (below) 32–68.

Ibn Athir 'Les Mosâfirides de l'Adherbaïdjân', translated C. Huart, *A Volume of Oriental Studies presented to E. G. Browne*, edited T. W. Arnold and R. A. Nicholson, Cambridge, 1922, 228–54.

Izedin, M. 'Un prisonnier arabe à Byzance au IXe. siècle: Haroun ibn Yahya', *Revue d'Études Islamiques* 15 (1941–46) 41–62.

Janin, R. *Constantine Byzantine, developpement urbain et répertoire topographique* (Archives de l'Orient chrétien 4, Inst. Français d'Études Byzantines) Paris, 1950.

Jankuhn, H. *Haithabu; ein Handelsplatz der Wikingerzeit* (4th edition) Neumünster, 1963.

Jenkins, R. J. H. (1949/1) *Translation of De Administrando Imperio* (with G. Moravcesik) Budapest, 1949.

(1949/2) 'The Supposed Russian Attack on Constantinople in 907', *Speculum* 24 (1949) 403–6.

(1962) *Commentary on De Administrando Imperio* (with others) London, 1962.

(1967) *Revised translation of De Administrando Imperio*, Dumbarton Oaks Texts, Washington, 1967.

Jones, G. (1960) *Egils Saga*, translated with introduction and notes, (American-Scandinavian Foundation) New York, 1960.

(1968) *A History of the Vikings*, Oxford, 1968.

(1967–8) 'The Legendary History of Olaf Tryggvason', W. P. Ker Lecture, University of Glasgow.

Jónsdóttir, Selma *An 11th Century Byzantine Last Judgement in Iceland*, Reykjavik, 1959.

Karsten, R. *The Religion of the Samek: Ancient Beliefs and Cults of the Scandinavian and Finnish Lapps*, Leiden, 1955.

Kazarov, G. I. (1938) *Die Denkmäler des thrakischen Reitergottes in Bulgarien (Dissertations Pannonicae* 2, 14) Budapest, 1938.

(1953) 'Zum Kult des thrakischen Reiters in Bulgarien' *Wissenschaftliche Zeitschrift der Karl-Marx Universität Leipzig* 3 (1953–4) 135–37.

Kendrick, T. D. *A History of the Vikings*, London, 1930.

Kerner, R. J. *The Urge to the Sea: the course of Russian History*, University of California, 1942.

Kiil, V. 'Hliðskjalf og seiðhjallr', *Arkiv för Nordisk Filologi* 75 (1960) 84–112.

Kivikosti, E. *Finland* (Ancient Peoples and Places 53) London, 1967.

Kleiber, B. 'Alstadsteinen i lyset av nye gravninger ved Kiev', *Viking* 29 (1965) 61–72.

Koutaissoff, E. 'Ohtheriana I, Kuznetsov on Biarmia', *English and Germanic Studies* II (1948–49) 20–33.

Krappe, A. H. 'The Snake Tower', *Scandinavian Studies* 16 (1940–41) 22–33.

Krause, W. 'Die Runeninschrift von Alt-Ladoga', *Norsk Tidsskrift för Sprogvidenskap* 19 (1960) 555–63.

Kuhn, H. 'Die Reiterscheiber de Völkwanderungzeit' *IPEK* 12 (1938) 95–115.

Kunkel, O. and Wilde, K. A. *Jumne, 'Vineta', Jomsburg, Julin; Wollin*, Stettin, 1941.

Kiel Papers Frühe Städte im westlichen Ostseeraum (Symposium des Sondersforschungsbereich 17, 'Skandinavien und Ostseeraumforschung', ed. H. Hinz Christian-Albrechts Universität, Kiel, 1972.

Lamb, J. W. *Saint Wulfstan, prelate and patriot* (Church Historical Society, MS. 16) London, 1933.

Lang, J. T. 'Illustrative Carving of the Viking Period at Sockburn-on-Tees', *Archaeologia Aeliana* (Series 4) 50 (1972) 235–48.

Laufer, B. 'Asbestos und Salamander', *T'Oung Pao* 16 (1915) 299–378.

Lazarev, V. *Old Russian Murals and Mosaics* from the XI to the XVI century, translated B. Roniger and N. Dunn, London, 1966.

Leach, H. G. *Angevin Britain and Scandinavia* (Harvard Studies in Comparative Literature 6) Cambridge, 1921.

Leake, J. A. *The Geats of Beowulf: a study in the geographical mythology of the Middle Ages*, Madison, Wisconsin, 1967.

Lemerle, P. '"Roga" et rente d'état aux Xe–XIe siècles', *Revue des études Byzantines* 25 (1967) 77–100.

Leo Diaconus *Corpus Scriptorum Historae Byzantinae*, Bonn, 1828.

Lewis, A. R. 'Byzantine Light-weight Solidi and Trade to the North Sea and the Baltic', *Studies in Language, Literature and Culture of the Middle Ages and Later*, edited E. B. Atwood and A. A. Hill, University of Texas, Austin, 1969.

Lid, N. 'Gand og Tyre', *Festskrift til H. Falk*, Oslo, 1927, 331–50.

Liden, E. 'Gullvarta-Sibilia', *Festskrift til F. Jonsson*, Copenhagen, 1928.

Liestøl, A. (1963) 'Runer fra Bryggen', *Viking* 27 (1963) 1–56.

(1965) 'The Maeshowe Runes: some new interpretations', *Fifth Viking Congress*, Torshavn, 1965, 55–61.

(1970) 'Runic Inscriptions', *Varangian Problems* (below) 121–31.

Linder, U.S. 'En upplandsk silverskatt från 800–talet', *Nordisk Numismatisk Arsskrift* (1938) 109–24.

Lindqvist, S. *Gotlands Bildesteine* (2 vols.) (Kungl. Vitterhets Historie och Antikvitets Akademien) Stockholm, 1941–2.

Liutprand *The Works of Liudprand of Cremona*, translated F. A. Wright, London, 1930.

Lopez, R. S. 'The Silk Industry in the Byzantine Empire' *Speculum* 20 (1945) 1–42.

Lot, F. *Les Invasions barbares et le peuplement de l'Europe* (2 vols.), Paris, 1937.

Lundström, P. 'Paviken I, ett vikingatida Varv på Gotland', *Gotlandskt Arkiv* 40 (1968) 99–114.

Macartney, C. A. 'The Petchenegs', *Slavonic (and East European) Review* 8 (1929-30) 342-55.

Macler, F. 'Armenie et Islande', *Revue de l'Histoire des Religions* 87 (1923) 236-41.

Magoun, F. P. 'Nikulás Bergsson of Munkaþvera and Germanic Heroic Legend', *Journal of English and Germanic Philology* 42 (1943) 210-18.

Mango, C. A. (1958) *The Homilies of Photius, Patriarch of Constantinople*, translation with introduction and commentary (Dumbarton Oaks Studies 3) Cambridge, Mass., 1958.

(1959) *The Brazen House: a study of the vestibule of the imperial palace* Archaeologisk Kunsthistoriske Meddelelser 4, 4) Copenhagen, 1959.

(1967) 'The Mosaics of Hagia Sophia', H. Kähler and C. Mango, *Hagia Sophia*, London, 1967.

Marwazi *Sharaf al-Zaman Tahir Marwazi*, translated with commentary by V. F. Minorsky (Royal Asiatic Society James C. Furlong Fund 22) London, 1942.

Melvinger, A. *Les premières incursions des Vikings en Occident d'après des sources arabes*, Uppsala, 1955.

Miller, D. A. *Imperial Constantinople*, New York, 1969.

Minns, E. H. *Scythians and Greeks: a survey of ancient history and archaeology on the north coast of the Euxine from the Danube to the Caucasus*, Cambridge, 1913.

Miskawaih *The Eclipse of the 'Abbasid Caliphate* (4 vols.) translated Margoliouth, Oxford, 1920-1.

Mongait, A. L. *Archaeology in the USSR*, translated M. W. Thompson (Pelican Book) Harmondsworth, 1961.

Nerman, B. (1929) *Die Verbindungen zwischen Skandinavien und dem Ostbaltikum in der jüngeren Eisenzeit*, Stockholm, 1929.

(1958) *Grobin-Seeburg; Ausgrabungen und Funde* (Kungl. Vitterhets Historie och Antikvitets Akad. 41) Stockholm, 1958.

Obolensky, D. (Prince) (1966) *Cambridge Medieval History* VI (1), Chapter XI, Cambridge, 1966.

(1971/1) *The Byzantine Commonwealth*, Oxford, 1971.

(1971/2) *Byzantium and the Slavs* (collected studies), London, 1971.

Oikonomides, N. *Les rangs de préséances byzantins des IXe. et Xe. siècles*, Paris, 1972.

Ostrogorsky, (1939) 'L'expédition du Prince Oleg contre Constantinople', *Seminarium Kondakovianum* 5 (Institute Kondakov, Prague) 11 (1939) 47 ff.

(1969) *The History of the Byzantine State*, translated J. Hussey (revised edition) New Brunswick, 1969.

Pargoire, J. 'Les Sainte-Mamas de Constantinople', *Transactions Russian Archaeological Institute in Constantinople* 9 (1904) 261–316.

Partington, J. R. *A History of Greek Fire and Gunpowder*, Cambridge, 1960.

Paszkiewicz, H. *The Origin of Russia*, London, 1954.

Pettazzoni, R. (1954) 'The Religion of Ancient Thrace', *Essays on the History of Religions*, translated H. J. Rose (Studies in the History of Religions 1) Leiden, 1954, 81–94.

(1956) *The All-Knowing God, researches into early religion and culture*, translated H. J. Rose. London, 1956.

Pipping, H. 'Om Pilgärdsstenen', *Nordiska Studier till. A. Noreen*, Uppsala, 1904, 175–82.

Ploss, E. E. *Siegfried-Sigurd der Drachenkämpfer, Untersuchungen zu germanisch-deutschen Heldensage.* . . (Beihefte Bonner Jahrbücher 17) Bonn, 1966.

Primary Chronicle   See Cross, 1953.

Prokofyeva, Y. D. 'The Costume of an Enets Shaman', *Siberian Shamanism* (below).

Psellus, M. *Chronographia*, translated E. R. A. Sewter (revised edition) Harmondsworth, 1966.

Peuchert, W. E. 'Germanische Eschatologien', *Archiv für Religionswissenschaft* 32 (1935) 1–37.

Ravdonikas, V. I. (1930) *Der Normannen der Wikingerzeit und das Ladogagebiet*, Stockholm, 1930.

(1935) '"Nadpis", inscriptions on swords from the Dnieper' (in Russian) *Izvestiya Gosudarstvennoy Akademii Istorii Material'noy Kul'tury*, 1933, 598–616.

(1951) Report on Ladoga (Soviet Academy 41, 1951) translated C. Stang, *Norsk Tidsskrift för Sprogvidenskap* 19 (1960) 478–86.

Ravndal, G. B. *Stories of the East Vikings*, Minnesota, 1938.

Riant, P. E. D. (Count) *Expéditions et Pèlerinages des Scandinaves en Terre Sainte au temps des Croisades* (Doctrinal thesis, Sorbonne) Paris, 1865.

Riasasnovsky, N. V. (1962) 'The Embassy of 838 revisited', *Jahrbücher für Geschichte Osteuropas* 10 (1962) 1–12.

(1969) *A History of Russia*, Oxford, 1969.

Rice, T. Talbot   *The Scythians* (Ancient Peoples and Places 2) London, 1957.

Rimbert   *Anskar, the Apostle of the North 801–865*, translated from *Vita Anskarii* of Rimbertus by C. H. Robinson (Lives of Early and Medieval Missionaries) London, 1931.

Ross, A. S. C. (1940) *The Terfinnas and Beormas of Ohthere* (University of Leeds Texts and Monographs 7) 1940.

Ross, A. S. C. (1954) 'Ohthere's Cwenas and Lakes', *Geographical Journal* 120 (1954) 337–45.

Runciman, Hon. Sir J. C. S. *A History of the First Bulgarian Empire*, London, 1930.

Ruprecht, A. *Die ausgehende Wikingerzeit im Lichte der Runeninschriften*, (*Palaestra* 224) Göttingen, 1958.

Sauvaget, J. *Introduction to the History of the Muslim East : a Biographical Guide*, translation, based on 2nd edition as recast by C. Cahen, University of California, 1965.

Sawyer, P. H. *The Age of the Vikings* (2nd edition) London, 1971.

Saxo *The First Nine Books of the Danish History of Saxo Grammaticus*, translated O. Elton, Folklore Society, London, 1894.

Schietzel, K. *Berichte über die Ausgrabungen in Haithabu*, edited Schietzel, Neumünster, 1969.

Schlauch, M. (1932) 'The Palace of Hugon of Constantinople', *Speculum* 7 (1932) 500–14.

(1934) *Romance in Iceland*, London, 1934.

Schlumberger, G. *L'épopée byzantine à la fin du dixième siècle* (3 vols.) Paris, 1896–1905.

Ševčenko, I. 'The Date and Author of the so-called fragments of Toparcher Gothicus', *Dumbarton Oaks Papers* 25 (1971) 117–88.

Shetelig, H. 'Traces of the Custom of Suttee in Norway during the Viking Age', *Sagabook of the Viking Club* 6 (1908–9) 180–208.

Siberian Shamanism Studies in Siberian Shamanism, edited H. N. Michael (Arctic Institute of North America, Anthropology of the North; Translations from Russian Sources 4) University of Toronto, 1963.

Sinor, D. '*Introduction à l'étude de l'Eurasie centrale*, Wiesbaden, 1963.

Skjaldedigtning Der norsk-islandske Skjaldedigtning edited F. Jonsson, Copenhagen, 1913–15.

Smyser, H. M. 'Ibn Fadlan's account of the Rus with some commentary and some allusions to Beowulf', *Medieval and Linguistic Studies in honor of Francis Peabody Magoun, Jr*, edited J. B. Bessinger and R. P. Creed, London, 1965, 92–119.

Sorlin, I. 'Les traités de Byzance avec la Russie au Xe. siècle', *Cahiers du Monde Russe et Soviétique* (1961) 313–60, 447–75.

Stelzer, O. 'Der Reiter', *Germania* 11 (1944) 410–17.

Stender-Petersen, A. (1934) *Die Varägersage als Quelle der altrussischen Chronik*, Acto Jutlandica 6, Aarhus, 1934.

(1953) *Varangica*, Aarhus, 1953.

Sternberg, L. 'Divine Election in Primitive Religion', *Congrès International des Américanistes* 21, Goteborg, 1925, 472–512.

Stokes, A. D. 'The Background and Chronology of the Balkan Campaigns of Svyatoslav Igorevich', *Slavonic and East European Review*, 40 (1961–2), 44–57.

Strandberg, R. 'Les broches d'argent caréliennes en forme de fer à cheval', *Eurasis Septentrionalis Antiqua* 12 (1928) 167–202.

Strömbäck, D. *Sejd: Textstudier i Nordisk Religionshistoria* (Nordiska Texter og Undersökningar utgivna i Uppsala av Bengt Hesselman, 5) Lund, 1935.

Studies in Shamanism Papers from the symposium at Abo, Finland, September 1962, edited Edsman, Stockholm, 1967.

Svärdström, E. 'Runorna i Hagia Sophia', *Fornvännen* 1970, 247–9.

Tallgren, A. M. 'Biarmia', *Eurasia Septentroinalis Antiqua* 6 (1931) 100–20.

Taylor, A. B. *Orkneyinga Saga*, translation with introduction and notes, Edinburgh, 1958.

Teall, J. L. 'The Grain Supply of the Byzantine Empire', *Dumbarton Oaks Papers* 13 (1959).

Thompson, M. W. *Novgorod the Great* (Summary of Russian publications on excavations at Novgorod), London, 1967.

Thomsen, V. *The Relations between Ancient Russia and Scandinavia and the Origin of the Russian State*, Oxford 1877. (A revised version in *Samlede Afhandlinger*, Copenhagen, 1919, 231ff.)

Toynbee, A. J. *Constantine Porphyrogenitus and his World*, Oxford, 1973.

Turville-Petre, E. O. G. (1966) 'Haraldr the Hard-Ruler and his Poets', Dorothea Coke Memorial Lecture, University College, London, 1966.

(1953) *Origins of Icelandic Literature*, Oxford, 1953.

Usher, A. P. *A History of Mechanical Inventions* (revised edition), Cambridge, Mass., 1954.

Vajda, L. 'Zur phaseikiguschen Stellung des Schamanismus', *Altaische Jahrbücher* 31 (1959) 456–85.

Varangian Problems Papers from the Symposium on 'The Eastern Connections of the Nordic Peoples in the Viking Period and Early Middle Ages', Aarhus, 1968, edited K. R. Schmidt and others, *Scando-Slavica* (Supplement I) Copenhagen, 1970.

Vasiliev, A. A. (1932/1) 'Economic Relations between Byzantium and Old Russia', *Journal of Economics and Business History* 4 (1931–2) 314–44.

(1932/2) 'Harun-ibn-Yahya and his description of Constantinople', *Seminaricum Kondakovianum* 5 (Institut Kondakov, Prague) 1932, 149–63.

(1936) *The Goths in the Crimea*, Cambridge, Mass., 1936.

Vasiliev, A. A. (1946) *The Russian Attack on Constantinople in 860*, Cambridge, Mass., 1946.

(1951) *The Second Russian Attack on Constantinople*, Dumbarton Oaks Papers 6, 1951.

Venedikov, I. 'Le syncretisme religieux en Thrace à l'époque romaine', *Acta Antiqua Philoppopolitane Studie Archaeologica*, Sofia, 1963.

Vernadsky, G. *Ancient Russia* (A History of Russia with M. Karpovich, vol. I), Yale University Press, 1946.

Vierck, H. 'Zum norrländischen Pelzwirtschaft in der zweiten Hälfte des 6 Jahrhunderts', *Goldbrakteaten aus Sievern* (see Hauck above), 380–390.

Vlasto, A. P. *The Entry of the Slavs into Christendom*, Cambridge, 1970.

Vogt, A. *Le Livre de Cérémonies* (2 vols., each with text and commentary) Paris, 1955.

Vries, J. de (1928) 'Die westnordische Tradition der Sage von Ragnar Lodbrok', *Zeitschrift für deutsche Philologie* 53 (1938) 257–302.

(1931) 'Normannisches Lehngut in den isländischen Königssagas', *Arkiv för nordisk Filologi* 47 (1931) 51–79.

(1956–7) *Altgermanisches Religionsgeschichte* (2 vols.) Grundriss der germanischen Philologie (edited H. Paul, 12) Berlin, 1956–7.

Vulpe, R. 'Ex voto au cavalier Thrace provenant de Callatis', *Dacia* 8 (1964) 335–43.

Wellesz, E. *Byzantine Music and Liturgy*, Cambridge Medieval History (1967), IV (2), 134 ff.

Wessen, E. *Historika Runinskrifter* (Kongl. Vitterhets Historie och Antikvitets Akademien) Lund, 1960.

Will, E. *Le Relief culturel Graeco-Romain*, Paris, 1955.

Wilson, D. M. 'East and West, a Comparison of Viking Settlement', *Varangian Problems* (above) 107–14.

Wright, J. K. *The Geographical Lore of the Time of the Crusades* (new edition) New York, 1965.

Yngvars Saga Yngvars Saga Viðfǫrla edited E. Olsen, Copenhagen, 1912.

Zeki Validi Zeki Validi Togan, *Ibn Fadlans Reisebericht* (*Deutsche Morgenlandische Gesellschaft*, Abhandlungen für die Kunde des Morgenlandes 24, 3) Leipzig, 1939.

Index

Abu al-Fida' 97
Achrida 239
Acre, siege of 260
Adalbert, Bishop of Hamburg 228
Adalsysla 20
Adam of Bremen: furs 97; geography 61; Harald's wealth 227–8; slavery 101; towns 70, 72, 73; Uppsala temple 271
Advice to an Emperor 208, 226, 228
Aegilsness 261, 265
Aesir 198, 270–2
Africa 61, 219
Ágrip 164, 165
Aifor 86–7
Alaborg 41, 47
Alanda river 25
Al-Biruni 111, 139
Aldeigjuborg 41, 45 ff, 63, 165, 294
Alexander I of Russia 256
Alexandria 274
Alexius I Comnenus of Byzantium 243; his Guard 182, 186, 191, 205; plot to gain throne 186; residence 195; saga references 236; use of Greek Fire 278; visits from Scandinavian kings 198, 257–9, 261–2
Alfred, of Wessex 24, 32, 33, 40, 71, 72
Al-Istakhri 309
Al-Kindi 111
al-magus 59

Al-Mas'udi 99, 124, 126 ff, 309
Al-Muqaddasi 99, 104
Al-Turtushi 72–3
Al-Ya'qubi 59
amber 71, 105
Anemas 115, 145, 146
Anglo-Saxon Chronicle 216
animal spirits 294
Anna, wife of Vladimir 150, 151, 179
Anna Comnena: burning of heretics 197; Greek Fire 276, 278; references to Guard 180, 186–187; silk armour 280, 281
An-Nadim 67
Annales Bertiniani 57, 117
Anskar, Bishop of Hamburg 21, 101, 104
Antioch: fighting at 241, 242, 243, 244; relics of Olaf I at 255
Anund of Sweden 20
Apostles, Church of the 204, 251
Apulia 22–3
Ardre, stone at 302
Arisdagus 241
Arithmus 178
Armenia 133, 241, 244, 313
Armenians, in Iceland 228, 313
Armod, poet 264
Arngrim of Sweden 40–1
asbestos 279–80
Asgard 271, 273
Asia Minor: campaigns in 188, 219, 239, 243, 244, 269; linked with Odin 272; relics from 247

Index

Askold and Dir 74, 75, 76, 123
Aslaug, Sigurd's daughter 281
Astrid, mother of Olaf I 103
Astrid, wife of Olaf II 165
Athens 220, 239, 246
Atil 112, 128, 138
Attaleiates 187, 190
Aud the Deep-minded 102
automata in Constantinople 195, 274 ff
Avars 121
Azerbaijan 127, 133

Baghdad: automata at 196; coins from 53; embassy from 64–65; taken by Turks 243; trade with 95
Baku 127
Baldwin of Jerusalem 260–1
Balearic Islands 260
Baltic 17 ff, 45, 47, 68 ff, 109, etc.
Banddrápa 47
Barðar Saga Snaefellsáss 296, 298
Bardas 143–4
Bardas Phocas 179, 241
Bardha'a 111, 113, 115, 133–5
Bardi Gudmundarson 234
Baruforos 86
Basil I of Byzantium 89
Basil II of Byzantium: campaigns 235, 239 ff, 244; founding of Guard 179–80, 183, 187; relations with Kiev 152, 170, 254
Beloozero 47, 50, 63
Beowulf 66, 279, 280–1
Berezan, island of 85, 93
Bergen: runes from 46; ship from 263–4
Biarmaland 32 ff, 109, 129, 159, 269, 293
Biorn of Hitdale, poet 154
birds: carrying fire 135, 213, 215–16; sacrifice of 85
Birka 54, 69 ff, 303, 308
Blachernae: Palace of 195; Virgin of 121, 204
black men 61, 160

Black Sea 81, 95, 117, 125, 126, 132, etc.
Blaland 60
Blöndal, S., work on Varangians 177
Blud, Slav general 148
Blues and Greens 198–9, 249
Bolverk Arnorsson, poet 208, 210–11
Book of Ceremonies 181, 201, 248 ff
booty 182, 222
Boris of Bulgaria 142
Bósa Saga 37
Bosporus 90, 124, 143, 171, 211, 226, 254
Bragi, poet 281
Brazen House (Chalce) 183, 201, 250
Brunanburh, Battle of 42
Brussels Chronicle 120–1, 122
Brynhild 151, 281, 311
Bucoleon, Palace of 185, 275
Bulgaria, campaigns in 208–9, 213, 220, 239, 279; the Great 60; journeys through 172, 266; stones in 303 ff.
Bulgars of the Danube 50, 92, 114, 132, 137, 139 ff, 220, 269
Bulgars of the Volga 50 ff, 64 ff; embassy to 64 ff; fighting with 109, 128, 137, 139, 151, 169; religion 203; towns of 74; contacts with 70, 88 (*see* Bulghar)
Bulghar: offered to Olaf II 165; route to 63, 88; trade at 52 ff, 65 ff, 74, 90, 99, 100, 104–5
Burislaf of Poland 156
Burizlaf (?Svyatopolk) 158 ff
Burtas 128, 139
Byzantium: attacks on 113 ff, 117 ff, 143 ff; campaigns of Emperors 239 ff; coins from 54; Harald of Norway at 208 ff; influences from 271 ff; life in 193 ff; links with Olaf I and II 255–7; pilgrimages to 247 ff;

Index

references in runes 236, 238; Eirik of Denmark at 257 ff; Olga of Kiev at 249 ff; Rognvald of Orkney in 263 ff; Sigurd of Norway at 261 ff

Caesarea (Asia Minor) 243, 244
Calocyras 140, 142
Cappodocia 144, 241
Caspian Sea: oil region 127, 276; raids on 95, 126 ff, 133 ff, route to 88, 169
Caucasus 269, 314, 316
Cedrenus: account of Svyatoslav's campaign 114, 143 ff; attack on Constantinople 170–1; baptism of Olga 248; defence of Constanza 246; Varangians in Asia Minor 188
chain across harbour 124, 226, 274
Chernigov 50, 76, 91, 157, 308
Cherson 84, 96, 132, 140, 152, 179
Chronicon Norwegiae 290, 294
Chronicles of Pseudo-Symeon 124
Chrysopolis, battle of 179
Chrysotriclinium 252, 253
Church of Varangians 191–2, 205–206, 222, 256
Cinnamus 191
cities, capture by trick 19, 213 ff
clocks 251, 274, 275
coins: brought back by Harald 228; finds in Scandinavia 52 ff; from Birka 70; from Byzantium 54; from Hedeby 69, 70; imitation of Greek coin 221
Colosseum 271
concubines 66, 79, 112
Constantine the Great 177, 200
Constantine VII Porphyrogenitus: *De Administrando Imperio* 77, 80 ff, 279; *Vita Basilii* 122; Host to Olga 136, 249 ff
Constantine (brother of John the Orphmotropus) 221, 224–5

Constantinople: attacks on 75, 117 ff, 130 ff, 146, 170 ff; embassy to 57 ff, 142; imprisonment in 185, 222; influence on North 270 ff; life in 193 ff; relics in 204 ff, 247; routes to 54, 80 ff, 248; sacking of 205, 315; technology of 274 ff; troops in 177 ff; visits to 136, 248 ff
Constanza 82, 244–6
Continuator Reginonis 248
Continuator of Theophanes 120
Conversion: of Olga 136, 248 ff; of Thorvald 254–5; of Vladimir 151, 180, 203, 254
Cornuti 177
Coronation ceremony 200
Cossacks 81, 85
costume of shaman 287
creation legends 315
Crimea: capture of Cherson 152; importance of 95–6, 138, 139; men from 88, 140; route to 84
Crusaders 180, 260 ff
Cwens 33 ff

Dagmale 24
Damusta Saga 274
Danube, river: estuary 82, 85; fighting near 140, 312; fire-ships on 115, 277; fortifications on 246; meeting on 116
Daphne, palace of 183, 250
De Administrando Imperio 80 ff, 279
Delean, Peter 209, 220
Dinogetia 140
Dnieper, river: area round 60, 117, 157; crossing of 84–5, 138, 156; mouth of 91; Pechinegs on 95, 141; route down 26, 54 ff, 58, 63, 75–6, 80 ff, 100, 120, 140, 152, 246, 248, 316
Dniester, river 82
Dobrynya 148, 149
Dorno of Kurland 19

334 Index

dragon: figureheads 262, 263–4; figures at Constanza 244 ff; killed by Harald 223; killed by Ragnar 280; spitting fire 278; *Yngvars Saga* 168–9
Dregovichi 55
dreng 237
Drevljane 55, 62, 74, 123, 135, 148
Dristra 114, 115, 140, 142, 144–6, 277
dromund 188, 264
drum of shaman 288, 290–1
Dublin 101
Dudo 217
duels 153 ff; of shamans 293 ff
Dvina (W. Dvina) 19, 26, 29, 30, 45; (N. Dvina) 34, 37, 39–40, 42, 43

Edda, Poetic 270, 271 (and separate poems)
Edda, Prose 270–2, 281, 315
Edessa 242
Edward the Confessor of England 180 (note), 255
Egils Saga 27, 33, 42, 51
Eilif Sprakalegg 235
Einar Skulason, poet 205
Eindridi the Younger 205, 235, 263 ff
Eirik Bloodaxe of Norway 42, 301
Eirik Emundarson of Sweden 24
Eirik Jarl 20, 47
Eirik the Good of Denmark 190, 195, 235, 257, 261, 262
Eirik the Victorious of Sweden 24, 167
Eiríksdrápa 259
Eiríksmál 301
Elbing, 27
Elbruz, Mount 314
Ellisif, Yaroslav's daughter 210, 226
Erfidrápa 37
Erling Crickneck 235, 263, 264
Erling Skjalgsson 102

Erp 102, 103
Essupi 84, 86
Estland 20, 24, 29, 103, 109
eunuchs 180, 221
Excubitors 178, 183
Eyjolf Dáðaskald, poet 47
Eymund, tale of 41, 158 ff, 164
Eyrbyggja Saga 231, 292–3, 294–295
Eystein of Norway 260, 265
Eyvind Bjarnarson 232

Fagrskinna 207, 211
Finland 24, 30
Finnbogi the Strong 232–3
Finnmark 32 ff
Finns 46, 90, 290 ff, etc.
Flateyjarbók 158, 191, 207, 222, etc.
Fostering by supernatural women 295 ff
Frodo I 19
Frodo IV 155
Frontinus 153, 226
Fulcher of Chartres 260
funeral: ceremonies 66, 114, 307 ff; of Emperor 201; feast 39, 135, 302; mock 213, 216–17
fur trade 97 ff; at Bulghar 74, 104–5; at Constantinople 86, 253; at Hedeby 69; in Crimea 96; in North 17; payment in 159; by Rus 64, 65, 76, 141
fur tribute: from Balts and Finns 43; from Biarmians 41; from Lapps 33–4, 39, 43; from Slavs 51, 63, 81

Galandri 86
gandr 292
Gastrikland, stones from 30
Gautreks Saga 301
Geisli 205, 235
Geoffrey of Monmouth 216
Georgia 241, 244
Gest Thorhallarson 190, 234
Gibraltar 248, 256, 264
Gilli the Russian 102

Index

Glum Geirason, poet 42
Glykas, Michael 185
Gnezdovo 55, 76
Godfred of Denmark 21, 68
gods, figures of 47, 65, 76, 271–3
gold: coins 54, 94, 221, 239, 242; figureheads of 262; gifts of 259, 262; horseshoes 262
Golden Gate 199, 204, 241, 262
Golden Hand 250
Golden Horn 124, 194, 211, 226, 274
Gorm of Denmark 23
Gotland Island of 17, 69, 73; gold in 54; stones of 13, 29, 99, 111, 120, 274, 300 ff, 312, 317
Gotlanders 23, 25, 27, 46, 62; etc.
Great Palace of Byzantium 183, 193 ff, 258, 272, 274
Greek Fire 92, 115, 131 ff, 144 ff, 169, 215, 242, 276 ff, 282
Greenland sagas 98, 285 ff
Grettis Saga 188, 234
Grim Hairy-cheeks 38
Grímnismál 271, 284
Gris Saemingsson 233
Grobin 22–3, 25, 26, 27, 45, 46, 74
Gudmund of Glasisvellir 298
Gudrun, Osvif's daughter 208, 230
Gudrun, wife of Olaf I 150
Guðrúnarhvǫt 281
Gunnstein 36–7
Gylfi of Sweden 272
Gyrgir (George Maniaces) 211

Hadingus 19, 215, 296–7
Haflidi Marsson 234
Hagbardus and Signy 310–11
Hagia Sophia 201 ff, 274; choir of 249, 251; clock 275; relics 204; runes 204, 246; services 118 ff, 195, 199, 200 ff
Hakon, supporting Yaroslav 157

Hákonarmál 301
Halfdan the Black 23
Halfdan the White 23
Hálfdanar Saga 41
Hálfs Saga 38
Halldor Snorrason 207, 214–15, 217–19, 222–3, 230
Hallfred, poet 165
Hallfreðar Saga 233
Halogaland 32, 33, 36, 38, 40, 75, 129
Hamburg 21, 22, 101
Hamðismál 281
Handvanus 19, 216
Harald Bluetooth of Denmark 23
Harald Fairhair of Norway 23, 33, 42, 158
Harald Greycloak of Norway 42
Harald Hardradi of Norway 47, 68, 191; in Byzantium 171, 182, 183, 189, 207 ff, 257, 261, 262–3
Harald of Sweden 169
Harald of Wessex 212
Harald Wartooth of Sweden 21, 157
Harun b. Yahya 199
Hedeby 21, 46, 68 ff, 72, 101
Heid, name of *vǫlva* 38, 284–5; giantess 43
Heiðarvíga Saga 190
Heimskringla 36, 47, 102, 103, 182, 205, 214, etc.
Helgi Poems 311
Hellespont 19, 61, 118
Hermes 304
Hero God of Thrace 306 ff
Herodotus 304
Hervarar Saga 20
Hetaireia 178, 181
Hippodrome 84, 193, 195, 197 ff, 253, 259, 262; statues in 198, 206, 271
Hjalmðers Saga 293
Hjalti Skeggjason 164, 165
Hneitir, sword of Olaf II 205–6
Holmgard 63 (*see* Novgorod)

Index

Holy Apostles, Church of 249
Holy Land: campaigns in 244, 257, 260, 269; pilgrimage to 165, 219, 235, 247 ff, 259, 260 ff
honey 51, 104–5, 142
Hoskuld Kollsson 66, 102
Hrafnkels Saga 232
Hudud al-'Alam 110, 134, 309
Hugon's Palace 275–6
hunt, significance of 304 ff

Ibn al-Faqih 134
Ibn Athir 112, 133, 134
Ibn Battuta 98
Ibn Fadlan: visit to Bulghar 64 ff, 88, 170; description of Rus 46, 74, 97, 98–9, 110, 136, 309
Ibn Hauqual 99, 113, 139
Ibn Isfandiyar 126
Ibn Khurdadbeh 95
Ibn Rusteh 63, 99, 109–10, 308, 309
Iceland: annals of 168; carving in 228; traditions taken to 105–106, 164 ff, 188, 207 ff, 230 ff, 269–70, 271 ff, 273 ff, 286, 315
Ignatius, Patriarch of Constantinople 120
Igor (?Ingvar) 92, 105, 123, 130, 135
Illugi of Bryndale (poet) 208
Impiltis 24–5
Incendiary weapons 115, 169, 264, 277–8
Ingigerd, wife of Yaroslav 24, 164 ff, 210
Ingvar of Sweden 87 ff, 167 ff, 236, 277–8
Ingvar (?Ikmor) 114–15, 145
Iranian influences 313 ff
Isaac Comnenus 187, 243
Islands of Princes 120, 224
Islendingabók 228
Ivar the Far-reacher of Sweden 20, 21
Izaslav 150, 166
Izborsk 63

James of Kiev 248
Jarisleif (Yaroslav) 158 ff
Jerusalem 219, 254, 260
John I Tzimisces of Byzantium 114, 131, 142–6, 187, 233, 236, 239
John II Comnenus of Byzantium 191, 205, 243
John Scylitzes 114, 132, 140, 143, 242, 312
John the Orphanotropus 221
Jomsborg 23, 72
Jomsvikings 109, 235
Jordan, river 220, 261, 265
Justinian 201; triclinium of 250, 251

Karelia 24, 34, 35, 36
Karli 36–7
Kaupang 71
Kazogs 155, 157
Keorki of Georgia 241
Ketil of Gardar 170
Ketil Salmon 38
Khagan 58, 64
Khazars 50–1, 55, 58, 59, 74, 139, 168, 269; alliances with 118, 126–7; fighting with 61, 77, 112, 127–8, 137 ff, 169, 241; mercenaries 178, 181; trade with 53, 64, 95, 105; tribute to 62, 63, 117, 123
Kiev: agreements with 89 ff, 93; attacks from 54, 117 ff, 137 ff, centre of Rus territory 62, etc.; embassies from 58; embassies to 80, 139–40, 151; founding of 74 ff, 117; Greek influence in 203–4; Olga's baptism 248–9; relations with Pechinegs 55, 152–3; route to Constantinople 81 ff, 120, 123 ff; rulers of 60, 95, 100, etc.; saga traditions at 128 ff, 148 ff, 253; tribute to 51, 63; Varangians at 148 ff, 316, etc.; wall-paintings at 203–4, 210

knots, tied by pilgrims 265
Kolskegg Hamundarson 233
Krivichi 55, 56
Kurland: alliance with 41; expeditions against 19, 22, 24, 109; forts in 25, 27; raids from 17; references on stones 29 ff

Ladoga, Lake 17, 36, 41, 43, 45
Laesi (Poles) 210
Landnámabók 99, 102, 233, 286
Lapps 32 ff, 269, 287; shamanism of 129, 288 ff
Last Judgement, Icelandic carving 228–9
Laxdaela Saga 66, 102, 105, 208, 230, 231
Layamon 216
Leanti 86
Leo VI of Byzantium 125, 185
Leo the Deacon 113 ff, 131, 135, 143 ff, 226
Liutprand of Cremona: *Antapodosis* 59, 130, 182, 185, 195–6, 200, 274, 277; *Relatio de Legatione* 94, 142

Manglabites 183, 209
Maniaces, Georgios 211, 213, 217, 221–2, 242
Manuel I of Byzantium 195, 235, 236, 243–4, 265
Mar Hunrodsson 211, 234
Maria (sister of Empress) 189, 213, 222
markets 68 ff, 98 ff, 102, 104 ff, 156
Marmora, Sea of 118, 120, 194
Marvazi 110, 134, 151
Marzuban 133, 134
Mercenaries 92, 123, 148, 177 ff, etc.
Mese 199
Michael I of Byzantium 226
Michael III of Byzantium 129
Michael IV (Katalak) of Byzantium 188, 211, 217, 220–1, 234, 236

Michael V of Byzantium 171, 180, 187, 209, 212, 217, 221–2, 224–5, 236
Michael VII Ducas of Byzantium 186, 190, 208
monuments in Constantinople 206
Moravia, 73, 75
Morkinskinna 165, 207, 209, 214, 217, 218, 234, 236
mosaics: in Hagia Sophia 203, 273; in Palace 253
Moses of Khorene 113
Mount Levunion, battle of 243
Mstislav 155, 157, 162, 166, 210
Myriocephalon, battle of 244

Nabites 182
Nicaea 243
Nicephorus I of Byzantium 178
Nicephorus II Phocas of Byzantium 94, 139, 142, 187
Nicephorus III Botaniates of Byzantium 186, 190
Nicephorus Bryennius 187, 242
Nicetas 120, 191
Nicholas, Abbot 259
Nineteen Couches, hall of 196, 201
Nordbrikt 185, 211
Normans 118, 178, 216, 243; conquest of England 180; William of Normandy 228
Novgorod: boats at 81; founding of 63–4, 74, 76, 117; rulers of 142, 148; sanctuary 75–6; Varangians at 156, 158 ff, 316
Numera 185, 222
Numeri 178

Obodrichi 21
Odd the Far-travelled 38 ff, 42, 123, 129 ff, 285, 296, 299
Odd the Little, poet 264
Odin: in Biarmaland 38; followers of 19, 20; heroic traditions of 109, 113, 274, 311–12; links with east 271 ff, 301 ff; resem-

blance to Thracian Rider 306 ff; shamanic powers 283
Ogmund (Kvillamus) 42, 299
Ohthere (Ottar) 32 ff, 40, 44, 71, 72
Olaf I of Norway, Tryggvason 47, 103, 150–1, 255 ff; Odd's Life of 103; sagas of 103, 255, etc.
Olaf II of Norway, the Holy 20, 36, 158, 208, 209, 275; cult of 191–2, 205, 224, 256, 261, 317; proposed marriage 24, 164; sagas of 102, 164, 165, 205, etc.
Olaf of Sweden, 24, 164 ff
Olaf the Peacock 103
Öland, isle of 303
Old Saxons 308
Oleg (Helgi), the Wise 40, 76, 123 ff, 128 ff
Oleg, son of Svyatoslav 149
Olga (Helga) of Kiev 123; as ruler 51, 179, 216; conversion 136; death 141; revenge on Drevljane 74, 135–6; visit to Constantinople 183, 196, 248 ff
Onega, lake 36, 41, 45, 47
Optimati 178
organs 249, 253, 274
Orkney, burial at 307
Orkneyinga Saga 235, 263 ff
Orvar-Odds Saga 38 ff, 90, 129, 285, 296
Ösel, isle of 20, 27, 30
Östergotland, stones from 21, 167, 236, 238
Øyvind 21

pay, of Varangians 181 ff
Pechinegs 55, 269; alliance with 132, 141; attacks by 84–5, 118, 141, 147, 152–3; defeat at Stara Zadoga 191, 205, 235; duel with champion 155; mercenaries 178; relations with Byzantium 89, 95, 139, 143, 191, 242 ff; shamanism 299; slaves 180

Pèlerinage de Charlemagne 275
Pereyaslavets 140–4
Pereyaslavl 82, 91
Permia 35 ff
Perun 75, 124
Peter of Bulgaria 140, 142
Pharangians 178, 181
Photius, Patriarch of Constantinople 118, 120 ff
Pilgrimage 247 ff, 274
Piraeus, lion from 220, 239
platform of shaman 284–6, 288, 290
Pliny 279
poets, Icelandic 269–70 (*see also* separate poets)
Poljani 55, 74
Polotsk 19, 50, 76, 148, 161–2, 217
pólútasvarf 182
Polyainus 152, 153
polyudie 51
Pomeranians 21
portages 50
priests, from Byzantium 228, 313
Primary Chronicle 62; account of Rus 45, 50, 63, 76, 117, 123; attacks on Byzantium 121, 122, 170, 278; Igor 105, 132–3; Oleg 128 ff; Olga 74, 135, 248, 253; Svyatoslav 136, 137 ff; treaties 75, 89 ff; Varangians 148 ff, 162; Vladimir 100, 148 ff, 203; Yaroslav 156 ff, 162, 166, 210
Procopius 202
Prose Edda 270–2, 281, 315
Prudentius, Bishop of Troyes 57
Pryetich, Slav general 141
Psellus, Michael 170–1, 180, 190, 221, 224–5, 277
Pskov 76

Radimichi 55, 123, 151
Ragnar (Eymund's Tale) 158 ff
Ragnar Lodbrok 280, 301
Ragnarok 313

Index

Ragnheid 148, 149–51
rapids on Dnieper 82 ff
Red Sea 169
relics 204, 247, 258, 261
Reply of Joseph 134
Report of Greek Toparch 137–8
Rhos 57, 59
Riekkala, island of 17
Rimbert, Bishop of Hamburg 21, 22, 26, 27, 69, 73, 101
robe of Virgin 121–2, 204
Robert Guiscard 216, 243, 262
Rognvald Jarl 165
Rognvald of Orkney 181, 235, 263 ff
Rognvald of Polotsk 148, 149
Romanus I Lecapenus of Byzantium 131
Romanus III Argyrus of Byzantium 171, 183, 211, 217, 242
Romanus IV Diogenes of Byzantium 243
Roskilde 258
Roslagen 59
Rukh-As 60, 272
Runes: at Berezan 85; Constantinople 185, 204; Constanza 246; Maeshowe 264; Novgorod 75; scales case 30; Staraja Ladoga 45, 46; Swedish stones 86, 99, 167 ff, 182, 236 ff, 247–8, 300 ff, 316
Ruprecht, A., work on runes 168, 236 ff
Rurik 45, 74, 75, 123
Rus 57 ff, etc.; burials 308

Saastamaa 20
sacrifices: animal 72, 114, 145; bird 85, 114; human 114, 145, 301, 307 ff
St Antonus, Life of 88
St Boniface 308, 310
St Gregory's Island 82, 85
St Irene, church of 204
St Mamas 90
St Sophia, Kiev 203–4, 210
Samarkand 53, 100, 196
Sarkel 60, 126, 138
Sarmatians 311
Saxo Grammaticus: Danes in Constantinople 181, 257 ff; duels 155; Frodo I 19, 217; Frodo IV 155; geography 61; Hadingus 19, 215, 296; Hagbardus and Signy 310; Harald Wartooth 157; Heid 284; Lapps 40, 293; Odin in Byzantium 272; Ragnar 280; towns 24
scales, of merchants 29, 70, 317
Schleswig 69
Schools (Candidati) 178, 183, 242
Sciringsceal 71
Scythia 19, 60–1, 316
Scythians 179, 180, 311
Seeburg 22
seiðr 283 ff
Seljuq Turks 243, 244
Semigallia 24, 29, 168
Serkland 60–1, 167, 219, 263
Severi 123
shamanism 38, 270, 283 ff, 287 ff
shield sign of truce 124
ship funeral 66, 71, 136, 288, 311
ships: of Rus 81, 125; given to Emperor 262
Sicily: campaign in 209, 210, 213, 219, 244; Roger of 260
Sidon, siege of 261
Sigrid the Proud 311
Sigurd the Crusader of Norway 158, 181, 198, 260 ff, 271, 301
Sigurd the Volsung 281, 311
Sigvat, poet 165
silk: given by Emperor 200, 262; in graves 69; made in Constantinople 82, 89, 93–4, 95, 104, 106, 141, 227, 259; sails of 124, 262; strengthened with asbestos 280–2
Silkisif 169
silver 52, 54, 70, 227–8; from Biarmians 36, 37, 39

sjónhverfing 292
Skipt 183
slave trade 99 ff; in Baltic 26, 29; in Bulghar 65 ff, 74; in Constantinople 81, 84, 86, 91, 93, 94, 253; in east 52; by Rus 64, 142
Slavs: army 141, 148, 156, 159 ff; in Baltic area 21, 24; boats 81 ff; funeral customs 308–9; language 80, 86; organisation 137, 148, 156, 162, round Kiev 55 ff; towns 64, 73 ff; tribute from 51, 63
Smaland 236, 238
Smolensk 50, 55, 63, 76
snake-pit, death in 273–4, 280
Snorri goði 230, 231
Snorri Sturluson: *Egils Saga* 27; *Haralds Saga* 208, 211 ff, 222 ff; *Prose Edda* 270, 272; sagas of Olaf I and II 24, 102, 103, 164; *Ynglinga Saga* 19–20, 60
Södermanland, stones from 29–30, 236, 237–8; support to Birka 69
Sǫgubrot af Fornkunungum 20
south road to Byzantium 248
spatharocandidatus 183, 209, 221
Spes 189
spirit wives 297 ff
Stamford Bridge, battle of 231
Stara Zagora, battle of 191, 205, 235
Staraja Ladoga 45 ff, 63, 65
Starkad 155, 301
Stefnir Thorgilsson 255
Stein 20
Stephanus, Admiral 211
Stiklastad, battle of 209, 257
Stora Hammars, Gotland, stones from 301, 302
Strabo 279
Strategicon 208
Strukun 86
Stuf the Blind, poet 208, 219
Sturlaugs Saga 37, 294

suttee, 76, 307, 311
Suzdal 50, 76
Sveigdir 19
Sveinald 149
Svinketil 144, 145
Svyatogor 293, 314
Svyatopolk 156–7, 166
Svystoslav: campaigns 113 ff, 137, 140 ff, 239, 246, 277, 312; death 85, 147; rejects Christianity 136; represented at Constantinople 252
Sweden the Great 19, 60
swords: in Baltic area 27; in Dnieper 85; in graves 55; of Rus 110, 111; of St Olaf 205, 256; trade in 95, 104
Symeon Logothete, Chronicle of 121, 122
Symeon of Bulgaria 140
Syria 241, 254

Tagmata 178, 220
Tatars 315, 317
Theodora of Byzantium 224–5
Theodore the Martyr 146
Thessalonica 220–1
Thjodolf Arnorsson, poet 208, 210, 219, 220
Thjodolf of Hvin, poet 20, 21
Thomsen, V. 57
Thor 38, 150, 272, 293
Thorarin Skeggjason, poet 208
Thorbjorg of Greenland 285 ff
Thorbjorn the Black, poet 264
Thorgeir Scotpoll, poet 264
Thorgerd Hǫlgabrudr 273
Thorgny of Tinundarland 24
Thorir Helsing 191, 235
Thorir Hund 36 ff, 257, 293
Thorir of Steig 227
Thorkel Thjostarson 232
Thorolf Kveldulfsson 33–4
Thorolf Skallagrimsson 42
Thorstein dromund 188–9, 234
Thorstein Oxleg 153
Thorstein Styrsson 190

Index

Thorvald the Far-travelled 254–5
Thracian Rider 303 ff
throne of Emperor 195, 274–5
Tmutorokan 60, 61, 64, 94, 120, 157
Tomis, Romania, stone from 306
Torks 151
Towns 68 ff; growth of 77
treaties with Byzantium 82, 89 ff, 123, 125, 132
Trebizond 241, 244
Trelleborg 23
Trondheim 205
Truso 27, 71–2
Þegn 237

Ulf Ospaksson 218, 222–3, 230–1
Ulsvorsi 86
Uppland: coins from 53; stones from 29, 30, 167, 182, 236–7, 248; support to Birka 69
Uppsala: dynasty of 167; Thing at 24, 164
Utgard-Loki 293

Valdemar of Denmark 223
Valgard of Voll 104, 208, 224
Valhalla 302, 307
valkyries 281, 299, 301 ff
Varangian Guard 105, 171, 177 ff; Harald of Norway in 221, 231; on campaigns 239 ff; visit from Eirik 257 ff
Varangians 62, 63, 77, 148 ff, etc.
Vartilaf 158, 161, 166
Varzuga river 32, 34
Västergotland, stones from 29, 236–7, 238
Västmanland, stones from 167
Vatnsdœla Saga 285
Vernadsky, G. 26, 60, 61
Vitichev 77–8, 82
Vladimir of Kiev 100, 148 ff, 179–80, 203, 239, 254–5

Vladimir, son of Yaroslav 172
voevoda 142, 148
Voles 124
Volga, river: route from Baghdad 88; route to Bulghar 47, 50, 54, 63, 70, 74, 151; route to Caspian 126 ff, 134, 168–9, 277–278; Rus on 65 ff, 309
Volk, Slav general 142
Volsungs 198, 281
Vǫluspá 313
vǫlva 38, 129, 285, 290
Vyshata, Slav general 172

Wace 216, 217
walnuts for fuel 216, 262
warrior on stones 301 ff
wax 51, 104–5, 142, 253
Wends 21, 72, 255, 308–9
west road to Byzantium 248
Westphalia, snake tower in 223
White Sea 32, 34, 36, 40, 43
William of Malmesbury 223
Wodan 307
woman with horn on stones 301 ff
women warriors 114–15, 311–12
Wulfstan, Archbishop of York 104
Wulfstan the traveller 24, 27, 71, 72

Yahya of Antioch 179
Yaropolk 148, 149, 154
Yaroslav 148, 156 ff, 182, 210, 226
Ymir 315
Ynglinga Saga 19, 60, 272
Ynglingatal 20
Yngvar 20
Yngvars Saga 87 ff, 163, 167 ff, 277–8

Zoe of Byzantium 211, 212, 214, 222, 224–5